The Story of the World Activity Book Two

The Middle Ages

From the Fall of Rome to the Rise of the Renaissance

Edited by Susan Wise Bauer

With activities, maps, and drawings by:
Suzanne Bryan, Sara Buffington, Sheila Graves, Lisa Logue, Justin Moore,
Tiffany Moore, Sarah Park, Kimberly Shaw, Jeff West, and Sharon Wilson

Peace Hill Press

www.peacehillpress.com

Printed in the U.S.A.
ISBN-13:   978-1-933339-13-9
ISBN-13 (looseleaf edition):   978-1-933339-14-6

ALSO BY SUSAN WISE BAUER

The Story of the World
History for the Classical Child
(PEACE HILL PRESS)

Volume 1: Ancient Times (revised edition, 2006)

Volume 2: The Middle Ages (revised edition, 2007)

Volume 3: Early Modern Times (2004)

Volume 4: The Modern Age (2005)

The Well-Educated Mind
A Guide to the Classical Education You Never Had
(W.W. NORTON, 2003)

The History of the Ancient World: From the Earliest Accounts to the Fall of Rome
(W.W. NORTON, 2007)

The History of the Medieval World: From the Conversion of Constantine to the First Crusade
(W.W. NORTON, 2010)

WITH JESSIE WISE

The Well-Trained Mind
A Guide to Classical Education at Home
(REVISED EDITION, W.W. NORTON, 2009)

For more on Susan Wise Bauer, visit her website,
at www.susanwisebauer.com

To find out more about *The Story of the World* series and
other titles published by Peace Hill Press, visit www.peacehillpress.com.

Rick Soldin at Electronic Publishing Services, Inc.,
assisted in composition and page design.

Table of Contents

Chapters

PHOTOCOPYING AND DISTRIBUTION POLICY

The illustrations, reading lists, and all other content in this Activity Book are copyrighted material owned by Peace Hill Press. Please do not reproduce reading lists, etc. on e-mail lists or websites.

For families: You may make as many photocopies of the maps and other Student Pages as you need for use WITHIN YOUR OWN FAMILY ONLY. Peace Hill Press publishes a separate set of Student Pages—which includes all maps, games, flags, timelines, and other consumable pages from the Activity Book. (These cost $11.95 for Volume 2. ISBN 978-1-933339-16-0.) It is often more economical for you to buy these separate pages than to photocopy the entire consumable section of the Activity Book. If you would like to purchase these, visit our website, at peacehillpress.com. Photocopying the pages so that the Activity Book can then be resold is a violation of copyright.

Schools and co-ops MAY NOT PHOTOCOPY any portion of the Activity Book. Smaller schools usually find that purchasing a set of the pre-copied Student Pages for each student is the best option. Other schools may purchase a licensing fee ($100 per volume, per year) that allows unlimited school and co-op duplication. For more information, please contact Peace Hill Press: e-mail info@peacehillpress.com; phone 1.877.322.3445.

How to Use This Activity Book

History is the most absorbing and enthralling story you can tell a young child, because it's true. A good history narrative is as strange and wondrous as a good fairy tale. Kings, queens, mummies, wooden horses, knights, and castles can be as fascinating as giants and elves—but they *really existed*!

In classical education, history lies at the center of the curriculum. The chronological study of history allows even small children to learn about the past in an orderly way; after all, the "best way to tell a story," as the King tells Alice in *Alice in Wonderland*, "is to begin at the beginning and go on to the end." When the study of literature is linked to history, children have an opportunity to hear the stories of each country as they learn more about that country's past and its people. History teaches comprehension; young students learn to listen carefully, to pick out and remember the central facts in each story. History even becomes the training ground for beginning writers. When you ask a young student to narrate, to tell back to you the information he's just heard in his own words, you are giving him invaluable practice in the first and most difficult step of writing: putting an idea into words.

This activity guide is designed to go along with Volume Two of Susan Wise Bauer's *The Story of the World: History for the Classical Child*. Think of each section in *The Story of the World* as a "springboard" into the study of world history. This book provides you with a simple, chronological overview of the progression of history. It isn't intended to be complete, but when you do history with young students, you're not aiming for a "complete" grasp of what happened in the Middle Ages. Instead, you want to give the child an enthusiasm for history, a basic understanding of major cultures, and an idea of the chronological order of historical events.

Using This Activity Book at Home

The Activity Book has two sections: a parents' guide in the front, and consumable Student Pages in the back. (Note the page numbers at the bottom of each page to see what section you're in.) For each section in *The Story of the World*, follow this pattern:

1) Read the child one section from *The Story of the World*. Longer chapters are divided into several sections; each section is appropriate for one session of history. Good readers can read the section to you instead.

2) **Review Questions:** These test the student's comprehension. When he has thoroughly studied the chapter, he should answer these questions orally without looking at the book. Encourage him to answer in complete sentences when possible. This is training in reading comprehension (and it will help you evaluate whether the child is listening with attention and whether he's really understanding what he's reading). Answers given are approximate; accept any reasonable answer. You can also make up your own questions.

3) **Narration Exercise:** Have the child tell you in two to five sentences what the history lesson was about. You can prompt the child with the Review Questions. Encourage the child to include the major facts from the history reading, but not EVERY fact. We have supplied sample narrations simply to give some idea of acceptable answers, not to imply that your child's narration should match word for word!

   Write down the child's narration if the child is not writing independently. Good writers can be asked to write the narration down themselves. To help with this process, listen carefully to the child's narration and repeat it back to her while she writes; this will help with "writer's block." For any given section, you can instead ask the child to draw a picture of her favorite part of the history lesson and then describe the picture to you. Write the description at the bottom of the picture. Put the narration or the picture in a History Notebook—a looseleaf notebook that will serve as the child's record of her history study.

4) When you have finished both sections of a chapter, stop and do **additional reading** and **activities** on the topic covered by that chapter. This Activity Book provides titles of books that you can find at your library for additional history reading, as well as maps, hands-on activities, and other projects. Some topics have many more resources available than others. Ask your local librarian for further suggestions.

When you reach a topic that has a wealth of interesting books and activities connected to it, stop and enjoy yourself; don't feel undue pressure to move on. Check your local library for titles before buying. The recommended titles range in difficulty from books for reading aloud to first graders to advanced books appropriate for fourth graders to read independently. When appropriate, ask the child to draw pictures, to narrate, or to complete brief outlines about the additional reading as well. Put these pictures and narrations into a three-ring History Notebook. This should begin to resemble the child's own one-volume history of the world. Don't ask the child to narrate every book or she'll grow frustrated; use this as occasional reinforcement for a topic she finds particularly interesting.

Because students from a wide range of grades will be using this Activity Book, we have tried to provide a range of activities, appropriate for different levels. Some are more appropriate for younger students; others will require more in-depth thought. We encourage you to select the projects that are most appropriate for you and your students.

5) **Maps:** Almost every section in Volume One of *The Story of the World* has an accompanying map activity. A blank map is in the Student Pages; an answer key showing the correct, completed maps begins on page 254.

6) We have provided **encyclopedia cross-references** to the appropriate pages in *The Kingfisher Illustrated History of the World*, *The Kingfisher History Encyclopedia* (revised), *The Usborne Book of World History*, and *The Usborne Internet-Linked Encyclopedia of World History*. Use these books for additional supplemental reading, especially for those topics that don't have extensive lists of age-appropriate library books.

7) Choose appropriate titles from the recommended **literature lists** and read these with your child. Classical philosophy discourages the use of "reading textbooks" which contain little snippets of a number of different works. These textbooks tend to turn reading into a chore—an assignment that has to be finished—rather than a wonderful way to learn more about the world. Instead of following a "reading program," consider using the "real books" from these literature lists. Following each title is a range of grades showing the appropriate reading level (RA=read aloud, IR=independent read).

8) Every four chapters, you should take one history class to prepare your history review cards. Photocopy the history cards (use stiff cardstock for longer-lasting cards) and cut them out; have the student color the picture. After the cards are completed, use them once or twice a week to review material already covered.

9) Optional: You can administer written tests (available separately from Peace Hill Press) if you desire a more formal evaluation or wish to develop your child's test-taking ability.

Multilevel Teaching

The Story of the World series is intended for children in grades 1–4, but is often used by older students: Volume One is written primarily for grades 1–4; Volume Two for grades 2–5; Volume Three for grades 3–6; Volume Four for grades 4–8. The maps and many of the activities in this book are also appropriate for children in grades 4–8. To use *The Story of the World* as the center of a multilevel history program, have your older child independently do the following: Read *The Story of the World*; follow this with the appropriate pages from the *Kingfisher History Encyclopedia*; place all important dates on a timeline; and do additional reading on his or her own level. For more book lists and detailed directions on classical education methods for both elementary and middle-grade students, see *The Well-Trained Mind: A Guide to Classical Education at Home*, by Jessie Wise and Susan Wise Bauer (revised edition, W.W. Norton, 2004), available from Peace Hill Press (www.peacehillpress.com) or anywhere books are sold.

An Important Note for Parents

Families differ in their attitudes towards teaching myths, in their willingness to view partially clothed people in ancient art, and in their sensitivity towards the (inevitable) violence of ancient times. We suggest that you skim through the activities in this book, glance through the literature that we recommend, and skip anything that might be inappropriate for your own family. In addition, both the *Kingfisher History Encyclopedia* and the *Usborne Internet-Linked Encyclopedia of World History* contain a number of pages on prehistoric peoples that may not agree with your family's convictions about humankind's beginnings. If this might pose a problem for you, preview these books before purchasing or using them.

Using This Book in the Classroom

Although this Activity Book was initially designed to be used by homeschooling families, it adapts well to the classroom. Following are suggestions on how each chapter may be taught:

1) The teacher reads aloud a chapter section while the students follow along in their own books. When you reach the end of a section, ask the review questions provided in this book to selected students. Depending upon the length of a chapter, you may read the entire chapter in one day or break it up over two days.

2) Using the review questions and chapter tests as a guide, type up a list of facts that the students should memorize, perhaps employing a fill-in-the-blank format. Give one to each student to help her prepare for the upcoming test. If you would like to administer formal tests, you can purchase them separately from Peace Hill Press.

3) Have the students do the map exercises.

4) Select one or two activities. Some are more appropriate for classroom use than others.

5) Each day there should be an oral or written review. You can make it fun by playing oral quizzing games such as "Around the World," "Last One Standing," or "Jeopardy!"

6) On the last day before the test, have the students color their chapter review cards.

7) Test the students.

8) Periodically review past lessons so your students will remember history chronologically.

Pronunciation Guide for Reading Aloud

Abbot Cuibert   —   AB uht QUEE bair

Aborigine   —   AB uh RIJ uh nee

Abu Bakr   —   AH boo BAH kur

Aegean Sea   —   uh JEE uhn (sea)

Agincourt   —   AHJ in kor

Agra   —   AH gruh

Ajanta caves   —   ah JAHN tuh (caves)

Akbar   —   AHK bar

Al Bakri   —   ahl BAHK ree

Aljama   —   AHL haw muh

Al-Amin   —   ahl ah MEEN

Al-Andalus   —   Ahl AN duh loos

Alcuin   —   AL kwin

Alhambra   —   ahl HAM bruh

Allah   —   AHL uh

Allemanni   —   all uh MAH nee

Almagest   —   AL muh jest

Al-Mansur   —   al man SEWER

Amaterasu   —   AH mah tay raw soo

Amerigo Vespucci   —   ah MAIR ee go ves PEW chee

Ananias Dare   —   AN uh NYE uhs (Dare)

Anne Boleyn   —   (Anne) bowl INN

Anne of Cleves   —   (Anne of) KLEEVZ

Antimony   —   AN tim OH nee

Aotearoa   —   ah oh TEER oh ah

Archbishop   —   ARCH BISH uhp

Asgard   —   AS gard

Augustine   —   AWE guh steen

Aztec   —   AZ tek

Babur the Tiger   —   BAW bur (the Tiger)

Baghdad   —   BAG dad

Barbarian   —   bar BEAR ee un

Bards   —   BARDZ

Bayeux tapestry   —   bye YUH (a mix between "yoo" and "yuh")

Bedouin   —   BED oo in

Beijing   —   BAY jing

Beowulf   —   BAY uh WOLF

Berber   —   BUR bur

Birbal   —   BUR bul

Bjarni   —   BYAR nee

Blondel   —   blon DEL

Bubonic   —   boo BON ihk

Buddha   —   BOO duh

Byzantine Empire   —   BIZ un teen (Empire)

Byzantium   —   bih ZAN tee uhm

Caffa   —   KAH fuh

Caliph   —   KAY lif

Canterbury   —   KANN tur burr ee

Castile   —   kah STEEL

Catherine of Aragon   —   (Catherine of) ARR uh gone

Catherine Parr   —   (Catherine) PAR

Celts   —   KELTS

Chandragupta   —   CHAHN druh GOOP tuh

Charlemagne   —   SHAR luh MAYN

Charles Martel   —   (Charles) mar TELL

Chieftain   —   CHEEF tuhn

Clotilda   —   kluh TIL duh

Clovis   —   KLO vis

Coliseum   —   KOHL ih SEE uhm

Conquistador   —   kon KEE stah DOR

Constantinople   —   kahn stan tuh NOH pul

Coronation   –   KOR uh NAY shun

Cracow   –   KRAK ow ("ow" rhymes with "cow")

Craith   –   KRAYTH

Croatan   –   CROW uh tan

Cuzco   –   KOOZ coe

Daimyo   –   DIE me oh (quickly slur syllables together)

Dais   –   DAY is

Danube   –   DAN yoob

Dauphin   –   doh FAN ("fan" with "a" like "apple"; barely say the "n")

Delhi   –   DEH lee

Diaspora   –   dye AS pur uh

Diocletian   –   dye oh KLEE shun

Donnacona   –   DAHH nah KOH nah

El Cid   –   EHL SID

Emir of Cordova   –   ay MEER (of) KOR doh vuh

Emu   –   EE moo

Ethelbert   –   ETH uhl burt

Ethelred   –   ETH uhl red

Ferdinand Magellan   –   (Ferdinand) muh JEL uhn

Francisco Vasquez de Coronado   –   fran SIS koh VAS kez day kor oh NAH doh

Fresco   –   FRESS koh

Frigg   –   FRIG

Gabriel   –   GAY bree uhl

Galileo Galilei   –   ga lih LAY oh ga lih LAY ee (the "a" in "ga" is like "apple")

Galleon   –   GAL ee uhn

Ganges   –   GAN jeez

Garderobe   –   GARD er ohb

Gaul   –   GAWL

Genghis Khan   –   JENG gihs KAHN

Ghana   –   GAH nuh

Ghazi   –   GAH zee

Giovanni Boccaccio   –   jee oh VAH nee boh KAH chee oh

Gladiator   –   GLAD ee ay tuhr

Goth   –   GAHTH

Granada   –   graa NAH duh

Grendel   –   GREN dul

Gulshan   –   GOOL shahn

Gupta dynasty   –   GOOP tuh (dynasty)

Guthorm   –   GOO thorm

Hagia Sophia   –   HAH zhee ah SOH fee ah ("zh" sound is like Zsa Zsa Gabor)

Haiku   –   HI koo (say "hah-ee" very quickly)

Hajj   –   HAZH ("zh" sound is like Zsa Zsa Gabor)

Halfdan   –   HALF dan ("hal" of HALF rhymes with "shall;" "dan" is like DANiel)

Hegira   –   HEH zheera ("zh" sound as above)

Hernan Cortes   –   ayr NANN kor TEZ

Hernando De Soto   –   ayr NAN doh day SO toh

Himalayas   –   HIM uh LAY uhz

Honingi   –   HOE neen ghee

Horns of Hattin   –   (Horns of) hat TEEN

Hrothgar   –   HRAHTH gahr

Huayna Capac   –   WHY nah kah PAHK

Huns   –   HUNZ

Hyde Abbey   –   HIDE AB ee

Humayan   –   hoo MY ahn

Ibn Athir   –   IB uhn ah THEER

Ibn Batuta   –   IB uhn bah TOO tah

Incas   –   EEN kuhz

Inti   –   IN tee

Isabella   –   IZ uh BEL uh

Islam   –   iz LAHM

Istanbul – IS tahn bool

Jabal Tariq – JAH buhl tair EEK

Jacques Cartier – ZHAHK kar tee AY

Jane Seymour – (Jane) SEE more

Jerusalem – juh ROO suh luhm

Johannes Gutenberg – yo HAN uhs GOO tuhn burg

John Cabot – KAB uht

Joyeuse – zhoy OOS ("zh" as in Zsa Zsa Gabor)

Julius Caesar – JEWL ee yus SEE zuhr

Justinian – juhs TIN ee uhn

Kamikaze – KAH mih KAH zee

Katanas – kah TAH nahs

Khans – KAHNZ

Kiev – KEE ef

Koran – kuh RAN

Kritovoulos – kree TOH vuh lohs

Kublai Khan – KOO blai KAHN

Kumargupta – koo mahr GOOP tah

Lake Texcoco – (lake) tex KOH koh

Lancastrian – lang KAS tree uhn

Leicester Abbey – LES tur AB ee

Leif Ericsson – LEAF ER ik suhn

Leo Africanus – ahf rih KAHN us

Li Yuan – LEE yoo AHH

Lutetia Parisiorium – loo TEE shee ah payr iss OR
          ee um

Macbeth – mac BETH

Magna Carta – MAG nuh KAR tuh

Mali – MAH lee

Manco Capac – MAHN koh kaw PAHK

Mansa Musa – MAWN saw MOO saw

Maori – MOU ree ("mou" rhymes with "cow")

Marianas Islands – MAIR ee AN uhs (Islands)

Maximilian – mack sih MIH lee ahn

Mayan empire – MY ahn

Mead – MEED

Mecca – MEHK uh

Medina – muh DEE nuh

Mediterranean Sea – MED ih tuh RAY nee uhn

Mehmed the conqueror – MEH med (the conqueror)

Merovius – meh ROH vee uhs or may ROH vee uhs

Midgard serpent – MID gard

Micmacs – MIHK macks

Ming – MEENG

Moghul – MOH guhl

Montezuma – MOHN tih ZOO muh

Moor – moohr

Morocco – muh ROK oh

Mosaic – moh ZAY ik

Mosque – mosk

Muhammad – moo HAM uhd

Muslims – MUZ lims

Newfoundland – NEW fuhn luhnd

Niccolo – NEEK koe low

Nicholas Copernicus – (Nicholas) koe PUR ni kus

Niña – NEE nyah

Norsemen – NORS mehn ("nors" rhymes with "horse")

Nottingham – NOT ing uhm

Oasis – oh AY sis (plural: Oases – oh AY sees)

Oda Nobunaga – OH dah NO boo NAH gah

Odin – OH dihn

Okuninushi – OH koo nee NOO shee

Onsen – OHN sehn

Orthodox – OR thuh doks

Ostrogoth – OS truh gahth

Othello – oh THELL oh

Ottoman – OT uh muhn

Pachamama – PAH chah mah mah

Paekche – PIKE shay

Pagoda Kofuku-ji – pah GOH dah koh foo KOOH jee

Pax Romana – PAHKS roh MAH nuh

Pedro Giron – PAY droh hee ROHN

Peking – pay KING

Pinta – PEEN tah

Portcullis – port KUHL ihs

Ptolemy – TOHL uh mee (second syllable is slurred)

Quetzalcoatl – ket SAHL koh ah tul (swallow the "l")

Ram Bagh – RAHM BAH

Ramadan – RAHM uh dahn

Refectory – rih FEK tuh ree

Relic – REL ik

Rheims – REEMZ

Roanoke Island – ROH uh noak

Robin of Lockesley – (Robin of) LOX lee

Roc - ROCK

Rodrigo Díaz de Vivar – rohd REE goh DEE ahz day vee VAHR

Rua – ROO ah

Rulu – ROO loo

Rune - ROON

Runnymede – RUN ee meed

Rurik – ROOR ik

Saladin – SAL uh deen

Salah – suh LAH

Salic law – SAH lik (law)

Samudragupta – SAH moo drah GOOP tah

Samurai – SAH moo rye ("rye" is really a quick "rah-ee")

Sanskrit – SAN skriht

Santa Maria – SANN tuh muh REE uh

Saracen – SAYR uh suhn

Sawm – sahm

Saxons – SAK suns

Scandinavia – SKAN duh NAY vee uh

Scourge – skurj

Scriptorium – skrip TOR ee uhm

Scyldings – SKEEL dings

Seppuku – sep POO koo

Shahadah – SHAH hah dah

Siege engines – SEEJ (engines)

Skandagupta – SKAHN dah GOOP tah

Skraelings – SKRAY leengs

Skymer – SKY mer

Songhay – SOHNG hye

Sui dynasty – SOO-EE (say quickly)

Suleiman – SOO lay mahn

Sultan – SUHL tun

Susano – SOO sah no

Sweyn Forkbeard – SVAYN FORK beerd

Tag Haza – TAHG ha ZHA ("zh" as in Zsa Zsa Gabor)

Tang Dynasty – TAHNG (dynasty)

Tariq Bin Ziyad – tar EEK bin zuh YAAD

Te Ika-a-Maui – TAY ee ka ah MOW ee ("mow" rhymes with "cow")

Tenochtitlan – teh NOCH teet lan

Terre-neuve – TAYR Noohv (somewhere between "nuhv" and "noov")

Tesserae – TESS er aye

Thane of Cawdor – THAYN (of) KAW dore

Thar Desert – TAR (desert)

Theodora – THEE uh DOR uh

Thialfi   –   thee AHL fee

Thor - THOR

Thorvald   –   THOR vuld

Tigris   –   TYE gris

Timbuktu   –   TIM buck TOO

Torah   –   TOR uh

Troy   –   troi

Tsar   –   zar

Tyr   –   tire

Valencia   –   vuh LEN see uh

Valhalla   –   val HAL uh

Valkyries   –   VAL keer eez

Vandals   –   VAN duls

Varangian Guard   –   vahr EN jee an (guard)

Vasco da Gama   –   VAS coe dah GAHM uh

Visigoth   –   VIZ ih gahth

Vizier   –   viz EER

Vladimir   –   VLAD uh meer

Vortigern   –   VOR tih gurn

Wani   –   WAH nee

Wessex   –   WEH siks

Wigwam   –   WIG wahm

William Caxton   –   (William) KAKS tuhn

Wittenberg   –   VIHT en burg

Woden   –   WOH dun

Xi'an   –   SHEE ahn

Yakka   –   YAK uh ("yak" as in "apple")

Yamato Dynasty   –   yah MAH toh

Yang Chien   –   YANG shee EN

Yangtze   –   YANG tzee

Yohanan ben Zakkai   –   yoh HAH nuhn ben zah KYE

Zakat   –   zuh KAHT

Zealot   –   ZEL uht

Xi'an   –   SHYAN

Xiling Ji   –   SHEE ling   JEE

Yangtze   –   YANG see   or   YANG dzu

The Glory That Was Rome

Encyclopedia Cross-References

Usborne Book of World History (UBWH), 88–91

Usborne Internet-Linked Encyclopedia of World History (UILE), 186–191, 194–195

Kingfisher Illustrated History of the World (KIHW), 114–119, 126–127, 140–142

Kingfisher History Encyclopedia (KHE),64–67, 80–81

WANDERING THROUGH THE ROMAN EMPIRE

REVIEW QUESTIONS

What was the most important city of the Roman Empire? (This city was called "The Ruler of the Whole World.") *Rome was the most important city of the Roman Empire.*

Can you remember one event that took place in the Coliseum? *Gladiator fights* OR *Chariot races* OR *Fights between lions and soldiers took place in the Coliseum.*

What was the leader of Rome called? *The leader of Rome was called the emperor.*

What does "Pax Romana" mean? *Pax Romana means "Roman peace." OR Everybody in the Roman Empire must obey Roman laws.*

Did the Celts obey the Pax Romana? *No, the Celts rebelled against the Romans.*

NARRATION EXERCISE

"The Roman Empire was very large and very powerful. The leader of the Roman Empire was called the emperor. Romans had very strict laws that everyone had to obey." OR

"I flew all around the Roman Empire on an imaginary magic carpet. I saw the emperor, Roman roads, and army camps. The Roman Empire was the most powerful empire in the world."

THE FALL OF ROME

REVIEW QUESTIONS

What problem was the Roman Empire having? *The Roman Empire became so large that it couldn't fight off invaders.*

Why did the Romans call the invading tribes "barbarians"? *The Romans called the invaders "barbarians" because the invaders didn't take baths, live in homes, or cook their food.*

Can you remember the name of one of the invading barbarian tribes? *The barbarians were called Huns (OR Vandals, Goths, Visigoths, Ostrogoths).*

What did the emperor Diocletian do? *He divided the Roman empire into two parts.*

What were the two parts of the Roman Empire called? *The two parts of the Roman Empire were called the Western Roman Empire and the Eastern Roman Empire.*

Did dividing the empire keep the Western Roman Empire strong and protected? *No, the barbarians conquered it anyway.*

Narration Exercise

"The Roman Empire got so big it couldn't fight off its enemies. Barbarians invaded it. An emperor decided to divide the Roman Empire into two parts, but the western part was conquered anyway." OR

"Wandering tribes invaded the Roman Empire. The Romans called them barbarians because they didn't take baths or cook their food. The barbarians conquered Rome."

Additional History Reading

Ancient Romans, by Daisy Kerr (Franklin Watts, 1996). An elementary guide to the Roman Empire, with text suitable for beginning readers; large print and color illustrations. (IR)

Costume of Ancient Rome, by David J. Symons (B. T. Batsford, 1987). This small book is actually a guide for stage costume designers, but children interested in dress will enjoy looking at the color paintings of Romans from all classes and the line drawings of armor, hairstyles, and accessories. (IR)

Gladiator, by Richard Watkins (Houghton Mifflin, 1997). Although the text of this dramatic book, illustrated with detailed black-and-white drawings, may be too complex for younger students, the pictures of each gladiator are captioned with one-paragraph descriptions which most children will be able to read. (RA 2–3, IR 4–5)

I Wonder Why Romans Wore Togas and Other Questions About Ancient Rome, by Fiona MacDonald (Kingfisher, 1997). Each page contains a simple question ("Why were Roman roads so straight?") and a 1–3 paragraph answer, written in large letters; color illustrations. (IR; may be RA for some second graders)

The Roman News: The Greatest Newspaper in Civilization, by Andrew Langley and Philip DeSouza (Candlewick Press, 1999). An entertaining and slightly tongue-in-cheek look at Roman life, Roman politics, and the greatest events in Roman history. (RA 2, although large summary paragraphs may be IR; IR 3–5)

Corresponding Literature Suggestions

Aesop's Fables, by Jerry Pinkney (SeaStar Books, 2000). Readable retellings and very attractive illustrations. Includes the story of Androcles and the Lion. (RA 1–2, IR 3–6)

Classic Myths to Read Aloud, by William F. Russell (Crown, 1992). A collection of Greek and Roman myths, designed to be read aloud to children five and older. (RA)

The Orchard Book of Roman Myths, by Geraldine McCaughrean, illus. Emma Chichester Clark (Orchard Books, 2001). Stories about Roman heroes (Aeneas, Romulus and Remus), Roman gods (Vulcan, Diana, Endymion, Mercury), and Roman legends (the geese who saved Rome from invading Gauls, the theft of the Sabine women), all retold for reading aloud. Each story is 6–8 pages, attractively illustrated. The previous version—and the one that many libraries may have—was published by Margaret McElderry Books and titled *Roman Myths*. (RA 2–4, IR 5)

Roman Myths and Legends, retold by Anthony Masters (Peter Bedrick Books, 2000). Beautiful (but sometimes scary) paintings illustrate these well-told stories from Roman mythology, including Romulus and Remus, Cupid and Psyche, Dido and Aeneas, and Horatius at the bridge. (RA 1–3, IR 3–5)

Rome Antics, by David MacCaulay (Houghton Mifflin, 1997). A homing pigeon soars through Rome, visiting ancient landmarks and ducking modern tourists. (IR)

The Roman Empire *(Student Page 1, answer 254)*

1. Color the Mediterranean Sea blue. It should look like a flying duck.

2. The center of the Roman Empire was the city of Rome. The emperor lived there. Circle Rome with purple, the color of royalty.

3. In yellow, outline the borders of the Roman Empire when it was at its largest point. Use the dotted line to help you.

COLORING PAGE   A Barbarian *(Student Page 2)*

PROJECTS

ART PROJECT   **Flying Around the Roman Empire**

Materials:
- ☐ Flying Carpet Figure *(Student Page 3)*
- ☐ Photograph of you (that you can cut up)
- ☐ Wall map

Directions:
1. Color the figure of the child on the flying carpet. Cut your own face out of the photograph and glue it over the blank face of the figure.

2. Now use your flying carpet to travel around the Roman Empire. Put your figure over the Mediterranean Sea. "Fly" it over to Italy. Then fly up Italy, over the Alps at the top of the "boot," and then over to Britain. Fly from Britain down to Spain, and then across the "nose" of the Mediterranean Sea, down into North Africa. Fly east (right) until you cross the Nile River. Turn north (up) and fly over Palestine and Asia Minor. Turn west (left) and fly across Greece and then back to Italy.

3. Now you can fly your "carpet" all around the house!

CRAFT PROJECT   **Make a Roman Legion's Signum or Standard**

Each legion in the Roman Army had its own *signum,* or standard, that it carried into battle. The first *signa* were made from bundles of straw tied to a pole. But as time passed, they became highly decorated. During the later part of the Roman Empire, most *signa* were decorated with ribbons, gold or silver eagles mounted at the top, and round metal disks. Each metal disk was carved with a picture of a fierce animal or a portrait of the emperor.

A special soldier called a *signifer* had the honor and responsibility of making sure the legion's *signum* was never lost in battle. The job was a dangerous one because the *signum* was so heavy that the soldier could not carry a weapon to protect himself. If a *signum* were lost during battle, the entire legion was shamed and disbanded as punishment. Follow the directions below to make your own Roman *signum* that you can use when you reenact a Celtic battle for Chapter 2.

Materials:
- ☐ Long cardboard tube (from wrapping paper)
- ☐ Construction paper
- ☐ Cardstock or lightweight cardboard
- ☐ Eagle or laurel templates *(Student Pages 4 and 5)*
- ☐ Aluminum foil
- ☐ Lengths of ribbon or yarn
- ☐ Glue, scissors, pen and crayons

Directions: 1. Cut several 6" round circles from the cardstock and wrap with aluminum foil. You may need to use some glue to hold the foil in place. Use a pen and press firmly on the foil to draw an outline of a fierce animal or an emperor's portrait. If you prefer, you can use pictures from magazines and glue them on instead.

2. Cut out the eagle or laurel template from the Student Pages. Color it. Glue it on a piece of cardstock. Cut the cardstock so it is the exact size of the template.

3. Next, cut out a 2" × 12" strip of cardboard. This will be used as the crossbar.

4. Assembly: Glue the eagle or laurel wreath at the top of the tube. Just below the eagle, glue the crossbar horizontally. Underneath the crossbar, space out and glue the "metal" disks into place on the tube. Be sure to leave enough room at the bottom of the tube so it can be held up. Allow the glue to dry completely. After everything is dry, cut long lengths of ribbon or yarn and tie, glue or staple them onto the crossbar. Your *signum* is now ready to use.

CRAFT PROJECT **Cookie Dough Roman Pillar**

Make a crumbled Roman building—and then be a barbarian and finish off your work!

Materials: ☐ Sugar cookie dough (a nice, sturdy recipe below)   ☐ Oven
☐ Spatula, kitchen knife and/or toothpick   ☐ Cookie sheet (greased)

Directions: 1. Remember that the pillars of the buildings of Rome fell.

2. Follow the recipe for the cookie dough.

3. Cover your hands with flour. Roll a lump of cookie dough into a thick pillar and lay it flat on your greased cookie sheet. Flatten lumps of dough into the base and top of the pillar and attach to the pillar. Carve the pillar with your knife or toothpick. If you like, you can sprinkle cinnamon sugar on the pillar to look like crumbling bits of stone.

4. Bake at 325 degrees for fifteen minutes (or until firm and lightly browned).

5. Once cooled take a picture of your sculpture. Then eat!

Sugar Cookie Recipe

Ingredients: ½ cup (1 stick) butter or margarine, softened   2 cups flour
½ cup sugar   1 teaspoon baking powder
1½ teaspoons vanilla, almond, or lemon extract   ½ teaspoon salt
1 egg
Sprinkles, colored sugar, candy pieces, and/or cinnamon sugar (optional)

Directions: 1. In a large bowl, cream butter and sugar. Beat in vanilla and egg.

2. In a small bowl, combine flour, baking powder and salt. Mix well.

3. Add dry mixture to the butter mixture little by little. Mix on low speed.

4. Press dough together with hands.

5. Divide dough into four balls. Wrap each in plastic wrap and chill for 2 hours in the refrigerator.

6. Use one ball of dough for the pillar (directions above). For remaining dough, roll each ball until ¼ inch thick. Cut with cookie cutters. Decorate with sprinkles, cinnamon sugar, colored sugars, or candy pieces. Place cookies on a greased cookie sheet.

7. Bake at 350 degrees for 8–10 minutes or until light brown.

Eat Like a Roman Soldier

Keeping the peace in Roman territories was hard work! Roman soldiers couldn't carry all of the comforts of home with them. Most ate food cooked over a fire. What do you think that would taste like? Try this and see!

Materials:
- ▨ Foil
- ▨ Hamburger shaped in patties
- ▨ Sliced onion
- ▨ Carrots, peeled and sliced long ways
- ▨ Fire pit outside (if possible), use a grill, or bake inside in oven
- ▨ New potatoes cut in medium chunks
- ▨ Other vegetables that you favor
- ▨ Salt to taste

Directions:
1. Prepare the food carefully on a clean cutting board or kitchen counter. Center a large square piece of foil on the work space. Put the hamburger patty down in the center of the foil, first. Add the onion and then the other vegetables.
2. Wrap up the foil packet sealing the ends carefully. This is an important step. The packet must be sealed securely because it acts as a pressure cooker when sealed correctly. Fold it over and pinch it down tight.
3. If it is possible, dig a hole in the ground in your backyard about the width of a tire. Adult should be in charge of building a small fire in the fire pit.
4. Place foil dinner into the fire with a stick and let it cook 35 minutes. (If necessary, you can also cook this in the oven at 350 degrees.)
5. Open and check if meat is cooked all the way through. It should not be pink in the center.
6. Use your clean hands to eat your foil dinner when it has cooled a bit. That's what the Romans did. No spoons or forks allowed!

Roman Empire from a Carpet View

What if that imaginary magic carpet of yours took you high enough that you could see the entire Roman Empire? What would it look like? Using your Chapter 1 map you can find out!

Materials:
- ▨ Masking tape
- ▨ Washable markers
- ▨ Wide end rolls of newsprint paper (available at your local newspaper printer, usually at a very low price)
- ▨ Chapter 1 map
- ▨ Large floor space

Directions:
1. Roll out two to three strips of newsprint—as long as you are tall—on to the large floor space that you'll be working on. Lay the strips with the sides touching. If three pieces are too wide, use only two.
2. Tape the strips of paper together at the seams where they are touching. Flip the taped pieces of paper over so that the taped sides are touching the floor and cannot be seen.
3. Look at your map. How will you put the same picture on to the large paper on the floor? This is where the game begins! Try to have the Mediterranean Sea in the middle of the paper. Don't worry about it looking perfect, just do your best. Decide where to start and with one eye on the map, follow it with a marker on to the map you are making on the floor.
4. Now look at the floor map. How does it look? Remember it doesn't have to be perfect. Label the places you remember from the chapter you just read.

The Early Days of Britain

CHAPTER 2

Encyclopedia Cross-References

UBWH 84–85, UILE 182–183
KIHW 112–113, KHE 68–69

THE CELTS OF BRITAIN

REVIEW QUESTIONS

What were the fierce, dangerous, blue-painted warriors of Britain called? *The blue-painted warriors were called Celts.*

What did the Celts do to the Romans in Britain? *The Celts drove the Romans out.*

What did "bards" do? *They memorized and sang stories that were never written down.*

In the story of the warrior Craith, what was the name of the giant? *The giant was named Giant Fovor of the Mighty Blows.*

Craith asked three warriors to help him rescue the princess. Each warrior had a different gift. Can you remember at least two of the gifts? *One warrior could see well, one could run fast, and one could hear the grass grow.*

NARRATION EXERCISE

"The Celts lived in Britain. They were strong and fierce warriors. They told stories about warriors to their children." OR

"A warrior named Craith wanted to marry a beautiful woman. He asked other warriors to help him. The warriors could run fast, see things far away, and hear well."

BARBARIANS COME TO BRITAIN

REVIEW QUESTIONS

Why did the Celtic king Vortigern ask the Angles and the Saxons to come over to Britain? *He wanted them to help him fight the other Celtic tribes.*

What did the Celts do once the Angles and the Saxons moved into their land? *Some Celts married the barbarians. Other Celts went and lived somewhere else.*

Do you remember what the kingdom of the Angles and Saxons became known as? *The kingdom of the Angles and Saxons became known as England.*

The Celts moved into the north and west of Britain. Can you remember two of the three countries where they settled? *The three countries are now called Scotland, Ireland, and Wales.*

What do we call this time in English history? *We call it the Middle Ages or the Dark Ages.*

Why do we call it the Dark Ages? *We call it the Dark Ages because the Angles and Saxons didn't write down any history or records.*

NARRATION EXERCISE

"The tribes of the Celts fought each other. A king of one of the tribes asked the barbarians to come over and help him fight the other Celts. The barbarians liked Britain so much that they stayed there." OR

"Angles and Saxons came to live in Britain. Now we call it 'England.' The Celts went to other parts of Britain to live. We call this the Dark Ages."

BEOWULF THE HERO

REVIEW QUESTIONS

What happened to the men who slept in the king's hall? *A monster came in and ate them.*

Who came to help the king kill the monster? *Beowulf, the mightiest man on the earth, came to help the king.*

When Beowulf and the monster Grendel were fighting, what painful thing happened to Grendel? *Beowulf pulled his arm off.*

Why did Beowulf decide to fight with bare hands? *Beowulf didn't think it would be fair to fight with weapons, since Grendel didn't have any.*

What did Grendel do after he was wounded? *He ran away and jumped into the water.*

How did the king thank Beowulf when he heard that Grendel had been defeated? *He had a great feast and gave Beowulf gold armor.*

NARRATION EXERCISE

"There was a monster that was eating all the warriors at night. Beowulf came and killed the monster. The king was so happy he gave Beowulf gold armor."

Additional History Reading

The Ancient Celts, by Patricia Calvert (Franklin Watts, 2005). An excellent guide to the Celts during Roman times, with many illustrations and a good clear explanation of the earliest Celtic tribes and their origins. (RA 1–3, IR 3–6)

The Celts (See Through History), by Hazel Mary Martell (Viking, 1996). A colorful and interesting guide to ancient Celtic culture. (RA)

The Celts: Lost Civilizations, by Allison Lassieur (Lucent Books, 2001). Plenty of maps and photographs, but the text is for slightly older students. Select a section to read out loud. (RA 1–4, IR 4–5)

Life in Celtic Times, by A.G. Smith (Dover, 1997). Focuses on the culture of the ancient Celts. (RA)

Raiders of the North: Discover the Dramatic World of the Celts and Vikings, by Philip Steele (Southwater Publishers, 2001). Focuses on the warlike nature of the Celts. (RA)

Corresponding Literature Suggestions

Beowulf, by Welwyn Wilton Katz (Groundwood Books, 2007). A prose retelling of the story of Beowulf, from the point of view of his young relative Wiglaf. Lengthy and somewhat difficult for younger children, but good for slightly older students. (RA 3–4, IR 5)

Beowulf the Warrior, by Ian Serraillier (Ignatius Press, 1997). Retells the story of Beowulf, in shortened form, in verse that preserves some of the alliteration; a few black-and-white illustrations. (RA 1–3, IR 4–5)

Celtic Fairy Tales, by Joseph Jacobs (Kessinger, 2003). A standard collection of wonderful tales. (RA)

Celtic Fairy Tales, by Neil Philip, illus. Isabelle Brent (Viking, 1999). Tales from Scotland, Ireland, Wales, Cornwall, and Brittany. Each story is longer than the stories in the Verniero book (below), but still appropriate for reading aloud. (RA 1–3, IR 4–5)

Celtic Memories, by Caitlin Matthews (Barefoot, 2003). Twelve traditional Celtic tales, suitable for reading aloud. (RA 1–3, IR 3–5)

Celtic Myths, by Sam McBratney, illus. Stephen Player (Hodder and Stoughton, 2005). Slightly more difficult tales for stronger readers. (IR 4–5)

Favorite Celtic Fairy Tales, by Joseph Jacobs (Dover, 1995). Eight longer tales for reading aloud or for good readers (the print is large and easy on the eye). (RA 1–4, IR 4–5)

Favorite Medieval Tales, by Mary Pope Osborne and Troy Howell (Scholastic Press, 2002). Wonderful (and brief) retellings of Beowulf, Gawain and the Green Knight, The Song of Roland, and other Celtic and early British tales, with full-color paintings as illustrations. Highly recommended! (RA 1–3, IR 4–5; may also be independent reading for strong third-grade readers)

One Hundred and One Celtic Read-Aloud Myths and Legends, by Joan Verniero (Black Dog and Leventhal Publishing, 2001). 101 well-written tales that can be read in ten minutes or less. (RA 1–2, IR 3–5)

MAP WORK

Barbarians Come to Britain *(Student Page 6, answer 254)*

1. Start on the mainland of Europe. Use a red crayon to circle the area that the Angles and Saxons originally lived (it is marked on your map).

2. Next draw an arrow across the North Sea to retrace the voyage the Angles and Saxons made to reach Britain. Use red to color the area they settled (this is the small area closed off by the dotted line).

3. Color the rest of Britain and Ireland (the large island west of Britain) blue to show where the Celts were living.

COLORING PAGE   Beowulf, ready to fight Grendel *(Student Page 7)*

PROJECTS

GAME ACTIVITY **Defeat the Romans**

The Celts and the Romans fought over control of Britain. Play this game to see who will gain control of the area.

Materials: ☐ Chess/checker board
☐ Red and blue colored card stock or paper
☐ Ruler, scissors and pencil

Directions: 1. This game can be played on a chess board, or by drawing an 8 × 8 grid on a sheet of paper.

2. Cut two sets of 17 1-inch square tokens, one set from each color of card stock/paper. Label 16 of the tokens with an "S" and one with a "G." These are the General and the Soldiers of your army. The blue tokens are the Celts, and the red tokens are the Romans.

3. Game Objective: The objective of this game is to capture all of the opposing army's men, before yours are captured.

4. Game Rules: Flip a coin to see which player goes first. Play begins by taking turns and placing tokens on any open square available on the board, one token at a time. When the tokens of both armies have been placed on the board, continue taking turns by moving a Soldier or General token one space at a time in any direction. Your goal is to try to sandwich the opponent's Soldiers in between two of your own. When this happens, you have captured that Soldier and can remove him from the board. The General token can be captured in a similar way, but he has the ability to jump over a Soldier into an empty spot (in other words, to capture the General you must surround him with two rows of opposing Soldiers). If an opponent's man is trapped between the General and one of his own men, the opponent's Soldier is captured and removed from the board. A player must always move a man when it is his turn, even if it results in the Soldier being captured. The first person to capture all of the opposing army's Soldiers wins. If a General is taken captive, the game is over immediately. Remember, protect your leader at all costs.

CRAFT PROJECT **Celtic Double-Headed War Axe**

Materials: ☐ A long cardboard tube from gift-wrap paper   ☐ Scissors, paintbrush, glue
☐ 10" × 17" poster board or other thick cardboard   ☐ Axe blade pattern *(Student Page 8)*
☐ Brown and silver paint   ☐ Optional: Aluminum foil
☐ 2 yards twine or string

Directions: 1. Use the axe blade pattern to draw one side of the blade head onto the cardboard. Flip the pattern over, line it up with the one just drawn, and trace the other side of the blade head. Use scissors to cut the pattern out.

2. Paint the cardboard tube brown (to simulate wood) and the blade head silver (to simulate metal). For a shinier blade head, cover it with a large piece of aluminum foil. A small piece of tape will hold down any stubborn edges.

3. Use a pair of scissors to make two parallel cuts in the cardboard tube. Make the cuts long enough (about 6") so that all but an inch of the middle spike is down inside the tube.

4. Use the twine/string to wrap around the blade head and axe handle in an "X" fashion. This will secure the blade from falling out and simulate how the Celts attached their blades into the wooden handles of their axes.

ACTIVITY PROJECT **Celtic Warrior Reenactment**

The Celts were known around the world as fierce, brave warriors. The ancient Greek geographer, Strabo, said of the Celts, "The whole race…is war mad." Before going into battle, the men would paint blue swirling patterns all over their bodies. They believed that the patterns had mystical powers and would protect them from harm during the battle. To make themselves look even fiercer, they used mud and clay to spike out their hair in all directions. It must have been a scary sight to see: hundreds of blue-painted men holding double-headed axes, screaming, yelling, and running toward you. To become a Celtic warrior, follow the directions below.

Materials: □ Double-headed axe, Celtic cloak and brooch
　　　　　□ Blue-colored face paint or eye shadow
　　　　　□ Hair mousse (extra firm holding)
　　　　　□ Optional items – old white t-shirt and blue fabric paint

Directions: 1. Use the blue face paint or eye shadow to paint blue swirling patterns on your body. Or, if you prefer, use an old t-shirt and draw the swirls with blue fabric paint.

2. Use the extra firm holding mousse to create the spikes in your hair. Do this by using liberal amounts of mousse and smaller portions of hair. If your hair is long, use a blow drier to help the mousse dry more quickly.

3. To make it even more fun, find a couple of friends to play the Romans in your reenactment.

CRAFT PROJECT **Celtic Brooch and Cloak**

The Celts lived in a colder climate and wore knee-length woolen cloaks to keep warm. To secure the cloak around their shoulders, the Celts would pin the cloak closed with a bronze brooch that had been decorated with red, blue, yellow and green enameling.

Materials: □ 1 yard of a solid color fabric　　　□ Large pin backing or safety pin
　　　　　□ Piece of light cardboard　　　　　□ Red, blue, green and yellow markers
　　　　　□ Dragon brooch pattern *(Student Page 9)*　□ Scissors and glue

Directions: 1. Glue the dragon brooch pattern to a piece of cardboard. After it has dried completely, cut it out and color it in with your markers.

2. After coloring the design in, turn the brooch over and glue the pin backing on. Use a liberal amount of glue to make sure the backing stays in place. A hot glue gun would work nicely for this too. Once the glue has completely dried, your brooch is ready to use.

3. Open up the fabric and use one of the short ends to drape over your shoulders and around your neck. Use your dragon brooch pin to secure the two ends. If the cloak is too long, have someone trim it to the desired length.

Christianity Comes to Britain

CHAPTER 3

Encyclopedia Cross-References

UBWH 97, 108–109, UILE 205, 236–237
KIHW 166–169, 180, KHE 102–103

AUGUSTINE COMES TO ENGLAND

REVIEW QUESTIONS

What did many Christians believe the pope's job should be? *They believed that the pope should take care of Christians all over the world.*

How did the pope first hear about Britain? *A slave trader told him.* OR *He saw boys from Britain being sold as slaves.*

What did the pope call the blond British boys? *He called them angels.*

Why did the pope send Augustine to Britain? *He wanted Augustine to teach the people there about Christianity.*

What did King Ethelbert say to Augustine when he arrived in Britain? *He said he could tell the people about Christianity.* OR *He asked if Augustine was going to put a spell on him.*

Augustine became the Archbishop of Canterbury. What was the Archbishop's job? *The Archbishop of Canterbury was the leader of all the Christians in England.*

NARRATION EXERCISE

"The pope saw boys being sold as slaves. They were from Britain. The pope sent Augustine to Britain to tell the people about Christianity." OR

"The pope sent Augustine to Britain. A king in Britain was worried that Augustine might put a spell on him. Augustine said that he would not do that, so the king let him come and live in Britain and tell people about his God."

MEDIEVAL MONASTERIES

REVIEW QUESTIONS

Who were the monks? *Monks are men who spend their lives praying and studying the Bible instead of getting married.*

What is a monastery? *A monastery is a place where the monks live together.*

Can you name two jobs that monks did in the story? *They were teachers, furniture-makers, or doctors.*

NARRATION EXERCISE

"Monks are men who pray and read the Bible. They don't get married, but live in a monastery. They work as doctors, teachers, and furniture-makers." OR

"Brother Andrew was a monk. He prayed and studied the Bible. He got up very early in the morning to go to church. He was making a table for the monastery."

REVIEW QUESTIONS

Why do we call the years after the fall of Rome the "Dark Ages" in England? *We call them the Dark Ages because most people couldn't read or write.*

Who taught the Anglo-Saxons to read and write? *Augustine and his companions taught the Anglo-Saxons to read and write.*

Who copied books by hand? *The monks copied books by hand.*

What did the monks write on? *The monks wrote on parchment* OR *on animal skins that had been soaked, stretched, and scraped.*

What were their pens made of? *Their pens were made of feathers, or quills.*

What was a *scriptorium*? A scriptorium *was a special room where the monks copied out books by hand.*

How did the monks decorate their books? *The monks decorated their books with paints made of egg whites* OR *with pictures in the margins and the tops of the pages* OR *with gold and silver.*

Why were books so expensive? *Books were expensive because they took a long time to make.*

NARRATION EXERCISE

"The Anglo-Saxons learned how to read from Augustine and his friends. Monks made books by hand. They wrote them on parchment and decorated them with paint and gold." OR

"Monks made parchment by scraping animal skins. They wrote with feathers and with ink made out of soot and tree sap. They copied the books in a special room called a *scriptorium*. Books were worth a lot!"

Additional History Reading

Across a Dark and Wild Sea, by Don Brown (Millbrook, 2002). This picture-book biography of the sixth-century Irish monk Comcille tells of his passion for words, his education in a monastery, and his adult life as scribe and monk. Beautifully done. (RA 1–2, IR 3–5)

Calligraphy, by Fiona Campbell (Children's Press, 1998). This book is an introduction to the art of calligraphy, filled with easy illustrations and projects using household items. (RA 1–2, IR 3–5)

The Church: Life in the Middle Ages, by Kathryn Hinds (Benchmark Books, 2002). Lavishly illustrated, clear text, good overview of medieval Christianity; selected chapters would make excellent read-alouds. (RA 1–3, IR 3–5)

How the Bible Came to Us: The Story of the Book That Changed the World, by Meryl Doney (Lion Children's Books, 1997). This history of the Bible for children, put out by an evangelical Christian press, includes sections on medieval monks and their copying work. (RA 1, IR 2–5)

Make Your Own Book: A Complete Kit, by Matthew Liddle (Running Press,1993). This kit contains everything needed to make a book—from binding the pages to illuminating, writing, and making a cover. (RA 1–2, IR 3–5)

What Were Castles For? (Usborne Starting Point History), by Phil Cox (EDC Publications, 2002). Answers different questions about life in and around a castle, with one section covering life in monasteries as well. (RA 1–2, IR 3–5)

Corresponding Literature Suggestions

Augustine Came to Kent, by Barbara Willard (Bethlehem Books, 1997). The British boy Wolf, brought to Rome as a slave, is set free by Pope Gregory and returns to Britain with Augustine's mission. One of the only books dealing directly with Augustine of Canterbury, this novel is too difficult for very young students but might make a good family read-aloud. (RA 1–4, IR 5)

The Holy Twins: Benedict and Scholastica, by Kathleen Norris, illus. Tomie DePaola (Putnam, 2001). This fictionalized picture-book biography of the founder of the Benedictine order is set in sixth-century Italy, but provides a good look at medieval monastic life and its ideals. (RA 1, IR 2–5)

The Last Snake in Ireland, by Sheila Callahan-MacGill, illus. Will Hillenbrand (Holiday House, 1999). A tongue-in-cheek story about St. Patrick, Ireland's snakes, and the Loch Ness Monster. (RA 1, IR 2–5)

Marguerite Makes a Book, by Bruce Robertson (J. Paul Getty Publications,1999). This beautifully illustrated book tells the story of how Marguerite came to help her father illuminate books. (RA 1–2, IR 3–5)

Otto of the Silver Hand, by Howard Pyle (Dover, 1967). Otto, raised in a medieval monastery, returns home to help his family. A long chapter book for good readers (IR 4–5)

Patrick: Patron Saint of Ireland, by Tomie DePaola (Holiday House, 1992). The story of Patrick's mission to Ireland, retold simply with many color pictures. (RA 1, IR 2–5)

Sir Gawain and the Green Knight, by Michael Morpurgo, illustrated by Michael Foreman (Candlewick, 2004). Morpurgo gives a much more complete retelling of the story than most other children's versions of this story. (RA 1–4, IR 5)

Sir Gawain and the Green Knight, retold by Selina Hastings (Walker, 1991). This medieval story comes from the days when Christianity in Britain was in conflict with the paganism represented by the Green Knight. (RA 2–3, IR 4–5)

The Story of Saint Patrick, by James Janda (Paulist Press, 1995). A retelling of the many legends surrounding Saint Patrick and his mission to Ireland. (RA 1–2, IR 3–5)

MAP WORK

From Rome to Canterbury *(Student Page 10, answer 254)*

1. King Ethelbert allowed Saint Augustine to start a church in Canterbury. Find the city of Canterbury in Britain and circle it in green.

2. Use a red crayon to show the route Saint Augustine might have taken if he had traveled from Rome to Canterbury by boat.

3. Use a brown crayon to show the route Saint Augustine might have taken if he had traveled mostly by land.

4. Use a blue crayon to color in the Mediterranean Sea, the North Sea and the Atlantic Ocean.

COLORING PAGES

Slave Boys from the Island of Britain *(Student Page 11)*

Medieval Manuscript—This type of lettering is called Insular Majuscule. Irish monks used this lettering, or calligraphy, when copying books. Color in the words "Deo Creavit," which means "God created." Then try copying some of the alphabet. You can trace it if you like. How long does it take you to copy your name? Can you imagine how long it took to copy a whole book this way? *(Student Page 12)*

CRAFT PROJECT   Make a Quill Pen and Ink

Materials:
- ☐ A good-sized feather (about 10" long)
- ☐ Cutting board, small sharp knife or scissors, straight pin
- ☐ Felt blotter (5" square of felt)
- ☐ Ink (store bought or Quill Ink Recipe, below. Grape juice also works. Better yet, use liquid grape juice concentrate.)
- ☐ Writing paper

Directions:
1. Place the feather in warm, soapy water and allow it to soak for 15 minutes. After the feather has finished soaking, have an adult remove the first 2" of feathers from the bottom of the quill with the knife or scissors. There is historic evidence that some people chose to remove all of the feathers from the quill stalk. Do whichever appeals to you the most.

2. Place the quill on a cutting board and trim the end of the quill stalk at an angle. This creates the point, or nib, of the pen. Use a straight pin to clean out any debris inside the stalk. The final step is to cut a small slit in the tip of the nib. This will help control the flow of ink while you write.

3. Learning to write with a quill pen takes practice. Dip the pen into the ink. Before writing, press the nib gently onto the felt blotter to remove any excess ink. The pen writes best when the nib is held at an angle to the paper. Practice on scratch paper to find the best angle and pressure you need to use to make the pen ink flow smoothly. When your pen runs out of ink, just dip it back into the inkpot, blot and continue writing.

4. If the nib of the pen should wear down or a piece of it chip off, simple follow the directions in Step 2 again.

Quill Ink Recipe

Ingredients:
Shells from 8–10 walnuts, crushed
1 cup of water
½ teaspoon vinegar

½ teaspoon of salt
Small empty jar

Directions:
1. In a small saucepan, bring the crushed walnut shells and the water to a boil. Reduce the heat and let the mixture simmer for 45 minutes. The water will turn a dark brown.

2. When the mixture has finished simmering, set it aside and allow it to cool down for 15 minutes. Using a strainer, pour the liquid into the small jar. Stir in the ½ teaspoon of salt and vinegar, until the salt has dissolved. Keep your ink jar covered while it is not in use, so that the ink will not dry out.

CRAFT PROJECT   Monk's Cross Necklace

When a man joined a monastery, he took a vow of poverty. This means that he gave up all of his possessions and worked solely for the benefit of God. One item that most monks did possess was a plain, carved wooden cross that was worn around their necks. Use the following instructions to make a cross of your own.

Materials:
- ☐ Air-drying clay
- ☐ Brown paint
- ☐ 1 yard brown rattail cord or twine
- ☐ Rolling pin, plastic knife, toothpick and markers
- ☐ Polymer Clay Option: Older children might prefer to use this material instead of air-drying clay. It takes a bit more skill to work with and requires baking to harden.

Directions:
1. Take a plum-sized piece of clay and roll it out into a rectangular shape that is about ½" thick. Use a marker to draw the cross designs on the clay, then cut away the unwanted portions with the plastic knife. If any of the cross' edges appear rough, use your fingers to gently push it back into place. Use a toothpick or sharpened pencil to place a hole in the top, center section of the cross. Allow the cross to dry overnight.

2. Use the brown paint to cover all areas of the cross. Depending on the thickness of the first coat, you might need to reapply the paint a second time. Allow for drying time between coats for the best results.

3. Using the rattail cord or twine, measure a length of the cord that will easily slip over the child's head when tied. Thread the cord through the hole in the cross and finish off by tying a slipknot at the end. Your cross is now ready to wear.

COOKING PROJECT **Prepare a Monk's Supper**

Monks were men who promised to live a quiet life of prayer and service to God. They lived together in a community called a monastery. These men worked together in the fields, ate meals together in the refectory and slept in dormitories. To experience a "taste" of what life was like as a monk, prepare a typical "monk's meal" for supper one night. You might like to pretend that it is Christmas, so you can have some butter on your bread!

Materials:
- ☐ Lentil or Split-Pea Soup (see recipes below)
- ☐ A crusty loaf of wheat bread
- ☐ Sliced cheddar cheese
- ☐ Sliced apples and pears
- ☐ Water or apple cider to drink

Lentil Soup Recipe

Ingredients:

1 onion chopped	¼ cup of olive oil
2 carrots, diced	2 stalks celery, chopped
2 cloves garlic, minced	1 teaspoon dried oregano
1 bay leaf	1 teaspoon dried basil
1 (14.5 ounce) can crushed tomatoes	1 cup dried lentils
8 cups water	½ cup spinach, rinsed and thinly sliced
2 tablespoons vinegar	Salt to taste, ground black pepper to taste

Directions:
1. In a large soup pot, heat the oil over medium heat. Add onions, carrots and celery; cook and stir until onion is tender. Stir in the garlic, bay leaf, oregano and basil; cook for 2 minutes.

2. Stir in lentils, and add water and tomatoes. Bring to a boil. Reduce heat, and simmer for at least 1 hour. When ready to serve, stir in the spinach and cook until it wilts. Stir in vinegar, and season to taste with salt and pepper. Makes 6 servings.

Split Pea Soup Recipe

Ingredients:

2 cloves garlic, minced
2 stalks celery, chopped
1¾ cups dried split peas
1 bay leaf
2 carrots, chopped
3 potatoes, peeled and cubed

1 onion, chopped
3 tablespoons olive oil
2 (14.5 ounce) cans chicken broth
2 ounces diced ham
2 teaspoons dried chervil
Salt and pepper to taste

(Potatoes were not introduced to Europe until the 1500s, so you can omit this ingredient if you want to be really authentic.)

Directions:

1. In a pressure cooker over medium heat, sauté the garlic, onion and celery in olive oil for 5 minutes, or until onion is translucent. Add the peas, broth, bay leaf and ham. Cook under pressure for 10 to 12 minutes. (***Note:*** If you do not have a pressure cooker, cook the peas over low heat for 3 to 4 hours or use a slow cooker.)

2. Once the peas are soft, stir in the potatoes, carrots and chervil and simmer for 15 minutes, or until the potatoes are tender. Season with salt and pepper to taste. Add water as needed to adjust the thickness of the soup.

CRAFT PROJECT   Medieval Letter Illumination

Illumination refers to the beautiful art work painted by the monks in the margins of their handwritten books. In most cases, the first letter of each page was enlarged and highly decorated. This craft project will provide you with an opportunity to try your own hand at illumination. There are several methods that can be used, so pick the one that best suits your artistic capabilities.

Materials:

☐ Card stock or heavy paper
☐ Illumination pattern *(Student Page 13)*
☐ Acrylic paints (for children with a steadier hand)
☐ Color markers or pencils
☐ Gold metallic paint or markers
☐ Optional: Gold leaf (this can be purchased at a craft store)

Directions:

1. Make two copies of the illumination pattern. One on regular paper and the other on card stock or heavy paper. The copy on the regular paper will be used to plan out the color scheme you will use on your final illumination.

2. After you have planned out your color scheme, use the gold metallic paint, markers or gold leaf to fill in the areas of your illumination that you want to be covered in gold.

3. After the gold paint has dried, use your paints, markers or color pencils to fill in the rest of the design. Medieval illuminations were done in very vibrant colors: blue, green, red and yellow. If you are using markers or color pencils, be sure to press hard and color in the areas heavily.

4. When you have completed your illumination, you can use it as the cover for your own handwritten book or you could mount it in a frame and display it on the wall.

Make a Monk's Robe

(Requires pattern purchased from fabric store)

During medieval times, monks dressed in long, hooded robes that were secured around the waist with a rope belt. McCall's Pattern 2854 can be used to make many different types of medieval clothing.

Materials:
- ☐ McCall's Pattern 2854, View F Tunic
- ☐ Brown fabric (refer to pattern directions for yardage)
- ☐ 2 yards medium size drapery cord
- ☐ Optional: Heat and bond seam tape

Directions:

1. Follow the pattern directions to complete the robe. If you do not have a sewing machine, this item can be made using Heat and Bond Seam Tape and an iron.

2. Use the length of drapery cord to make a belt. Tie a slip knot at each end of the cord to stop it from unraveling. Tie the belt around the child's waist using a square knot. The ends of the cord should hang down to about the mid-calf on the child. If the belt is too long, cut off the unneeded length and retie the knots at the ends of the cord.

3. Now, put on your Monk's Cross Necklace and get your picture taken for your History Notebook. It would be fun to wear your robe while you are having your monk's meal.

The Byzantine Empire

CHAPTER 4

Encyclopedia Cross-References

UBWH 92–93, UILE 202–203
KIHW 162–164, KHE 100–101

THE BEAUTY OF CONSTANTINOPLE

REVIEW QUESTIONS

What happened when the Roman Empire got too big for one ruler? *The Roman Empire was divided into two parts.*

What were the two parts known as? *The two parts were called the Western Roman Empire and the Eastern Roman Empire.*

What was the capital city of the Eastern Roman Empire? *The capital city was Constantinople.*

What do we call the last surviving part of the Eastern Roman Empire? *We call it the Byzantine Empire.*

What was the capital city of the Byzantine Empire? *The capital city was Constantinople.*

If you were a child in Constantinople, where would you be during the day? *In school.*

Describe some of the things you might see in Constantinople. *People in togas; shops selling silks, jewelry, and food; a beautiful church with a gold ceiling.*

Was Constantinople a big, beautiful, rich city or a poor, ugly city? *A big, beautiful city!*

Do you remember how many palaces were in Constantinople? *There were fourteen palaces in Constantinople.*

NARRATION EXERCISE

"Constantinople was the capital city of the Byzantine Empire. It was very large and rich." OR

"Constantinople was a beautiful city. It had good roads, shops with food and jewelry, big churches, and lots of palaces. The biggest church was called the Hagia Sophia."

JUSTINIAN, THE JUST EMPEROR

REVIEW QUESTIONS

Did Justinian come from a rich family? *No, his parents were poor peasants.*

Why did Justinian want to go to Constantinople? *He wanted to go to school.*

What did Justinian join, after he finished school? *He joined the army.*

Once Justinian became the emperor of the Byzantine Empire, what did he do? *He sent his armies to conquer the lands that were once ruled by the Roman Empire.*

When he had conquered these faraway lands, what problem did he encounter? *They all followed different laws.*

How did he solve this problem? *He made a new set of laws that everyone had to follow.*

What were some of the laws from the Code of Justinian? *Everyone could go to the beach or the river; if you found treasure washed up by the river, you could keep it; you could own slaves; thieves must repay the owner of the stolen object; you must warn people below if you are trimming a tree near a road; preachers must be loud enough for everyone to hear.*

NARRATION EXERCISE

"Justinian was a peasant who worked hard and became emperor. He took back a lot of the land that had belonged to the Roman Empire. He came up with a new set of laws for all the people of his empire to follow." OR

"Justinian was a good emperor of the Byzantine Empire. He conquered many lands and wrote a new set of laws for everyone to follow. Some of the laws were that the sea belonged to everyone and that people couldn't mistreat their slaves."

THE EMPRESS THEODORA

REVIEW QUESTIONS

What did Theodora do before she became the empress? *She was a circus clown, an actress, and a wool spinner.*

Why did Theodora become a Christian? *She wanted a different kind of life.*

Who did she marry? *She married Justinian.*

How did Theodora save the Emperor Justinian's throne? *She convinced her husband to stay and fight the rebels and not run away.*

NARRATION EXERCISE

"Theodora married Justinian and became the empress of the Byzantine Empire. Justinian listened to Theodora before he made a decision. He listened to her when she told him to stay and fight some rebels and to not run away." OR

"Theodora was a famous actress. Then she married Justinian and became empress. She was very wise and helped her husband remain emperor of the Byzantine Empire."

THE CHURCH IN THE EAST

REVIEW QUESTIONS

What happened to the Hagia Sophia in the riots? *It was mostly destroyed.*

What is a mosaic? *A mosaic is a picture made by arranging little colored pieces, called tesserae, into a pattern.*

Do you remember what many people believed the pope's job should be? *Many people believed that the pope should look after all Christians.*

Did Christians in Constantinople think that the pope should be able to make decisions for all Christians? *No, they thought that all the leaders of churches in important cities should join together to make decisions.*

What do we call Christians who continued to believe in the authority of the pope? *We call them Roman Catholics.*

What do we call Christians further east, who called their leaders patriarchs? *We call them Orthodox OR Eastern Orthodox.*

In the story, why did Nicholas give money to the girls? *Because they were poor, and they needed money to marry their true loves.*

What is a "saint"? *A person who has a special relationship with God.*

What name is St. Nicholas often called by today? *Santa Claus!*

NARRATION EXERCISE

"There were a lot of Christians in Constantinople. They built big churches with beautiful mosaics in them. They believed that the leaders of many churches, not just the pope, should make decisions all together. We call them Eastern Orthodox." OR

"The Christians in the Byzantine Empire told a story about a man named Nicholas. He gave money to three poor girls so that they could get married. Today we call him St. Nicholas or Santa Claus."

Additional History Reading

Byzantine Fashions, by Tom Tierney (Dover, 2002). A fun introduction to Byzantine culture, via its clothes. (RA 1–2, IR 3–5)

Cities Through Time: Daily Life in Ancient and Modern Istanbul, by Robert Bator (Lerner Publications, 2000). A descriptive look at Constantinople from its birth as Byzantium through its renaming as Constantinople and its capture by the Turks. Advanced fourth-grade reading level, but many pictures make it suitable for a read-aloud (pick and choose different sections). (RA 1–4, IR 4–5)

Cultural Atlas for Young People: The Middle Ages, by Mike Corbishley (Oxford University Press, 2003). This dictionary-like book is filled with maps, pictures, and factual paragraphs; it profiles Justinian's achievements with a brief mention of Theodora and includes pictures of the mosaic work at Ravenna. (RA 1–3, IR 4–5)

Famous Men of the Middle Ages, ed. Cyndy and Robert Shearer (Greenleaf Press, 1992). This read-aloud features the life of Justinian in Chapter 6. (RA 1–4, IR 4–5)

I Am Eastern Orthodox, by Philemon D. Sevastiades (Rosen Publishing Group, 1996). This very simple account by an Eastern Orthodox child describes the history and practices of the Eastern Orthodox Church. (IR 2–4)

Mosaics (Step by Step), by Michelle Powell (Heinemann Library, 2001). This project book describes mosaic techniques and then describes projects recreating objects from ancient African, Egyptian, Greek, Aztec, and Indian cultures. (Projects are do-alone for grades 4–5, substantial help required for grades 1–3).

Corresponding Literature Suggestions

How the Monastery Came to Be on the Top of the Mountain, by Alvin Alexi Currier (Conciliar Press, 1999). A lovely picture-book tale of a medieval Eastern Orthodox monastery on the top of a Romanian mountain. (RA 1–2, IR 3–5)

The Legend of Saint Nicholas, by Demi (Margaret K. McElderry, 2003). (RA 1–3, IR 3–5)

The Miracle of Saint Nicholas, by Gloria Whelan (Bethlehem Books, 1997). The story of a Christmas miracle in a church named after Saint Nicholas; explains Orthodox practices with beautiful illustrations. (RA 1, IR 2–5)

Saint Nicholas, by Ann Tompert (Boyds Mills Press, 2000). This picture book retells the story of Nicholas's life from childhood on, with detailed illustrations (one is a little bit frightening) made to look like mosaics. (RA 1, IR 2–5)

Saints: Lives and Illuminations, by Ruth Sanderson (Eerdmans, 2007). Forty short biographies, one of which is on Theodora. (RA 1–2, IR 3–4)

Who in the World Was the Acrobatic Empress? The Story of Theodora, by Robin Phillips (Peace Hill Press, 2006). Focuses briefly on Theodora's childhood, and then on how she helped her husband, Emperor Justinian, during the Nika Revolt. (RA 1–2, IR 3–4)

MAP WORK

The Byzantine Empire at the Time of Justinian *(Student Page 14, answer 254)*

Simple map work

In 527, Justinian became emperor of the Roman Empire in the east, which we now call the Byzantine Empire. His dream was to rebuild the Roman Empire. In 533 he began with campaigns against the Vandals and Ostrogoths in Africa and Italy. In 552 he conquered parts of southern Spain. In 565, Emperor Justinian died, having seen some of his dream fulfilled.

1. Find the box in the key that shows the Byzantine Empire. Shade the box in orange. Then color the territory Justinian ruled as Emperor of the Byzantine Empire on the map (this is the area in the dotted lines).
2. Locate the beautiful Constantinople on the map. Circle Constantinople in brown.
3. Use blue for the water and river outlines.

Advanced map work *(Student Page 15)*

Justinian built many Byzantine churches and monasteries. But he was not the only one! As the Byzantine Empire grew, so did the number of churches and monasteries. Color the pictures on *Student Page 15,* cut them out, and place them on the map close to the city where they were located.

COLORING PAGES

Empress Theodora helped Justinian rule the Byzantine Empire. *(Student Page 16)*

Justinian rebuilt the Hagia Sophia and made it more beautiful than ever. *(Student Page 17)*

PROJECTS

ACTIVITY PROJECT Make a "Code of Justinian"

Look back through the laws Justinian included in his code. Many scribes and leaders helped Justinian to form his code. They looked at the Roman and Greek laws. Maybe they even looked over Hammurabi's laws. Remember him? (See pages 46 through 50 in *The Story of the World; Volume 1: Ancient Times, revised edition.*) Hammurabi had his laws carved on a tall stone. When you studied about Hammurabi, you might have written up some rules that are in your home. (See page 26 in *The Story of the World Activity Book One, revised edition.*) As we look at Justinian, we're going to write up some laws that are in our town, state, or country.

Justinian used helpers, so you should gather your own helpers (your parents, siblings, or friends.) What laws should govern your house? Remember that laws often have to do with property—who is allowed to use what, and under what conditions? Laws also govern how people should behave towards each other. When are they allowed to tell each other what to do? When do they have to obey each other? What is the penalty for hurting (offending) another person?

Now imagine that each person in your family could make their own laws. How would these laws be different? Would they conflict with each other? (Justinian had this problem when he ruled over many different countries.) How could you make these laws together into one code?

Write your laws down in a notebook or folded-paper booklet. Make sure that everyone knows where the laws can be found!

CRAFT PROJECT **Crown of the Empress Theodora**

Ravenna was an important city conquered by Justinian. Can you locate it on your map? (*See* "Advanced Map Work.") The church of San Vitale, in Ravenna, was special to Justinian. This church contains a famous mosaic of Justinian and Theodora bringing gifts to the altar. This mosaic shows us the kind of crown Justinian and Theodora wore.

Materials:
- Template of Empress Theodora's Crown (*Student Page 18*)
- One sheet of purple posterboard
- Beans, buttons, craft jewels, painted rocks, macaroni, rice, sand or other small things
- White craft glue
- Medium-sized craft pearls (or use dried white lima beans)
- Thread and needle

Directions:
1. Photocopy and enlarge the crown template. Using the template, cut out two pieces from the purple posterboard. Do not include the circular disc on the second tracing. That is the front of the crown.

2. Staple one side. Wrap around the wearer's head until it fits snug, but not too tight. Mark the place, and leaving an inch on the back end to staple together once finished, cut off excess.

3. Place the crown flat on a table covered with newspaper for protection. Glue pearls or beans onto crown.

4. Finish top disc with your own special arrangement of decorations.

5. Let dry completely. Staple the crown together.

6. With the needle and thread, make a long string of pearls. Empress Theodora wore several long strands of pearls which hung from the bottom edge of her crown and draped down past her shoulder. Measure how long your strands need to be to create the same look. Attach one strand in front of the ear and two behind the ear. Use the needle to poke through the posterboard. Then tie the strands to the crown.

OPTION: Instead of gluing the different pieces, color or paint the different layers of decorations onto the posterboard. Add the dangling pearls for added effect!

CRAFT PROJECT **Jeweled Earrings of the Empress Theodora**

In the mosaic at San Vitale, the Empress has large hoop earrings with a long strand of pearls and jewels dangling from the hoops and blending with the pearl strands hanging from her crown. Here's a way for you to create the same look.

Materials:
- Craft clip-on earrings, with holes in the disc, about the size of a nickel (at craft stores in the jewelry findings section)
- Hot glue gun (parental supervision advised)
- Glue sticks
- Two gold buttons with no shank (⅝ inch or less)
- Craft pearls
- Plastic, round "jewel" beads of your choice
- Gold craft wire
- Scissors

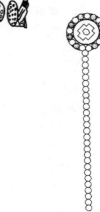

Directions: 1. Decide on the design of your earrings. If the gold buttons cover the whole disc on your earring, continue on designing your long pearl strand.

2. Measure out how long you want your strand to dangle from your ears. Add an inch to the total and double length to have enough for both earrings.

3. String your first pearl onto the middle of your wire. Bend it around, securing the bottom so that none of the beads can slide off. Fold the wire up so that both ends can be threaded together. Keep wire straight and taunt to provide the easiest success with the threading.

4. Finish stringing the beads, leaving an inch on the end.

5. Tuck the two ends into the bottom middle hole of the earring clip. Go from the front side to the back and then thread it up one more hole from the back to the front.

6. Bend it down and secure when you add the gold button to the top disc with hot glue.

7. If you still have some space around your button, add your pretty jewel beads around the outer edges.

8. Repeat with second earring, following the exact pattern of your first earring.

9. Use with your Empress Theodora crown!

CRAFT PROJECT · Make Justinian and Theodora Paper Dolls

Materials:
- ☐ Colored pencils
- ☐ Scissors
- ☐ Scotch Removable Double-Stick Tape
- ☐ Photocopy of the paper dolls *(Student Page 19)* on card stock
- ☐ Photocopy of paper doll clothes *(Student Pages 20 and 21)* on regular white paper

Directions: 1. Color the paper dolls and their clothes. Cut them all out. Though the mosaics of Justinian and Theodora use muted brown, creams, reds and greens, they also wore bright purples and blues! (For pictures of the mosaics, see *Cultural Atlas for Young People: The Middle Ages,* by Mike Corbishley, pages 16–20.)

2. Use the removable double-stick tape to keep the outfits on your dolls.

ART PROJECT · Byzantine Mosaic

Materials:
- ☐ Clean gallon milk jug, top cut off (leave at least four inches from the bottom)
- ☐ Beads, beans, marbles, beach glass, or broken tile pieces (call ahead and see if tile stores have broken pieces they will give away!)
- ☐ Large paperclip, with the large end cut off, forming a hook for the mosaic
- ☐ Petroleum jelly
- ☐ Plaster of Paris
- ☐ Piece of paper and pencil
- ☐ Disposable plastic tub to mix the plaster in
- ☐ Craft knife

Directions: 1. Trace the bottom of the milk jug onto a piece of paper. This will be your working space. Draw up your idea for your mosaic. Remember the more detailed your drawing is, the more difficult your mosaic will be. After you draw your picture, arrange your mosaic pieces on it.

2. Generously smooth on the petroleum jelly onto the inside of the clean milk jug. This helps prevent the mosaic foundation from sticking after it dries.

3. Pierce the milk jug on the side with the paperclip end from the outside so that the cut off side is poking into the jug as far as you can. Make sure it is one inch from the jug's bottom. Leave a bit of the rounded side sticking out as the hanger after you're finished. This will be the top of your mosaic.

4. Mix the Plaster of Paris in the disposable tub according to the directions on the box.

5. Once it is smooth and creamy, pour into the milk jug. Make sure it fills up at least two inches to give it a good foundation.

6. Wait until the mix is out of the soupy stage. Begin by pressing in your design, following the pattern you've already made on your paper. If your design begins sinking, wait a few more minutes and try again.

7. Let it dry at least for a day and night. Then tap the sides. Use a craft knife or sharp pair of scissors, to cut down the side of the jug, freeing the hanger. Gently lift the mosaic out of the rest of the carton and let it dry one more day. Hang it up and enjoy your mosaic!

Please Note: You should NEVER pour liquid plaster down the sink or wash items that have plaster on them in the sink! Plaster can set under water and will clog your pipes!!

ACTIVITY PROJECT **A Secret Act of Kindness**

Reread the story of Nicholas. Can you think of someone who did something nice for you? For your family? For your neighborhood?

Today, think of something you could do for someone else. Make sure when you do it that they do not know it was you who did it! Nicholas did his good deeds in secret (that is why Santa Claus is always said to come in the middle of the night, when everyone else is asleep). After you do your secret good deed, remember that Nicholas never told the three girls who brought their dowry. His kindness remained secret!

The Medieval Indian Empire

CHAPTER 5

Encyclopedia Cross-References

UBWH 83, 116–117, UILE 174–175
KIHW 136–137, KHE 78–79

A KING NAMED SKANDAGUPTA

REVIEW QUESTIONS

Why was travel in the Middle Ages dangerous? *You might get caught in a battle between war leaders.*

Why was it safer to travel in the Byzantine empire? *Justinian and the other emperors made sure that their people obeyed the laws.*

What is a "dynasty"? *A dynasty is a family that rules in a place for many years.*

What dynasty united all the little kingdoms of India? *The Gupta dynasty united India.*

What was the first Gupta king named? *The first Gupta king was called Chandragupta.*

What was the time of peace and wealth during the Gupta dynasty called? *This time is called the Golden Age of India.*

Who invaded India during the Gupta dynasty? *The Huns invaded India.*

What is King Skandagupta known for? *He defeated the invading Huns.*

Although the Indians succeeded in driving back the Huns, what happened to India when the fighting was over? *Its Golden Age ended—India became poorer and weaker.*

NARRATION EXERCISE

"India was united during the Gupta dynasty. India became peaceful and rich. Then the Huns invaded. Although King Skandagupta managed to drive them out, the fighting made India poor and weak." OR

"India was ruled by a family called the Guptas. India became very rich and peaceful. The barbarians invaded, but India fought back and won."

MONKS IN CAVES

REVIEW QUESTIONS

Whose teachings did the monks of India study and follow? *They followed the teachings of Buddha.*

Where did some of the monks live? *The monks lived in caves.*

How did the monks crack the cliffs so that they could dig their caves? *They put logs into trenches and then soaked the logs with water so they would swell and crack the cliffs.*

How did the monks decorate the caves? *They carved sculptures out of the stone and painted frescoes on the walls.*

What is a fresco? *A fresco is a painting made on wet plaster.*

What are the caves called? *The caves are known as the Ajanta Caves.*

Who rediscovered the Ajanta Caves? *Two soldiers out hunting tigers discovered the Ajanta Caves.*

"The monks in India followed Buddha. Some lived in caves. They created sculptures and painted frescoes on the wall. A fresco is a picture painted on wet plaster." OR

"Some Indian monks lived in caves. They dug out the caves with tools, logs, and water. They decorated the caves with paintings and sculptures. These caves are called the Ajanta Caves."

Additional History Reading

Buddha, by Demi (Henry Holt, 1996). The story of Siddhartha's life and a brief introduction to the teachings of Buddhism. (RA)

Country Insights: India, City and Village Life, by David Cumming (Raintree Steck-Vaughn, 1998). This guide to the different parts of India describes daily life in a number of different settings; covers modern India, but also the climate and countryside. (RA 2–3, IR 4–5)

I Am a Hindu, by Devi S. Aiyengar (PowerKids Press, 1996). A very simple introduction to Hindu practice; the child featured is an Indian who explains Indian customs and basic Hindu beliefs. (IR)

In the Heart of the Village: The World of the Indian Banyan Tree, by Barbara Bash (Sierra Club Books for Children, 1996). The activity in and around a banyan tree reveals daily life in rural India; the book begins with the retelling of an ancient India creation legend. (RA 2–3, IR 4–5, although some children may resist the unusual font)

India (Countries of the World), by Michael S. Dahl (Bridgestone, 1997). Focuses on the modern culture of India, with occasional glances back at the past. (RA)

My Friend's Beliefs: A Young Reader's Guide to World Religions, by Hiley H. Ward (Walker Publishing, 1988). Pages 13–40 discuss Hinduism and Buddhism. (RA)

Snake Charmer, by Ann Whitehead Nagda (Henry Holt, 2002). The story of a young Indian whose father is teaching him to be a snake charmer; set in modern India, but informative about ancient customs. Photographs and simple text. (RA 2, IR 3–5)

We Come From India, by David Cumming (Raintree Steck-Vaughn, 2000). This easy-to-read, highly photographic book is about life in modern India, but also covers aspects of Indian life that have not changed since ancient times. (IR)

World Religions, by John Bowker (Dorling Kindersley, 1997). Pages 18–41 cover Hinduism, and pages 54–75 cover Buddhism. (RA)

Corresponding Literature Suggestions

A Coloring Book of Ancient India (Bellerophon Books, 1989). Uses images from ancient Indian culture. (RA and activities)

The King's Chessboard, by David Birch, illus. Devis Grebu (Dial Books, 1988). A traditional Indian tale about pride, with a mathematical puzzle at its center. (RA 1, IR 2–5)

Once a Mouse…, by Marcia Brown (Atheneum, 1961). This Caldecott Medal book retells, very simply, an animal fable featuring an Indian hermit. (IR)

The Prince Who Became a Beggar, by Amina Okada, illus. Dominique Thibault (Creative Education, 1993). A retelling of the Buddha's life, incorporating myths and legends; simple text, but a little long for reading out loud unless you select individual chapters. (RA 2–3, IR 4–5)

The River Goddess: A Hindu Tale, by Vijay Singh, illus. Pierre de Hugo (Creative Education, 1993). The story of the river goddess Ganges and her descent to earth, one of the foundational creation myths of India; sidebars cover different aspects of ancient Indian civilization. (RA 2–3, IR 4–5)

The Very Hungry Lion: A Folktale, by Gita Wolf, illus. Indrapramit Roy (Annick Press, 1996). This Indian folktale about Singam the Lion is illustrated with traditional Indian folk paintings. (IR)

The Wisdom of the Crows and Other Buddhist Tales, by Sherab Chodzin (Tricycle Press, 1998). A nice collection of Buddhist moral tales from India, Burma, Tibet, China, and Japan. (RA)

The Wizard Punchkin, by Joanna Troughton (Peter Bedrick Books, 1988). A folk tale from ancient India about a wizard who keeps his heart outside of his body. (IR) (**Out of print;** check your local library)

———————————————— **MAP WORK** ————————————————

The Gupta Empire *(Student Page 22, answer 255)*

1. The Ganges is the most important river in India. Trace the path of the river in blue. The arrows all point to the Ganges River.

2. The Ganges floods every year, leaving good soil for crops to grow on. Color the area around the Ganges River green.

3. One of the borders of the Gupta empire was formed by the Himalaya, the highest mountains in the world. Color each of the mountains red, because the Gupta empire "stopped" there.

4. The monks built caves in Ajanta. Circle Ajanta Caves in brown and color it in to look like a cave entrance.

Coloring Page   During the Gupta dynasty, villagers rode on elephants. *(Student Page 23)*

———————————————— **PROJECTS** ————————————————

ART PROJECT   ## Say "Welcome" with Sand Art

Diwali is a Hindu New Year celebration. Followers of the Hindu religion hang beautiful sand pictures on their doors as part of the New Year festivities.

Materials: ☐ Paper
             ☐ Pencil
             ☐ Glue stick
             ☐ Colored sand (purchase at craft or art supply store or see Colored Sand Recipe, below)

Directions: 1. On the piece of paper, sketch out a drawing. Simple is better with this project.
             2. Using the glue stick, trace all the areas you want to be one color (say blue).
             3. Sprinkle colored sand on the gluey areas. Shake off any excess sand.
             4. Repeat steps 2–3 with another color until your picture is completed.
             5. Hang your picture in your front hallway or on your bedroom door.

Colored Sand Recipe

Materials: Sand
Food coloring
Zip-close baggies

Directions: 1. Measure one cup of sand and put it in a baggie.

2. Add a couple drops of food coloring and zip-close the baggie.

3. Shake the bag of sand until the color is spread evenly throughout.

Make as many colors as you like!

CRAFT PROJECT Weave Your Own Woolen Cloth

The peoples living in the Himalayan Mountains needed strong, warm clothing to make it through the harsh winters. They would make yarn from the wool of their mountain sheep. This yarn would be woven into lengths of fabric to make cloth for clothes. Follow the directions below and make your own woolen fabric.

Materials: ☐ Piece of corrugated cardboard (the larger the piece, the larger the finished cloth)
☐ Yarn in several colors (small scraps can also be used)
☐ Pencil, ruler, large nail, scissors, large plastic sewing needle and tape

Directions: 1. To make the loom, use the ruler and pencil to mark a dot every ½" along the top and bottom of the piece of cardboard. When this has been done, use the nail to punch a hole in each dot, being sure to go all the way through the cardboard.

2. Take a small piece of tape and wrap it tightly around the end of a piece of yarn. This will be our needle to help thread the yarn through the holes in the loom. Starting at the top left hand corner, thread the yarn up and down through the holes. Continue doing this until all the holes have been threaded. When this has been done, tie a large knot at each end leaving a long tail. This threading has created the "warp" thread of our cloth.

3. Now use any combination of colored yarns to begin your weaving. Thread your yarn through the large plastic needle (tape would work again) and starting at the bottom, weave the yarn over and under the warp threads. Periodically, you will need to use your fingers to push or "pack" down the yarns to create a denser weave. If you would like to change colors, simply join the new yarn with a knot and continue weaving. Be sure to hide the knotted ends behind the weaving.

4. Once you have finished your weaving, turn your loom to the wrong side. Working with two of the warp threads at a time, clip them in the middle and tie them off together at the top and bottom.

Paint an Ajanta Cave Fresco

The frescoes discovered in the Ajanta Caves, like those found in ancient Minoan Crete and Roman Pompeii, are still bright centuries after their creation. Follow the directions below to create your own beautiful wall fresco.

Materials:
- ☐ Box of Plaster of Paris mix
- ☐ Water
- ☐ Plastic spoon and mixing bowl
- ☐ Small aluminum foil pan
- ☐ Water color paints and brushes
- ☐ Planned drawing to be painted

Directions:
1. Fresco painting requires accuracy, because you cannot correct any mistakes you might make. So for best results, have your design and color choices planned out on paper first.
2. Follow the directions on the box of Plaster of Paris* to create the plaster mix. Quickly pour the plaster into a small aluminum pan. Using the back of a plastic spoon, smooth the surface of the plaster.
3. When the plaster is firm but still damp to the touch, it is ready to be painted.
4. Use the watercolors to paint your picture. As the plaster dries, the pigments from the paint will be permanently set into the plaster.
5. When the plaster has completely dried, remove the tile from the pan and display.

   * *Please Note:* You should NEVER pour liquid plaster down the sink or wash items that have plaster on them in the sink! Plaster can set under water and will clog your pipes!!

ACTIVITY PROJECT **Touch the Fresco**

After the Ajanta Caves were discovered, thousands of people came to see the caves. Hundreds of people would touch the frescoes every day. Let's see how a picture of yours holds up to the same treatment.

Materials:
- ☐ One picture drawn by the child

Directions:
1. Hang the picture up in an area of the house that people often pass (suggestion: the refrigerator door). Hang it at about the height of your nose so everyone in the family can reach it easily. You may also want to put a sign over the picture that says, "Touch me."
2. Have everyone run their fingers across the picture several times a day, especially after cooking or eating!
3. After one week, look at the picture. Does it look as nice as it did at first?

The Rise of Islam

CHAPTER 6

Encyclopedia Cross-References

UBWH 98, UILE 206–207
KIHW 174–175, KHE 106

MUHAMMAD'S VISION

REVIEW QUESTIONS

What is the land of the Arabian Peninsula like? *It is a hot, dry desert.*

Do you remember the name we give to the tribes of people who lived there? *We call them Bedouins.*

How were the Bedouins expected to behave? *They were supposed to be kind to the poor, the strangers, and the sick.*

Did the Bedouins actually behave this way? *No, Muhammad saw them treating others badly, gambling, and drinking too much.*

What did Muhammad see, in his vision in the cave? *He saw a silk scroll with words of fire.*

What did the mighty voice of the angel command Muhammad to do? *The angel commanded Muhammad to read the scroll.*

What was the angel's name? *The angel said that his name was Gabriel.*

NARRATION EXERCISE

"Muhammad was a Bedouin. He wanted the Bedouins to treat each other better. One night, he was thinking about this when an angel appeared to him and told him to read a scroll." OR

"Muhammad was called 'The Trustworthy One.' He used to go into the desert at night to think about how to make men be better. An angel appeared to Muhammad. The angel told Muhammad that he would be the messenger of Allah."

MUHAMMAD FLEES TO MEDINA

REVIEW QUESTIONS

What were the followers of Muhammad's teachings called? *Muhammad's followers were called Muslims.*

What did Muhammad tell the people of Mecca when he preached to them? *Allah is the one true God. Don't worship idols. Give your money to the poor.*

How did the rich and powerful people of Mecca respond to Muhammad and his teachings? *They did not like what he said—they didn't want to give their money away to the poor! They made life for Muslims very difficult.*

Why did Muhammad finally leave Mecca for Medina? *Because soldiers in Mecca wanted to kill him.*

Why didn't the soldiers go into the cave where Muhammad was hiding? *Because there was a spider web across the entrance. They thought Muhammad could not have entered the cave without breaking the web.*

Do you remember the special name for Muhammad's journey from Mecca to Medina? This name is part of the Muslim way of counting the years. *His journey is called the Hegira.*

Narration Exercise

"Muhammad preached about Allah in Mecca. The rich people did not like him, so they chased him out of town. He went to Medina instead. His journey was called the Hegira." OR

"Muhammad preached to the people in Mecca. Those who followed his teachings were called Muslims. One night, soldiers in Mecca tried to kill Muhammad. He hid in a cave to avoid them."

THE KORAN: ISLAM'S HOLY BOOK

Review Questions

How did Muhammad's friend Abu Bakr assemble the Koran, Islam's holy book? *He asked people to bring him all the teachings of Muhammad that they had written down or memorized.*

What is the name of the five duties every Muslim should do? *The five duties are called the Five Pillars of Islam.*

Can you tell me at least two of the Five Pillars? *Believe that Allah is the one true God; Pray to Allah five times a day; Give away part of your money every year to the needy; Do not eat or drink in the daytime during Ramadan; Try to go to Mecca at least once in your life.*

Narration Exercise

"Muhammad's teachings were put together into one book called the Koran. The Koran says that you should obey the Five Pillars of Islam. The pillars tell you to pray to Allah and give your money to those who need help." OR

"Muhammad's friend asked everybody to bring him the teachings of Muhammad that they had memorized or written down. He collected them all into one book called the Koran. The Koran tells people how to live a good life."

Additional History Reading

I Am Muslim (Religions of the World), by Jessica Chalfonte (Powerkids Press, 1997). A gentle, easy-reader introduction to Muslim beliefs. **Out of print,** but many libraries carry the Religions of the World series. (IR 1–3)

Muslim Holidays, by Faith Winchester (Bridgestone Books, 1996). Briefly describes Muslim beliefs and the eight most important Islamic celebrations. (RA 1–2, IR 3–5)

Ramadan, by Suhaib Hamid Ghazi (Holiday House, 1996). A young boy celebrates Ramadan with his family, while learning the meaning and importance of the holiday. (RA 1, IR 2–5)

Ramadan: Rookie-Read-About Holidays, by David F. Marx (Children's Press, 2002). A simple beginning-reader introduction to the feast which stands at the center of the Fourth Pillar. (IR 1–3)

The Story of Religion, by Betsy and Giulio Maestro (Mulberry Books, 1999). Brief explanations of the basic beliefs and practices of the world's major religions, including the Muslim faith. (RA 1–2, IR 3–5)

The Usborne Book of World Religions, by Susan Meredith (EDC Publishing, 1996). More detailed explanations of the world's religions than *The Story of Religion,* for those who would like to explore further. (RA 1–3, IR 4–5)

This Is My Faith: Islam, by Anita Ganeri (Barron's Educational Series, 2006). (RA 2–3, IR 4)

Corresponding Literature Suggestions

The Enchanted Storks: A Tale of Baghdad, retold by Aaron Shepard (Clarion Books 1995). When the Caliph of Baghdad finds himself trapped in the body of a stork, only the evil sorcerer with designs on his throne knows the magic word that will restore the Caliph to human form. **Out of print.** (RA 1, IR 2–5)

Forty Fortunes: A Tale of Iran, by Aaron Shepard (Clarion Books, 1999). A well-intentioned fortune-telling peasant unwittingly tricks a band of local thieves into returning the king's stolen treasure; set in the area of ancient Babylonia. **Out of print;** check your local library. (RA 1, IR 2–5)

The Hundredth Name, by Shulamith Levey Oppenheim (Boyds Mill Press, 1997). A young boy named Salah wants to lift his camel's sadness, and so prays that the camel will learn Allah's hundredth name, which is unknown to man. (RA 1, IR 2–5)

The Three Princes: A Tale from the Middle East, by Eric Kimmel (Holiday House, 1994). A princess promises to marry the prince who finds the rarest treasure. (RA 1, IR 2–5)

—————————————————— **MAP WORK** ——————————————————

The Birthplace of Islam *(Student Page 24, answer 255)*

1. Color the Arabian Peninsula light brown.
2. Locate Mecca on the map and circle it with a purple crayon.
3. Locate Medina and circle it with a red crayon.
4. Trace Muhammad's route from Mecca to Medina in green.

COLORING PAGE   A Bedouin and his camel *(Student Page 25)*

—————————————————— **PROJECTS** ——————————————————

COOKING PROJECT   Make an Edible Oasis

In a desert there is normally very little water. Plants need water to grow. Animals and people need water to drink. An oasis is an area in a desert where water is present and plants can grow. When caravans went through the Arabian Desert, they hoped to find an oasis on their journey.

Materials:
- ☐ Small paper plate
- ☐ Light brown sugar
- ☐ Tootsie Rolls
- ☐ Blue M&Ms, Skittles or other blue candy
- ☐ Green candy fruit slices or candy spearmint leaves
- ☐ Animal cookies (like Mother's Circus Animals or Barnum's Animals—make sure camels are included)
- ☐ Toothpicks
- ☐ Small amount of frosting (to use as "glue")
- ☐ Scissors
- ☐ Knife

Directions:
1. Place the sugar (sand) on the plate.
2. Create a place in the sugar for an area of blue candies (water).
3. Cut a toothpick in half and place it at one end of a Tootsie Roll.
4. Then, using a knife, cut the green fruit candies lengthwise into three or four slices. These will be the leaves of your palm trees. Carefully poke the toothpick end of the Tootsie Roll through the green candy (leaves).

5. Clear space in your sugar and use a little frosting to help your palm tree stick on the plate.

6. Now invite cookie camels to come "drink" in the oasis.

Low-Sugar Variation

Materials:
- Small paper plate
- Wheat cracker crumbs for sand
- Slim Jims for palm tree trunks
- Glue
- Snow peas or fresh spearmint leaves for palm tree leaves
- Natural animal cookies from a health food store or plastic toy camels
- Aluminum foil for water
- Toothpicks
- Scissors

Directions:
1. Cut a small amount of aluminum foil (water) and glue on plate.

2. Surround this area with crushed crackers.

3. Cut Slim Jims into 2-inch "palm tree trunks."

4. Cut the toothpicks in half and place in one end of the Slim Jims.

5. Carefully poke the snow peas with the toothpick end of the Slim Jims.

6. Clear a space within the cracker crumbs and glue the palm tree in place.

7. Now let the camels come and enjoy their little oasis.

ACTIVITY PROJECT ## Make a Pilgrimage

Muslims go on a Hajj, or pilgrimage, to fulfill their obligations to Allah. Go on your own pilgrimage across the house or yard. Try to go in the same direction that Muslims travel for their Hajj.

Materials:
- World map or globe

Directions:
1. To find the direction that Muslims travel, you must first figure out where you are in relation to the city of Mecca. On a world map or globe, put your finger on where you live.

2. Now put another finger on Mecca (or more generally on Saudi Arabia).

3. Looking at the compass on the map, figure out in which direction Mecca lies from your home. (**Note to Parent:** You may need to assist the child with this part.)

4. If Mecca lies east of you, start at the western end of your home or yard. Ask your parent to give you a helpful task to do that involves traveling east. (**Note to Parent:** Ask the child to fetch you something or do a chore at the eastern end of the house).

5. When you are finished with the task, return to your starting place. Now you have completed your pilgrimage.

ACTIVITY PROJECT ## The Five Pillars of Islam

Using the blank picture of five pillars provided (*Student Page 26*), label the five pillars of Islam. Write "Islam" on the roof (top triangle). Label each pillar with:

Shahadah, or Faith
Salah, or Prayer
Zakat, or Giving

Sawm, or Fasting
Hajj, or Pilgrimage

Then color the pillars.

The Shahadah, Confession

When someone wants to become a Muslim, they recite the Shahadah, or the Confession of their belief. But just saying the words will not make you a Muslim. A true Muslim is someone who is completely aware of the meaning of the Confession, who speaks it with heartfelt devotion, and who follows all that is required, living as if the Confession is truly believed. Many Islamic artists used the words from the Shahadah in their artwork. The letters are written in calligraphy because the Koran, the Muslim holy book, contains the eternal words of Allah which should always be expressed with as much beauty and care as possible. This tile is a copy of many that are made as a reminder of this confession.

Materials:
- ☐ Large, white tile (from the hardware store)
- ☐ Acrylic paints and thin brushes
- ☐ Copy of the Shahadah *(Student Page 27)*
- ☐ Pencil
- ☐ Glue
- ☐ Newspaper to cover the work spot

Directions:

1. Place the newspaper on the area where you are going to do your painting. Wash and dry your white tile.

2. Cut out the copy of the Shahadah or the other words you are going to highlight. Glue it on to the center of the tile and let dry.

3. With a pencil, draw a picture of flowers along the sides of the tile. (Use the illustration at the right as a guide.) Paint over your design with acrylic paint colors, using a thin brush so that lines are smooth and fluid. Let dry.

Islam Becomes an Empire

CHAPTER 7

Encyclopedia Cross-References

UBWH 112–113, 122–123, UILE 208–209
KIHW 176–177, 190–191, KHE 106–107, 116

THE FIGHT FOR MECCA

REVIEW QUESTIONS

Muhammad was more than a prophet. What other job did he have in Medina? *He was also a ruler and a judge.*

What problem did the people of Medina have? *They were hungry. There wasn't enough food.*

What solution did Muhammad have for the food shortage? *He told his followers to attack the caravans bringing food to Mecca and take the food back to Medina.*

How did Meccans respond to their caravans being attacked? *They were angry and fought Medina.*

Do you remember how many years the two cities fought? *The two cities fought for seven years.*

How did the fight end? *Muhammad's army defeated Mecca.*

What did Muhammad declare Mecca to be? *He declared Mecca to be the Holy City of Islam.*

What is every faithful Muslim supposed to do, at least once during his life? *He should visit Mecca.*

NARRATION EXERCISE

"The people of Medina didn't have enough food so they took food from Mecca. The army of Mecca attacked Medina, but they were defeated. Muhammad took over the city of Mecca and said that only Muslims could live there." OR

"Muhammad had many followers. He lived in Medina, but he wanted Mecca back again. Muhammad and his large army defeated Mecca in battle. He declared Mecca to be the Holy City of Islam. Every faithful Muslim is supposed to visit Mecca."

THE SPREAD OF ISLAM

REVIEW QUESTIONS

Who was the new ruler of Mecca? *Muhammad now ruled over Mecca.*

What happened to make all the Muslims worried and concerned? *Muhammad died. They didn't know who should lead them.*

Who became the new leader, or caliph, of the Islamic empire? *Muhammad's old friend, Abu Bakr.*

Was Abu Bakr a strong caliph? *Yes.*

How did the Islamic empire do under the rule of the caliphs? *It became very large and powerful. Many people converted to Islam.*

What city became the new capital of the Islamic empire? *Baghdad became the new capital.*

"Muhammad died and everyone was worried. They didn't know who should lead them. Muhammad's friend Abu Bakr became their leader. The Islamic empire became very big and powerful." OR

"After Muhammad died, the Islamic empire was ruled by caliphs. It became very large. Many people became Muslims. The center of the empire became the city of Baghdad."

THE CITY OF BAGHDAD

REVIEW QUESTIONS

Can you name two things that the city of Baghdad became known for? *Baghdad was known for beautiful buildings, running water, public libraries, and scholars (or thinkers).*

In the story, why did Sinbad decide to become a sailor? *Because all his life he had only spent money and enjoyed himself. He wanted to have a real adventure and be a great explorer.*

What did the beautiful island turn out to be? *The island turned out to be a big fish!*

What did Allah send to Sinbad so that he would not drown in the sea? *Sinbad found a wooden bathtub.*

When Sinbad found a large, white dome on an island, what did it turn out to be? *The dome turned out to be the egg of a gigantic bird.* OR *A roc's egg.*

NARRATION EXERCISE

"Sinbad wanted to be a great explorer. He sailed to an island that turned out to be the back of a huge, sleeping fish. Then Sinbad went to another island where a gigantic bird lived." OR

"The city of Baghdad became the capital of the Islamic empire. A famous book called *The Thousand and One Nights* was written there. In the book, a sailor named Sinbad has many adventures."

SINBAD IN THE VALLEY OF THE SNAKES

REVIEW QUESTIONS

How did Sinbad escape the island with the giant bird? *He tied a piece of cloth to himself and to the leg of the bird. When the bird flew away, Sinbad went with it.*

Sinbad landed in a beautiful valley—but what new terror was located in the valley? *The valley was filled with huge snakes.*

What did Sinbad fill his pockets with in the valley of the snakes? *He filled his pockets with diamonds.*

How did Sinbad get up the cliff to the men above? *Sinbad held onto a piece of meat. An eagle grabbed the meat and flew up to the men above.*

INSTEAD OF A NARRATION EXERCISE

Ask the child to draw a picture of Sinbad and the eagle.

Additional History Reading

The Arabs: In the Golden Age (Peoples of the Past Series), by Mokhtar Moktefi and Veronique Ageorges (Millbrook Press, 1996). A fascinating look at early Arabic civilization, with information on history, art, religion, culture, science, and more. **Out of print.** (RA 1–3, IR 4–5)

The Golden Age of Islam: Cultures of the Past, by Linda S. George (Benchmark Books, 1998). This series is designed for fourth and fifth graders, but the clear text and large type makes it child-friendly. Selected chapters would serve as good read-alouds. (RA 1–3, IR 4–5)

Islam, by Neil Morris (Peter Bedrick Books, 2001). Covers the life of Muhammad, the Koran, and some of the most important events in the history of Islam. Many illustrations; most of the text is on an advanced third-grade level. (RA 1–3, IR 3–5)

Muhammad, by Demi (Margaret McElderry, 2003). Another in a series of biographies written by the famous author/illustrator, this beautifully illustrated biography has simple text, but the small font may trouble some young readers. (RA 1–2, IR 3–5)

Corresponding Literature Suggestions

Ali, Child of the Desert, by Jonathan London, illus. Ted Lewin (New York: Lothrop, Lee & Shepard, 1997). A Moroccan boy travels to market with his father and encounters a sandstorm. **Out of print,** but worth finding at your local library. (RA 1–2, IR 3–5)

The Golden Sandal (A Middle Eastern Cinderella Story), by Rebecca Hickox (Holiday House, 1999). A retelling of the Cinderella story in a Mesopotamian context. (RA)

An Illustrated Treasury of Read-Aloud Classics for Young People, edited by Becky Koh (Black Dog & Leventhal, 2003). Tales written for reading aloud, from a variety of sources—from *Cinderella* to a chapter of *A Wrinkle in Time.* Includes a tale from the Arabian Nights, retold in classic style by Andrew Lang, which takes place in the same area that Sargon conquered. (RA 1–4, IR 5–up)

Muslim Child: Understanding Islam Through Stories and Poems, by Rukhsana Khan (Albert Whitman & Co., 2002). Good introduction to the daily life of a Muslim child. Includes several full-page illustrations, as well as helpful information sidebars. (RA 2–3, IR 3–6)

Sinbad in the Land of Giants, by Ludmila Zeman (Tundra Books, 2001). An exciting retelling with colorful illustrations. **Out of print.** (RA 1–2, IR 3–5)

———————————— MAP WORK ————————————

The Spread of Islam *(Student Page 28, answer 255)*

1. Color all the areas inside of the dotted lines light brown. This shows the Islamic empire.
2. Locate the Red Sea, the Persian Gulf and the Arabian Sea and color them blue.
3. Baghdad, the Round City, became the center of the Islamic empire. The caliph lived there in a splendid palace. Put an orange star over the city of Baghdad.

COLORING PAGE   Sinbad the adventurer *(Student Page 29)*

GAME ACTIVITY **From Mecca to the World Game**

Use chapters 6 and 7 for this game. It will test your memory of the events surrounding the birth and growth of Islam.

Materials:
- *The Story of the World, Volume 2*, chapters 6 and 7
- Game board *(Student Page 30)*
- Game pieces: beans, coins, buttons or small plastic toys to serve as player markers
- One die or two, depending on how fast you want the game to go

Directions:
1. Before the game:
   a. Enlarge the game board to fit on an 11 × 14-inch sheet of paper.
   b. Color the board and the designs on it.
   c. Glue game board onto cardboard or posterboard to add strength. (optional)
   d. Cover with clear contact paper. (optional)
   e. Select game pieces, one for each player.
2. To play:
   a. All players begin at the place marked "Start".
   b. Roll the dice and the lowest number gets to be first. Go clock-wise from the first player.
   c. Follow the circle pathway to the end.
   d. If you land on a circle connected to a box, answer the question and follow the instructions.
   e. The first one to the end who can answer the last question correctly wins the game.

CRAFT PROJECT **Sinbad Spoon Puppets**

The story of Sinbad from *1001 Nights* can be recreated with these easy-to-make spoon puppets, a few chairs, a blanket and your imagination.

Materials:
- The Sinbad Spoon Puppets *(Student Page 31)*
- A box of plastic spoons (different colors are fun!)
- Glue
- Scissors
- Colored pencils

Directions:
1. Color the pictures of the seven spoon characters from the story of Sinbad found in chapter 7 of *The Story of the World, Volume 2*. Cut them out and glue them on the plastic spoons.
2. Using two chairs with a blanket draped over it, create a puppet theater.
3. Act out the story with your puppets. Or make up your own!

COOKING PROJECT **Make Ali Baba "Open Sesame" Biscuits**

Read the story of *Ali Baba and the Forty Thieves* (from the Arabian Nights). In some retellings of this story, Ali Baba sent sesame biscuits with his brother, Cassim, to help him remember the secret password to open the cave, "Open, Sesame!"

Ingredients:
1 cup whole wheat flour
1 cup white flour
1 tablespoon baking powder
¾ teaspoon salt
Small amount of olive oil to grease cookie sheet

4 tablespoons butter
¾ cup plus 2 teaspoons milk
2 tablespoons sesame seeds

Directions:
1. Preheat oven to 425 degrees.
2. Mix flours, baking powder, salt, and 5 teaspoons of sesame seeds.
3. Cut in butter using two knives (like scissors). Do this until mixture is crumb-like.
4. Stir in milk until mixture is doughy.
5. Put dough on floured surface. Knead about 12 times.
6. Use a floured rolling pin and roll dough until it is about ½ inch thick.
7. Use a round biscuit cutter to cut out biscuits.
8. Lightly grease a cookie baking sheet with some olive oil.
9. Place biscuits on the cookie sheet. Sprinkle the remaining sesame seeds on the biscuits.
10. Bake 12–15 minutes. Let cool and enjoy!

ACTIVITY PROJECT **Make a Hanging "Valley of Snakes"**

Hang these "swirling snakes" from your ceiling. Turn on a fan to see them twist and twirl.

Materials:
☐ Lightweight paper plates
☐ Pencil
☐ Button
☐ String (2 feet or more for each snake)
☐ Scissors
☐ Markers or crayons (perhaps also glitter and glue)

Directions:
1. Make a hole in the center of a paper plate with a sharpened pencil.
2. Decorate both sides of the plate with the crayons, markers, and/or glitter. Let dry if needed.
3. Starting on the outside, cut a spiral design on the plate. Stop a little short of the center.
4. Tie a button to the end of a piece of string.
5. Thread the string up through the hole in the center of the plate. The plate should "sit" on the button when hung, making a coil.
6. Hang your snakes from the ceiling. Make as many as you wish!

Make Your Own Royal Scimitar

Medieval historians describe crescent-shaped swords, or scimitars, used by Muslim warriors in the Middle Ages. This type of sword, light and flexible, was an excellent cutting weapon, especially when used by a warrior mounted on a horse.

Materials:
- ☐ Photocopy of the scimitar template *(Student Page 32)*, enlarged onto 11" × 17" paper
- ☐ Cardboard piece the length and width of the enlarged template
- ☐ Carpet knife or Exacto knife
- ☐ White craft glue
- ☐ Silver, gold, black and one jewel color acrylic paint
- ☐ Craft paint brushes
- ☐ Newspaper to protect working area

Directions:
1. Cut out the photocopy of the scimitar and trace onto the cardboard.
2. Using the carpet knife carefully cut out the cardboard scimitar.
3. Following the pattern on the template, paint the blade silver, the decorative top of the hilt gold and paint the jewel the color of your choice. Paint the handle black and the stripes gold. Paint the bottom scroll gold, also.
4. Let that side dry then do the same on the other side.
5. When dry, take a picture of yourself with your new royal scimitar!

The Great Dynasties of China

Encyclopedia Cross-References

UBWH 118–119, UILE 268–269
KIHW 170–171, KHE 104–105

YANG CHIEN UNITES NORTH AND SOUTH

REVIEW QUESTIONS

What did the people of North and South China think of one another? *They didn't like one another at all.*

Do you remember the name of the general who united them? *Yang Chien united them.*

Was Yang Chien from the north or from the south? *He was from the north. He invaded the south and won.*

What dynasty did Yang Chien found? *He founded the Sui dynasty.*

Why couldn't northerners and southerners travel easily to each other's territory? *Two rivers blocked their way.*

What two rivers blocked their way? *The Yellow River and the Yangtze River blocked their way.*

How did the Sui emperors connect northern China with southern China? *They had a new "river," called the Grand Canal, dug.*

How did the emperors find enough workers to dig the Grand Canal? *They forced men, women, and children to work on the canal.*

Which emperor went for a ride on the Grand Canal when it was finished? *Yangdi went for a ride on the Grand Canal.*

Did the people of China love Yangdi? *No—they rebelled against him and killed him.*

NARRATION EXERCISE

"A general from North China invaded South China and united them. He founded a new dynasty called the Sui dynasty. The Sui emperors had the Grand Canal built." OR

"Yang Chien united North and South China. He founded the Sui Dynasty. To keep North and South China together, the Grand Canal was dug out to connect two rivers. But the people of China were angry because they were forced to work on the Canal."

THE TANG DYNASTY

REVIEW QUESTIONS

Can you remember two things that Li Yuan, the first emperor of the Tang dynasty, did to make his people happy? *He made the cities stronger and cleaner; he told the people they could follow any religion they wanted; he encouraged trade with other places.*

Why is the Tang dynasty called the "Golden Age" of China? *It was the "Golden Age" because everybody was happy and wealthy. They told stories and made music and art.*

How did the Chinese print books? *They carved words into wooden blocks and dipped the blocks into ink.*

What did the Chinese do with the sap from lacquer trees? *They painted it on wood and cloth. It hardened to make a smooth surface.*

What did Chinese scientists spend years trying to figure out? *They tried to figure out how to make gold.*

What did they invent by accident? *They invented gunpowder.*

What did the horses do that frightened the soldiers? *The horses danced to the music.*

Narration Exercise

"During the Tang dynasty, China was peaceful and rich. The Chinese invented gunpowder, painted things with lacquer, and printed books with wooden stamps. The emperor even had a hundred dancing horses!" OR

"The Tang dynasty is known as the 'Golden Age' of China because it was rich and peaceful. Artists made beautiful things, and the people dressed in gorgeous clothes and ate fancy foods. The emperors were so powerful that they had their own gates!"

Additional History Reading

Ancient China Treasure Chest: 2000 Years of History to Unlock and Discover, by Chao-Hui Jenny Liu (Running Press, 1996). Text would be a read-aloud. Projects include: Chinese calligraphy (brush, ink and instructions), Chinese fan, I Ching coins, charts, stickers, and a booklet (overview of dynasties, inventions, and principles of Taoism). Small children will need help with most of the projects. (RA and activities)

Empress of China, Wu Ze Tian, by Cheng-An Chiang (Victory Press, 1998). This beautiful picture book tells the story of the only Tang dynasty emperor who was female. (RA 1–2, IR 3–5)

The Grand Canal of China, by Lyn Harrington (Rand McNally, 1967). **Out of print**, but this children's introduction to the Grand Canal is worth finding at your library or buying second-hand. (IR 1–3)

Long Is a Dragon: Chinese Writing for Children, by Peggy Goldstein (Pacific View Press, 1992). Explains how Chinese writing developed and demonstrates how to write seventy-five Chinese characters, using detailed instructions and examples. (RA)

Science in Ancient China (Science of the Past), by George Beshore (New York: Orchard Books, 1998). Detailed and interesting descriptions of the achievements of the Chinese in science, medicine, astronomy, and cosmology; includes innovations such as rockets, wells, the compass, water wheels, and moveable type. (RA 1–3, IR 4–5)

Corresponding Literature Suggestions

Cat and Rat: The Legend of the Chinese Zodiac, by Ed Young (Henry Holt & Co, 1998). This book tells how the Jade Emperor held a race to determine which twelve animals would have a year named after them in the Chinese calendar. It also explains why Cat and Rat are enemies to this day. (IR 1–4)

The Legend of the Kite: A Story of China, by Jiang Hong Chen (Soundprints Corp Audio, 1999). A young boy loses his kite during the spring kite festival. To cheer the boy up, his grandfather tells him about the legend behind the festival and inspires him to build a new kite. (RA 1, IR 2–4)

Lon Po Po: A Red Riding Hood Story From China, Ed Young (Philomel Books, 1989). This Caldecott winner tells of three sisters who save themselves from being eaten, by tempting Lon Po Po (the granny wolf) up a tree and to her death. (IR 1–4)

The Lord of the Cranes: A Chinese Tale, by Kerstin Chen (North South Books, 2000). The Lord of the Cranes descends from Heaven to test people's kindness. He is able to find only one innkeeper willing to help him, so he rewards him with a painting of three dancing cranes that come to life when music is played. (RA 1–2, IR 3–4)

Two of Everything, by Lily Toy Hong (Albert Whitman & Company, 1993). An old couple finds a magic pot that doubles everything they put into it. It brings them good luck until the old woman accidentally falls into the pot. (IR 1–4)

The Warlord's Puzzle, by Virginia Walton Pilegard (Pelican Publishing Co, 2000). A warlord is presented with a beautiful blue tile that is accidentally broken into 7 pieces. A great contest is held to see who can solve the puzzle and put the tile back together. A sample tangram is provided at the end of the book for the reader. (RA 1, IR 2–5)

Yeh-Shen: A Cinderella Story From China, by Ai-Ling Louie (Philomel Books, 1982). This book is based on the original Chinese version of the tale, which dates back to the Tang Dynasty (619–907AD). (IR 1–4)

———————————————— **MAP WORK** ————————————————

China and the Grand Canal *(Student Page 33, answer 255)*

1. Use a yellow crayon to trace the route of the Yellow River as it runs from west to east (from left to right).

2. Use a blue crayon to trace the route of the Yangtze River as it also runs from west to east.

3. Use a red crayon to highlight the Grand Canal that the Sui emperors made the Chinese peasants build.

4. Remember, on a map the directions are as follows:

    a. North is located at the top of the page,

    b. South is located at the bottom of the page,

    c. East is located on the right-hand side of the page, and

    d. West is located on the left-hand side of the page.

COLORING PAGE   A statue of a Tang warrior *(Student Page 34)*

———————————————— **PROJECTS** ————————————————

CRAFT PROJECT   **Make a Jade Bead Necklace**

To the ancient Chinese, jade symbolized nobility, perfection, constancy and immortality. Jade was believed to contain the essence of both heaven and earth and served as a symbolic link between man and the spiritual world. The Chinese thought that jade would protect them from harm and bring them good fortune. One emperor was so sure of jade's ability to ensure immortality that he had himself buried in a suit of armor made from jade that covered him from head to toe. Follow the directions below to make a jade necklace for yourself.

Materials: ▫ Toothpicks   ▫ Petroleum jelly
             ▫ Blunt knife   ▫ Length of string or cord
             ▫ Greenish-blue modeling clay (Fimo or Sculpey)
                (You can combine blue and green in a food processor to get the perfect color)

Directions: 1. Break off a piece of the modeling clay and work it between your fingers until it becomes pliable.

2. Roll the clay into a "snake" shape, about ½" thick. Use the knife to slice the "snake" into ½" lengths.

3. Make the beads round, by slowly rolling them in the palm of your hand. To make the whole in the center of your beads, grease toothpicks with petroleum jelly and carefully push one toothpick through the center of each ball. Do not remove the toothpicks.

4. Cook the beads, following the instructions on the package of clay. This usually takes about 20 minutes. Once the beads have baked, remove them from the oven and allow them to cool slightly. Remove the toothpicks and allow the beads to completely cool before stringing them on a length of cord.

COOKING PROJECT Learn to Eat with Chopsticks

The Chinese have been using chopsticks for about five thousand years. It is believed that people first used these sticks to help them cook meat over open fires. As time passed, people began chopping their food into smaller sized pieces so they would cook faster. The cooking sticks were then used for eating as well as cooking. Chopsticks are two long, thin pieces of wood that have been tapered at the bottom. They are usually made from bamboo, but other materials have been used such as animal bone, ivory, and jade. During the Middle Ages, Chinese emperors preferred to use chopsticks made from silver because they thought the metal would turn a different color when it came into contact with poison. (Being poisoned by your enemies was a common problem back then!) Follow the directions below and try your hand at eating with this ancient utensil.

Materials: □ Set of chopsticks (your local Chinese restaurant can supply these)
□ Strip of paper (½" × 11")
□ Rubber band
□ ¼ cup dry rice

Directions: 1. Rubber band the two chopsticks together tightly near the top of the sticks.

2. Roll up the strip of paper until it is rolled to a diameter of ⅜".

3. Tuck the paper roll between the two chopsticks close to the rubber band. They will now function like tweezers and allow small children the enjoyment of using them.

4. Cook rice. Add ¼ cup of dry rice to ½ cup water and bring to a boil on the stovetop. Cover and reduce heat to simmer. Simmer for 30–45 minutes. Toss rice with pat of butter and a sprinkle of salt.

5. Now try eating the rice with your chopsticks!

CRAFT PROJECT Make a Chinese "Lacquered" Bowl

Lacquer is a resin from the lacquer tree and can be very poisonous in its natural form. The lacquer was made by collecting the sap from the trees, straining it, and then placing it over heat to remove any extra moisture in the sap. Once the lacquer had "cooked," coloring was sometimes added. Lacquer was painted onto tableware, boxes made from wood, and other materials. Black and red were the most common colors, and were usually highlighted with gold painted designs. Follow the directions below to make your own "lacquered" bowl.

Materials: □ Air-drying clay (or clay such as Sculpey)   □ Paintbrushes
□ Craft paint (black, red and gold)   □ White glue or spray sealer

Directions: 1. Use a large amount of clay and form it into a bowl shape. Allow the piece to dry overnight (or bake according to instructions).

2. Paint the inside of the bowl red and the outside black. Allow the bowl to dry between colors to make it easier to paint. You may need to apply a second coat of paint for even coverage. Once the paint has dried, use the gold paint and a thin, round paintbrush to paint a design on the outside of the bowl. A cherry tree branch with blossoms would be very nice (*see* image to the right).

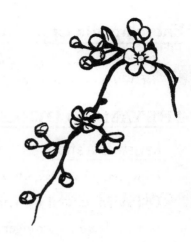

3. After the design has been applied and allowed to dry completely, make the "lacquer" from one part white glue to two parts water. Apply the "lacquer" with a paintbrush and allow it to dry completely between coats. If you would prefer, you can purchase a can of spray sealer from a craft store and use that instead.

CRAFT PROJECT String Block Printing

China was the first country to use carved wooden blocks to print on paper. To print this way, a wooden block would be carved with a picture or words, dipped into ink, then pressed onto a sheet of paper. This allowed the Chinese to make many copies of a book quickly, instead of using the labor-intensive process of writing each book out by hand. Follow the directions below to make a printing block of your own.

Materials:
- ☐ Pieces of corrugated cardboard
- ☐ String
- ☐ White glue
- ☐ Paper plates
- ☐ Craft paint
- ☐ Paper

Directions: 1. Use a pencil or marker to make a simple, open design on the piece of cardboard. Next, pour some glue onto a paper plate and drag lengths of string through the glue to completely coat them. If needed, run the glued string between your fingers to remove any excess glue. Arrange the string along the lines of the design on the cardboard, but be sure to not overlap the strings. Continue this process until the entire design has been covered. Allow the glue to dry

2. When the print block has been finished, pour some craft paint onto another paper plate. Use your finger or a spoon back to spread the paint around into a large, thin puddle.

3. Dip your printing block, string side down, into the paint then press it firmly and evenly onto a clean sheet of paper. You can usually get a couple of prints from the block before you will need more paint. Once you have your technique down, you can use your printing blocks to make gift-wrap on butcher paper or several layers of tissue paper. You could also use it to make greeting cards.

East of China

CHAPTER 9

Encyclopedia Cross-References

UBWH 120, UILE 170, 268
KIHW 146–147, KHE 84–85

THE YAMATO DYNASTY OF JAPAN

REVIEW QUESTIONS

How many large islands make up Japan? *Japan is made up of four large islands.*

Did Japan start off with one king? *No, many different clans ruled in Japan.*

Which clan grew stronger than all the rest and became emperors of Japan? *The Yamato dynasty became emperors of Japan.*

The Yamato emperors said that they were descendents of what Japanese goddess? *The sun goddess, Amaterasu.*

Why was Amaterasu's brother, the sea-god Susano, jealous? *Susano was jealous because the sky was larger than the sea.*

Did Susano win his war against his sister Amaterasu? *No, he lost and had to run down to earth.*

Why were the old man and the old woman weeping? *They were weeping because an eight-headed serpent had eaten seven of their daughters.*

To keep the girl hidden from the serpent, what did Susano change her into? *He changed her into a hair comb.*

After Susano chopped the serpent into eighty pieces, what did he find inside its body? *He found a magical sword.*

How many sons did Susano and his wife have? *They had eighty sons.*

When Amaterasu saw that Japan was noisy and full of battles, what did she do? *She sent her favorite grandson to rule.*

Can you name two of the three sacred objects that Amaterasu gave to her grandson, Honingi? *She gave her grandson a mirror, beads, and the magic sword to help him rule.*

NARRATION EXERCISE

"The god of the sea, Susano, saved a girl from a serpent by turning her into a comb. His sister sent her grandson to rule Japan. His descendents are the Yamatos, the dynasty that united Japan." OR

"The god of the sea and the goddess of the sun were fighting. The sea god gave her a magic sword as a peace offering. She eventually gave the sword to her grandson to help him rule Japan."

A TALE OF THREE COUNTRIES: KOREA, CHINA, AND JAPAN

REVIEW QUESTIONS

Korea is a peninsula. How many sides of the country are surrounded by water? *It is surrounded by water on three sides.*

What large country invaded Korea and ruled over part of it? *China invaded Korea.*

The Koreans drove the Chinese back into the north of their country. How many kingdoms was the rest of Korea divided into? *Korea was divided into "The Three Kingdoms."*

Why did the king of Paekche want to make friends with Japan? *He was hoping that Japan would help him conquer the other two Korean kingdoms.*

Of all the gifts that the king of Paekche gave to the emperor of Japan, what gift most fascinated the emperor? *The emperor liked the book written with Chinese letters.*

What did the Korean tutor Wani teach the Japanese prince how to do? *Wani taught the prince to read and write in Chinese.*

What religion did the Japanese learn from the Koreans? *The Japanese learned about Buddhism.*

What country eventually conquered the kingdom of Paekche? *China conquered it.*

What did the Japanese people call China? *They called China "The Land of the Setting Sun."*

What did the Japanese people call Japan? *They called Japan "The Land of the Rising Sun."*

How did the Yamato emperor of Japan try to protect his country from China? *He broke off all ties with China and stopped sending young men there.*

Narration Exercise

"Korea is a small country located next to China. They learned the Chinese way of writing, Chinese religion, and many Chinese customs. The Koreans then taught the Japanese these things. Then China conquered Korea, but Japan managed to keep itself separate from China." OR

"Korea was once divided into three separate kingdoms. One of these kingdoms made friends with Japan and taught the people about Chinese writing and ideas. Many Japanese traveled to China and learned how to read, write, and dress like Chinese. But then the Japanese emperor broke ties with China."

Additional History Reading

Cool Melons—Turn to Frogs! The Life and Poems of Issa, with story and translations by Matthew Gollub, illus. Kazuko G. Stone (Lee & Low Books, 1998). Wonderful to use before doing the haiku project described in this section, this picture book tells the story of the eighteenth-century haiku master Issa, and translates and illustrates more than thirty of his most famous poems. The story is written on a third-grade level; most second graders will be able to read the poems with help. (RA 1–2, IR 2–5)

Easy Origami, by John Montroll (Dover Publications, 1992). This book describes the traditional Japanese art of paper-folding and provides a collection of 32 projects, ranging from a very simple hat, cup and pinwheel, to the more challenging designs of a penguin or piano. Clear illustrations and easy-to-follow instructions. (RA 1–2, IR 3–5)

Heroines: Great Women Through the Ages, by Rebecca Hazell (Abbeville, 1996). Brief (4–6 pages) biographies of great women in history, each including a page-long description of the heroine's time and country. Includes Lady Murasaki Shikibu, the tenth-century Japanese writer credited with the invention of the novel. (RA 2, IR 3–5)

Japan (Make It Work), by Andrew Haslam (Two-Can Publications, 2001). This book provides information on different areas of ancient Japanese life: clothing and housing, geography and agriculture, artwork and religion. It contains easy-to-follow directions to make several craft projects, including a samurai's armor, a pagoda and a carp fish kite. (RA 1–2, IR 3–5)

Japan: The Culture (Lands, People and Cultures #6), by Bobbie Kalman (Crabtree Publications, 2000). A well-photographed guide to the social customs, manners, and celebrations of Japan. (RA 1–3, IR 4–5)

Japan: The Land (Lands, People and Cultures #4), by Bobbie Kalman (Crabtree Publications, 2000). A well-photographed guide to the geography, weather, and history of Japan. (RA 1–3, IR 4–5)

Japanese Kimono Paper Dolls in Full-Color, by Ming-Ju Sun (Dover Publications, 1986). Two paper dolls and 26 kimonos are based on eighteenth and nineteenth century woodcuts; this is a little later than the period under study, but the dolls do show the evolution of a uniquely Japanese style. (RA 1–3, IR 4–5)

Japanese Prints Coloring Book, by Ed Sibbett (Dover Publications, 1982). This 48-page coloring book contains pictures of old Japanese prints, which show many aspects of life during medieval times. (IR)

Corresponding Literature Suggestions

A Carp for Kimiko, by Virginia Kroll (Charlesbridge Publishing, 1996). A little girl wishes for a calico carp kite, just like the one her brothers fly on Children's Day. But Japanese tradition dictates that only boys get to have the colorful kites on that day. The story introduces the reader to the Japanese customs and traditions surrounding the celebrations of Children's Day and Doll's Day. (RA 1–2, IR 3–5)

The Boy Who Drew Cats, by Margaret Hodges (Holiday House, 2002). This Japanese story is based on a legend about a 15th century artist named Sesshu Toyo. The drawings he made in a Zen monastery were so realistic that people believed they could come alive. (RA 1–2, IR 3–5)

The Crane Wife, by Odds Bodkin, illus. Gennady Spirin (Harcourt Brace, 1998). A medieval Japanese tale about a mysterious girl who marries a Japanese villager; lovely Japanese-style illustrations. (RA 1–2, IR 3–4)

In the Moonlight Mist: A Korean Tale, by Daniel San Souci (Boyds Mills Press, 1999). This book is a beautiful retelling of an old Korean tale about goodness and sacrifice. A poor, but good-hearted, woodcutter rescues a magical deer from a hunter and is rewarded for his efforts by being told how he can make his greatest wish come true: to have a wife and family of his own. (RA 1–2, IR 3–5)

Little Oh, by Laura Krauss Melmed, illus. Jim Lamarche (Lothrop, Lee & Shepard, 1997). When a Japanese woman makes an origami doll, the doll comes to life, gets lost, and travels through Japan before becoming real. (RA 1–2, IR 3–5)

Mr. Pak Buys a Story, by Carol Farley (Albert Whitman & Company, 1997). A Korean farmer and his wife send their servant to the city to buy a story for their entertainment. A thief tricks Mr. Pak into buying a ridiculous story to take home instead. But a wonderful thing happens when the story scares off a band of robbers about to enter the house. (RA 1, IR 2–5)

MAP WORK

Korea, China, and Japan *(Student Page 35, answer 256)*

1. Color Korea orange.
2. Korea is a peninsula, meaning that it is surrounded by water on three sides. Outline the coast of Korea in dark blue.
3. Color the water in the Sea of Japan, the Yellow Sea, and the East China Sea in light blue.
4. Japan is made up of four large islands. Color those islands yellow.
5. Color China pink.
6. The Koreans taught the Japanese all about Chinese culture, language, and religion. So ideas went from China to Korea and on to Japan. Using black, draw a line from dot 1 to dot 2 (China to Korea) and another line from dot 2 to dot 3 (Korea to Japan).

COLORING PAGE   Susano *(Student Page 36)*

CRAFT PROJECT **Make a Japanese Carp Kite**

The Japanese celebrate the holiday of Boy's Day on May 5th. On this day, each boy is given a kite that is flown from a tall bamboo stick outside his home. Because of the carp's fight to swim against the current, the fish symbolizes strength, courage and determination. These are all qualities that Japanese parents wanted their sons to develop.

Materials
- ☐ 20" x 30" piece of white broadcloth fabric
- ☐ 1½" × 13" strip of thin cardboard
- ☐ Black Sharpie marker
- ☐ Scissors
- ☐ Hole punch
- ☐ Fabric glue, fabric paints, paintbrushes
- ☐ Tape and string
- ☐ Long piece of dowel or an old stick
- ☐ Newspaper

Directions:

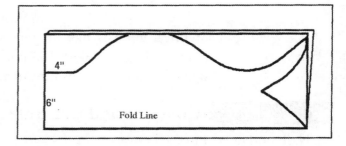
Figure A

1. Fold the fabric in half lengthwise. Use the black Sharpie to draw the carp design on the fabric, as shown in Figure A. Use the scissors to cut the pattern out.

2. Open the fabric up and place right side up on some newspaper. Use the Sharpie marker to draw the eyes, scales and tail on the fish, as shown in Figure B.

3. Use the fabric paints to color in the fish (**Note:** other types of craft paint can be used, but they will dry a bit stiffer). Allow the paint to dry completely.

4. Run a line of fabric glue along the open side of the fish. Be sure to leave the mouth and tail sections open, so that air will be able to flow through.

5. Use a hole punch to place two holes 3½" in from either end of the cardboard strip. Use a piece of tape to form the strip into a circle. Place the cardboard strip 2" deep inside the mouth opening. Run a bead of glue around the inside of the mouth opening; fold the fabric to the inside of the mouth. This will enclose the cardboard strip in between the fabric. Allow the glue to dry.

Figure B

6. Use a sharp point (scissor tip or nail) to punch through the fabric covering the holes. Cut two lengths of string 24" long. Thread each string through a hole in the cardboard and tie a knot. Take the other ends of the string and tie them around the dowel or stick. Your kite is ready to be tested in the wind.

Design a Japanese Kimono

The kimono is the traditional dress of Japan. It consists of a long-sleeved robe that is tied around the middle with a sash. Kimonos were made of many fabrics, from simple cotton to the most luxuriously embroidered silks. Take your crayons, glitter pens, paints or markers and design your own kimono fabric pattern. If you prefer, you could use scraps of fabric or pieces of glossy magazine pictures to make a collage instead.

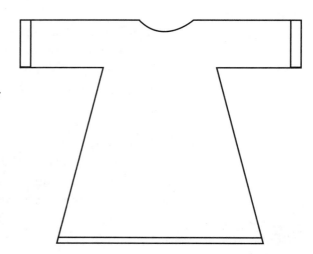

Materials: □ Large piece of paper
□ Assorted art supplies

Optional: fabric scraps, glossy magazine pictures and glue

Directions: 1. Take a pencil and lightly sketch the shape of a kimono onto a sheet of paper (*see* illustration).

2. Then gather up all of your art supplies and get to work. Designs from nature and mythical animals like dragons were very popular. Highly colorful kimonos were a sign of wealth and power in Ancient Japan.

Compose and Illustrate a Haiku

Haiku originated in Japan over 700 years ago and is considered the oldest surviving poetic form still in use today. Haiku is unique in that it is short (usually only three lines), non-rhyming, and talks about nature. (***Note to Parent:*** this writing activity may be too difficult for some learners. If that is the case, check out a book of haikus from the library. Have the child pick their favorite and skip ahead to step 4 of this activity.)

Materials: □ Sheet of paper and a pencil
□ Haiku poetry book from the library or the examples below
□ Drawing supplies

Directions: 1. All haikus occur during a specific season. Pick a season: fall, spring, winter, summer.

2. Think of as many words as you can that relate to the season. They should all be words about nature. (For example, if the season is summer: watermelons, seashore, minnows, dandelions, thunderstorms, or mosquitoes but NOT beach balls, sun hats, convertibles, or pools.)

3. Pick a word from your list and spend a few minutes brainstorming words that describe that topic or describe a thought that comes to mind when you think about the topic. (For example, if you pick minnows: darting, shallow pools, sunny water, little shadows, quick, the beach, the tide, swirling, school of fish, speed, grace, nervous movement, hard to catch, swirling sand, craggy rocks, etc.)

4. Use your favorite words from your brainstorm in your haiku. When composing your haiku, keep these rules in mind:

a. Haikus have only three lines. The first line of a haiku should have 5 syllables; the second line 7 syllables; the third line 5 syllables. But if you can't get your haiku to fit that rule exactly, it's okay.

b. The haiku should describe an impression or picture, not a story or sequence of events. For example, this haiku tries to tell a story:

> The grasshopper eats,
> Sleeps, leaps among the grasses—
> Darting to and fro.

There are too many events in that poem: eating, sleeping, leaping. It is better to pick just one picture or instant. This poem is about just the leap of the grasshopper:

> The grasshopper leaps
> He is quick, quiet, and sly—
> Grass sleeps beneath him.

c. Most haikus are not one long sentence. There is usually a dash or a colon at the end of the first or second line:

> Footprints in the snow:
> The rising sun will soon melt
> Night's beautiful ice.

5. Copy your haiku onto paper and illustrate it.

COOKING PROJECT   Make a Japanese Meal

Osumashi (Clear Soup): Soup is a standard item at breakfast in most Japanese households and it is also served at other meals. It can be served plain or it can be garnished with tofu squares, thinly sliced vegetables or small amounts of shredded meat. The Japanese eat soup by drinking it directly from a bowl. If vegetables or meat are added to the soup, those are eaten first with chopsticks.

Ingredients: 3 cups of chicken broth   ½ teaspoon of soy sauce
4 mushrooms, sliced   1 tablespoon chopped chives

Directions: 1. Pour the chicken broth into a 1–quart saucepan and bring to a boil. Stir in the soy sauce and boil for 2 minutes longer.

2. Remove from the heat. Pour the soup into 4 small bowls and garnish with the sliced mushrooms and chopped chives.

Gohan (Rice): The Japanese word for rice is *gohan* which means "honorable food." It was brought to Japan by the Chinese and quickly became the staple food of Japan. Rice can be served at every meal, even dessert.

Ingredients: 2 cups short-grain white rice, uncooked   2½ cups of water
1 teaspoon salt

Directions: 1. Rinse the rice in cold water and allow it to drain in a sieve.

2. Place the rice, water and salt into a 1-quart covered saucepan and allow it to come to a fast boil. Reduce the heat and simmer the rice until all of the water is absorbed (this can take about 20–30 minutes).

3. After the rice is cooked, remove it from the heat and allow it to steam for 10 minutes.

Goma-ae (Sesame Seed Dressing): This dressing is tossed with fresh green vegetables (green beans, broccoli, spinach, cabbage or cauliflower) that have been steamed or boiled first.

Ingredients: 1 pound fresh green vegetables   3 tablespoons sesame seeds
3 tablespoons soy sauce   1 tablespoon sugar

Directions: 1. Toast the sesame seeds by placing them in a dry frying pan over a medium heat. Shake the pan constantly so the seeds do not burn. When the seeds are a golden brown (about 3 minutes) remove them from the heat.

2. Place the browned seeds in a small bowl and crush them lightly with the back of a spoon. Add the rest of the ingredients, stir well and set aside.

3. Cook the vegetables in whatever manner you prefer (steaming or boiling). When they have finished cooking, drain well, place in a serving bowl and toss with the dressing.

Yakimono: In Japan, dishes that have been prepared in the "yaki" manner are cooked over a high heat so that the outside of the food is crispy and the inside is juicy and tender. This way of cooking can be done with all types of meats, fish, and vegetables. Our recipe, Beef Teriyaki, will be marinated in a sauce before it is grilled.

Ingredients: 1 pound flank steak   1 cup of beef broth
¼ cup soy sauce   1 tablespoon onion, minced
½ teaspoon garlic, minced   ½ teaspoon grated ginger root
½ tablespoon lemon juice, freshly squeezed   1 tablespoon honey

Directions: 1. Slice the steak diagonally across the grain into ½" × 1-inch strips and place in a shallow pan or large bowl.

2. Mix the remaining ingredients and pour over the meat. Let the meat marinate for 2–3 hours in the refrigerator, turning the meat 3 or 4 times.

3. Thread meat on skewers (pre-soak bamboo skewers). Grill the meat to the desired degree of doneness.

Learn to Play Kai-awase (Shell Game)

Kai-awase was a game played by the ladies of the emperor's royal court. The game was played with clamshells that had first been painted gold and then were painted with pairs of identical faces on the inside of the shells. The rules of the game are identical to those of Memory.

Materials:
- 12" × 20" sheet of paper
- Sheet of gold foil wrapping paper
- Markers, colored pencils, rubber stamps or stickers
- Glue, scissors, ruler and pencil

Directions:
1. Glue the gold foil paper onto the sheet of paper. Press down well. Let dry and trim excess gold paper.

2. Use the ruler and pencil to mark off a 2" × 2" square grid over the entire sheet of paper. Cut out the 60 squares with scissors. To make the playing cards look like shells, make a shell template on the gold side of each card and trim away the excess with scissors. Use the image of the clamshell on *Student Page 77.*

3. Use your art supplies to make pairs of identical cards. Some examples of designs would be: words, geometric shapes, and pictures of any kind. The only requirement is that they be identical.

4. *Rules of Play:* To start the game, the shells are all placed face down. One player at a time turns over two shells. If the patterns match, the player keeps the shells. If the patterns do not match they are turned back over and it becomes the next players turn to select. The winner of the game is the person who ends up with the most shells.

The Bottom of the World

CHAPTER 10

Encyclopedia Cross-References

UBWH not included, UILE 274–275
KIHW 76, KHE 88–89, 141

THE FIRST PEOPLE OF AUSTRALIA

REVIEW QUESTIONS

How many continents are in the world? *There are seven continents.*

Let's chant their names together. (Repeat this list several times with me!) *North America, South America, Antarctica, Africa, Europe, Asia, Australia.*

Did the first people of Australia live in houses? *No, they were nomads.*

What do we call these Australian nomads? *Aborigines.*

Do you remember what the Latin words *ab origine* mean? *They mean "from the beginning."*

Rulu lived in a *clan*. What is a clan? *A clan is a group of people all related to each other.*

What types of things did Rulu and the other aborigines eat in the story? *They ate moths, bats, sea cows, snakes, lizards, kangaroos, and emus.*

What did Rulu call all of the grown-up men and grown-up women of his clan? *Father and mother.*

How did Rulu and the "fathers" keep the kangaroos from smelling them? *They covered themselves with a paste of mud and ashes.*

How did Rulu get water out in the desert? *He squeezed water out of a water-frog!*

What is the Dreamtime? *The Dreamtime is a long-ago time when spirits still lived on earth.*

NARRATION EXERCISE

"Nomads lived in Australia. They lived in a clan and moved from place to place. They hunted for food like sea cows, snakes, and kangaroos. We call the nomads aborigines." OR

"Rulu is an aborigine in Australia. Australia is one of the continents. Rulu lives in a nomad clan. He calls all the grown-ups in his clan mother and father. He hunts and eats kangaroos and bats and gets water from a water-frog."

THE LONG JOURNEY OF THE MAORI

REVIEW QUESTIONS

How many islands belong to the country of New Zealand? *New Zealand has two islands.*

When did the Maori first come to New Zealand? *They came to New Zealand during the Middle Ages.*

Do you remember what islands the Maori people came from? *They came from the Polynesian Islands (in the Pacific Ocean).*

What were Maori canoes and sails made from? *The canoes were made from trees and the sails were made from coconut fibers.*

How did the Maori people prepare for their long sea-journey to New Zealand? *They filled the boats with fruits, vegetables, and animals so they would have plenty of food on their journey.*

When the Maori people first saw New Zealand from their canoes, what did they think the islands looked like? *They thought it looked like a long, white cloud.*

Why wouldn't Maui's brothers let him fish? *They said he was too little.*

What did Maui end up catching? *He caught a gigantic fish!*

What did his brothers do to the fish? *They chopped at it with* meres, *sharp-edged wooden clubs.*

What happened to the fish when the sun shone on it? *It turned into land.*

How were the islands of New Zealand *really* formed? *Volcanoes rose out of the sea and their lava turned to stone.*

Narration Exercise

"The Maori people traveled to New Zealand in canoes they had made. They tell a story about a boy who caught a giant fish that turned into an island. New Zealand is really made out of lava that turned into stone and collected dirt. It has many mountains, valleys, and hot springs." OR

"People in New Zealand tell a story about how their country was made. Maui's brothers would not let him fish because he was too little. He went anyway and ended up catching the biggest fish of all. That fish turned into an island. The story explains why New Zealand has mountains, valleys, and volcanoes."

Additional History Reading

1000 Years Ago on Planet Earth, by Sneed B. Collard III, illus. Jonathan Hunt (Houghton Mifflin, 1999). This wonderful book goes all the way around the world, describing life on every continent in 1000 AD and ending with the Aboriginal peoples of Australia. **Out of print.** (RA 2–3, IR 4–5)

An Adventure in New Zealand (Simon & Schuster, 1992). This Cousteau Society-produced book takes children through New Zealand's countryside with beautiful photographs and simple text. **Out of print.** (RA 1–2, IR 3–5)

Australia: Rookie-Read-About Geography, by Allan Fowler (Children's Press, 2001). This simple-reader guide to Australia's deserts and coast should be an independent read for most young students. (RA 1, IR 2–4)

Destination: Australia, by Jonathan Grupper (National Geographic Society, 2000). Many photographs and brief-but-interesting text take the reader through a full day in Australia. (RA 1, IR 2–4)

Look What Came from Australia, by Kevin Davis (Orchard Books, 2000). A simple guide to customs, language, and items originating in Australia. (RA 1, IR 2–5)

Corresponding Literature Suggestions

Dingoes at Dinnertime, by Mary Pope Osborne (Random House, 2000). A chapter book for independent readers. The Magic Tree House pair end up in the Australian desert and find themselves in the company of unusual animals. (IR 2–5)

Home of the Winds, by Ronald Leonard Bacon (Child's Play International, 1989). A retelling of a traditional Maori tale. **Out of print.** (RA 1, IR 2–4)

Maui and the Sun: A Maori Tale, by Gavin Bishop (North South Books, 1996). A trickster tale from Maori legend, with bright poster-like illustrations. **Out of print.** (RA 1, IR 2–4)

The Pumpkin Runner, by Marsha Diane Arnold, illus. Brad Sneed (Dial, 1998). A farmer in the Australian outback likes to run around his ranch; pumpkins give him enough energy to run in the big race from Melbourne to Sydney. (RA 1–2, IR 3–5)

―――――――――――――――― **MAP WORK** ――――――――――――――――

Australia and New Zealand *(Student Page 37, answer 256)*

1. Australia is one of the seven continents in the world. Color the continent of Australia green.

2. The islands of New Zealand were formed by hot lava from spewing undersea volcanoes. Color the islands of New Zealand bright orange like hot lava.

3. New Zealand is surrounded by ocean, and the Maori people used to paddle out in their canoes to fish. Color a blue border around the islands of New Zealand to show the areas where the Maori used to fish.

COLORING PAGE   Maori warrior's face *(Student Page 38)*. Color this Maori warrior's face with bright, warlike patterns!

―――――――――――――――― **PROJECTS** ――――――――――――――――

COOKING PROJECT   **Make Moth Mix**

The Aborigines eat a variety of foods, including certain insects. Popcorn and Bogong moths make for a crunchy snack. This recipe substitutes peanuts for moths—but you can still pretend!

Ingredients: ½ cup popcorn   ½ cup peanuts (cocktail or dry roasted)
              1 tablespoon cooking oil   1 tablespoon honey

Directions: 1. Put oil in a large saucepan.

2. Add popcorn kernels. Place lid on saucepan. Cook over high heat, moving the pan continually so the kernels don't burn.

3. When the corn has finished popping, remove from heat. Cool.

4. Add peanuts and honey to popcorn. Stir to coat.

CRAFT PROJECT   **Make a Boomerang**

The Aborigines used boomerangs for a number of purposes: hunting birds, and tools for cutting, scraping, and lighting fires. Boomerangs were even decorated and used in religious ceremonies. A boomerang strikes an object with more force than a stone or a stick. Although some types of boomerangs return to the thrower, the Aborigines used non-returning boomerangs that were shaped like a cross.

Materials: ☐ Two paint stirring sticks (available at any paint supply store)
             ☐ Sandpaper (medium grain)
             ☐ 2 rubber bands
             ☐ Markers or acrylic paint

Directions: 1. Using the sand paper, round the edges of each paint stick.

2. Decorate the sticks. If you use paint, it needs to be painted on smoothly.

3. Cross the paint sticks at the center. Snip two rubber bands in half. Wrap and tie them around the center of the paint sticks to form a cross with four even spokes (like the cross the American Red Cross uses).

4. Go outside to an open area and throw your boomerang. Be careful not to throw it at anybody!

ACTIVITY PROJECT **Become a Maori Warrior**

Maori warriors of New Zealand painted their faces and bodies to frighten enemies.

Paint your face like a Maori warrior. You can use face paint, or items from your home (tinted sunblock, lipstick, eyeliner, washable magic marker). If you'd like, use the picture of a Maori fighter on *Student Page 38* as a guide.

ACTIVITY PROJECT **Take the Journey of the Maori**

The Maori sailed from the Polynesian Islands far out in the Pacific to get to New Zealand. They loaded their canoes with pigs and chickens and fruits and vegetables. Make a "canoe" that sails to New Zealand. You will need two people to send the canoe across the sea.

Materials:
- □ 2 1-liter plastic soda bottles, caps off
- □ Duct tape
- □ 2 12-foot strings
- □ 2 (6 pack) plastic ring soda holders
- □ Paper
- □ Crayons or markers

Directions:
1. Cut the two soda bottles in half around the middle. (Have an adult help you with this.) Discard the bottom half of each bottle.

2. Using the remaining top halves of the soda bottles, duct tape the wide end of bottle 1 with the wide end of bottle 2.

3. Thread both pieces of string through the connected soda bottles.

4. Snip each of the two plastic six-rings in half, length-wise, to make four two-loop handles.

5. Tie a two-loop handle to each end of the string.

6. Wrap the soda bottle in construction paper and draw a canoe on the side. Fill the canoe drawing with Maori people as well as chickens, pigs, fruit, and vegetables.

7. Have Person 1 grab one set of handles and Person 2 grab the others. Person 1 will be Polynesia and Person 2 will be New Zealand.

8. Person 1 pulls apart his arms and says, "Goodbye Polynesia! Hello New Zealand!" and sends the canoe to New Zealand. Person 2 keeps his arms together.

9. Now Person 2 gets to be Polynesia. He spreads his arms apart and also says, "Goodbye Polynesia! Hello New Zealand!" Play the game as often as you like.

The Kingdom of the Franks

CHAPTER 11

Encyclopedia Cross-References

UBWH 91 (map only), UILE 204
KIHW 156, KHE 114

CLOVIS, THE EX-BARBARIAN

REVIEW QUESTIONS

What happened to the barbarians who settled in Roman territory? *They learned Roman customs and became civilized.*

What barbarian tribes invaded the land of Gaul? *The Franks invaded Gaul.*

Roman citizens already lived in Gaul. Two more tribes settled there too. Can you remember either of the names of these tribes? *The Allemani and the Burgundians also settled in Gaul.*

The leader Merovius united the tribes. Did Merovius belong to the Franks, the Romans, the Allemani, or the Burgundians? *He was a Frank.*

Why did the tribes of Gaul decide to follow Merovius? *They wanted to drive off the Huns.*

What was the name of Merovius's grandson? *His name was Clovis.*

What was the goal of Clovis, the leader of the Franks? *He wanted to unite all of Gaul into one empire.*

What do we call Clovis's empire today? *We call it France.*

What deal did Clovis make with God? *Clovis agreed to become a Christian if God let him win the battle against another tribe.*

Did he win the battle? *Yes, he won the battle and became a Christian.*

NARRATION EXERCISE

"Barbarian tribes moved into Gaul and settled next to the Romans. A leader named Merovius brought them all together to fight the Huns. The tribes didn't stay together, but Merovius's grandson Clovis finally united them into one empire." OR

"Gaul was united when Clovis, the leader of the Franks, conquered the other tribes. Clovis was the grandson of the man who first made all the tribes come together in one army. Gaul became known as the Frankish empire. Today we call it France."

FOUR TRIBES, ONE EMPIRE

REVIEW QUESTIONS

The Frankish empire had four different kinds of people living in it. Can you remember their names? *They were Franks, Romans, Burgundians, and Allemanni.*

What city did Clovis make the capital of the Franks? *He made Paris the capital city.*

Why did Clovis choose Paris as the capital city? *It was on a hill, so it was easy to defend from attack, and there were good Roman roads leading to it.*

Why did Clovis say that everyone in his empire should become a Christian? *He thought it would unite the people. People of the same religion usually don't fight one another.*

Clovis made one capital city and one religion for his new empire. What was the third thing that Clovis did to unite the people of his empire? *He made laws called the Salic Laws that everyone had to follow.*

Can you remember one of the Salic Laws? *People had to pay money if they attacked each other; calling names was against the law; you couldn't move to a new village if the people didn't want you.*

Were the laws fair? *The laws were not as fair to the Romans as they were to the Franks!*

NARRATION EXERCISE

"Clovis wanted to keep the people of his empire united. He chose a capital city, made everyone become a Christian, and made a new set of laws that everyone had to follow. The laws were called the Salic Laws."
OR

"Clovis had to rule four different groups of people. So he did three things to keep the Frankish empire together. He made Paris the capital city. He made everyone become a Christian. He also made one set of laws for everybody to follow."

Additional History Reading

Famous Men of the Middle Ages, edited by Cyndy and Robert G. Shearer (Greenleaf Press, 1992). This book contains a read-aloud chapter on Clovis. (RA 1–3, IR 4–5)

The Life and Times of Charlemagne, by Jim Whiting (Mitchell Lane Publishers, 2005). A fairly advanced junior biography of Charlemagne, readable and well illustrated. Sections are suitable as read-alouds. (RA 1–3, IR 4–7)

Medieval Paris: Journey to the Past, by Anna Cazzini Tartaglino, illus. Aldo Ripamonti (Raintree/Steck-Vaughn, 2001). Written for slightly older children, this book traces the history of Paris from its founding by Clovis through its medieval expansion; the sections on Clovis are easily read aloud. (RA 1–3, IR 4–5)

Paris, by Renzo Rossi (Enchanted Lion Press, 2003). Written for younger readers, Rossi's heavily illustrated book spends less time on Paris's beginnings but is simpler to read. (RA 1–2, IR 3–5)

Corresponding Literature Suggestions

The Duke and the Peasant: Life in the Middle Ages, by Sister Wendy Beckett, (Prestell USA, 1997). A beautiful children's book that uses colorful paintings from the Duc de Berry's *Book of Hours,* which depicts each month of the year in medieval France. The text explains the lives of the rich and the poor, as well as giving details about the artwork itself. **Out of print.** (RA 1–3, IR 4–5)

Favorite Medieval Tales, by Mary Pope Osborne (Scholastic Press, 1998). Wonderful (and brief) retelling of *The Song of Roland* (a Charlemagne legend), and other Celtic and early British tales, with full-color paintings as illustrations. Highly recommended! (RA 1–3, IR 3–5)

Marguerite Makes a Book, by Bruce Robertson (J. Paul Getty Museum, 1999). Though written about a Parisian family in the 1400's, the illustrations in the beginning of the book show how the city of Paris was located on the island in the middle of the Seine River. Read this with an eye on how Clovis chose this stunning place as his own capital. (RA 1–2, IR 3–5)

Medieval Tales that Kids Can Read and Tell, by Lorna MacDonald Czarnota (August House Publishers, 2000). Very brief tales along with historical background and tips for kids who want to tell them out loud; includes tales from the Song of Roland, a medieval fable about Charlemagne. **Out of print.** (RA 2, IR 3–5)

―――――――――――――――――――― **MAP WORK** ――――――――――――――――――――

The Frankish Empire Under Clovis *(Student Page 39, answer 256)*

1. Color the Mediterranean Sea and the Atlantic Ocean blue.

2. Color the North Sea and the Baltic Sea blue.

3. Underline the word "Allemanni" in yellow.

4. Underline the word "Burgundians" in pink.

5. Underline the word "Franks" in light blue.

6. Clovis united all three tribes into one empire. Outline the territory of the Frankish Kingdom in dark blue to show the unification.

COLORING PAGE   Clovis eventually ruled over all of Gaul. *(Student Page 40)*

―――――――――――――――――――― **PROJECTS** ――――――――――――――――――――

ACTIVITY PROJECT   **Design Your Own Dynasty**

Clovis began as just another Frankish Barbarian ruler who had inherited his father's land. But Clovis had a dream to make his father's northeastern empire larger. Through cunning, deceit, strength, persuasion, and fortune, his empire grew to include most of what is now France and Germany. He left a great empire for his heirs, who fought over the inheritance. The line of the Merovingian Dynasty is filled with both brutality and goodness. Slowly Clovis's great vision of a grand Frankish Empire dissolved as his descendents pursued pleasure and self-benefit over the good of the kingdom. Finally, Pepin the Short, Charlemagne's father, stepped in and stripped the last Merovingian king of his power, establishing a new dynasty.

Clovis had an idea of what his kingdom was going to look like when he started. Design your own kingdom—and complete it with your own dynasty.

Materials: ▨ Colored Pencils
             ▨ White paper with no lines
             ▨ Construction paper of your favorite color

Directions: 1. Think through what a kingdom of your own imagination might look like. Would it be small and controllable or vast and wide? Would it be set in the mountains, the seaside, or the desert? Would it contain lakes, rivers, and seas, or border an ocean? Where would you place your capital city and what would you name it? Draw a map of your kingdom on a white sheet of paper. Use the colored pencils and add symbols for things like mountain ranges, lakes, cities, deserts, and rivers. Don't forget to make a key saying what each symbol means.

             2. Using the Merovingian Dynasty family tree as an example, make up your own dynasty tree. Use your family if you want, or make up people and tell what they are like.

             3. Glue your map and your dynasty family-tree on pieces of construction paper.

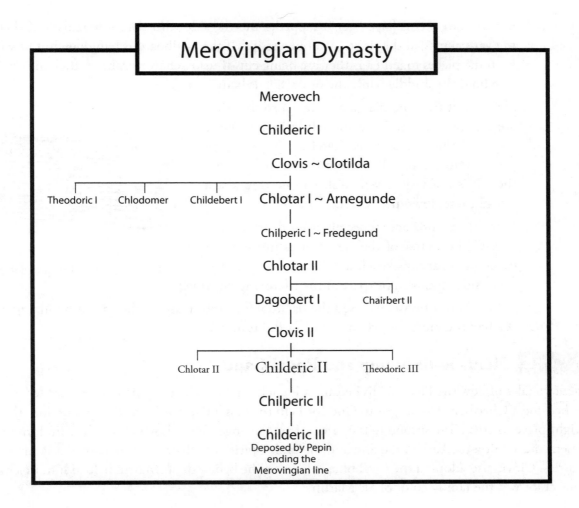

Merovingian Dynasty

Merovech
|
Childeric I
|
Clovis ~ Clotilda
|
Theodoric I — Chlodomer — Childebert I — **Chlotar I ~ Arnegunde**
|
Chilperic I ~ Fredegund
|
Chlotar II
|
Dagobert I — Chairbert II
|
Clovis II
|
Chlotar II — **Childeric II** — Theodoric III
|
Chilperic II
|
Childeric III
Deposed by Pepin
ending the
Merovingian line

CRAFT PROJECT   **Long-Haired Kings**

Before the Franks were conquered by the Romans, the chieftains wore their hair long and flowing. When they met Roman aristocracy and saw that the Romans cut their hair short, they changed to the Roman way. As Rome weakened, Clovis and other Frankish leaders saw their chance to throw off Roman rule. Part of the rebellion was to grow their hair long again. Clovis also braided the front part of his hair on both sides. The Merovingians adopted this look as their own.

Materials:
- 2 skeins of yarn (yellow, tan, black, or brown)
- Large sheet of cardboard at least 15" × 15" (or use the back of a chair or any area that would give you 30-inch strands*)
- Scissors
- Felt strip the same color as yarn, 1" × 9" (use an outline of a ruler to make the strip)
- Straight pins
- Sewing machine or needle
- Thread same color as the yarn

Directions:
1. Wrap the yarn around the legs of a chair or a large sheet of cardboard, tightly, spreading out the yarn evenly. When one skein is finished make sure you end and begin on the same side. Mark that side.

2. When both skeins have been wrapped, note the side with the loose ends. On that side cut the yarn across all the tightly wrapped strips. If the cardboard is lying down, this will help to keep the pieces together as they are being cut. If using chair legs, have someone on the uncut side hold the middle while the other side is being cut.

3. Stretch out the long pieces on a table, so that they are relatively even. Place the felt strip under the center of the yarn strands. Carefully pin the yarn pieces onto the felt. Bunch up the strands so that the felt is not visible. An adult will need to sew a straight line down the center.

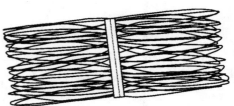

4. Once the stands are secure all around, try on the wig. Gather a few of the yarn stands in the front on one side, and make a braid. Do the same on the other side. You are now part of the Merovingian tribe!

Note: At our house, we used the barstool legs and wrapped the yarn around and around it. We had the most fun when two of us did it together.

CRAFT PROJECT **Fleur-de-lis Stamp and Royal Cape**

There are two tales of how the Fleur-de-lis became a French symbol. The first one tells of a battle Clovis fought after he became a Christian. He prayed to God for help to cross a river and found a trail of lilies that led him to the right place to cross. The second tells of a visit from an angel of God, who brought with him the symbol to represent the Trinity: the Father, the Son and the Holy Spirit. The fleur-de-lis remained a symbol of France for centuries. Clovis also adopted the royal blue color after, he believed, St. Martin helped him in a battle. The royal blue color was the family color of St. Martin.

Materials for Stamp:
- 1 sheet of foam board any color (stay away from yellow or gold so the paint shows when you are working with the stamp)
- Cut out of the fleur-de-lis pattern *(Student Page 41)*
- Craft knife or scissors
- Thick tacky glue or hot glue
- Block of wood, the size of your palm (check in hardware stores for free end pieces)
- Craft paintbrushes
- Yellow or gold paint

Directions:
1. Trace pattern onto foam board and cut out.
2. Glue onto block of wood.
3. Let stamp sit until dry.

Materials for a Royal Cape:
- 1½ yards of inexpensive, satin-looking, royal blue fabric
- Thread to match
- Iron and ironing board

Directions:
1. Iron the edges under about ¼ inch all the way around.
2. Stitch this edge down. OR If you have a serger, serge the cape's sides securely.

3. Place some paper on a working table. Put cape on top, satin side up. Smooth away any creases.

4. Brush on a smooth coat of yellow or gold paint onto the fleur-de-lis stamp. (Do not dip the stamp into the paint as this will give it too much paint and distort the design.) Create a design around the edges of your cape, and/or in the middle.

5. Let dry. Use with the Frankish wig and Merovingian brooch.

CRAFT PROJECT **Merovingian Brooch**

As the Merovingian dynasty grew, so did the demand for beautiful goods fit for a king and his entourage. Grave goods discovered from as far back as Clovis's father's day show beauty, gifted workmanship, and intricate designs. Try your hand at using simple metal techniques and Sculpey to create an artful cloisonné look from the past.

Materials:
- □ White unlined paper
- □ Pencil
- □ Gold, blue, red and yellow Sculpey (polymer clay found at craft stores)
- □ Copper wire, at least 16 gauge (at hardware store)
- □ Wire cutters or old scissors
- □ Hammer
- □ Drinking glass
- □ Glass pie plate
- □ Pin back (at craft stores)

Directions:
1. Use the glass to make a round circle on the white paper. This will be the size of your brooch. Decide what kind of design you would like to make and sketch it out on your paper circle.

2. Stretch out a strand of copper wire about the size of your arm. In the garage, or someplace where you can pound on cement, lay the wire down and hammer the wire so that it is thin and flat.

3. Roll out half of the Sculpey brick. Using the drinking glass, cut out a round circle. Lay it flat in a glass pie plate. This will be your working surface.

4. Now bend your copper wire to make the design you sketched out. Wire may break, but don't worry. Once you've molded your design, press the wire down on a table and make sure it lies relatively flat. Press the wire design into the Sculpey circle where you want it. Make sure the wire is sticking out some.

5. Bake for 20 minutes at 250 degrees. Let it cool.

6. Press into the wire areas different colors of Sculpey, forming a raised design.

7. Attach the pin back to the back of the brooch by using a thin rectangle of gold Sculpey to hold it in place.

8. Bake again for 20 minutes at 250 degrees. Let it cool.

9. Use to hold the royal cape on at the shoulder of one side.

The Islamic Invasion

CHAPTER 12

Encyclopedia Cross-References

UBWH 98, UILE 207, 258–259
KIHW 176, KHE 107

THE ISLAMIC INVASION

REVIEW QUESTIONS

Which barbarian tribe settled in the land of Spain? *The Visigoths settled in Spain.*

Why did the Visigoths start to quarrel among themselves? *They couldn't agree on who would be the next king.*

Who invited Tariq bin Ziyad to Spain? *The sons of the dead king.*

Why did they want his help? *They wanted to drive out the warrior Rodrigo, who had taken the throne.*

What empire did Tariq belong to? *He was a Muslim commander who fought for the Islamic Empire.*

What area did Tariq help to conquer with his armies before coming to Spain? *He conquered much of North Africa.*

Did Tariq want to help the sons of the dead king regain power? *No, he wanted the land for his empire!*

What incredible thing did Tariq order his armies to do when they first arrived in Spain? *He ordered them to burn their ships.*

When Spain was under Islamic rule, what did Spanish followers of Islam become known as? *They were called Moors.*

Do you remember any of the new crops that they planted? *They planted cherries, apples, almonds, and bananas.*

The rock where Tariq stood to watch his ships come in was called *Jabal Tariq,* the "mountain of Tariq." What do we call it today? *We call it the rock of Gibraltar.*

NARRATION EXERCISE

"The Muslim warrior Tariq was invited to Spain to help the sons of the dead king become king. He ended up taking the land for himself, and Spain became part of the Islamic Empire. The Spanish Muslims were called Moors. They built mosques, used Arabic numbers, and planted gardens." OR

"The Visigoths settled in Spain. But then they fought over who would be king. A Muslim commander named Tariq invaded. He told his army to burn their ships. He said they would either take over the land or die trying. His army won, and the land of Spain became part of the Islamic Empire."

Additional History Reading

Count Your Way through the Arab World, by Jim Haskins (Carolrhoda Books, 1991). This counting book gives the Arabic name for each numeral and explores various aspects of the Islamic world. (IR, may be RA for some second graders)

Look What Came from Spain, by Kevin Davis (Franklin Watts, 2003). A simple guide to Spanish influence on American culture and history, written on an advanced second-grade level. (RA 1–2, IR 2–4)

Spain: Festivals of the World, by Susan McKay (Gareth Stevens, 1999). This introduction to Spanish culture is centered around Spanish holidays, some of which are Islamic-influenced. (RA 1–2, IR 3–5)

Spanish and Moorish Fashions, by Tom Tierney (Dover, 2003). Many pictures; brief text explaining the Arab influence on Spanish clothes. An entertaining way to review the effect of the Islamic invasion! (RA 1, IR 2–5)

Corresponding Literature Suggestions

The Beautiful Butterfly: A Folktale from Spain, by Victoria Chess (Houghton Mifflin, 2000). One of the oldest and most popular Spanish folktales, retold in a colorful easy-to-read picture book format. (RA 1, IR 2–4)

Muslim Child: Understanding Islam Through Stories and Poems, by Rukhsana Khan (Albert Whitman & Co., 2002). Good introduction to the daily life of a Muslim child. Includes several full-page illustrations, as well as helpful information sidebars. (RA 2–3, IR 3–5)

The Three Golden Oranges, by Alma Flor Ada, illus. Reg Cartwright (Atheneum, 1999). This traditional Spanish tale of Blancaflor is retold in picture-book style, with beautiful illustrations of the Spanish countryside. (RA 1–2, IR 3–5)

—————————————— **MAP WORK** ——————————————

The Islamic Empire *(Student Page 42, answer 256)*

Simple map work

1. The Muslim commander Tariq bin Ziyad conquered much of North Africa including the city of Tangier. Underline the word "Tangier" in blue.

2. Tariq sailed from Tangier to Gibraltar to conquer Spain. Draw a blue line from Tangier to Gibraltar to represent Tariq's journey. It was a short trip!

3. Once he landed in Gibraltar, Tariq ordered the ships to be burned. Circle Gibraltar in orange to represent fire.

4. Tariq conquered Spain for the Islamic Empire. Color Spain in purple.

5. The Islamic Empire included much of North Africa and Arabia. You've already colored in Spain. Color the rest of the Islamic Empire (within the dotted lines) in purple. Be sure not to cross into either the Byzantine Empire or the Frankish Kingdom.

Advanced Map Work *(Student Page 43)*

Coloring Page   A Moorish mosque and fountain *(Student Page 44)*

—————————————— **PROJECTS** ——————————————

Activity Project   ## A Moorish Ruler's Tunic and Robe

The years of the Islamic rule in Spain saw advances in medicine, science, and philosophy. The caliphs set about to build great libraries, some boasting 500,000 books. Cultural centers such as Granada became rich in learning and influence. The Islamic rulers displayed their wealth by dressing in sumptuous fabrics of rich designs and colors. Follow these simple steps to make your own Moorish ruler's tunic and robe.

Materials:
- 5 yards of white muslin
- Rit dye, color of your choice
- Scissors
- Sewing pins
- Sewing machine
- White thread
- Iron and ironing board
- Acrylic paint (use bright colors, especially gold and silver)
- Brush
- Stamps

Directions: 1. Cut the fabric in half. One half will be for the under tunic and the other for the rich ruler's robe.

2. Follow the Rit dye directions and dye the robe half. Dry in the dryer and iron.

3. Fold the tunic fabric in half and lay it on the floor. Have the wearer of the Moorish Tunic lay down on the fabric in the center with his head over the edge, off the fabric. Arms should be extended out on both sides in a cross-like fashion.

4. Keeping about 4 inches from the body, cut out the tunic like diagram A.

5. Pin the edges.

6. Sew the seams straight down from the arm, turning at the corner and down to the bottom.

7. Fold the tunic in half lengthwise and make a semi-circle for the head.

8. Turn inside out and press.

9. Repeat the process with the robe material. When cutting the head hole, cut down the center of the robe on the front only, from the top to the bottom (Diagram B). Turn under ¼" with iron and sew edges.

10. Use the stamps and paint (or go freehand!) and decorate the edge of the robe all along the front opening and around the bottom and arm edges.

11. Let dry on a hanger and enjoy the beauty of your Moorish Ruler's Tunic and Robe.

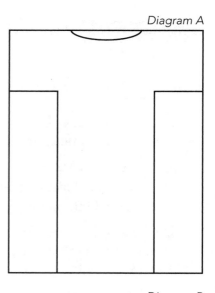

Diagram A

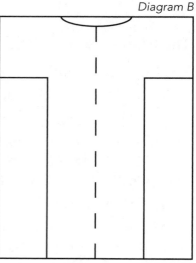

Diagram B

CRAFT PROJECT **Moorish Stamps**

This stamp activity can be used to decorate the edges of your ruler's robe.

Materials:
- □ 1 sheet of foam board any color (the thicker the better)
- □ Cut out of the Moorish symbols patterns *(Student Page 45)*
- □ Craft knife or scissors
- □ Thick tacky glue or hot glue
- □ Block of wood, the size of your palm (check in hardware stores for free end pieces)
- □ Craft paintbrushes
- □ Acrylic or fabric paints

Directions: 1. Trace pattern onto foam board and cut out.

2. Glue onto block of wood.

3. Let stamp sit until dry.

4. Brush paint on the stamp and apply to surface. Let dry before use.

ACTIVITY PROJECT **Moorish Ruler's Turban**

Not only did the Moors use the traditional Islamic garb, but a group called the Mozarabs, Christians who kept their faith but adopted Muslim culture, also dressed in the flowing robes and turbans of the day.

Materials: ▢ 1 yard of colorful fabric or white muslin dyed to match the robe

Directions: 1. Drape the cloth so the head is in the center of the front part of the fabric (like a biblical costume of Mary, for example).

2. Gather the ends and twist until they make two separate ropes in the back.

3. Cross the two rope sides and wrap around the front of the head, following the fabric edge along the front.

4. Twist them together and tuck them into each side. Note that one side will tuck into the top and the other side will tuck into the bottom. Tuck in loose fabric. Use with long tunic and decorated robe.

COOKING PROJECT **A Moorish Feast**

In the Iberian Peninsula, which includes Spain and Portugal, there are many varieties of food. Because the peninsula is surrounded by the sea on three sides, fish and seafood are dietary staples on the coast. Chicken and lamb are more common inland.

The Moors dined at a long, low table with cushions scattered around it. Feast as the Moors did—find or make a low table (or go picnic style), sit on floor pillows, listen to music, and eat Moorish food.

Materials: ▢ Stools, chunks of wood, or bricks   ▢ Islamic music from the library
              ▢ Pillows in colorful pillowcases   ▢ Candle light
              ▢ Several colorful tablecloths   ▢ Moorish Recipes
              ▢ Moor tunic, robe and turban
              ▢ Flat piece of board that can accommodate those who will be dining

Directions: 1. Using the stools or bricks under the slab of wood, make a low table and cover it with your favorite tablecloths or colorful fabric.

2. Place pillows around to accommodate each guest.

3. Try the following Moorish recipes.

4. Play the music, light the candles (no electricity during this era) and enjoy your experience!

Moorish Recipes: *Easy Arroz con Pollo*

Ingredients: 2 cups chicken broth   ½ teaspoon salt
              1 grocery store roasted chicken, cut up   Ground pepper to taste
              1 14½ ounce can of Italian flavored stewed tomatoes, drained   1 tablespoon butter
              1 box of Spanish style rice (Farmhouse or Rice-a-Roni)

Directions: 1. Place all ingredients above in to large pot and bring to a boil.

2. Lower heat, cover, and let simmer 20 minutes.

3. Serve on a plate, placing chicken pieces on top of rice.

4. Serve with green or red grapes, pita bread and red grape juice.

Medieval cookbook translator Steve Bloch made these suggestions when asked how to introduce kids to a Moorish cuisine.

- Give a pile of marzipan (invented in Islamic Spain, 11th century) to kids and have them sculpt things for one another to eat. These sculptures can be painted with food coloring. Keep in mind, he writes, the Islamic prohibition against making depictions of living things. Marzipan, also called almond paste, is found in grocery or cake decorating stores.

- One of my favorite simple recipes from the medieval Islamic world, Bloch says, is *Sekanjabin.*

Ingredients: Sugar or honey
    Water
    Vinegar
    Crushed mint leaves (in grocery store's herb section)

Directions:
1. Dissolve sugar or honey in half as much water.
2. Add a little vinegar.
3. Simmer for a good while (half an hour or more).
4. Remove from heat, and add crushed mint leaves. You now have syrup that will keep un-refrigerated for months. For a refreshing summer drink, mix one part of syrup with 7–10 parts of cold water. I've also mixed it with hot water to drink when I have a sore throat or a cold.
   (*Note:* Similar recipes are made from equal amounts of lemon juice and sugar, or equal amounts of pomegranate juice and sugar.)

- In the Middle Ages, cooking and medicine were closely tied together. Many medieval recipes were also cures for ailments. According to medieval medicine, somebody with a cold has an excess of cold and moist "humors," and needs to balance them by eating and drinking warm and dry things.

CRAFT PROJECT   Make a Spanish History Wind-Chime

Follow this project and learn some of the early highlights from Spanish history.

Materials:
- ☐ 1 (12 ounce) frozen juice can, washed and dried
- ☐ 4 juice can lids
- ☐ Large sewing needle
- ☐ Thread, fishing line or string
- ☐ Glue
- ☐ Spray polyurethane
- ☐ 4 circle pictures *(Student Page 46)*
- ☐ 5" × 9" rectangular piece of paper
- ☐ Tape
- ☐ Colored pencils
- ☐ Nail and hammer

Directions:
1. Color and cut out the pictures for this craft: a long rectangle picture and 4 circle pictures.
2. Decorate the rectangular piece of paper. You may write "Highlights from Spanish History" on the paper. Glue or tape it around the side of the empty juice can.
3. Cut four pieces of string all the same length (about 7 to 8 inches long).
4. Glue the string onto the center of the juice can lids. Glue the picture overtop of the string.

5. Using the sewing needle, gently poke holes evenly around the open end of the juice can about a half of an inch from the edge. Follow with the nail if you are using a thicker string.

6. With the nail and hammer, poke two holes close to each other on the bottom of the juice can. Thread a piece of string through the holes and tie ends in a knot so you can hang up your wind-chime when it is done.

7. Spray the juice can and the lids with polyurethane spray. (*Note:* Do this outside or in a well-ventilated area.) This will help the wind-chime to be rainproof.

8. Tie the strings attached to the pictured lids to the holes in the juice can. Hang each pictured lid in order.

9. Hang your wind-chime outside where you can hear it!

The Great Kings of France

CHAPTER 13

Encyclopedia Cross-References

UBWH 99, UILE 198, 216
KIHW 186–187, KHE 114–115

CHARLES THE HAMMER

REVIEW QUESTIONS

After the Muslim fighters invaded Spain, where did they plan to go next? *They planned to charge up into France and conquer the Franks.*

What was the nickname of Charles Martel, the new king of the Franks? *His nickname was "Charles the Hammer."*

What city did the Muslims and Franks fight their huge battle at? *They fought at Tours.*

In the story told by the Arab historian, why was the Muslim general worried about his men? *He thought that they were too worried about their plunder and not worried enough about the battle.*

Why did the Muslims ride back to their tents during the fight? *They wanted to protect the wealth inside their tents.*

Who won the fight? *Charles the Hammer and the Franks won!*

NARRATION EXERCISE

"The Muslim armies wanted to invade the land of the Franks. Charles the Hammer was the new king of the Franks. When the Muslims invaded his land, he fought them at Tours and won." OR

"Charles, the king of the Franks, was called Charles the Hammer because he kept 'hammering' his foes until he won. He even drove back the powerful Muslims when they tried to invade his land! "

THE GREATEST KING: CHARLEMAGNE

REVIEW QUESTIONS

Who was the greatest Frankish king of all? *Charlemagne.* OR *Charles the Great.*

Who was Charlemagne's grandfather? *Charles the Hammer was Charlemagne's grandfather.*

The story listed three ways in which Franks were becoming more like barbarians. Can you remember two? *They weren't going to church; they weren't having their children baptized (OR They were forgetting about Christianity); the children weren't learning how to read and write.*

Name at least two ways that Charlemagne tried to improve the lives of his people. *He had more copies of the Scriptures made; he built new roads and bridges; he started schools for boys; he taught the people better ways to farm; he told families to bring their children to church; he fought wars and expanded his kingdom.*

Why did Charlemagne's people call him the "Emperor of the Romans"? *They were telling him that he was as powerful as the old Roman emperor, and that his kingdom had a peace like the Pax Romana.*

Although Charlemagne was a great and powerful ruler, what did he never learn to do well? *He never really learned how to write his letters.*

"Charlemagne was the greatest king of the Franks. He was afraid that the Franks were becoming barbarians again. He tried to make the lives of his people better, and he fought wars to expand his empire. He told the Franks to teach their children about Christianity and how to read and write. But he never learned how to write himself." OR

"Charlemagne was a great Frankish king. He started schools, built new roads and bridges, and fought wars to make his empire larger. He also wanted everyone in his empire to become a Christian. His empire grew so big and peaceful that people thought it was like the old Roman empire. So he became known as the 'Emperor of the Romans.'"

Additional History Reading

Charlemagne and the Early Middle Ages, by Miriam Greenblatt (Benchmark Books, 2002). This biography, which covers both Charlemagne's life and everyday life in France at the time of his rule, is for slightly older children. However, the chapters are very brief and selected chapters would make good read-alouds. (RA 1–4, IR 4–5)

Famous Men of the Middle Ages, edited by Cyndy and Robert G. Shearer (Greenleaf Press, 1992). Includes a read-aloud section on Charlemagne. (RA 1–3, IR 4–5)

Getting to Know France and French, by Nicola Wright (Barrons, 1993). A colorful large-print introduction to the land, culture, and language of France. (RA 1–2, IR 3–5)

Ten Kings and the Worlds They Ruled, by Milton Meltzer, illus. Bethanne Andersen (Orchard Books, 2002). Illustrated, read-aloud biographies of ten kings, 8–12 pages each. Includes Charlemagne; definitely the best read-aloud biography for young children. (RA 2–4, IR 4–5)

Corresponding Literature Suggestions

Little Red Riding Hood (Puffin Easy to Read), by Harriet Ziefert (Puffin, 2000). This classic tale is written just for this level of readers and includes the woodcutter's heroic victory (for those of us who need Perrault tweaked now and then). (RA 1–2, IR 2–4)

Puss in Boots, by Fred Marcellino (Farrar, Straus and Giroux, 1990). Another Perrault retelling with beautifully painted illustrations; a Caldecott Honor Book. (RA 1–2, IR 3–5)

Son of Charlemagne, by Barbara Willard, illus. Emil Weiss (Bethlehem Books, 1998). Written for slightly older readers, this tale of Charlemagne's reign is told by his oldest son. (IR 4–5)

———————————————— MAP WORK ————————————————

The Empire of Charlemagne *(Student Page 47, answer 257)*

Simple map work

1. The Muslim armies who invaded the land of the Franks came from Spain. Color Spain red.

2. The army of Charles Martel met the Muslim army at the city of Tours in France. Circle the city in orange.

3. Charlemagne ruled over an enormous empire. Trace the edges of his empire (the Frankish Empire) in purple. If you want, you can color it in when you are finished.

Advanced map work *(Student Page 48)*

COLORING PAGES *(Student Pages 49, 50, 51, and 52)*

Witikind—Witikind led a rebellion against Charlemagne and avoided capture for twelve years! Finally, Charlemagne offered Witikind terms for surrender, and the rebel swore a lifetime allegiance to Charlemagne and received a Christian baptism.

Charlemagne—One of the great leaders in the history of Western culture, Charlemagne dressed and ate like a commoner. He loved hunting and sport; his biographer wrote that Charlemagne was strong and tall, well-built with flowing white hair, and that "his eyes were piercing and unusually large." He carried his sword with him wherever he went, along with a blue cloak to keep him warm. He would not give his daughters away in marriage for diplomatic gain, and they stayed with him till he died. His sons rode with him during war campaigns.

Louis—Charlemagne and Hildegard's third son was crowned king of Aquitaine by Pope Hadrian on Easter Sunday, 781. He was three years old. Like his brothers, he was educated and trained under his father's supervision. He also learned the arts of hunting and war from his father, but he was not as athletically inclined as his brothers. Once he was older, he proved his military skills by conquering Spanish lands all the way to Barcelona. When his older brothers died, he became Charlemagne's heir. Louis proved to be a remarkable leader, though very different from his father.

Einhard—Charlemagne's biographer came from a noble family and was very well educated. He was also Charlemagne's most trusted advisor. Einhard wrote down the details of Charlemagne's life for us and called Charlemagne the most outstanding leader that ever lived.

Hildegard—Charlemagne's second wife came from a noble Frankish family. She had three sons and four daughters and enjoyed traveling with her husband on his journeys. They also took their children along with them, all around the country, since Frankish custom meant that the king had no one permanent "court." Hildegard even gave birth to their third son, Louis, in Spain! But she died in 783.

Alcuin of York—Charlemagne's spiritual advisor and friend, Alcuin was born to a wealthy family in northern England. Knowing his excellent reputation as an educator, Charlemagne asked him to become the Minister of Education at Aachen in 781. Alcuin established schools and monasteries there and in other parts of Charlemagne's empire. Charlemagne also had his help in overseeing the education of both his sons and his daughters.

Carloman/Pepin—Charlemagne and Hildegard's second son was crowned king of Italy by Pope Hadrian on Easter Sunday, 781. He was four years old. Later in his life, Pepin conquered territory for his father and brought even more wealth to the Frankish kingdom. He died on July 8, 810.

Charles—Charlemagne and Hildegard's first son was the heir of Charlemagne's kingdom and groomed to be the next king of the Franks. He spent lots of time at his father's side; Charlemagne monitored his education and taught him to hunt. As Charles grew, he took over military responsibilities and became his father's best general. He died December 4, 811, at 39 years of age. His death devastated Charlemagne.

Roland—Charlemagne's good friend and trustworthy knight (or *paladin*, which means chosen knight) died in an ambush carried out by hostile tribes at the top of a mountain, while he was trying to cross the Pyrenees. There is a marker at the supposed spot of the attack today. This story is told in a medieval legend called *The Song of Roland*.

Ganalon—In every story there is a villain. In *The Song of Roland*, Ganalon is one of Charlemagne's twelve favorite knights. However, he persuades Charlemagne not to answer Roland's call for help!

ACTIVITY PROJECT Tent Full of Spoils

The Muslim army camped outside of the city of Tours. Their tents were full of spoils they had captured: wealth, food, clothing, horses, and gold. Construct your own "tent full of spoils." Make a tent out of sheets and blankets. Collect things to keep inside of it: coins, your favorite clothes, trophies, costume jewelry, stuffed animals, and snacks (ask your parent if you can eat inside the tent). Of course when the army of the Franks comes, you'll have to flee!

CRAFT PROJECT Puppet Retelling

Materials: ☐ Coloring pages *(Student Pages 50, 51, and 52)*
☐ Colored pencils
☐ Glue sticks
☐ Popsicle or craft sticks (or plastic silverware)
☐ Long blanket or tablecloth
☐ Two chairs

Directions: 1. Color and cut out the portraits of Charlemagne's friends and family on the coloring pages. Paste each picture at the top of a Popsicle stick.

2. Using the chairs, drape the long cloth between them, stretching the chairs far enough apart so that you have a good, wide puppet stage. See how much of Charlemagne's life you can remember. Or make up your own stories with the characters!

CRAFT PROJECT Charlemagne's Crown

Many of the official paintings of Charlemagne include a jeweled, elaborate crown. Make this crown for yourself.

Materials for one crown:
☐ Enlarged copy of the Charlemagne crown template *(Student Page 53)*
☐ 1 piece of aluminum dryer vent (at hardware stores for about $1.50)
☐ Permanent ink pen
☐ 1 tube of caulking with caulking gun   ☐ Glue gun and five to ten glue sticks
☐ Scissors or tin snips   ☐ Cardstock
☐ Craft wire   ☐ Acrylic paints
☐ Hammer and a nail   ☐ Gold acrylic paint
☐ Craft jewels   ☐ Craft paint brush
☐ 1 bag of medium-sized craft pearls (at craft store)

Directions: 1. The day before, it is best for a parent to prepare the crown as follows:

a. First, measure your child's head size. If larger than 21 inches, you can make an adjustment with the extra panel on the template.

b. Trace the crown template onto the silver side of the aluminum with a permanent ink pen.

c. Cut out the crown carefully as the aluminum may be sharp.

d. After crown is cut, bend it at each panel so that it curves around with ease forming the crown shape.

e. Check by slipping the crown over your child's head before you pound the holes. For smaller heads, you may skip the extra panel, but for larger heads you may use the extra panel to give you the needed size.

f. Using the nail and hammer, lay the edges down on a hard surface and pound several holes through both ends. The nail will make holes through both sides.

g. Use the craft wire and thread it through, pulling the crown edges to the size needed.

h. Using the caulking, go around all of the edges, covering every rough spot. This will be painted gold at the end and also adds a nice finished look. Make sure you also go around the bridge edges and cross edges. This can be done by laying them on a piece of foil while drying.

i. Note that the caulking may need to be pushed into the sharp aluminum if it slips off, but in a week this will be hard and stable.

2. One day later, the child may:

a. Cut out the cross from the template. Trace it onto a piece of cardstock. Cut out.

b. Repeat step "a" for the scalloped ridge.

c. Paint the cross and the scalloped ridge gold. Let dry.

d. Glue the cross to the front of the crown. Glue the scalloped ridge from the top of the cross, along the right side of the cross, and to the crown. (So when the crown is worn, the scallop should be on the right side of the person.) Let dry.

e. Decorate the crown with the paints and jewels. The crown was very lavish and covered thickly with jewels. Now you look just like the emperor Charlemagne! Kneel down and have someone place the crown on your head, saying, "Hail to Charles, crowned by God, the great and peace-bringing Emperor of the Romans!"

Easy Version of Charlemagne's Crown

Materials:
- Posterboard
- Charlemagne crown template *(Student Page 53)*
- Aluminum foil or metallic craft paint
- Pencil
- Scissors
- Stapler
- Glue stick
- Craft jewels (or shiny flat buttons, painted dried beans)
- Glue gun

Directions:
1. Measure your child's head size. If his head exceeds 21 inches, you can make an adjustment with the extra panel on the template.

2. Trace the template onto the posterboard. The crown should be your child's head size plus 1½ inches.

3. Cut out the crown. Wrap it around the child's head to double check the size. Staple the two ends together to form a crown (sharp ends of staple should face away from the child's head to prevent scratching).

4. Cut out the crown and scalloped edge from the template. Trace onto the posterboard. Cut out.

5. Glue the cross to the front of the crown. Glue the scalloped ridge from the top of the cross, along the right side of the cross, and to the crown. (So when the crown is worn, the scallop should be on the right side of the person.) Let dry.

6. If you are using paint, paint the entire crown gold or silver (including cross and scallop). If you are using aluminum foil, wrap the crown in it. Secure any loose ends of foil to the inside of the crown with glue.

7. Fasten the jewels (or buttons or beans) to the crown. Decorate it lavishly. Now you look just like the emperor Charlemagne! Kneel down and have someone place the crown on your head, saying, "Hail to Charles, crowned by God, the great and peace-bringing Emperor of the Romans!"

The Arrival of the Norsemen

CHAPTER 14

Encyclopedia Cross-References

UBWH 100–101, UILE 210–213
KIHW 204–205, 234–235, 216–219, KHE 130–131

THE VIKING INVASION

REVIEW QUESTIONS

What happened to the old Roman Empire? *Barbarians attacked it.*

What do we call the "barbarians" who attacked the Franks? *They were called "North-men," or Norsemen.*

What peninsula did the Norsemen come from? *They came from Scandinavia.*

Do you remember the three kingdoms of Scandinavia? *The Scandinavian kingdoms are Norway, Denmark, and Sweden.*

What other name were the Norsemen known by? *They were also called "Vikings."*

What is the advantage in having a flat-bottomed boat? *The boat can float in shallow water. You can row it right up to the sand on the beach!*

Why was it easier for the Vikings to invade the Franks after Charlemagne died? *The kingdom was divided among Charlemagne's three grandsons and was no longer strong and united.*

What did the Franks do to stop the Vikings from invading the western part of France? *The Franks gave the Vikings a piece of the land called Normandy.*

Once the Vikings had been in Normandy for a while, how did they start to speak and act? *They started to act just like the Franks!*

What had the Vikings become? *They had become Normans.*

NARRATION EXERCISE

"The Vikings came from the north and invaded the Frankish empire. They sailed right up onto the beaches in their flat-bottomed boats. Eventually the Franks gave the Vikings some Frankish land. This land was called Normandy, and the Vikings were called Normans." OR

"After Charlemagne died, the kingdom of the Franks was divided and could not fight off the Vikings. The Vikings invaded France so often in their longships that they were eventually given some of the land. After living there for awhile, they started to act just like the Franks!"

ERIC THE RED AND "ERIC'S SON"

REVIEW QUESTIONS

Why did Eric the Red have to leave Iceland? *He killed two neighbors in a fight.*

What name did Eric the Red give to the land that he discovered so that other Viking settlers would come there? *Greenland.*

What was Greenland really like? *Greenland was cold, dark, icy, treeless, and full of mountains.*

How did the Viking settlers in Greenland get enough grain to live? *They traded sealskins, polar bear furs, tusks, and other items to visitors.*

Did they have enough to eat? *No; they had so little food that they did not grow very tall!*

Why did Eric the Red's son, Leif Ericsson, decide to go exploring? *He wanted to find the land that Bjarni saw from a distance but never explored.*

What fruit did Leif Ericsson find in the new land that he discovered? *He found grapes.*

What did he name the new land? *He named it Vineland.*

What made the new settlers of Vineland give up their settlements? *The Native Americans (or Skraelings) of the land defended their territory and fought the Vikings.*

What land had Leif Ericsson discovered? *He had discovered North America.*

Narration Exercise

"The Vikings were great explorers. Eric the Red sailed to cold, icy Greenland. His son, Leif Ericsson, sailed to North America. He called it Vineland and tried to settle there, but the settlers were chased away by the Native Americans." OR

"The Viking explorer Eric the Red tried to get settlers to come to the cold, icy land that he had discovered by calling it Greenland. His son, Leif Ericsson, was also a famous explorer. He sailed to North America long before Columbus! He named the new land Vineland because it was full of grapes."

THE NORSE GODS

Review Questions

Where did the Vikings believe that the gods lived? *The gods lived in Asgard, above the sky.*

How was Asgard connected with the earth? *Asgard was connected to earth by a rainbow bridge.*

What is one way a Viking could get into Valhalla, the feasting hall of the gods? *A Viking who died in battle would be taken to Valhalla by a Valkyrie.*

Who was Thor? *Thor was the thunder-god.*

Why did Thor want to go to Skymer's home? *Thor wanted to steal Skymer's giant kettle of mead.*

What became of the goat bones and skins that were eaten the night before? *Thor turned them back into live goats.*

Why did one of the goats limp? *The goat limped because the son of the house cracked one of its bones open.*

What did the five caves turn out to be? *The caves were the fingers of the giant Skymer's lost glove.*

When Thor was drinking from Skymer's horn of mead, what was he really doing? *He was drinking from the ocean.*

When Thor wrestled with the cat, what was he really wrestling with? *He was wrestling with the world serpent, the Midgar Serpent.*

Why couldn't Thor conquer the old woman? *She was Old Age. Not even the strongest man can beat age.*

Narration Exercise

"The Vikings believed in many gods. The thunder god Thor tried to steal a giant's mead kettle. Thor thought he was drinking from a horn, wrestling with a cat, and fighting an old lady, but he was really drinking from the sea, lifting up the world serpent, and fighting against Old Age." OR

"The Vikings believed that their gods and goddesses lived in Asgard. A warrior could get into Valhalla by dying in battle. The Norse god Thor set off on a journey to steal mead from the giant Skymer. Skymer tricked Thor by asking him to do nearly impossible things. Thor was angry when he couldn't defeat Skymer's old nanny, but he was really wrestling against Old Age."

Additional History Reading

The Grandchildren of the Vikings, by Matti A. Pitkanen and Reijo Harkonen (Carolrhoda Books, 1995). This lavishly photographed book shows modern-day children of Scandinavia and traces their connection with the Vikings of old. (RA 1–4, IR 5)

The Vikings (Treasure Chests), by Fiona MacDonald (Running Press, 1997). Activities includes: sun dial compass, Viking board game, Viking boat, and map with stickers. Plus, there are other stickers, a mini poster of Viking ships, a Viking Mythology tree, and a little booklet about the Vikings. Small children will need help with most of these projects. (RA 2–3, IR 4–5 and activities)

Who Were the Vikings? (Starting Point History Series), by Jane Chisholm (EDC Publications, 2002). A simple Internet-linked guide to Viking history, with easy-to-read text. (RA 1, IR 2–4)

Corresponding Literature Suggestions

Beorn the Proud, by Madeleine Polland, illus. Joan Coppa Drennen (Bethlehem Books, 1999). This chapter book tells about the friendship between a Viking boy and an Irish farm girl kidnapped by Viking invaders; a good independent read for strong readers or family read-aloud for younger students. (RA 1–3, IR 4–5)

East O' the Sun and West O' the Moon and Other Norwegian Fairy Tales, by George Webbe Dasent (Dover, 2001). Includes ten short stories from Norway. (RA 1–3, IR 4–5)

Magic Tree House #15, Viking Ships at Sunrise, by Mary Pope Osborne (Random House, 1998). Travel back in time, visit a monastery in medieval Ireland and meet some Vikings! (RA 1–2, IR 3–5)

Odin's Family: Myths of the Vikings, retold by Neil Philip, illus. Maryclare Foa (Orchard Books, 1996). These short, large-print retellings are good for younger readers and cover all of the major themes in Norse mythology. (RA 2, IR 3–5)

Yo, Vikings! by Judith Byron Schachner (Dutton Books, 2002). In this wildly colorful picture book, Emma imagines that she's a Viking, reads up on Vikings at the library, renames herself Emma the Red, buys a Viking ship with her allowance, and takes her friends off on an adventure. (RA 1, IR 2–4)

_____ **MAP WORK** _____

Viking Lands *(Student Page 54, answer 257)*

1. The Vikings of Scandinavia invaded the kingdom of the Franks. Let's trace the path of the Viking longships in green. Start at the dot in Scandinavia (the dot between Norway and Sweden) and draw down through the waters until you get to the dot in the Frankish Kingdom.

2. Eventually the Vikings were given some of the Frankish land. This land was called Normandy. In orange, trace the path the Viking settlers took from Scandinavia to Normandy.

3. Some Vikings sailed across the Atlantic Ocean to Iceland. Trace the path from Scandinavia to Iceland in blue.

4. The Viking explorer Eric the Red sailed west from Iceland hoping to find a new home. He found Greenland. Trace the path of his journey from Iceland to Greenland in red (for Eric the Red).

5. Eric's son, Leif Ericsson, went exploring like his father. He found a new land that he named "Vineland." Today we call that new land Newfoundland. In purple, trace Leif's journey from Greenland to Newfoundland.

COLORING PAGE   A Viking longship *(Student Page 55)*

────────────────────────────── **PROJECTS** ──────────────────────────────

ACTIVITY PROJECT   **A Viking Funeral**

Viking chieftains had elaborate funerals. The chieftain was dressed in his best clothes and laid on a Viking longship with all his weapons and precious possessions. Then the longship was set on fire and pushed onto the water to burn.

Hold your own Viking funeral. Put an action figure or doll in a toy boat. You can dress your chieftain in fine clothes and add weapons, jewelry, and coins to the boat if you wish. Then float the toy boat in your bathtub!

CRAFT PROJECT   **Make a Viking Boat**

Materials:
☐ Both templates for boat copied on cardstock *(Student Pages 56 and 57)*
☐ 6" square piece of paper for sail
☐ Colored pencils or crayons
☐ Scissors
☐ Glue or tape
☐ Drinking straw for mast
☐ Small amount of air-drying, blue foam clay for stand (optional)

Directions:
1. Color and cut out all the pieces of the Viking boat.
2. On both ends of the hull, cut on dotted lines then fold tabs to inside and glue A to B and C to D.
3. Fold the dragon's head and tail down the middle and cut out where indicated, then unfold and glue to hull where indicated. Match up the 2 sides of the head and glue together. Repeat for tail.
4. Glue the shields to the sides of the hull.
5. Cut a small slit in top of hull between shields and insert oars in slits.
6. Put a glob of hot glue in bottom of hull and insert straw for mast. Glue sail to mast.
7. Make a stand that looks like ocean waves from the clay.

CRAFT PROJECT   **Make a Viking Brooch or Thor's Hammer Pendant**

Materials:
☐ Photocopy of templates *(Student Page 58)*
☐ Hole punch
☐ Colored pencils, water color pencils or markers
☐ Sandpaper
☐ Deli plastic containers, #6 recyclable
  (Or use "Print & Shrink" oven-bake crafts sheets found at department or office supply stores.)
☐ Scissors
☐ Cording for pendant
☐ Safety pin for brooch
☐ Glue

Directions: 1. Cut up a deli plastic container, freeing the useable top and bottom. Sand one side of the plastic until it is cloudy and you can feel the roughness on every part of it (delete this step if using the "Print & Shrink" craft sheets). This is so the color will stick. Or if using Print & Shrink sheets and you have a scanner, scan templates and print on the sheets. Color as directed in step 2.

2. Lay the plastic on top of the template pattern. Trace the pattern on the plastic, making sure you are working on the scratched side. Then color the pattern. For the most vivid color use watercolor pencils that are moist.

3. Decide where you want to punch your hole if you are making a pendant and use the hole punch to create the hole.

4. Once you are finished, cut the template out and place on a cookie sheet. Bake at 250 degrees for about 10 to 15 minutes. Check often. (Burning plastic is not good for you to breathe!) Take out when the items are lying flat and are thicker. Your item will shrink and the colors will intensify.

5. Use the cording to hang the pendant around your neck. Glue a safety pin on back of the brooch.

Thor's hammer was drawn from one found at Romersdal on Bornholm Island in Denmark. It dates back to about 1000 A.D. Thor was the god of rain and thunder and protector of the Viking farmer in Norse mythology. The hammer was Thor's symbol.

The Viking ship brooch was found in a grave at Lilevang, Bornholm, Denmark. A Viking woman often wore two brooches or buckles, one on each shoulder to fasten her clothing.

CRAFT PROJECT | Make a Viking Long House

Materials:
- ☐ Card stock
- ☐ Scissors
- ☐ Glue or tape
- ☐ Ruler
- ☐ Pencil

Directions for base:

1. Measure 2½" around edges of card stock and draw lines on each side. Fold on each line. Cut on dotted lines as shown in picture.
2. Fold all tabs marked A to the inside and glue or tape to pieces marked B (see picture).

A	B	A
	house base	
A	B	A

Directions for roof:

1. Trim 1½" off long edge of one side of card stock. Measure 2½" on each short end, mark it, and fold the paper to the inside along each mark.
2. With those ends folded in you will have a 6" by 7" piece. Bring both 6" ends together and fold like a taco.
3. Cut on dotted lines as shown in picture. On each end fold one end flap on top of the other and glue or tape. Trim end pieces even with edges of roof. This will form the triangular shape on the ends of the roof.

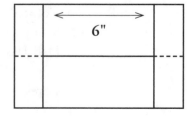

Decorate your long house:

During Viking times, there weren't any local hardware stores, so Vikings had to use whatever materials were available to make their homes. If they lived near a wooded area, they built log or plank homes. In areas where no lumber was available, they built homes from sod. At times Vikings used rocks around the foundation of their homes. Their roofs were usually made from thatch, but some Vikings used sod for their roofs and then planted grass, which grew right on the roof! Look around the area where you live and make a list of the materials you would use if you were building a Viking home.

Suggested materials:

- ☐ Dry twigs (for a log house)
- ☐ Craft sticks or toothpicks (for a plank house)
- ☐ Pebbles (if you want a rock foundation)
- ☐ Cut grass, straw or shredded wheat for the roof
- ☐ Glue
- ☐ Mud (if you want a sod house)
- ☐ Grass seeds (for sod house roof)

Directions for log or plank house:

1. If you are using pebbles for a rock foundation, glue those around the base of your house first.
2. For a log house, break twigs to fit and glue in place. For a plank house glue craft sticks or toothpicks in place.
3. Crumble shredded wheat and glue on roof or use grass or straw. Use spray-on glue after the material is in place.

Directions for a sod house:

1. Spread mud on your house and over roof.
2. Sprinkle grass seeds on roof.
3. Gently mist every day. (Don't get the house too wet or it will buckle.)

COOKING PROJECT **Make Viking Bread**

The Vikings made bread out of barley, oats and rye. Since they ground their own flour by hand, the bread had a gritty texture.

Ingredients: 3 cups whole wheat flour (can also use part oat, barley or rye flour)
2 cups white flour
1 teaspoon baking soda   2 cups warm water
1 teaspoon sea salt   1 cup oats

Directions:

1. In a large bowl, mix flour, baking soda, and salt.
2. Add and stir in ¾ cup of oats (save ¼ cup for later).
3. Slowly add the 2 cups of warm water. Stir well. The mixture will become difficult to stir.
4. Knead the mixture until the mixture becomes stiff.
5. Form into a circle and place on a greased cookie sheet.
6. Sprinkle the remaining oats on top.
7. Put the cookie sheet into a cold oven. Then turn the oven to 375 degrees. Bake bread for one hour.
8. Cool slightly and enjoy!

The First Kings of England

CHAPTER 15

Encyclopedia Cross-References

UBWH 100–101, UILE 214–215, 218
KIHW 222–223, 226–227, 234–235, KHE 122–123, 132–133

THE VIKINGS INVADE ENGLAND

REVIEW QUESTIONS

The Vikings invaded many parts of the world. Five are listed in the beginning of your story. Can you name at least three of them? *The Vikings invaded Iceland, Greenland, North America, France, and Britain.*

Britain is divided into four parts. Can you name them? *Britain is made up of England, Scotland, Ireland, and Wales.*

The Celts first lived in Britain. Who tried to conquer the Celts? *The Romans tried to conquer the Celts.*

Who came to Britain next? *The Angles and the Saxons came to Britain next.*

Where did the Vikings go to find new land to farm? *To Britain (or England).*

Why were the Celts and the Anglo-Saxons so frightened of the Vikings? *The Vikings weren't Christians, so they didn't leave priests, monks, churches, and monasteries alone; they also kidnapped women and children.*

Why didn't the British drive the Vikings out of their country? *Because they were divided into seven smaller kingdoms and didn't have a strong king to unite and lead them.*

What was the huge band of Viking invaders that landed in England called? *It was called "The Great Army."*

Who were its two leaders? *It was led by brothers, Halfdan and Ivar the Boneless.*

NARRATION EXERCISE

"The Vikings wanted new land to farm so they invaded Britain. The British were divided in small kingdoms, so they were too weak to defend themselves. The Great Army marched through England, fighting and looting, and the Vikings settled down and took English land for their own farms." OR

"When the Vikings invaded Britain, they treated the English badly. But the English were too weak to resist them. The English were divided and did not have a strong king to unite them. The Vikings were led by two brothers named Halfdan and Ivar the Boneless. These brothers wanted to conquer England right down to the sea."

ALFRED THE GREAT

REVIEW QUESTIONS

Where was the kingdom of Wessex? *Wessex was in the south of England.*

When the people of Wessex saw that the Vikings were planning to invade their land, what did they first do to avoid an attack? *They paid the Vikings lots of gold.*

Why did Guthorm threaten to invade Wessex? *He decided that he wanted the kingdom anyway.*

When paying off the Vikings didn't work, whom did the people of Wessex appoint as their leader? *They appointed Alfred (the Great).*

When Guthorm's army mounted a surprise attack at Christmastime, where did Alfred go? *He went to the countryside and hid, pretending not to be king.*

Why did the peasant's wife scold Alfred? *He wasn't paying attention and he burned her cakes.*

Why did Alfred decide to stay in hiding until spring? *He wanted his farmers to plant their crops before they started fighting.*

Meanwhile, what happened to Guthorm's army? *It was getting smaller—his warriors were bored and settled down on farms.*

Where did the great battle between the Vikings and Alfred's army take place? *The battle was fought at Salisbury Plain.*

When Alfred finally did launch his attack against the Vikings, who won? *Alfred the Great won!*

What happened to Alfred's body? *No one knows for sure.*

Narration Exercise

"The Vikings wanted to invade Wessex. At first, the people of Wessex paid them gold to stay away, but the Vikings invaded anyway. The people made Alfred their king. At first, he had to hide from the Viking army, but then he collected his own army together and defeated the Vikings at Salisbury Plain." OR

"The people of Wessex chose Alfred to be their king and help them defeat the Vikings. Alfred pretended not to be king and hid in the country until his army was strong enough to fight off the Vikings. He let his farmers plant their crops before the battle. Then he attacked the Vikings and drove them away."

THE BATTLE OF HASTINGS

Review Questions

What Viking king became king of England? *Sweyn Forkbeard became king of England.*

Once the Vikings began to rule England, did they still think of themselves as Vikings? *No, they started to think of themselves as "English."*

Edward the Confessor had no sons. What nobleman did his advisors appoint to be the next king? *They appointed Harold of Wessex.*

Why did William of Normandy think he should be king? *He was married to an English princess and he was related to the king.*

Why didn't the English advisors want William to be king? *Because he wasn't even English. He was French (Norman)!*

How did William trick Harold at the feast? *William told Harold to swear with his hands on a table that he would give the throne to William. The table turned out to be a box filled with the bones of saints! Now he had to keep his promise.*

When Edward the Confessor died, did Harold honor his promise to William? *No.*

What "bad omen" did the people of England see when Harold became king? *They saw Halley's Comet.*

What is the name of the famous battle where William's and Harold's armies fought one another? *It is called the Battle of Hastings.*

Who won the battle? *William and his army won the battle.*

What was the new name given to the man who conquered the English in the Battle of Hastings? *He became known as William the Conqueror.*

What name was carved on Harold's tomb? *He was called "Harold the Unfortunate."*

"The English wanted Harold to be king, but William of Normandy also wanted to be king. He tried to force Harold to give him the crown. Then he invaded England with an army. Harold and William fought the Battle of Hastings, and Harold lost. William became known as 'William the Conqueror.'" OR

"After Alfred died, the Vikings invaded again and took over the throne. Then the Normans invaded. Their leader was William the Conqueror. He attacked the English at the Battle of Hastings. The English lost, and the Normans became the new rulers of England."

Additional History Reading

Cathedral: The Story of Its Construction, by David Macaulay (Houghton Mifflin, 1981). This book follows the construction of a fictional cathedral, modeled after the cathedral at Chartres; the Normans brought the technique of cathedral construction from France to England. All construction details are accurately portrayed. (RA 1–2, IR 3–5)

Great Building: Stories of the Past, by Peter Kent (Oxford University Press, 2001). Easy to follow and engaging, this book covers the construction of nine great buildings, beginning with the Great Pyramid and ending with Hong Kong's airport. The section on the Beauvais Cathedral describes the change from low Roman-style churches to huge stone cathedrals under Norman influence. (RA 1–3, IR 4–5)

Corresponding Literature Suggestions

Adventures With the Vikings, by Linda Bailey (Kids Can Press, 2001). In this easy chapter book, three children enter a magical travel agency and find themselves back to the time of invading Norsemen. (RA 2, IR 3–5)

Sword Song, by Rosemary Sutcliff (Farrar Straus & Giroux, 1998). Written for slightly older readers (unfortunately, there is little fiction for younger readers on this topic), this historical novel tells about a Viking mercenary who finds himself banished to Scotland. Good for advanced readers or as a family read-aloud. (RA 1–4, IR 4–5)

We Just Moved! By Stephen Krensky (Scholastic, 1998). For beginning readers; this volume in the "Hello Reader!" series is an easy-reader story about a medieval boy who moves from one castle to another. (IR 1–2)

Who in the World Was the Unready King? The Story of Ethelred, by Connie Clark (Peace Hill Press, 2005). Connie Clark tells the story of Ethelred, the boy king who handed England over to the Vikings. (RA 1–2, IR 3–4)

MAP WORK

England and Normandy *(Student Page 59, answer 257)*

1. Alfred hid from the Vikings in the wild countryside of his kingdom, Wessex. Underline Wessex in green.
2. Alfred battled the Vikings on Salisbury Plain. Alfred won, so put a green box around Salisbury Plain.
3. Harold had been crossing the English Channel between England and Normandy when his ship encountered a storm. Color the English Channel blue.
4. William was from Normandy. Underline Normandy in yellow.
5. Harold and William fought at the Battle of Hastings. William won, so put a yellow box around Hastings.
6. Draw William's path from Normandy to Hastings in yellow.

Alfred the Great—this was drawn from a statue that stands in Oxfordshire. *(Student Page 60)*

The Bayeux Tapestry commemorates the Battle of Hastings. *(Student Page 61)*

_____ **PROJECTS** _____

CRAFT PROJECT **Make an Alfred the Great Statue**

Materials:
- ½ gallon milk carton
- Brown paper bag
- Glue
- Poster board
- Craft stick
- Alfred the Great coloring page *(Student Page 60)*

Directions:
1. Measure and draw a line around the milk carton 3 or 4 inches from the bottom.
2. Cut around the line so you have the bottom part of the milk carton. This is the base upon which the statue will stand.
3. Cut down the side of the bag so it is one flat sheet of paper. Now crumple it into a small ball, uncrumple it and crumple it again.
4. Place several drops of glue on each side of the statue base. Glue the crumpled paper onto the base working on one side at a time. Do not straighten the paper out so it will look more like a rock when finished.
5. Glue the coloring page on the poster board and cut out around the picture of Alfred.
6. Glue the craft stick on the back of the statue so one end sticks out about 2" past Alfred's feet.
7. Cut a slit in the top of the statue base and push the craft stick through so Alfred the Great will stand up. You may need to stuff the left over paper bag into the milk carton bottom to anchor the craft stick.

See the copy work project in this chapter to finish your statue.

COPY WORK PROJECT **Write the Inscription from Alfred the Great's Statue**

Materials:
- Paper
- Marker or pen

Directions:
1. Use your best handwriting to copy all or part of the inscription on the base of Alfred the Great's statue.
2. With your parent's help use the dictionary to find the meaning of any words you don't understand in the inscription.
3. In your own words tell about the good things that this inscription says Alfred the Great did.
4. Glue your inscription to the front of the statue you made.

Alfred found learning dead and he restored it
Education neglected and he revived it
The laws powerless and he gave them force
The church debased and he raised it
The land ravaged by a fearful enemy from which he delivered it
Alfred's name will live as long as mankind shall respect the past

William the Conqueror and Harold Game

Have Chapter 15 handy as you race to win the Harold and William Game! If you have more than two players, divide up into teams and answer the questions as a group. The questions will cover all the information in Chapter 15 of *The Story of the World, Volume 2*.

Materials:
- ☐ *The Story of the World, Volume 2*
- ☐ Game board *(Student Page 62)*
- ☐ Game pieces, beans, coins, buttons or small plastic toys to serve as player markers
- ☐ Game cards cut out and folded once *(Student Pages 63, 64, and 65)*
- ☐ Large bowl

Directions:
1. Before the game:
   a. Enlarge the game board to fit on an 11 × 14-inch sheet of paper.
   b. Color the board and the designs around it.
   c. Glue game board onto cardboard or posterboard to add strength. (optional)
   d. Cover with clear contact paper. (optional)
   e. Select game pieces, one for each player.
   f. Place folded game card questions into the bowl.

2. To play:
   a. Choose whose side you'll be on and put your game piece on the name at the top.
   b. The player on Harold's name gets to draw a game card from the bowl first.
   c. Answer the question and move once. If the answer is wrong, place the question back into the bowl and do not move forward.
   d. Questions that have been answered correctly do not go back into the bowl.
   e. The first one to the end who can answer the last drawn question correctly wins the game.

Memorize *Norman and Saxon* by Rudyard Kipling

Rudyard Kipling was an internationally famous poet and writer. When Kipling was very young he lived in India. Then he moved to England where he went to school. He worked as a reporter when he was only sixteen years old! Later he traveled around the world and lived in the United States and again in England. Mr. Kipling wrote many remarkable poems and stories like *The Jungle Book* and *Just So Stories*. He was offered several awards and honors for his stories and poems but he did not want to accept those honors. In 1907 he accepted the Nobel Prize for Literature. Here is a poem he wrote about the Normans and Saxons.

Materials:
- ☐ Copy of poem provided
- ☐ Tape recorder (optional)

Directions:
1. Read the poem several times a day until you can remember every word. Or read the poem into a tape recorder and play it over and over until you can say the poem.
2. Practice saying the poem in front of a mirror.
3. Recite the poem for your friends and family.

Norman and Saxon

The Saxon is not like us Normans. His manners are not so polite.
But he never means anything serious till he talks about justice and right.
When he stands like an ox in the furrow with his sullen set eyes on your own,
And grumbles, 'This isn't fair dealing,' my son, leave the Saxon alone.

By Rudyard Kipling

4. Answer these questions.

What is more important to the Saxon in the poem, manners or being treated fairly?

Why do you think the Norman says to leave the Saxon alone?

Answers for Parent:

1. being treated fairly

2. The Saxon takes fairness and justice very seriously; you don't want to upset him!

COOKING PROJECT   Alfred Cakes

Ingredients:

1 cup of all purpose flour
¼ cup sugar
½ tablespoon baking powder
¼ teaspoon salt
½ teaspoon nutmeg
3 tablespoons of butter, cut up in little pieces

¼ cup currants or raisins
¼ cup cut-up dates
1 large egg
⅛ cup heavy whipping cream
⅛ cup orange juice

Directions:

1. Set oven at 425 degrees.
2. Mix together all the dry ingredients in a large bowl: flour, sugar, salt, and nutmeg.
3. Using a pastry blender or knives, cut in the butter so it looks like small breadcrumbs.
4. Stir in the currants and dates.
5. In a smaller bowl, mix together the egg, cream, and juice.
6. Make a small well in the middle of the dry ingredients in the large bowl.
7. Pour in the egg mixture into the well of the dry ingredients and mix together until all is moist.
8. Flour your hands. Gather dough in a ball in the bowl and knead gently.
9. Divide dough into four parts and make a round "cake" with each.
10. Place on a baking sheet and bake for 8–10 minutes, or until lightly browned. Watch them carefully so you don't end up with burned cakes!

CRAFT PROJECT   A Day in Your Life Bayeux Tapestry

The coloring page of the Bayeux Tapestry shows how some very creative people told the story of a very influential battle that happened in early English life, The Battle of Hastings. Using the materials below, tell the story of a favorite day by just using pictures, paint, and a long strip of material! Try to draw your story so that another person can tell what happened by just looking at your pictures.

Materials:
- ☐ Several sheets of white paper, clear tape, and a pencil
- ☐ 1 yard of inexpensive white material (the original was stitched on fine linen, but muslin will work well for this project)
- ☐ Iron fusing tape (at fabric stores)

□ Acrylic paint in different colors
□ Craft paint brushes of different sizes
□ Newspaper
□ Long table as a working space

Directions:

1. Stick together several sheets of white paper lengthwise. This will be your planning sheet for your story picture. Draw out your tale and design boarders to decorate your story on the top and bottom of your page, like the Bayeux Tapestry.

2. Fold the material lengthwise and iron. Cut the material along the ironed line. Using the fusing tape, iron the two pieces end to end so that it will lay like a long table runner.

3. Place newspaper on a long table to work on.

4. Following your paper guide, paint your story onto the material. Once dry, hang it up on your wall, or place along a long table. Your story will tell the tale of your favorite day and remind you that many more favorite days are to come!

Option: Use a long sheet of white paper (or several pieces stuck together) and tell your story using paint, colored pencils or crayons instead of painting on the cloth.

England After the Conquest

CHAPTER 16

Encyclopedia Cross-References

UBWH 104–107, UILE 224–229
KIHW 252–253, KHE 140–141

THE ENGLISH LANGUAGE

REVIEW QUESTIONS

What is the name of the original language of the Angles and the Saxons? (Hint: It is known as the first form of English.) *The Angles and the Saxons spoke Old English.*

Do you remember any words that came from Old English? *Man, house, sheep, dog, wood, field, work, drink, laughter, the, this, here, and that are all from the Old English.*

What language did the Celts speak? *They spoke Celtic.*

When the Angles and the Saxons heard a useful word in another language, what did they often do? *They added it to their own language.*

Did they add Celtic words to their language? *They did not add very many Celtic words.*

Name some languages that the Angles and the Saxons took words from. *They borrowed from Latin, Greek, Scandinavian (the language of the Vikings), and French.*

Can you remember any of the Scandinavian words that came into English? *Leg, skin, skull, angry, cut, crawl, die, drown, hungry, weak, egg, steak, and dirt are all Scandinavian words.*

Who is Thursday named after? *Thursday is named after Thor, the thunder god.*

When did the French language come to England? *French came to England when the Normans invaded and settled down.*

Do you remember any French words that became English? *Peace, curtsy, beef, chair, curtain, garden, castle, judge, jury, honor, courage, and rich are all French words.*

NARRATION EXERCISE

"The Angles and the Saxons spoke a language called Old English. When they heard useful words in other languages, they would add those words to English. That is how today's English language came to be." OR

"English is a mixture of several different languages. The Angles and the Saxons added words from Latin and Greek when they learned about Christianity. They added Viking words when the Vikings invaded. And they added French words when the Normans invaded."

SERFS AND NOBLEMEN

REVIEW QUESTIONS

Before the Norman invasion, who owned the land in England? *Each family owned its own small piece of land to farm.*

Before the Norman invasion, how did the English form armies? *All of the farmers banded together to fight, and the king was the warleader.*

Who did William the Conqueror think owned the land in England? *He thought that the king owned the land.*

If the king of England gave land to knights, what did he expect in return? *He expected the knights to fight for him and to give him money to keep the army strong.*

When knights gave land to farmers, what did they expect in return? *They expected part of everything the farmers grew.*

What were these farmers called? *They were called peasants or serfs.*

Everyone in England served someone, and the person they served had a duty to give them back something in exchange. What was this way of life called? *This was called feudalism.*

What did the house of a serf look like? *It had a dirt floor, walls of mud and sticks, a thatched roof (a roof made of straw), a pile of leaves for a bed, and a fireplace.*

What did the knights eat for dinner in their grand castles? *Meat like eel and pigeon, pies, bread baked into shapes, salads of flower petals, fruit, and cheese.*

What would a knight have to do if a foreign army invaded England? *He would have to go and fight.*

NARRATION EXERCISE

"In England, the knights fought for the king and the king gave them land. The knights gave land to the serfs to farm and the serfs gave food to the knights. This was called feudalism. Serfs lived in small houses and ate vegetables, fruit, and only a little meat. Knights lived in castles and ate fancy meals." OR

"Feudalism is a system where people serve others in exchange for something. The English knights served the king in exchange for land. They would have to go and fight if there were a war. The serfs gave food to the knights in exchange for some of the knights' land. Serfs couldn't ever be forced to leave their land."

STONE CASTLES

REVIEW QUESTIONS

Originally the Norman knights built wooden houses. Why did they start building stone castles instead? *Because the peasants didn't like the Norman knights. The peasants tried to burn down the wooden houses. So they built stone castles, because stone does not burn.*

What was the portcullis used for? (Hint: The portcullis was on the front gate.) *The portcullis is a wooden gate on the front gate of the castle. If enemies are seen, the portcullis can be dropped to close off the entrance to the castle.*

The tall square tower in the center of the castle was called the keep. If enemies attacked, what was the keep used for? *Everyone could go inside the keep for protection. The keep had food and weapons inside.*

What were some of the smaller buildings inside the castle courtyard? *The kitchen tower, the prison tower, the outdoor laundry, and the garderobe (outhouse) were in the courtyard.*

What was soap made out of? *It was made out of animal fat and wood ash!*

NARRATION EXERCISE

"Knights and their families lived in stone castles. A castle had towers and a large wall around it so it could be defended. There was also a kitchen, a laundry room, and a smelly outdoor bathroom!" OR

"Anne and William decided to play hide-and-seek in the big stone castle. They went to the keep, the kitchen tower, the outdoor laundry, the garden, and even the outside toilet called the garderobe."

Additional History Reading

Clothes and Crafts in the Middle Ages, by Imogen Dawson (Gareth Stevens, 2000). This book begins with a map and a little basic history before discussing the materials available and how craftsmen used them to create useful, beautiful things. It ends with a section showing children how to make medieval kirtles, tunics, jewelry, a pilgrim's badge, and an illuminated manuscript. (RA 1–2, IR 3–5)

A Farm Through Time, by Eric Thomas (DK Publications, 2001). Through the use of detailed illustrations, the author shows the development of a farm from the Middle Ages to the present. Colored drawings with plenty to identify; text varies in difficulty, but much of it can be read by an advanced second-grade reader. (RA 1–2, IR 2–5)

Knights, by Philip Steele (Kingfisher, 1998). Bright and colorful pictures on oversized pages, with a fairly simple central text covering the life of a knight, heraldry, arms and armor, and a knight's world; more complex text serves as picture captions. *Note:* This book was republished in 2000 along with another Kingfisher volume as the paperback *The Medieval World.* (RA 1–3, IR 4–5)

Life in a Medieval Castle and Village Coloring Book, by John Green (Dover Pub, 1991). This book provides a brief overview of life in the Middle Ages. The line drawings and text give clear views of many elements of medieval society. They illustrate the skills needed for defense and hunting as well as those needed in the business of weaving, milling, blacksmithing, lumbering, and marketing. (RA 1–2, IR 3–5)

The Middle Ages, by Jane Shuter (Heinemann Library, 2000). Two-page sections introduce the various elements of life in the Middle Ages, covering religion, family life, food and castles. (RA 1–3, IR 4–5)

A Street Through Time, by Anne Millard (DK Publications, 1998). This book illustrates the development of a Stone Age camp into a twentieth-century city. The sections covering the Iron Age to the Black Plague are particularly applicable to this chapter. Detailed illustrations with plenty to identify; text varies in difficulty, but much of it can be read by an advanced second-grade reader. (RA 1–2, IR 2–5)

A Three-Dimensional Medieval Castle, by Willabel L. Tong, illus. Phil Wilson (Viking Children's Books, 1997). A detailed pop-up castle with drawbridge, secret passages, a tower, and much more. Buy, rather than find at the library, so that you can use the press-out figures and furniture. It has been available for several years at metmuseum (dot) org (forward slash) store. (RA 1, IR 2–5)

Till Year's Good End: A Calendar of Medieval Labors, by W. Nikola-Lisa, illus. Christopher Manson (Atheneum, 1998). With colored illustrations styled after medieval woodcuts, this book reviews the labors of a medieval peasant month by month. (RA 1–3, IR 4–5)

Corresponding Literature Suggestions

Castle Diary: The Journal of Tobias Burgess, Page, by Richard Platt (Candlewick Press, 1999). This tale of a young page who lives at his uncle's castle provides many details about everyday life in medieval times. (RA 1–2, IR 3–5)

Castles, by Gillian Osband, illus. Robert Andrew (Orchard Books, 1991). This beautifully illustrated book leads young readers through an adventure in a pop-up medieval castle. (RA 1, IR 2–5)

Knight's Castle, by Edward Eager (Odyssey, 1999). One of a series, this book, first published in 1956, follows the adventures of four children who are magicked back in time to the days of Ivanhoe, where they encounter lots of Saxon-Norman hostility. A chapter book, too long for reading aloud (but look for the book-on-tape version at your library). (RA 1–3, IR 4–5)

A Medieval Feast, by Aliki (Harper Trophy, 1986). This Reading Rainbow book describes the many preparations made by the manor inhabitants for a great feast in honor of the visiting King and Queen. (IR 1–4)

The Reluctant Dragon, by Kenneth Grahame, illustrated by Inga Moore (Candlewick, 2004). Written by the author of *Wind in the Willows,* this book tells of Saint George's predicament when he comes upon a dragon that would rather recite poetry than have a good fight. (RA 1–2, IR 3–5)

Saint George and the Dragon, by Margaret Hodges (Little, Brown and Company, 1990). This Caldecott Winner retells part of Spenser's *The Faerie Queene.* George, the Red Cross Knight, slays the dreadful dragon that has been terrorizing the countryside for years and brings peace and joy to the land. (RA 1–2, IR 3–5)

——————————————————— **MAP WORK** ———————————————————

England After the Conquest *(Student Page 66, answer 257)*

1. English is a mix of many languages. One of those languages is Old English, brought to England by the Angles and the Saxons. Draw a red line from this land to England.

2. English also borrowed from the Celtic language, which is still spoken today in Ireland, Scotland, and Wales. Draw a blue line from the "G" in England to Ireland, Scotland, and Wales.

3. English also took Greek and Latin words. Draw a green line from Greece and Italy to England.

4. Viking words were also taken. Draw a yellow line from Scandinavia to England.

5. When William the Conqueror of Normandy took the English throne, French was spoken by all the rich and important people of England. Draw a brown line from Normandy to England.

COLORING PAGE

The Normans began to build heavy stone castles instead of wooden houses. *(Student Page 67)*

——————————————————— **PROJECTS** ———————————————————

ACTIVITY PROJECT **Blending Languages**

When English-speakers heard a useful word in another language, they would take it and mix it in with all of their English words—and soon that word would *be* English. This simple exercise shows how many languages were "mixed up together" to make today's English.

Materials: ☐ Assorted colors of Play-Doh (red, blue, green, yellow, orange)
          ☐ Pencil

Directions: 1. English is a mix of many languages. One of those languages is Old English, brought to England by the Angles and the Saxons. Roll out a small piece of red Play-Doh and carve the words "Old English" into it with a pencil.

2. English only borrowed a small number of words from the Celtic languages. Roll out a small piece of blue Play-Doh and carve "Celtic" into it.

3. English also took Greek and Latin words. Roll out a piece of green Play-Doh and carve "Greek and Latin" into it.

4. Viking words were also taken. Roll out a piece of yellow Play-Doh and carve "Viking" into it.

5. French was spoken by the important people of England. Roll out a piece of orange Play-Doh and carve "French" into it.

6. Now mash all of the Play-Doh colors together until they are evenly mixed. Roll out this big lump of Play-Doh and write "English" on it. What color is this new English Play-Doh? Does it look anything like the colors of Play-Doh that went into it?

COOKING AND ACTIVITY PROJECT **Edible Mini Norman Castle**

The Normans introduced castles with a motte and bailey. The motte was a high mound that the castle stood on and the bailey was the large walled area in front of the motte. Normans also built square "keeps" (large, tall towers) in the center of the castle (like the Tower of London). Before William's Norman victory, the English built whole towns behind the protection of the castle walls. Now, only the castle was placed behind the protective walls. The town was built outside, with its own walls to protect it. Build this Norman Castle and include the parts shown in the diagram. Build the castle on wax paper, and use toothpicks to help stick the castle pieces together.

Ingredients: 3 tablespoons of melted butter
1 10 ounce package of marshmallows
6 cups of cereal (pick a kind that will look like stone, like Kix, or Cocoa Puffs, or for a colorful castle, choose Fruity Brontosaurus Blasts)
1 stick of soft butter

Directions: 1. Place a large pot on the stove and turn to low heat. Pour melted butter and marshmallows into the large pot and stir until melted. Take off heat and let it cool for a few minutes.

2. Add the cereal and mix until completely coated.

3. Using the stick of butter, butter your hands.

4. Divide the cereal mix into thirds. Mold ⅓ of the cereal into 4 square walls. Divide another third into 4 parts to make the cornered wall towers. Roll a glob of the cereal mix like a snake, adding to it to make the thickness desired. Stick the towers to the wall pieces and form your bailey.

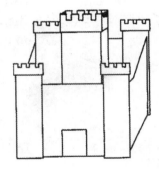

5. Build your tall keep with the last third of the mix. If possible add windows and an entrance. The windows on the lower side of a castle wall were very narrow so that no one could climb in. But the windows higher up were wider. There was usually one main gate, and sometimes there was a ditch of water around the whole castle wall and another gate tower on the other side of the ditch with a drawbridge that added protection to those in the castle. Make your castle exactly how you would envision it in the middle of a quaint village on a foggy British morning!

6. Once your castle is finished, take a picture of it. Then enjoy eating it with a tall glass of milk!

Make an Almoner or Coin Purse

Clothing made during the Middle Ages did not have pockets. People had to carry their money and other possessions in a small coin purse called an almoner. After the purse had been closed, it would be tied onto the person's belt for safekeeping. Thieves who would try to steal such purses on market days or at holy festivals were known as "cut purses." They would sneak up behind a person and use their sharp knives to quickly cut the "purse strings" and be off with the money. Even today, we use the term "purse strings" when referring to money.

Materials:
- 14" square of scrap material
- 12" round dinner plate
- 2 yards of ribbon or string
- Colored marker and scissors

Directions:
1. Place the fabric right side down onto the table. Turn the dinner plate upside down and center it on the fabric. Use the colored marker to draw around the plate to create the purse pattern. Cut out the circle with scissors.

2. With a sharp pair of scissors, snip small holes (about ½" apart) all the way around the circle. Next, weave the ribbon in and out of the holes to create the drawstring.

3. After the ribbon has been threaded through the holes, hold both ends of the ribbon and push the material towards the end to close the pouch. Use the drawstrings to tie the purse to your belt.

GAME ACTIVITY **Medieval Fox and Geese**

The game Fox and Geese is a battle fought out by two players of unequal power, and appears to have originated in Northern Europe.

Materials:
- Fox and Geese Game Board (*Student Page 68*)
- 13 pennies (The Geese)
- 1 dime (The Fox)

Directions:
1. Toss a coin to see which player gets to be the Fox (the loser of the coin toss will be the Geese). The Geese (the thirteen counters of one color) should be placed so as to fill up all the points on one side of the board, as shown below:

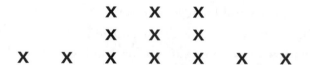

The Fox can be placed on any vacant point that is remaining.

2. The Fox moves first. Each player moves only one counter during his or her turn. Both the Fox and the Geese counters move along a line forwards, backwards, or sideways, to the next spot.

3. The Fox may move along a line or jump over a goose to an empty spot. This results in the capture of the Goose and its removal from the board. The Fox may capture two or more Geese in one turn, as long as he is able to jump to an empty point after each capture. The Fox wins the game if he captures the gaggle of Geese to a number (5 or less) that makes it impossible for them to trap him.

4. The Geese cannot jump over the Fox or capture the Fox. For the Geese to win, they must successfully trap the Fox into a corner and make it impossible for him to make a move.

Knights and Samurai

CHAPTER 17

Encyclopedia Cross-References

UBWH 102–103, 120–121, UILE 220, 223, 270–271
KIHW 224–225, 244–245, 254–255, 314–315, KHE 150–151, 156–157

THE ENGLISH CODE OF CHIVALRY

REVIEW QUESTIONS

At first, what did knights do when there were no wars to fight in? *They wandered around fighting, stealing, and killing.*

Under the code of chivalry, knights owed loyalty to the king and to whom else? *They owed loyalty to God and the church.*

Whom did knights swear to take care of? *They swore to take care of the weak (women, monks, priests, widows, and orphans).*

When did boys begin to learn to be knights? *They began their training at the age of seven.*

After a boy had served as a young page, what did he become? *He became a servant to one particular knight—a squire.*

What things did you have to learn before you could become a knight? *How to carry a shield and use a sword, how to ride a horse, how to put on heavy armor, how to speak politely and eat neatly, and how to behave.*

In the knighthood ceremony, what three colors did a knight wear and why? *He wore white to remind him of purity, red to remind him of the blood he would spill, and brown to remind him of the earth where he would be buried.*

What was wrong with chain mail? *It would not stop the blade of an axe or the point of a lance.*

What sort of armor did knights begin to wear instead? *They wore armor made of plates of steel.*

What might happen to a knight who had broken the rules of chivalry and been rude to a lady? *She could point him out, and he would have to leave the tournament.*

NARRATION EXERCISE

"You had to learn how to fight and how to behave before you could become a knight. Knights served the king and also God. They competed in tournaments to practice their skills." OR

"Knights swore loyalty to the king and to God. They protected the weak and defended the church under the code of chivalry. They had to fight well and behave properly."

THE SAMURAI: JAPANESE KNIGHTS

REVIEW QUESTIONS

Besides England, what other country had knights and lords? *Japan had knights and lords.*

What were the Japanese knights called? *They were called samurai.*

How many islands make up the country of Japan? *Four long thin islands and almost four thousand smaller ones!*

Did the emperor of Japan run his country? *No, he was almost never seen and he left ruling to his noblemen.*

Do you remember what the Japanese noblemen were called? *They were called daimyo.*

What was samurai armor made from? *It was made from iron plates, lacquered and tied together with silk and leather strips.*

Do you remember any of the code called "the way of the warrior"? *A samurai had to defend his daimyo (lord); he had to either win or die when fighting for his lord; he had to kill himself if he showed cowardice or fear.*

Besides fighting, what other things did samurai do? *Samurai wrote poetry, made gardens, and even danced.*

NARRATION EXERCISE

"Japan had knights called samurai and lords called daimyo. The daimyo gave land to the samurai, and the samurai had to defend the daimyo. The samurai were fierce warriors, but they also wrote poetry, made gardens, and danced." OR

"Samurai were knights on the island of Japan. Samurai were expected to win a fight or die. They served a lord called a daimyo who served the emperor of Japan. Samurai lived by a warrior code that told them not to show any fear or cowardice."

Additional History Reading

Design Your Own Coat of Arms, by Rosemary Chorzempa (Dover Publications, 1990). This book contains step-by-step instructions for creating your own family coat of arms. It contains sample coats of arms that belonged to some of the world's most famous figures. (RA 1–3, IR 4–5)

Eyewitness: Knights, by Christopher Gravett (Dorling Kindersley Book, 2000). This book (slightly more difficult than the following recommendations) uses detailed color photographs and informative text to trace the history of knighthood, starting from its early origins to its eventual decline. It also has details on the development and construction of armor, and life in a medieval castle. (RA 1–3, IR 4–5)

Harold the Herald: A Book About Heraldry, by Dana Fradon (Dutton Children's Books, 1990). Although this book is **out of print,** it is worth finding if you have a fourth–fifth-grade-level reader interested in heraldry; it covers the basics of heraldry through a story about Harold, a medieval herald. (RA 3, IR 4–5)

How Would You Survive in the Middle Ages?, by Fiona McDonald (Orchard Books, 1997). Poses questions to the reader: how would you cope with common problems and dilemmas of medieval life? (RA 1–3, IR 4–5)

Knights, by Philip Steele (Kingfisher, 1998). Bright and colorful pictures on oversized pages, with a fairly simple central text covering the life of a knight, heraldry, arms and armor, and a knight's world; more complex text serves as picture captions. This book was republished in 2000 along with another Kingfisher volume as the paperback *The Medieval World.* (RA 1–3, IR 4–5)

Knights, by Catherine Daly-Weir (Grosset & Dunlap, 1998). This book describes the life of a young knight-in-training. He has to learn fighting, horseback riding, and manners—and attend a medieval banquet—before he can become a knight. (RA 1, IR 2–4)

Knights Treasure Chest, by Marilyn Tolhurst (Running Press, 1995). This treasure chest includes a paper-model castle, a working catapult, heraldic stencils and many other things. Younger students will need help completing the projects. (RA 1–3, IR 4–5 and activities)

Lift the Lid on Knights, by Straun Reid (Running Press, 2001). This activity box provides the child an opportunity to explore the medieval world of chivalry, adventure and to build his very own knight. (RA 1–2, IR 3–5 and activities)

Step Into Ancient Japan, by Fiona MacDonald (Anness Publishing Ltd., 1999). This book describes the marvels of Japan, from shoguns and emperors to tea ceremonies and martial arts. The worship of Shinto gods and the Zen Buddhist code that the samurai followed are also discussed. Instructions are included for several projects that will help children better understand this culture. Some text is fairly difficult, while other paragraphs are simple; many color illustrations. **Out of print**, but worth looking for. (RA 1–3, IR 4–5)

Corresponding Literature Suggestions

Eyewitness Readers: Days of the Knights—A Tale of Castles and Battles, by Christopher Maynard (DK Publications, 1998). This third-grade reader combines a story with factual information about castles, battles and knighthood. (RA 1–2, IR 3–4)

In the Time of Knights: The Real-Life History of History's Greatest Knight, by Shelley Tanaka (Hyperion/Madison Press Book, 2000). A story based on the life of William Marshal, who became a knight at the age of thirteen and fought in England during a time of civil war. Contains photos of historical sites and artifacts, as well as original art. (RA 1–3, IR 4–5)

The Inch-High Samurai, by Ralph McCarthy (Kadansha International, 2000). Inchy Bo is a tiny person who refuses to let his small size keep him from performing mighty deeds. (RA 1, IR 2–4)

The Knight at Dawn: Magic Tree House Series #2, by Mary Pope Osborne (Random House, 1993). Eight-year-old Jack and his younger sister Annie are transported back in time to the Middle Ages, where they explore a castle and are helped by a mysterious knight. (RA 1–2, IR 3–5)

Knights of the Round Table: Bullseye Step into the Classic Series, by Gwen Gross, illustrated by Norman Green (Random House, 1991). In short chapters, the author tells the tales of King Arthur, Excalibur, and the Knights of the Round Table. (RA 1–2, IR 3–5)

The Making of a Knight, by Patrick O'Brien (Charlesbridge Publishing, 1998). Seven-year-old James becomes a page and, after years of faithful service, earns his knighthood. Beautiful oil illustrations. (RA 1–2, IR 3–5)

Saint George and the Dragon, retold by Margaret Hodges, illus. Trina Schart Hyman (Little, Brown, & Co, 1990). This Caldecott Medal winner, a retelling of an episode from Edmund Spenser's *The Faerie Queene,* illustrates the chivalric values held by English knights. (RA 2–3, IR 4–5)

Sam Samurai (The Time Warp Trio), by Jon Scieszka (Viking Children Books, 2001). The Time Warp Trio are working on a haiku writing assignment for school when they are accidentally sent back in time to medieval Japan. The boys go through many adventures before they can find their time travel book and return home. A chapter book for independent readers. (RA 1–2, IR 3–5)

Sir Cumference and the First Round Table: A Math Adventure, by Cindy Neuschwander (Charlesbridge, 1997). Sir Cumference works with the help of his wife, Princess Di of Ameter, and his son, Radius, to find the perfect shape for King Arthur's table. (RA 1–2, IR 3–5)

Sword of the Samurai: Adventure Stories from Japan, by Eric Kimmel (Harper Trophy, 2000). This read-aloud book contains a collection of 11 traditional stories that illustrate the code of the samurai. (RA 1–3, IR 4–5)

Three Samurai Cats, by Eric Kimmel (Holiday House 2003). A lighthearted fable set in samurai-era Japan. (RA 1, IR 2–4)

From England to Japan *(Student Page 69, answer 258)*

1. The country of Japan is about the size of the state of California, and it has varied climates. The northern island of Hokkaido is very cold. It is covered in snow for up to four months a year. Color that island blue.

2. The southern parts of Japan are warm with sunny beaches. Color the island of Kyushu red.

3. Most of Japan has a mild, temperate climate. Color the islands of Honshu and Shikoku green.

4. The Sea of Japan separates Japan from China and Korea. Draw blue waves in the Sea of Japan.

COLORING PAGES

A knight in armor *(Student Page 70)*

A samurai warrior *(Student Page 71)*

PROJECTS

CRAFT PROJECT ## Design Your Own Coat of Arms

Medieval knights did not go into battle wearing uniforms like soldiers do today. Instead they covered themselves from head to toe in chain mail and armor. It was very difficult to tell a friend from a foe during the heat of battle, so knights began wearing unique and colorful coats of arms. In the beginning, the designs of a knight's coats of arms were very simple. They usually consisted of large colorful shapes or bands that could easily be seen from far away. As time passed, the designs became more elaborate. People would pick things that told something about their families or their character (for example a lion design was used to show courage). Now it's time to design a coat of arms for yourself!

Materials:
- ☐ Shield Template *(Student Page 72)*
- ☐ White cardstock or piece of cardboard
- ☐ Ruler, pencil, glue stick
- ☐ Colored markers or paint in red, blue, black, green, purple, silver and gold

Directions:
1. On a scrap sheet of paper or a copy of the shield template, plan out your design and color combinations. You can use just colored bands and shapes, or you can personalize it with a design that shows some hobby, sport, or animal you are interested in.

2. Glue the blank shield template onto a piece of cardstock/cardboard and allowed it to dry completely.

3. Trace out your design on the template with a pencil and ruler. Once the design has been drawn, use colored markers or paints to fill in the different areas.

4. After your coat of arms has been filled in with paint, allow it to dry completely before using your scissors to cut it out. Some children might need help with this, due to the added thickness of the cardstock. Your coat of arms is now ready to be displayed.

ACTIVITY PROJECT ## King Arthur and His Knights Word Search Puzzle

King Arthur and his Knights of the Round Table are the most famous knights in history. Their adventures have been read through the ages, and are still exciting today. Take a few minutes to find King Arthur and the names of his twelve knights in the word search puzzle *(Student Page 73)*.

| CRAFT PROJECT | ## Make a Pair of Knight's Spurs

When a squire had been selected to join the ranks of the knighthood, he had to go through a ceremony first. During the ceremony, he would receive a sword, a helmet, a shield and a set of gold spurs. The young knight would then kneel in front of his sponsor. The sponsor would bestow upon him the honor of knighthood by tapping him lightly on his shoulders with a sword. Follow the directions below to make your own pair of gold spurs.

Materials:
- 8" × 20" piece of gold cardstock
- Copy of spur template and rowel (star-shaped piece) pattern *(Student Page 74)*
- 1 yard of ½" gold ribbon or string
  Optional: plain cardstock and gold metallic paint

Directions:
1. Using the spur template provided, trace and cut out two of each piece from the cardstock. If you are using regular cardstock, cut out the pieces and paint them with the gold metallic paint. Allow them to dry before assembling them.
2. Fold the spur in half, being sure to match the back extensions as best as you can.
3. Glue the rowel (star-shaped piece) between the two back extensions and allow the glue to dry completely.
4. Cut the yard of ribbon in half, one half for each spur. Thread the ribbon through the front holes of the spur. Place the spur around the child's shoe, making sure the ribbon goes under the foot. Bring the ribbon ends to the top of the foot and tie in place.

| CRAFT PROJECT | ## Make an Origami Samurai Helmet

Origami is the ancient art of paper folding and was brought to Japan by the Chinese over 1,500 years ago. Origami continues to be a popular craft in Japan and school children are taught how to do it at a very young age. The word *origami* literally means *to fold* (ori) *paper* (kami). Try your hand at this ancient art by following the simple instructions below.

Materials:
- 22" × 22" square piece of wrapping paper
  Optional: 10" × 12" piece of thin cardboard, scissors and stapler

Directions:
1. Place the paper face down on a flat surface. Fold the paper in half diagonally and crease well. You now have a large triangle.
2. Turn the paper so the folded edge is facing you. Take the right-hand corner and fold it over so the point touches the opposite edge, crease well along the new fold. Repeat the same procedure with the left-hand corner. You should now have a five-sided shape that looks like a house.
3. Fold the top layer of the "roof" point down as far as it will go and crease well. Flip the paper over and repeat the same procedure to the final "roof" point.
4. Separate the opening of the hat and place it on your head. For added decoration, you can cut out a horn embellishment from the cardboard and staple it to the front of your hat.

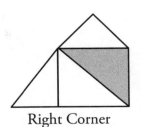

Right Corner

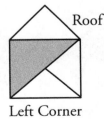

Roof

Left Corner

Design a Samurai's Family Crest (Ka-mon)

Just like the knights of Europe, the Samurai had a difficult time identifying people during battle. They solved this problem by displaying a family crest, or *ka-mon*, on their kimonos, armor and battle flags. Originally the crest was a simple, symmetrical design that depicted flowers, animals or geometric shapes. Over time, the crests became more elaborate and detailed, just like the knight's coat-of-arms did in Europe. Even today, many Japanese cities and businesses adopt crests for their logos and trademarks. Follow the directions below to cut your own *ka-mon* from thin sheets of colored paper.

Materials: □ 4" × 4" squares of wrapping paper, origami paper or bond paper
(Thinner paper is easier to cut)
□ Scissors, pencil, large sheet of drawing paper and glue
Optional: colored markers to decorate the plain bond paper

Directions: 1. To make a flower: fold your square in half diagonally three times. You now have a small triangle ready to be cut. Use the pencil to draw the petal shape of the flower on the part of the triangle that has the opened ends. If you would like the center open on your flower, cut off the tip at the top of the fold.

2. Experiment folding your paper in different ways and see what designs you can create. After you have finished making several designs, select a few of your favorites and mount them with glue onto your large sheet of drawing paper to display them.

3. If you used plain bond paper to make your designs, add additional color with the markers.

The Age of Crusades

CHAPTER 18

Encyclopedia Cross-References

UBWH 99, 110–111, UILE 240–241, 259
KIHW 242–243, KHE 148–149, 200

A COMMAND FROM THE POPE

REVIEW QUESTIONS

What empire grew even larger than the old Roman empire? *The Islamic empire grew larger than the Roman empire.*

Why was Jerusalem such an important city for the Muslims? *Muslims believed that Muhammad ascended to heaven from a rock inside the city.*

Why was Jerusalem holy for Christians? *Jesus was crucified there.*

Why was Jerusalem holy for Jews? *It was the city of David and the ruins of the Temple were there.*

What was a pilgrim? *A pilgrim made a trip to show his or her devotion to God, and sometimes to ask forgiveness for sins.*

When the Byzantine emperor sent a message asking the pope to help defend the city of Constantinople, how did the pope respond? *He sent armies to recapture Jerusalem.*

What did the pope promise the knights who went to recapture Jerusalem? *They would get rewards in heaven and even have their sins forgiven!*

What were the attempts to recapture Jerusalem called? *They were called crusades.*

What was a crusader? *A crusader was a knight who went on a crusade.*

What did crusaders learn in Arab countries? *They learned to take baths more often!*

NARRATION EXERCISE

"Jews, Christians, and Muslims all wanted to go to Jerusalem. But the Muslims began to keep Christians and Jews from visiting the city. The pope wanted to recapture the city of Jerusalem from the Islamic empire. So he sent knights to fight for the city." OR

"The Islamic empire spread to Jerusalem and then came close to Constantinople. The Byzantine emperor asked the pope for help to defend the city. Instead the pope sent knights on crusades to recapture the city of Jerusalem. The pope promised that any knight who went to fight in the Crusades would receive a reward in heaven."

RECAPTURING JERUSALEM

REVIEW QUESTIONS

What did Peter the Hermit tell people to do? *He told ordinary people to go on a crusade.*

Was this "People's Crusade" successful? *No, it was a disaster!*

How long did it take the knights of the First Crusade to get from Constantinople to Jerusalem? *It took them two years.*

Who were Saracens? *Saracens were the Muslim fighters who attacked the knights of the First Crusade.*

Getting inside the walls of Jerusalem was difficult. How did the knights of the First Crusade finally manage to do it? *They broke apart ships and used the wood to build siege towers. They climbed up the siege towers and over the wall surrounding Jerusalem.*

What did the crusaders do when they entered the city? *They killed thousands of Muslims and Jews.*

What did the crusaders do with the land around Jerusalem? *They divided the land into little kingdoms and ruled over it.*

Did crusaders and Muslims become friends? *Although they learned to live together, they were never really friends.*

NARRATION EXERCISE

"The knights of the First Crusade had a difficult time fighting the Muslims of Jerusalem. They could not find a way to get inside the city. So they built tall towers, climbed over the walls of Jerusalem, and recaptured the city. When they were inside, they killed many, many people who weren't even soldiers. Afterwards, the Muslims and the crusaders lived together, but they were never really at peace." OR

"The pope sent knights to get back the city of Jerusalem from the Muslims. It took the knights of the First Crusade two years to get to Jerusalem. Then they had to get over the thick walls of the city. After they recaptured the city, they divided the land into little kingdoms. Crusaders were the princes of these kingdoms."

SALADIN OF JERUSALEM

REVIEW QUESTIONS

Why did knights set out to fight a Second Crusade? *They heard that the Saracens had defeated one of the kingdoms near Jerusalem.*

Did the Second Crusade succeed? *No, it failed.*

What was the name of the Muslim commander who took back the city of Jerusalem? *His name was Saladin.*

What was Saladin known for? *He was known to be a model Muslim who was just and fair.*

When King Guy of Jerusalem heard that the Muslim armies were approaching, did he stay behind the walls of the city or did he rush out to fight the Muslim army? *He rushed out to fight the army.*

What happened to his army? *His army grew so hot and thirsty that Saladin's army defeated them easily.*

What did Saladin do when he entered Jerusalem? *He sold the Christians as slaves and let the weak and old go free. He let pilgrims enter Jerusalem again.*

Were any future crusades successful? *No.*

NARRATION EXERCISE

"Saladin was a Muslim soldier who wanted to take back Jerusalem from the Christians. He led an army against King Guy of Jerusalem and defeated him. Then he took over Jerusalem and sold the Christians as slaves. But he let weak people and old people go free, and he let pilgrims visit the city." OR

"The king of Jerusalem was foolish. He ran out to fight the Muslim armies instead of staying behind the city walls. The king lost, and the leader of the Muslim army, Saladin, became the new ruler of the city. Saladin was known to be a just and fair ruler. The crusaders didn't have any more successful crusades."

Review Questions

What was the "Reconquest of Spain"? *It was the time when Christian kingdoms pushed the Muslim rulers out of Spain.*

What was the Islamic kingdom of Spain called—where the Moors lived? *It was called Al-Andalus.*

How did Al-Mansur treat the Jews and Christians of Spain? *He made them pay higher taxes and kept them from meeting together.*

Where did the Christians go? *They went up north to the Christian kingdoms in Spain.*

Why did El Cid (Rodrigo Diaz de Vivar) let his beard grow so long? *The king of Castile banished him, and he swore to let his beard grow until he was pardoned.*

What does El Cid mean? *It means "the lord" or "the boss."*

Did El Cid fight for Christians or for Moors? *He fought for both sides!*

Why did Alfonso of Castile send for El Cid? *An army of Muslim warriors was coming to Spain from North Africa, and he was afraid that they would defeat the Christian kingdoms of Spain.*

How did El Cid defeat the larger Muslim army at Valencia? *He met them on a small field where only a few warriors could fight at one time.*

Narration Exercise

"Spain was mostly ruled by the Moors, but there were Christian kingdoms in the north. These kingdoms fought against the Moors. El Cid was the greatest Spanish warrior. He helped to defeat the Muslim armies from North Africa. After this, Spain became mostly Christian again. We call this the Reconquest of Spain." OR

"El Cid was a warrior of Spain. He was banished from Castile by the king, and he swore to let his beard grow until he was pardoned. The king of Castile needed help fighting against the Muslims, so he called El Cid to help him. El Cid fought them on a small field and defeated them. It was a great victory for the Christian kingdoms."

Additional History Reading

El Cid, by Geraldine McCaughrean (Oxford University Press, 1999). A picture-book biography of the great Spanish warrior, with simple, poetic, and entertaining but somewhat lengthy text; as a read-aloud, this book might take two or three days. **Out of print,** but worth looking for at your local library. (RA 1–3, IR 4–5)

Knights, by Philip Steele (Kingfisher, 1998). This book about life as a knight covers many different facets of medieval life, but contains a section specifically focused on the Crusades. (RA 1–2, IR 3–5)

Saladin: Noble Prince of Islam, by Diane Stanley (Harpercollins, 2002). Stanley's biography notes Saladin's compassionate and just acts, but doesn't turn him into a fairy-tale hero. The text will be read-aloud for second grade students, but the full-color paintings will hold the attention of even younger children. (RA 1–2, IR 3–5)

Corresponding Literature Suggestions

Canterbury Tales, by Barbara Cohen (Lothrop, Lee & Shepard, 1988). This book contains four of Chaucer's stories, retold in clear prose suitable for young readers and beautifully illustrated throughout. (RA 1–3, IR 4–5)

The Canterbury Tales: Oxford Illustrated Classics, by Geraldine McCaughrean (Oxford University Press, 1999). This is a complete retelling of Chaucer's 14th century masterpiece about pilgrims on their way to Canterbury and the tales they tell to keep themselves entertained on the long journey. (RA 1–3, IR 4–5)

Chanticleer and the Fox, by Chaucer (Harper Trophy, 1989). This Caldecott Award-winning picture book retells Chaucer's tale of a rooster and a fox, both undone due to flattery and vanity. (RA 1, IR 2–4)

Chess: From First Moves to Checkmate, by Daniel King (Kingfisher, 2004). Many instructive, computer-generated graphics will help parents teach younger children in this introduction to chess. Includes a section on the history of the game. (RA 3–4, IR 5–6)

Medieval Tales that Kids can Read and Tell, by Lorna MacDonald Czarnota (August House Publishers, 2000). Very brief tales along with historical background and tips for kids who want to tell them out loud; includes tales about Saladin. (RA 2, IR 3–5)

Saint Francis, by Brian Wildsmith (Oxford University Press, 1995). This lovely picture book about Francis of Assisi describes his journey to the Holy Land during the Crusades. (RA 2, IR 3–5)

―――――――――――――――――――― **MAP WORK** ――――――――――――――――――――

The World at the Time of the Crusades *(Student Page 75, answer 258)*

1. Circle the holy city of Jerusalem in green.

2. Circle the city of Constantinople in brown.

3. The pope called on knights from countries with Christian kings to go take back the city of Jerusalem from the Muslims. Using blue, draw a dotted line from Italy to Jerusalem, from France to Jerusalem, and from England to Jerusalem.

4. The Islamic empire was huge. Color the parts of the Islamic empire on the map in green. The Islamic empire was so large that the whole empire does not even fit on this map.

COLORING PAGE   A copy of a medieval painting of the Crusades *(Student Page 76)*

―――――――――――――――――――― **PROJECTS** ――――――――――――――――――――

CRAFT PROJECT **Make Your Own Pilgrim's Badges**

Once a pilgrim had visited a holy shrine, he would purchase a souvenir badge to show that he had actually been there. He would pin the badge onto his shirt or hat for all to see. These badges were usually made out of material or tin. Here are a few badges to shrines that a pilgrim might visit!

Materials: ▫ Copy of Pilgrim's Badges *(Student Page 77)*
             ▫ Light cardboard, glue, scissors, color pencils or markers, tape and safety pin

Directions: 1. Cut each of the Pilgrim's Badges out and paste them on a piece of cardboard. Allow the glue to dry completely, and use the scissors to trim away any excess cardboard you want removed.

              2. Use your color pencils or markers to decorate the badge. After the badge is completed, use a piece of masking tape to secure the safety pin onto the back of the badge. The Pilgrim Badges are now ready to be placed on your hat or crusader's surcoat.

CRAFT PROJECT	**Make El Cid's Beard**

Materials:
- 1 piece black sticky-back felt
- Skein of brown or black yarn
- Elastic string
- Scissors

Directions:

1. Cut the felt so it is the right size to give you a 3" long beard. (You may need a parent help you figure out what size to cut for your face.)

2. Cut the yarn into 1½ to 2 foot lengths.

3. Remove the paper from the felt to expose the sticky side. Attach one end of the two-foot lengths of yarn to the sticky felt to give you a long and flowing beard.

4. Add as many pieces of yarn necessary to give you a nice, bushy beard.

5. With scissors, snip tiny holes on each side of the beard.

6. Tie a piece of elastic string from one hole to the other, so that the beard can fit snugly over your head like a headband.

When you are finished making your beard, braid it just like El Cid used to do. Secure the end with a rubber band. You can also knot the braid like El Cid used to do before battles.

CRAFT PROJECT	**Make a Crusader's Surcoat**

A surcoat was a garment worn over a knight's armor. It was open down both sides and secured around the waist with a belt. Surcoats were decorated on the front with the knight's coat of arms; this helped identify him during a battle. When a knight left for the Crusades, he usually traded in his surcoat for a white one that had a large red cross on the front. The red cross served as a visual reminder to him and his enemy, the Saracens, of his Holy Mission.

Materials:
- Old white sheet or cotton fabric (see Step 1 for amounts)
- Red fabric paint
- Paint or sponge brush
- Pencil or chalk, scissors
- Heat and Bond Seam Tape

Directions:

1. Take the child's shoulder measurements and add 3". Next, measure the child from the top of his shoulders to the top of his knees.

2. Using the above measurements cut two pieces from the old sheet or from fabric. If you are worried about the sides raveling, turn under a ½" hem and use Heat and Bond to "sew" the hem.

3. With a piece of chalk or a sharpened pencil, sketch out the design of a large cross on the front of the surcoat. Fill in the design with red fabric paint and allow it to dry completely.

4. Cut two 3" strips of Heat and Bond Seam Tape and follow the package instructions for application. On the right side of the painted piece, place a strip of seam tape at the top of the shoulders. Line the seam tape up with the outside edge of the fabric and iron in place. Do this on both sides. Next, peel off the paper backing of the seam tape, place the other fabric piece on top, matching corners, and iron the two sections together. This creates the shoulder seams of your surcoat and it is now ready to be worn.

GAME ACTIVITY **Learn to Play Chess**

The game of chess is considered to be the oldest game of skill in the world and historians have traced its origin back to ancient China. Traders brought the game to India and from there it moved to the Middle East. Knights liked to play the game during peacetime and sieges. It allowed them to practice their strategic skills, which were so valuable during battle. Perhaps during periods of peace, the Crusaders played this game against their Muslim opponents! It was during this time that the game pieces were given the names that we know them by today: king, queen, bishop, knight, rook or castle, and pawn.

Chess is still a very popular game throughout the world and major tournaments are held each year to find the best players.

Materials: ☐ Chess board and pieces
☐ A "How To" Book (see Suggested Literature for recommendations)

CRAFT PROJECT **Conquest and Reconquest Flipbook**

Spain became the center of many battles. Each wave of conquerors—Visigoth, Moorish, and Christian—left its mark.

Materials: ☐ Spanish Conquest and Reconquest page *(Student Page 78)*
☐ Scissors or paper-cutter
☐ Stapler

Directions: 1. Number the squares, 1 through 16, beginning in the upper left corner and moving down the column. When you get to the bottom of a column, move to the top of the next one and continue numbering, moving down.

2. Cut out all of the squares along the black line. *Note:* a smooth, even cut will have the best results.

3. Place in order according to the number on the corner.

4. Make sure that the right side is lined up evenly.

5. Staple on the left side.

6. Hold your book and flip it from the first to the last to see the changes in authority in Spain.

A New Kind of King

CHAPTER 19

Encyclopedia Cross-References

UBWH 110, UILE 221, 241, 243
KIHW 262–263, KHE 148–150, 162–163

RICHARD THE LIONHEARTED

REVIEW QUESTIONS

What did Richard do as soon as he became king? *He raised an army and went to fight in the Crusades.*

Why did the king of France leave the Holy Land when Richard arrived? *Richard quarreled with him.*

Did Richard recapture Jerusalem? *No, he never even reached the city.*

Why did Richard start back to England? *He heard that John, his brother, was trying to steal his throne.*

Why did the Duke of Austria imprison Richard? *Because Richard had insulted him during the Crusades.*

According to legend, how did Blondel find Richard? *He hummed an English tune and he heard Richard hum the rest of it.*

Why did the Duke of Austria release Richard? *The English paid him a huge amount of money.*

How did Richard die? *He died in France, fighting over a French city that Richard claimed belonged to him.*

NARRATION EXERCISE

"When Richard became king of England he went off to fight in the Crusades. He quarreled with the King of France and the Duke of Austria. On his way home, he was put in prison by the Duke of Austria. His friend Blondel found him, and England paid a ransom to get him back. He died fighting in France." OR

"Richard the Lionhearted was not a very good king. He only wanted to go off and fight battles. While he was gone, his brother John tried to rule in his place. He was captured on his way home from the Crusades, and the people of England had to pay a lot of money so that he would be released. He died fighting in France."

JOHN LACKLAND AND THE MAGNA CARTA

REVIEW QUESTIONS

What nickname did the people of England give to John? *They called him John Lackland.*

Why did they call him Lackland? *His brother Richard "inherited" England; John was the younger brother and didn't inherit anything.*

Did John look like a king? *No; he was short, plump, and going bald.*

What did John do to prove that he was just as kingly as his brother? *He fought many battles in France.*

What did King John do that angered the noblemen? *He made them pay him lots of money (and he had his nephew murdered).*

What is a civil war? *A civil war is when soldiers fight in their own country, against their own people.*

The noblemen made John sign a paper stating that the king now had to obey the law too. What was that "charter" called? *It was called the Magna Carta.*

How did the Magna Carta change the way that the king behaved? *Now he had to follow the law like everyone else.*

Do you live in a country where the leaders have to follow the law? *Yes. Your representatives have to give the leaders permission to start a war or raise taxes.*

Narration Exercise

"King John fought many battles and raised money by forcing noblemen to pay him. The noblemen got together and marched into London with an army. They forced King John to sign the Magna Carta. Now the king had to obey the law too, instead of doing whatever he wanted." OR

"King John wanted to prove he was as kingly as his brother Richard. So he fought in France. He needed money, so he took it from his noblemen. They forced him to sign a paper saying that he would obey the law, rather than starting wars and raising taxes whenever he wanted to. Now, in many countries, leaders have to get the permission of the people to start wars and raise taxes."

ROBIN HOOD

Review Questions

Why were the peasants unhappy under John's reign? *John took money from the noblemen, so the noblemen took money from the peasants and serfs.*

How did Robin Hood help the poor serfs of England? *He stole money from the noblemen and gave it to the poor.*

What disguise did Robin Hood wear to gain entrance into the Sheriff's home? *He dressed up as a butcher.*

What did Robin say to get the Sheriff to travel with him into the woods with lots of money? *He told the Sheriff he would sell him more meat.*

What were Robin Hood's "herds"? *Robin's herds were the deer in Sherwood Forest.*

What happened to the Sheriff at the end of the story? *Robin Hood's men left him at the edge of the forest.*

Narration Exercise

"Robin Hood stole money from the rich and gave it to the poor. One day he dressed himself up as butcher and convinced the Sheriff to come into the forest to buy meat. But then he took the Sheriff's money to give to the poor. He told the Sheriff that Richard, not John, was the true king of England." OR

"Robin Hood stole money from the noblemen and gave it to peasants. He was loyal to Richard, not to John. Once he tricked the Sheriff of Nottingham into bringing a bag of gold into the woods. Then Robin robbed him and gave the money away to the poor."

Additional History Reading

The Adventures of Robin Hood, by Roger Lancelyn Green (Everyman's Library, 1994). This classic retelling of the Robin Hood cycle of tales will make a good read-aloud; older students can read independently. (RA 1–3, IR 4–5)

Heroines: Great Women Through the Ages, by Rebecca Hazell. (Abbeville, 1996). Brief (4–6 pages) biographies of great women in history, each including a page-long description of the heroine's time and country. Includes Eleanor of Aquitaine, mother of Richard and John, along with information on feudal England. (RA 2, IR 3–5)

Lives of Extraordinary Women: Rulers, Rebels, and What the Neighbors Thought, by Kathleen Krull, illus. Kathryn Hewitt (Harcourt Brace, 2000). Very brief (3–4 pages) and interesting biographies, including that of Eleanor of Aquitaine, who went on the Second Crusade. (RA 2–3, IR 4–5)

Magna Carta, by Walter Hodges (Coward-McCann, 1970). Children's books on the Magna Carta are hard to find; this one is a little too detailed for second grade but would be excellent for third and fourth graders. Unfortunately **out of print;** check your library. (IR 3–5)

Ten Queens: Portraits of Women of Power, by Milton Meltzer, illus. Bethanne Andersen (Dutton Children's Books, 1998). Ten interesting biographies for reading aloud; each is 8–14 pages, with color illustrations. Includes Eleanor of Aquitaine, a fascinating French princess who married into the English royal line and became the mother of John and Richard. (Mentions King Henry's mistresses and affairs.) (RA 2–4, IR 5)

Corresponding Literature Suggestions

Adventures in the Middle Ages, by Linda Bailey, illus. Bill Slavin (Kids Can Press, 2000). Josh, Emma and Libby travel back in time to the days of knights and castles in this entertaining book which is part comic strip, part story, and part fact-book. (RA 1–2, IR 3–5)

Castle Diary: The Journal of Tobias Burgess, Page, by Richard Platt, illus. Chris Riddell (Candlewick Press, 1999). A thirteenth-century page boy keeps his diary over the course of a year; lengthy, but very entertaining. (RA 1–3, IR 4–5)

Eyewitness Classics: Robin Hood, by Neil Philip, illus. Nick Harris (Dorling Kindersley, 1997). This retelling is on a fairly difficult level, but includes beautiful illustrations and numerous informative sidebars on different aspects of life during the time of Robin Hood. (RA 2–3, IR 4–5)

——————————————————— MAP WORK ———————————————————

Richard and the Crusades *(Student Page 79, answer 258)*

1. Richard I was king of England. Color England in orange.
2. Richard I went to Jerusalem on a crusade. Use a green crayon to trace the dotted line from England to Jerusalem.
3. When Richard heard that his brother John was trying to take over his kingdom, he decided to go home. He took a shortcut through Austria. Circle Austria with purple.
4. Then the duke of Austria captured Richard and put him in prison! Draw a red dotted line from Jerusalem to Austria.
5. The duke agreed to free Richard I for a huge sum of money. The sum was paid. Draw another red dotted line from Austria to England to show Richard's trek home.

COLORING PAGE   The people of England told stories about Robin Hood, a mysterious man who lived in the royal forests with a band of outlaws. *(Student Page 80)*

CRAFT PROJECT | **Simple Robin Hood Quiver and Arrows**

Robin Hood was an expert archer—he could hit anything with his bow and arrows! When he and his men were hungry, they would hunt with their bows, shooting deer, rabbits, and other animals for food. The arrows were kept in cases, called quivers, worn across their backs. Make your own quiver full of arrows.

Materials:
- ☐ 1 paper towel tube
- ☐ Brown paper (either construction paper, craft paper, or the inside of paper grocery bags)
- ☐ Tape
- ☐ White glue
- ☐ Pencil
- ☐ Cord, rope, or braided yarn (2½ to 4 feet)
- ☐ String
- ☐ Tape
- ☐ 6 drinking straws (preferably the non-bending kind)

Directions for Quiver:

1. Cut out the brown paper so that it fits around the length of the paper towel tube. Secure it with tape.
2. Cut out a circle of brown paper a little larger than the end of the paper towel tube. Punch a hole through the center of the circle with a pencil.
3. Setting the paper towel tube in the middle of the brown circle, trace with a pencil the circumference of the tube onto the paper. Set the tube aside.
4. Squeeze glue on the pencil line.
5. Set the tube on the glue. Let dry.
6. Thread the cord through the hole in the paper circle and up through the tube. Cut and tie the cord so that you can sling the quiver over your shoulder.

To make a decorative fringe:

7. Cut a strip of brown paper the length of the tube and 3" wide.
8. Make short snips (about 2") up the length of the paper to create a fringe.
9. Glue the fringe to the tube.

Directions for Arrows:

1. Snip the end of one straw at an angle.
2. Push the end of the cut straw into the end of an uncut straw to make one long straw.
3. Repeat steps 1–2 two more times to create three long straws.
4. Draw 3 arrowheads on the brown paper. Tape one arrowhead to one end of each long straw. If you want, tie a piece of string at the base of the arrowhead.
5. Put the arrows in your quiver.
6. Now if you are hungry and want a snack from the kitchen, make sure you bring your quiver full of arrows!

SEWING PROJECT ## Make a "Merry Men's" Cape and Hat

(Requires Pattern from Fabric Store)

To blend well with the trees in Sherwood Forest, Robin Hood and his band of Merry Men made their clothes from a local fabric called Lincoln Greene. The fabric was dyed blue first, and then it was dyed yellow to make the color. In his book *The Faerie Queene*, Edmund Spenser (1552–99) wrote this description of Robin Hood: "All in woodman's jacket he was clad of Lincolne Greene, belay'd with silver lace." Use Spenser's description to make your own version of a Merry Man's Lincoln Greene cape and hat.

Materials:
- ☐ Cape – McCall's Pattern 2853, View G Cape
- ☐ Hat – McCall's Pattern 2853, View G Hat
- ☐ Medium Green felt or fabric (see pattern back for fabric requirements)
- ☐ Metallic Rickrack (Silver)
- ☐ Long feather
- Optional: Heat and Bond Seam Tape

Directions:
1. Cape: Follow the pattern directions to complete the cape using the green felt or fabric. If you do not have a sewing machine, these items can be put together using Heat and Bond Seam Tape and an iron. Finish off the cape by sewing silver rickrack around the edges.

2. Hat: Follow the pattern directions to complete the hat. Then embellish it with the feather.

3. Dress in a long shirt first, and fasten a belt around your waist. Add a sword or bow and arrows, and complete your "Merry Man" outfit with the cape and hat.

CRAFT PROJECT ## Make King Richard's Shield

King Richard's coat of arms was well known throughout Medieval Europe. The design was composed of three golden lions standing against a blood-red background. Historically, the lion has symbolized strength, courage and power. King Richard I had all of these qualities and more, so it comes as no surprise that he was called Coeur de Lion, or Richard the Lionhearted. Use the directions below to create your own replica of this great king's shield.

Materials:
- ☐ Cardboard or poster board
- ☐ Red paint and gold crayon or pencil
- ☐ Scissors, glue, paint brush
- ☐ Lion design (*Student Page 81*)

Directions:
1. Decide on the shape of your shield and cut it out from the cardboard. Popular shapes at this time were circles, ovals, rectangles and curved triangles. After the shield has been cut out, paint the entire surface with red paint and allow it to dry completely.

2. Make three copies of the lion design below. Color each of them with a gold crayon or pencil, then cut out and glue onto your red shield background. If you would like to, change the size of each copy of the lion and glue them on the shield from large to small.

3. To add handles on the back of your shield, cut two pieces of cardboard that are each 2" × 12" long. At the ends of each piece, fold back a 3" tab. This creates the tabs that will be glued onto the back of the shield. When gluing the tabs down, be sure to allow enough room for the child's hand and forearm to slide through easily.

Make a Magna Carta for Your Bedroom

The noblemen of England forced King John to sign the Magna Carta. This meant that even though John was king of England, he had to follow the laws of the land just like everyone else. The Magna Carta spelled out the laws that every Englishman (including King John) had to obey. Make a Magna Carta for your land: your bedroom! Follow the directions for making "aged" paper if you want your Magna Carta to have an authentic look.

Materials:
- ☐ Scrap Paper
- ☐ Paper (see directions for "aged" paper below)
- ☐ Pen or marker

Directions:
1. Write several silly "laws" for your bedroom that everyone who enters has to obey. (For example, anyone who enters must sing, "I'm a Little Teapot;" impose a "Raisin Tax"—to enter the bedroom you must be given a raisin.) Have a parent approve your laws to make sure they are reasonable.
2. Copy your laws onto the dried antiqued paper. Title it: "My Magna Carta." Have everyone in the house sign your Magna Carta and follow your bedroom laws for a day.

Materials for "aged" paper:
- ☐ White or cream paper (construction paper works best)
- ☐ 9" × 13" baking pan
- ☐ 3 black tea bags
- ☐ 3 cups very hot water
- ☐ Spoon
- ☐ 2 spatulas
- ☐ Dish towel

Directions for "aged" paper:
1. Steep 3 tea bags in 3 cups of very hot water. Steep for 5 minutes.
2. Pour the tea into the 9" × 13" pan.
3. Submerge paper in the tea. *Caution:* Don't touch the hot water—use a spoon to sink the paper.
4. Let the paper sit in the water for 1 to 3 minutes, or until the paper turns the desired color.
5. Carefully remove the paper (using the two spatulas) from the tea. Set it to dry on the dish towel.

The Diaspora

CHAPTER **20**

Encyclopedia Cross-References

UBWH 90, UILE 233
KIHW 178–179, KHE 108–109

THE SCATTERING OF THE JEWS

REVIEW QUESTIONS

How did the Roman Empire treat the Jews? *Some of the governors made the Jewish people pay taxes, arrested and executed Jews, and wouldn't let them worship God.*

Because the Roman Empire was taxing them and treating them unfairly, what did the Jews of Jerusalem decide to do? *They decided to revolt and take the city for their own.*

Who were the Zealots? *They were Jewish freedom fighters.*

What did the Romans do when they broke into Jerusalem? *They burned the Temple.*

After the Romans squashed the revolt, what did they force the Jews to do to make sure a revolt would never happen again? *They forced the Jews to leave Jerusalem.*

Why was it particularly upsetting for the Jews to leave the city of Jerusalem? *They thought that worshipping in the Temple of Jerusalem made them Jewish.*

How did the Jewish scholar Yohanan escape the city of Jerusalem? *He got in a coffin and pretended to be dead. His followers carried him outside the city walls, saying they were going to bury him.*

How did Yohanan think the Jews could remain Jews without worshipping in the Temple? *He thought that if the Jews studied the sacred writings of the Torah and continued to worship God in synagogues (or "little temples"), they would still be Jews.*

What were "rabbis"? *Rabbis were teachers who could read and explain the Torah.*

Why did other countries often view the Jews with suspicion? *The Jews were loyal to God rather than to any one country.*

What is the Diaspora? *The Diaspora is the scattering of Jews through many different countries.*

NARRATION EXERCISE

"The Jews revolted against the Romans in Jerusalem. The Romans fought back and forced the Jews to leave the city. The Jews went to many different countries, but they always remained Jews. The countries they lived in were suspicious of them, because they thought the worship of God was more important than loyalty to a country." OR

"The Romans burned the Temple and forced the Jews to leave Jerusalem. The Jews were worried they would not be Jews if they could not worship in the Temple. But they studied the sacred writings and continued to worship God. Rabbis read the Torah in synagogues all over the world, so that the Jewish people could remain Jews."

REVIEW QUESTIONS

What did the Emir of Cordova decree? *He said that the Jews must leave Cordova and not return.*

Why did the clever rabbi go to see the Emir? *The Emir was going to ask him three questions. If the rabbi a[nswered] them correctly, the Jews could stay in the city.*

How did the rabbi answer the question about how many stars are in the sky? *He told the Emir to go and co[unt] them if he didn't believe the answer.*

What was the distance between the truth and a lie? *It was the same as the distance between eyes and ears.*

In the third test, what did the rabbi do with the paper he drew from the bowl? *He ate it.*

Why did he eat the paper? *He was sure they both said "Go."*

NARRATION EXERCISE

"The Jews tell a story of a ruler who wanted the Jews to leave his city so he asked a rabbi three impossible questions. The rabbi outwitted the ruler and answered the questions correctly, so the Jews were allowed to stay in the city." OR

"The clever rabbi knew how many stars were in the sky and the distance between the truth and a lie. He also drew the right paper out of the bowl when the Emir told him that one paper said 'Go' and the other said 'Stay.' He outsmarted the Emir, so the Jews were able to stay in Cordova."

Additional History Reading

Dance, Sing, Remember: A Celebration of Jewish Holidays, by Leslie Kimmelman, illus. Ora Eitan (HarperCollins, 2000). Simple descriptions of the historical and Scriptural traditions behind twelve holidays. (RA 2, IR 3–5)

Israel, by Adele Richardson (Creative Education, 2001). A simple, heavily illustrated history of Israel from Biblical times until the present. (RA 2, IR 3–5)

Jewish Holiday Treats, by Joan Zoloth (Chronicle Books, 2000). Stuffed with recipes, craft ideas and patterns, explanations and ideas for celebrating the whole year! Ideas are applicable to many different celebrations while the recipes are creative and unique. Don't miss the Amazing Honey Cake! (RA 1–3, IR 4–5)

The Jewish Kids Catalog, by Chaya M. Burstein (Jewish Publication Society of America, 1984). Full of historical facts, timelines, crafts, definitions and ideas. (RA 1–3, IR 4–5)

Corresponding Literature Selections

The Rabbi Who Flew, by Renate Dollinger (Booksmythe, 2001). A folktale about the rabbi of a small village; he is so holy that when he prays he rises into the air, but then everyone can see the holes in his shoes! (RA 2, IR 3–4)

Raisel's Riddle, by Erica Silverman, illus. Susan Gaber (Farrar, Straus & Giroux, 1999). In this picture-book version of the Cinderella tale, the heroine is a Diaspora Jew, brought up by her rabbi grandfather in eastern Europe. (RA 1–2, IR 3–5)

The Scattering of the Jews (Student Page 82, answer 258)

1. The Jews in Jerusalem revolted against the Romans. Underline the city of Jerusalem twice in orange.

2. The Romans forced the Jews to leave Jerusalem. The Jews went to Egypt, North Africa, Spain, Italy, France, Austria, Poland, England, and Russia. Circle each of these places in purple.

3. Draw a purple arrow from Jerusalem to Egypt. Then draw another purple arrow from Jerusalem to North Africa. Repeat this process for all the places that you circled in purple. This scattering of the Jews is called the Diaspora.

COLORING PAGE   Herod's Temple, which stood in the city of Jerusalem, was destroyed by the Romans in 70 A.D. (Student Page 83)

PROJECTS

ACTIVITY PROJECT Communicating the Responsa Way

Once the Jewish people were scattered around Europe, North Africa, Russia and in the Middle East, how were they going to communicate their ideas and questions about God with each other? The great leaders in the Middle Ages communicated through letters of guidance on the Torah, the Jewish scriptures, called "responsa." These leaders set up Yeshiva, or Jewish religious schools, so that the people would learn about the truth in the Torah. There were many questions for these leaders to talk about, and so they sent letters of guidance on the Jewish law to communities all over the world.

Try your own responsa. Find as many as you can who will join you for an hour or more (see how long you can go) in only using written messages to communicate. You can draw a picture of your question or you can write it out on a slip of paper. Remember, no talking! See how many of your questions you can get answered this way. What does it feel like? What are some good things about communicating this way? What are some difficulties?

COOKING PROJECT Charoset, Part of Remembering

Even though the Jews were scattered all over the world, they kept special traditions that helped them to remember their history and the promises God had given them. One tradition is to remember the Passover. The Book of Exodus tells us that, when the Jewish people were freed from slavery in Egypt, the Angel of the Lord passed over everyone who put a special mark on their doorpost, showing that they belonged to God. The Jews call this the Passover. There are special things they eat on the night they celebrate and remember the Passover.

The Passover reminded them of God's promises to them. Each part of the Passover meal meant something special.

The matzo is unleavened bread, eaten three times in the meal. A **lamb bone** represents the sacrifice of a lamb. An egg reminds the Jews to stay determined, even in adversity, just as an egg gets harder in heat. **Greenery** (like parsley or lettuce) reminds them of new life. **Salt water** reminds them of the tears of the slaves under the hard toil in Egypt. Four cups of **red wine** or grape juice represent the four promises of freedom which God gave to them. **Charoset** represents the mortar the slaves used between the bricks. At the Passover meal there is also an extra cup of wine on the table. A door is left open. Both are for the prophet Elijah who will reappear to proclaim the coming of the Messiah, the Jewish savior. They conclude the Passover meal with the words "*Next year in Jerusalem*," because they miss their homeland.

Though the Jews kept their traditions, they had different recipes according to what was available in their new country. Here are three recipes for Charoset. Use one, or try all three on Matzo bread that you can find in large grocery stores.

Special thanks to Julie Gray who sent these recipes.

Ashkenazi Jewish Charoset

Ashkenazi is the name given to the Jews that settled along the Rhine River in northern France and western Germany. They then moved to Poland.

Ingredients: 1 apple, peeled, cored, and chopped
½ cup crushed walnuts
1 teaspoon cinnamon
2 teaspoons sugar or honey
2 tablespoons sweet wine or grape juice

Directions: Combine all ingredients in a bowl and chill.

Sephardic Jewish Charoset

Sephardic Jews found great freedom under the liberal Christian and Muslim empires of Spain and Portugal. In the 1400s, however, they were expelled, and many made their homes in the Netherlands.

Ingredients: ½ cup dates, pitted and chopped
½ cup dried apricots, chopped
½ cup chopped walnuts
1 tablespoon apple juice

Directions: Combine all ingredients in a bowl and chill.

Italian Jewish Charoset

Italian Jews had lived in Italy since the days of the Romans but in the 1200s were strongly urged to convert to Christianity. In the 1500s they were required to live in only Jewish communities, separate from the rest of the people. These communities were called ghettos.

Directions: Make the Ashkenazi Charoset, but add one chopped hard-boiled egg.

CRAFT PROJECT   Make a Tzedakah Box

Tzedakah, or giving generously to help others in need, is a very important part of the practice of Judaism. In the Middle Ages, the great Jewish scholar Maimonides wrote, "Even a poor person who lives entirely on tzedakah must also give tzedakah to another." Tzedakah is viewed as an act of religious duty, a righteous act, giving the poor their due. It is required of every Jew and some sages have said it is the highest commandment of all.

Making your own Tzedakah box:

Special thanks to Joan Q. Horowitz of Massachusetts for the inspiration for this craft.

Materials:
- [ ] Clean baby-food, jelly or peanut butter jar and lid
- [ ] Nail and hammer
- [ ] Symbols *(Student Page 84)*
- [ ] Colored pencils
- [ ] Glue
- [ ] Fabric such as felt or flannel (optional)
- [ ] Ribbon, rick-rack or glitter (optional)
- [ ] Coins

Directions:
1. Color the Jewish symbols and cut them out. Glue them onto the sides of the jar.
2. Using the nail and hammer, hammer a hole into the jar lid in a line, forming an opening the size of a quarter. Do this on a cement floor, like one in a garage. Make sure any sharp edges are facing the inside of the lid. You may want to cover the inside with fabric with a circle cut out using the top lid pattern as a cut-out guide.
3. With your glue, cover the top of the lid, flat side, with a paper circle piece that you can make by using the lid as a guide. Color a reminder to give to those who don't have as much as you.
4. Use ribbon, rick-rack or glitter along the sides of the jar lid if you want.
5. Place coins in your jar. When full, give away the coins to someone in need. Start saving again!

CRAFT PROJECT   **Make a Mezuzah**

Special thanks to Rick Bialac of Georgia for the inspiration for this craft.

A mezuzah is a small container-like case that the Jewish people place on the doorposts of their houses to remind them that the presence of God is there with them always. It is made out of wood, plastic or metal. Inside the container is a piece of parchment which has written on it the "Shema," which means "hear." Shema is the command found in Deuteronomy 6:4 which says, *"Hear O Israel! The Lord our God, the Lord is one!"* On the outside of the mezuzah is the *shin*, the letter which makes a "sh" sound in Hebrew, and which stands for the Shema. The box is usually nailed on at an angle because, as the story goes, the rabbis of old couldn't decide whether to place it across or up and down. A compromise has it at a tilt.

Materials:
- [ ] Two empty matchboxes
- [ ] Foil
- [ ] Masking tape
- [ ] Craft jewels, pearls or sequins (optional)
- [ ] ½ cup of instant coffee in a shallow bowl (optional)
- [ ] Flathead tacks
- [ ] Hebrew *shin* and "Shema" message *(Student Page 85)*

Directions: 1. Take the drawers out of both matchboxes. Bend back one end-side in both boxes so that they form an opening. Cut off the hanging ends. Connect the two open ends of the drawers together with tape, forming one long drawer.

2. Place the two outside boxes together on their ends, so they are lying flat. Tape them together on both sides. Wrap the two boxes with a thin layer of foil. Cut the foil off at their ends so that the drawer can fit back in (check to make sure). Decorate the box front with the Hebrew *shin* ("sh") from the Student Page. Add any craft jewels, pearls or sequins that you want onto the top of the covered box.

3. Cut out the "Shema" on the Student Page. For added effect, crinkle up the paper and dip it in instant coffee for 5 minutes to create the parchment look. Dry with a hand dryer or let dry naturally. Then, roll up and tuck into the drawer.

4. Tack or tape the outside box of your mezuzah onto a doorway. Pick one that you go through often. Remember to place it at an angle. Once it is secure, slip the drawer carefully into the box.

CRAFT PROJECT | **Clever Rabbi of Cordova Finger-Puppets**

Materials:
- ☐ One rubber glove
- ☐ Glue
- ☐ Scissors
- ☐ Colored pencils
- ☐ Your fingers
- ☐ Character puppets *(Student Page 86)*

Directions: 1. Color the faces of the characters from the Clever Rabbi of Cordova story as told in chapter 20 of *The Story of the World, Volume 2.* Cut them out.

2. With your scissors, cut off the fingers of the rubber gloves. Glue the faces on the pad of the fingers. You may need to stick your finger inside for added help. Hold the glued face between your thumb and finger for a short time to aid in securing the faces on.

3. Act out the story with your puppets. Or make up your own!

The Mongols Devastate the East

CHAPTER 21

Encyclopedia Cross-References

UBWH 114–115, UILE 250
KIHW 270–273, KHE 170–171

GENGHIS KHAN, EMPEROR OF ALL MEN

REVIEW QUESTIONS

What invaders did China and Japan have to worry about? *They had to worry about the Mongols.*

Where did the Mongols come from? *They came from the mountains north of China.*

What was the name of the fierce leader of the Mongols? *He was named Genghis Khan.*

What city did Genghis Khan want to attack? *He wanted to conquer Beijing.*

Genghis wanted to invade China, but what did he need to do first? *He needed to unite all the Mongol tribes under him.*

After Genghis Khan conquered Beijing, what did he do? *He turned west and attacked the Islamic empire.*

How did people react to the Mongols? *They were very afraid of them!*

What nickname did Muslims give to Genghis Khan? *They called him "The Scourge."*

Where is Genghis Khan buried? *No one knows, because his men killed everyone who saw the funeral procession pass.*

NARRATION EXERCISE

"Genghis Khan united all the Mongol tribes and declared himself their leader. Then he led the Mongols into China to attack Beijing. After that, he began to attack the Islamic empire. People were too afraid of the Mongols and Genghis Khan to fight back!" OR

"China and Japan were afraid of the Mongol invaders. The greatest Mongol leader was Genghis Khan. He conquered parts of China and some of the Islamic empire over to the Caspian Sea. When he died, he was buried in a place that no one knows about."

THE MONGOL CONQUEST OF CHINA

REVIEW QUESTIONS

The Mongols conquered land that belonged to two empires. What were they? *They conquered land that belonged to the Byzantine Empire and to the Islamic empire.*

Who was Kublai Khan? *He was Genghis Khan's grandson. He became the emperor of China.*

How did the Chinese defend themselves against the Mongols? *They made poisonous and choking fogs.*

Once Kublai Khan became emperor of China, what did he make people do to show that they were beneath him? *He made them take off their shoes and bow down before him until their foreheads touched the floor.*

What city did Kublai Khan make his capital? *He made Peking his capital.*

What happened both times Kublai Khan tried to invade Japan by sea? *A huge storm blew in and caused many Mongol ships to sink.*

What is a "kamikaze"? *It is the Japanese name for a "divine wind."*

After Kublai Khan died, what happened to his large kingdom? *It was divided up into smaller kingdoms.*

NARRATION EXERCISE

"Kublai Khan conquered China and became the emperor. He lived in a great palace and forced people to bow down and touch the floor in his presence. But both times he tried to invade Japan, he was defeated by storms. His empire was very large, but after he died it fell apart." OR

"The Mongol dynasty of China began with Kublai Khan. He ruled over a giant empire, but he never managed to conquer Japan. He was the emperor of China and the Great Khan of the Mongols, but after his death, his empire was divided into small pieces."

Additional History Reading

Ancient China (Journey Into Civilization), by Robert Nicholson (Chelsea House Publications, 1995). This book is full of wonderful illustrations that complement the short selections on crafts, food, clothing, city life, inventions, etc., in China. (RA 1–3, IR 4–5)

Ancient China (Treasure Chest), by Chao-Hui Jenny Liu (Running Press, 1996). The treasure chest contains an informative book on Chinese history and includes a brush-and-ink set with instructions on how to create Chinese characters, as well as many other activities and projects. Younger students will need assistance. (RA 1–3, IR 4–5 and activities)

The Great Wall of China, by Leonard Everett Fisher (Aladdin Paperbacks, 1995). This book provides a brief history of the Great Wall of China and how it was built over 2,000 years ago to keep out marauding Mongol invaders. (RA 1–3, IR 4–5)

Ten Kings and the Worlds They Ruled, by Milton Meltzer, illus. Bethanne Andersen (Orchard Books, 2002). Illustrated, read-aloud biographies of ten kings, 8–12 pages each. Includes Kublai Khan. (RA 2–4, IR 4–5)

Corresponding Literature Suggestions

Fa Mulan: The Story of a Woman Warrior, by Robert San Souci (Hyperion Books, 1998). A retelling of the Chinese legend about a brave young girl who disguises herself and goes off to fight the Tartars (Mongols) who are invading her country. (RA 1, IR 2–5)

The Hunter, by Mary Casanova (Atheneum, 2000). The story of a young hunter who saves his village from starvation, and then is faced with the choice to preserve his own life or save the same villagers from a devastating flood. (RA 1, IR 2–4)

The Legend of Mu Lan: A Heroine of China, by Wei Jiang (Victory Press, 1997). A young girl disguises herself so that she can take her father's place in the army. (RA 1, IR 2–5)

Liang and the Magic Paintbrush, by Demi (Henry Holt and Company, 1980). This Reading Rainbow selection is about a poor Chinese boy who receives a magical paintbrush that turns everything he paints to life. (RA 1, IR 2–4)

The Paper Dragon, by Marguerite Davol (Simon & Schuster, 1997). The unassuming scroll painter Mi Lei is the only one in the village brave enough to confront a dragon that is terrorizing the people. (RA 1, IR 2–4)

The Mongol Empire at Its Height *(Student Page 87, answer 259)*

1. The Mongols came from the cold, mountainous region called Mongolia. Underline Mongolia in blue. Then, draw three mountain symbols (like an upside down "v") and color them blue as well.

2. Genghis Khan invaded the city of Beijing in China. Draw a blue line from Mongolia to Beijing.

3. Genghis Khan's grandson, the emperor Kublai Khan, built a huge palace in the city of Beijing. Draw a yellow star over Beijing.

4. After Genghis Khan died, the Mongol Empire continued to grow. The empire stretched from the Yellow Sea in the east all the way to the Black Sea in the west. Trace the borders of the Mongol Empire in bright yellow. Then, color the Yellow Sea and the Black Sea red to show that the Mongol Empire "stopped" there.

COLORING PAGE Genghis Khan, leader of the Mongol hordes *(Student Page 88)*

CRAFT PROJECT **Make a Ger**

The Mongols were nomads, so they didn't have permanent homes. They could pick up and move their homes whenever they needed to! Today we call the Mongol homes *gers*. Gers are circular homes with a roof that slants upward, but not as much as a teepee. Each ger has a smoke hole at the top, two center poles that help support the ger, and a wooden door. The size of the ger varies, depending on how many people live in it!

Materials:
- Two sheets of thin cardboard or thick construction paper
- Markers
- Two dark-colored sheets of felt
- Glue or tape

Directions:
1. Make a cylinder out of the cardboard that is wider than it is tall. How big you make the ger is really up to you. Do not attach the ends of the cardboard because before you do, you need to create "lattice work." Now, using an orange or brown marker, draw intersecting diagonal lines to make "lattice work" (like a trellis) all along the cardboard.

2. Now attach the ends of the cardboard with tape or glue so that you have a complete cylinder.

3. Using another piece of cardboard, fold it into a cone, leaving a hole at the top where the smoke hole would be. The gers are not as steep as teepees, so make your cone a little flatter than you would if you were constructing a teepee. Attach the ends with tape or glue and cut off the excess cardboard at the bottom so that the bottom is circular.

4. Attach the ceiling cardboard and the cylinder "walls" cardboard with glue or tape.

5. Cut an upside-down "L" in the wall to make the door. The "L" shape allows you to open and close the door. This should not be as tall as the walls. If you want, you can color the inside of the door orange and draw lines on it to represent boards.

6. Cover your ger with felt. Use one piece of felt for the walls and another piece of felt for the roof. You can attach the felt with tape or glue, but make sure to cut out a piece for the door and also leave space for the smoke hole.

7. Look inside your ger and pretend you live there!

ACTIVITY PROJECT **Put History Back in Order!**

Cut out the events on *Student Page 89*. Glue them in the correct order onto a blank sheet of paper. Illustrate!

MEMORY PROJECT **Memorize the First Lines of "Kublai Khan"**

Samuel Taylor Coleridge wrote a poem about Kublai Khan's palace. Memorize the first few lines:

> In Xanadu did Kublai Khan
> A stately pleasure-dome decree:
> Where Alph, the sacred river, ran
> Through caverns measureless to man
> Down to a sunless sea.

ACTIVITY PROJECT **Make a Watermelon Warship**

Watermelon grows very well in the dry climate of China. Carve a watermelon into a ship to symbolize the Mongols' attempt to invade Japan. It failed miserably, so have fun eating the Mongol ship! You can just carve the ship if you wish, or you can make the fruit salad to go inside.

Ingredients: 1 cup lemon juice   1 honeydew, cut into cubes or balls
                 1 cup sugar   1 cantaloupe, cut into cubes or balls
                 2 tablespoons flour   1 pint fresh strawberries, sliced
                 2 eggs, beaten   ½ pound green grapes
                 1 watermelon
                 1 cup whipping cream whipped (or 1 cup whipped topping;
                    if using topping cut the sugar to only ½ cup)

Directions for fruit sauce:

1. In a saucepan, bring lemon juice, sugar, and flour to a boil. Reduce heat to low. Stir ¼ of the hot mixture into the eggs (to temper them). Add egg mixture to saucepan. Cook and stir for fifteen minutes but do not boil. Cool mixture; fold in whipped cream. Cover and chill until ready to serve.

Directions to carve the ship:

1. Cut a thin slice from the watermelon base so that it can sit flat.
2. With a marker, draw a line about 2" above the center of the watermelon, all along the top of the watermelon. This will be your cutting line.
3. With a knife, cut along the line you drew.
4. Carefully pull the top off the watermelon.
5. Scoop out the watermelon with a melon ball scoop or slice it into cubes.

To serve watermelon with fruit salad:

1. Mix the cubed watermelon, honeydew, cantaloupe, strawberries, and grapes in a bowl.
2. When ready to serve, mix the fruit with the chilled sauce from earlier.
3. Put the fruit salad in the watermelon boat and serve.

COOKING PROJECT ## Make Chicken in Peanut Sauce

Try this traditional Chinese food!

Ingredients: 2 tablespoons vegetable oil   ¼ cup water
2 chicken breast halves, cut into 1" strips   2 tablespoons soy sauce
1 clove garlic, minced   2 tablespoons peanut butter
1 green onion, chopped   1 tablespoon red wine vinegar
1 teaspoon ground ginger   2 cups Broccoli florets
1 cup cucumber, seeded and sliced

Directions: 1. Heat oil in wok till hot, add chicken, garlic and green onion. Stir-fry until the chicken has been cooked through.

2. Reduce heat and add the water, ground ginger, soy sauce, peanut butter and vinegar. Stir well and simmer for 5 minutes.

3. Add the broccoli and cucumber. Cook for about 7 minutes, or until vegetables are crisp but tender. Serve dish over rice. Makes 4 servings.

CRAFT PROJECT ## Make a Chinese Hanging Lantern

Materials: ☐ 12" × 18" sheet of paper
☐ Long stick or dowel
☐ 3 lengths of string about 1 foot long
☐ Glue, scissors, ruler, hole-puncher
☐ Pencil and assorted art supplies

Directions: 1. Paint or color a picture on the sheet of paper. Possible suggestions include an outdoor scene of a mountain with a branch of cherry blooms or pine trees in the foreground, or a family of cranes catching fish on a lake. After the painting has completely dried, fold the paper in half lengthwise.

2. Use the ruler and a pencil to lightly draw a straight line 1½" from the open edges of the paper. This will be the stopping line when you are cutting the openings for the lantern.

3. Starting at the folded edge cut a straight line up to the stopping mark. Keep making similar cuts that are spaced 1" apart (*see* diagram below).

4. To assemble the lantern, unfold the paper and glue the uncut edges to form the top and bottom of the lantern, being sure to overlap the edges about 1". Allow the glue to dry. Use the hole-puncher to make three holes spaced evenly around the top of the lantern. Tie a piece of string through each hole in the lantern, then tie the three strings together around the top of the stick.

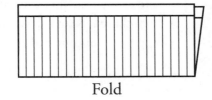

Fold

Exploring the Mysterious East

CHAPTER 22

Encyclopedia Cross-References

UBWH 118–119, UILE 251, 269, 273
KIHW 270–273, 282–283, KHE 174–175, 180–181

•MARCO POLO GOES TO CHINA

REVIEW QUESTIONS

What was the road called that led into China? *It was called the Silk Road.*

Can you remember three of the things that merchants found at the end of the Silk Road? *They found gold, cloves, ginger, jade, lacquer, flowers, wine, sweet-smelling wood, rugs, and silk.*

Why did Kublai Khan encourage merchants from other countries to come to China? *He knew that trade would make China richer.*

What was the name of the traveler who wrote a book about his journey to China with his father? *His name was Marco Polo.*

What errand did Kublai Khan send Niccolo Polo on? *He sent Niccolo for one hundred wise men who could explain Christianity and some holy oil from Rome.*

How long did it take Marco and Niccolo to get to China? *The journey took four years.*

Can you remember two new things that Marco saw in China? *He saw ice cream, pears that weighed ten pounds, and coal.*

What did Marco Polo do in China? *He governed different cities in Kublai Khan's empire and judged between Chinese officials. (He was also asked to find out whether soldiers were plotting against Kublai Khan.)*

NARRATION EXERCISE

"Marco Polo traveled the Silk Road to China when he was a boy. He wrote a book about all that he saw there. He saw the Khan's marble palace, a gold-painted dining hall, ice cream, and coal. He stayed in China for twenty years and worked for Kublai Khan. When he went home, his relatives didn't recognize him." OR

"The emperor of China, Kublai Khan, encouraged merchants to travel to his country along the Silk Road. He knew that this would make China rich, so he sent his soldiers out to make the road safe. One of these merchants, Marco Polo, wrote a book about all that he saw in China, including the magnificent buildings, the large amounts of food, and the beautiful clothes."

THE FORBIDDEN CITY OF THE MING

REVIEW QUESTIONS

After Kublai Khan died, what happened to the land between Europe and China? *Mongol leaders divided it and fought with each other.*

Why didn't the Ming emperors want any contact with other countries? *They thought China was perfect. They had nothing to learn from others!*

We talked about three things that the Ming emperors did. Can you remember two of them? (Hint: Two of these things have to do with building, and one is a law forbidding the Chinese to do something.) *They made the Great Wall stronger; they made it illegal for sailors to sail to other countries; they built a palace at the center of Peking.*

What was the name of the new palace built in the center of Peking? *It was called the Forbidden City.*

Why was it called the Forbidden City? *It was as large as a small city, and foreign visitors were forbidden to see it.*

How did the builders get stones into Peking (also called Beijing)? *They dug wells, poured water along the road, waited for it to freeze, and then slid the stones on the ice.*

What were the bricks of the Forbidden City made of? *They were made of rice and lime.*

Do you remember the names of two of the halls inside the Forbidden City? *They were called the Hall of Supreme Harmony, the Hall of Military Might, the Hall of Peace, and the Hall of Terrestrial Tranquility. The throne room was called the Hall of Celestial Purity.*

What was the job of the royal food-taster? *He had to take a bite of each of the emperor's dishes to make sure that none of the food was poisoned.*

What little creature did the children of the emperor keep as pets? *They kept crickets!*

Narration Exercise

"The Ming emperors of China did not want any contact with other countries. They even made it against the law for sailors to sail to other countries! Instead, they built a beautiful palace called the Forbidden City which no outsiders were allowed to enter. They lived in the Forbidden City with their families until they were driven out." OR

"The Ming emperors of China were not like Kublai Khan. They wanted nothing to do with trade or foreigners. They spent their time building the Forbidden City, a great palace with many magnificent buildings. The palace had halls decorated with gold dragons and yellow paintings. Children who lived there could see plays, go ice skating, and play with crickets."

Additional History Reading

Ancient China (Ancient and Living Cultures: Stencils), by Roberta Dempsey (Goodyear Publishing, 1994). A simple guide to China's stories, celebrations, and culture, with five easy-to-do art projects. (RA 1–2, IR 3–5)

China (Ancient Civilizations), by Tami Deedrick (Raintree/Steck Vaughn, 2001). This book covers a span of 700 years in Chinese history, providing plenty of information about medieval dynasties (not just ancient emperors) and the daily life, culture, and inventions of China. (RA 1–2, IR 3–5)

China (First Reports), by Susan Sinnott (Compass Point Books, 2000). This independent reader focuses on the unique geography, culture, and history of China, including Confucius, the Great Wall, the Silk Road, Marco Polo, Communism, language, calligraphy, the opera, food and Chinese festivals. (RA 1, IR 2–4)

Marco Polo: A Journey Through China, by Fiona MacDonald (Franklin Watts, 1998). The books covers Marco Polo's expeditions, with each two-page spread (illustrated by watercolors) dealing with a different aspect of Polo's life and travels. (RA 1–2, IR 3–5)

Marco Polo and the Wonders of the East, by Hal Marcovitz (Chelsea House Publishers, 2000). An excellent, slightly longer biography of Marco Polo which also covers the Silk Road and trade during the rule of the Mongol Empire. (RA 2–3, IR 4–5)

Marco Polo for Kids, by Janis Herbert (Chicago Review Press, 2001). A retelling of Marco Polo's journey to China, with descriptions of the peoples he met along the way and 21 craft projects from these different countries. (RA 1–2, IR 3–5)

The Silk Road: 7,000 Miles of History, by John Major (Aladdin, 1999). A picture-book with beautiful illustrations and a fair amount of text, covering the history of the route between China and Persia and describing one typical journey around 700. (RA 1–3, IR 4–5)

Corresponding Literature Suggestions

Beautiful Warrior: The Legend of the Nun's Kung Fu, by Emily Arnold McCully (Arthur A. Levine Books, 1998). The Chinese girl Jingyong learns martial arts, becomes a Buddhist nun, and teaches little Mingyi how to defeat the village bully. Beautiful pictures and text, with the focus on strong and resourceful women. (RA 1, IR 2–5)

Bestiary: An Illuminated Alphabet of Medieval Beasts, by Jonathan Hunt (Simon & Schuster, 1998). This book describes the imaginary beasts thought to inhabit the world of the East (and elsewhere!). (RA 2, IR 3–5)

Bitter Dumplings, by Jeanne M. Lee (Farrar, Straus & Giroux, 2002*).* Three unhappy people find a new beginning when they meet in a Chinese village long ago. Pretty illustrations and a lovely story, although the print is quite small. (RA 1–3, IR 4)

The Dragon Prince: A Chinese Beauty and the Beast Tale, by Laurence Yep (Harper Collins Juvenile Books, 1999). In this Chinese version of the popular fairy tale, Dragon Prince threatens to harm a poor fisherman unless one of the farmer's daughters marries him. (RA 1, IR 2–4)

The Emperor and the Kite, by Jane Yolen (Philomel Books, 1967). A little girl is ignored by her family until she proves her worth by saving her kidnapped father, the emperor. (RA 1, IR 2–5)

The Empty Pot, by Demi (Henry Holt & Company, 1996). A young boy dares to appear before the Emperor of China with an empty pot and is chosen to become the next ruler of his country. (IR)

Kat and the Emperor's Gift, by Emma Bradford (Just Pretend Inc, 1998). In this chapter book, a young girl named Kat travels in her time machine to the court of Kublai Khan and helps a Mongolian princess. (IR 4–5)

The Weaving of a Dream: A Chinese Folktale, by Marilee Heyer (Viking Press, 1989). This is a tale of a young son's love for his mother; he searches for a tapestry that will save her life. (RA 1, IR 2–5)

Yeh-Shen: A Cinderella Story from China, by Ai-Ling Louie, illus. Ed Young (Paper Star, 1996). An orphan girl earns her right to marry the king in this Chinese version of the ancient story. (RA 1–2, IR 3–5)

—————————————————— **MAP WORK** ——————————————————

The Ming Dynasty and the Silk Road *(Student Page 90, answer 259)*

1. The long road that led to China was called the Silk Road. Shade the words "The Silk Road" in purple.
2. Starting at the left side of the map, trace the path of the Silk Road to the end of the Yellow River.
3. The Silk Road passed by several deserts. Circle the Taklamakan and Gobi Deserts in yellow.
4. The Silk Road also bordered the Great Wall. Shade the words "Great Wall" in orange.
5. Trace the length of the Great Wall in orange.
6. The Forbidden City is located in the city of Beijing. Circle Beijing in green.

―――――――――――――――――――――― **PROJECTS** ――――――――――――――――――――――

`CRAFT PROJECT` **Make a Chinese Farmer's Hat**

Toiling in a rice field was very hard work, especially when the weather was bad. To protect themselves, farmers would weave a cone-shaped hat from reeds or bamboo to keep the sun and rain off their heads and necks. Follow the easy directions below to make a hat of your own.

Materials:
- ☐ Brown paper grocery bag
- ☐ 4 foot length of yarn
- ☐ Scissors, brown marker, tape or stapler

Directions:
1. Cut open the brown grocery bag so that it lies flat on the table. Use a marker to draw a 13" circle on the bag and cut out.
2. Use the brown marker to draw a brick-like pattern to make it appear that the hat has been woven from bamboo.
3. Make a straight cut from the edge of the circle to the middle. Overlap the cut edges a couple of inches to form a cone-shape. Use tape or a stapler to keep the lapped edges in place.
4. Cut the length of yarn in half to make two ties. On each side of the hat, make a small hole and thread the yarn through it and tie a small knot. You might need to use a piece of tape to keep the knot from coming through the hole. Your hat is now ready to wear. Place it on your head and tie it under your chin.

`CRAFT PROJECT` **Make Handmade Paper**

In 105 AD, a Chinese court official named Ts'ai Lun invented paper. He mixed mulberry bark, hemp and rags with water and mashed it all into a pulp. The liquid was then pressed out and the thin mat of pulp was left in the sun to dry. This humble mixture would begin a communication revolution. After the invention of this paper, both art and literature flourished in China. It was not until 1009 AD that this great invention reached Europe, when the Arabs started the first paper mill in Xativa, Spain.

Materials:
- ☐ White or colored construction paper
- ☐ Blender (with adult supervision)
- ☐ Water
- ☐ Rectangular pan
- ☐ 2 pieces of screen (larger than pan)
- ☐ Old towels and newspapers
- ☐ Rolling pin

Directions:
1. Tear the scrap paper into small pieces and place in the blender until the blender is half full.
2. Add enough water to the blender to make it ¾ full. Place the lid on the blender and run on medium speed until the scrap paper has been turned into a watery pulp. If the mixture looks too thick, add a little bit more water and blend again.
3. Place one piece of screening over the pan and slowly pour the pulp mixture over it. Use a knife or spoon back to spread the pulp into a square or rectangular shape. Let the water drain off the pulp for about an hour.
4. To remove additional water, place a folded towel on top a stack of old newspapers. Carefully lift the screen from the pan and place on top of the towel. Place the other piece of screening on top of the paper and use the rolling pin to press out the water.

5. When as much water has been removed as possible, lift off the top piece of screen. Carefully flip it over onto the other folded towel and gently peel off the other piece of screening. Place the towel in the sun and allow it to completely air dry. If the paper curls too much during the drying process, cover the paper with a pressing cloth and iron it flat.

CRAFT PROJECT **Paint a Chinese Scroll**

Instead of hanging framed pictures in their homes, the Chinese prefer to use painted scrolls. These scrolls tend to be pictures of nature and usually have several Chinese calligraphy characters written down the side. Use the directions below to make your own nature scene or paint one of a place that is special to you.

Materials:
- 10" × 24" piece of paper
- Two 12" dowels or straight sticks
- 20" length of ribbon
- Watercolors, paintbrush, glue or tape

Directions:
1. Use the watercolors to paint an outdoor scene on the piece of paper. To imitate the Chinese style of painting, keep the composition simple and include Chinese characters down one side. Let dry.
2. Fold back a 1½" tab at the top and bottom of the paper. Place a piece of doweling (or stick) under the flap, glue or tape the flap in place. Repeat the same procedure at the other end of the paper.
3. Tie the ribbon to both ends of the top dowel. Your Chinese scroll is now ready to be hung.

CRAFT PROJECT **Make an Artist's Signature Chop**

When an artist in China finished a painting, he did not sign his name at the bottom of the painting with his paintbrush. Instead, he would sign his painting by dipping his wooden signature chop (block) into red ink and pressing it on the painting. Follow the directions below to create your own signature chop.

Materials:
- Large pencil eraser
- Pencil
- Metal paper clip
- Red ink pad
- Finished piece of artwork

Directions:
1. With the pencil, write your initials on the eraser. Be sure to draw them backwards so that they will print correctly when you use it on your artwork.
2. Unfold the paper clip and use it to scrape your initials into the eraser. This works best when you try to scrape it away in several thin layers.
3. When the carving is completed, press the eraser face down on the red ink pad. Then press the inked eraser on a finished piece of your artwork. *Note:* Chinese artists did not limit themselves to placing their signatures at the bottom of their paintings. In most instances, the signature chop design became an integral part of the finished painting.

ACTIVITY PROJECT **Travel the Silk Road**

Follow the Silk Road around the house!

Materials:
- Paper
- Pens
- Activity Map from this Chapter *(Student Page 90)*
- Sunglasses

- ☒ 2 snacks (like raisins, trail mix, a granola bar)
- ☒ 1 glass of water
- ☒ Makeshift "oar" (meter stick, wiffle bat, broom, etc.)
- ☒ Sheets for a fort
- ☒ Chinese trading goods (silk or silky cloth; "gold objects" like trophies, gold glitter, Christmas ornaments, or gold candy like Werther's Originals; "ivory objects" like white plastic silverware or white soap; stuffed animals)

Directions for set-up:

1. Make signs that say: "Taklamakan Desert," "Tun-huang-shih," "Gobi Desert," "Loyang-shih," "Yellow River," and "Peking."

2. Post the signs around your house in this order:

   Put "Taklamakan Desert" on a wide space of floor.

   Put "Tun-huang-shih" on a comfy chair. Put a snack (like trail mix) next to the chair.

   Put "Gobi Desert" on another wide space of floor. Put a glass of water near it.

   Put "Loyang-shih" on another comfy chair or couch. Put a snack nearby.

   Put "Yellow River" on a set of stairs or in a hallway. Put the makeshift oar nearby.

   Put "Peking" at the end of the Yellow River. Construct a fort out of blankets and place the "Chinese trading goods" inside.

Directions for the journey:

1. Take your chapter map. You'll need this map to help you find your way on your journey. You are starting from the west (the left-hand side of your map).

2. You are a western traveler following the Silk Road to trade for silk, gold, ivory, and exotic plants and animals. First you had to pass by the hot, dry Taklamakan Desert. This desert is treacherous to cross and many travelers have lost their lives there. You have enough supplies to make it safely across the desert. Put on a pair of sunglasses to cross this desert (on your map, you're taking the southern, or bottom, route through the desert).

   Interesting fact: Although it is very dangerous, the Taklamakan Desert also has its own music! The shifting sand, sand dunes, and falling sand cliffs create sounds that echo all across the desert. Marco Polo claimed that he saw and heard spirits singing as he passed through this desert. He probably did hear music, but the "spirits" were probably just a mirage brought on by thirst, hunger, and heat.

3. Oasis settlements along the way offer a place to rest and recover from your weary travels. The settlement of Tun-huang-shih will give you a chance to relax. Take a seat in the comfy chair, take off your sunglasses, eat a snack, and relax.

4. The Silk Road also passed to the south of another desert: the Gobi Desert. Unlike the Taklamakan, this desert has some oases where you can get water. Drink a glass of water as you pass through this desert.

5. Take a rest at Loyang-shih. Relax and eat a snack.

6. You decide to take the Yellow River to Peking (also called Beijing). Grab your oar and paddle down the river.

7. You have finally arrived at the marble palace of the Khan in the city of Peking. Here you trade for Chinese goods. Go inside the palace and retrieve the gold, ivory, silk, and exotic animals. Stay and relax in the emperor's palace before you begin your journey home.

The First Russians

CHAPTER 23

Encyclopedia Cross-References

UBWH 128, UILE 145, 256–257
KIHW 382–383, KHE 226–227

THE RUS COME TO CONSTANTINOPLE

REVIEW QUESTIONS

Three groups of people tried to conquer Constantinople. Can you remember them? *Muslim warriors, Mongols, and the Rus all tried to conquer Constantinople.*

Who was Rurik? *He was a Viking who settled down in central Europe.*

What people already lived in Rurik's new home? *The Slavs already lived there.*

Why did the Rus sail down to Constantinople? *They traded ivory, honey, wax, nuts, and slaves for silk, glass, and silver.*

When the Rus became tired of traversing treacherous waters to trade with Constantinople, what did they decide to do? *They decided to attack Constantinople and take it for themselves!*

We listed four reasons why Constantinople was hard to conquer. Can you remember two? *It was surrounded by water on three sides; it was surrounded by three walls and a moat; it had towers where archers could stand and shoot out to sea; a chain was stretched across the water so ships couldn't get close to the shore.*

What secret weapon did the Byzantine army use to make sure the Rus ships could not approach the city of Constantinople? *They used sea fire—oil that burned even on water.*

After the Rus failed to conquer Constantinople, what did the Rus prince Vladimir do instead? *He made friends with the Byzantine emperor.*

What gift did Vladimir give to the Byzantine emperor? *He sent many Rus warriors who became the emperor's bodyguard.*

What happened to Vladimir? *He married a Byzantine princess and was baptized as an Eastern Orthodox Christian.*

Today, what do we call the land of the Rus? (Hint: It is named after the Rus.) *We call it Russia.*

NARRATION EXERCISE

"The Rus were descended from Vikings who settled down with Slavs. They tried to take the city of Constantinople, but the Byzantine army's weapon of sea fire burned their ships before they could reach the city. So the Rus decided to make friends with the Byzantine emperor instead. The Rus prince, Vladimir, even married a Byzantine princess. Their country became known as Russia." OR

"Constantinople had been attacked by many different tribes. When the Rus sailed to attack the city, the Byzantine army spread burning oil, called sea fire, across the water. The Rus were unable to conquer the city. Later, the Rus befriended the emperor of Constantinople. They even sent warriors to be the bodyguard for the emperor. Today we call their land Russia."

REVIEW QUESTIONS

Was Russia one unified country? *No, it was several tribes ruled by warriors.*

What was Ivan the Great's big accomplishment? *He united the Russian cities into one country.*

What city did Ivan the Great first rule? *He ruled in Moscow.*

Who tried to make Ivan pay tribute? *The Mongols wanted Ivan to pay tribute.*

After Ivan the Great defied the Mongols, what did he do next? *He captured Kiev and three other cities.*

What is the Kremlin? *It is a fortress in the middle of Moscow. It became Russia's center of government.*

Why did the people of Moscow call their city the "Third Rome"? *It was the most important city after Rome and Constantinople. (It was also the center of Eastern Orthodoxy after Constantinople fell to the Turks* [see footnote in Story of the World, Vol. 2].*)*

What did Ivan the Terrible start calling himself to show he was as powerful as the ancient Roman emperors? (Hint: It means "Caesar" and sounds a little bit like it too.) *He called himself the Tsar.*

What happened after Ivan's wife died? *He started to go mad; his hair started to fall out; he thought people were plotting against him.*

What was the job of the secret police? *They were supposed to look out for anyone who might be plotting against the tsar.*

Can you describe what they looked like? *They rode black horses with black saddles and bridles, and they had a flag with a broom and a dog's head on it.*

What did Ivan the Terrible do that caused him so much grief he tried to jump from a tower? *He struck his son and killed him.*

NARRATION EXERCISE

"Ivan the Great united the Rus. But his grandson, Ivan the Terrible, was a very cruel ruler." OR

"There are two famous Russian 'Ivans.' Ivan the Great united the different Rus cities to make them into one country. Ivan the Terrible was a wicked tsar who treated his people very badly."

Additional History Reading

Daily Life in Ancient and Modern Moscow, by Patricia Toht, illus. Bob Moulder (Runestone Press, 2001). This middle-grade guide to Moscow begins with the city's early Slavic existence, covers the rise of the czars, and continues on from Peter the Great through communist and post-communist times. The first twelve sections deal with Moscow in the time of the Slavs, Moscow under Rurik, the coming of the Mongols, Moscow as "Third Rome," and the Ivans; each section would make a good 2–3 page read-aloud. (RA 1–3, IR 4–5)

Moscow: Rookie-Read-About Geography, by Allan Fowler (Children's Press, 2000). A simple, early-reader guide to the city and its buildings. (IR 1–3)

Russia: First Reports, by Susan H. Gray (Compass Point Books, 2002). Simple text and many photographs make this easy-reader guide to Russia a good choice for young students; little information on Russia's history, but an excellent guide to the country and culture. (RA 1, IR 2–4)

Welcome to Russia, by Alison J. Auch (Compass Point Books, 2002). Another beginner's guide to the country, with spectacular photographs. (RA 1, IR 2–4)

Corresponding Literature Suggestions

Baboushka and the Three Kings, by Ruth Robbins, illus. Nicolas Sidjakov (Houghton Mifflin, 1960). This Caldecott Medal picture book retells the Russian folk tale, handed down from the early days of Eastern Orthodoxy in Russia, of an old woman invited to journey with the Three Kings to see the Christ Child. (RA 1, IR 2–4)

Baba Yaga and Vasilisa the Brave, by Marianna Mayer, illus. K. Y. Craft (William Morrow, 1994). A young girl triumphs over the schemes of a wicked stepmother and marries the czar in this Russian Cinderella story. (RA 1, IR 2–4)

Clay Boy, by Mirra Ginsburg, illus. Jos. A. Smith (Greenwillow Books, 1997). A Russian couple makes a boy out of clay—and he eats EVERYTHING. (RA 1, IR 2–4)

The Littlest Matryoshka, by Corinne Demas Bliss, illus. Kathryn Brown (Hyperion Books, 1999). The tale of a traditional ancient Russian toy taken to modern-day America. (RA 1, IR 2–4)

A Perfect Pork Stew, by Paul Brett Johnson (Orchard Books, 1998). A retelling of a traditional Ivan the Fool tale in picture-book style. (RA 1–2, IR 3–5)

Russian Fairy Tales, by Gillian Avery (Everymans Library, 1995). A collection of traditional tales for reading aloud, with lovely illustrations. (RA 1–3, IR 4–5)

―――――――――――――――――― **MAP WORK** ――――――――――――――――――

The Territory of the Rus *(Student Page 92, answer 259)*

1. Vikings from Scandinavia invaded land in central Europe. Color Scandinavia (the part of it shown on this map) in yellow.

2. These Vikings were called the Rus. Circle the land of the Rus in orange.

3. Draw a yellow arrow from Scandinavia to the land of the Rus.

4. The Rus decided that they would conquer the city of Constantinople. Put a blue box around the dot that marks Constantinople.

5. Draw an orange line from the land of the Rus to the city of Constantinople.

6. When the invasion failed, the Rus prince of Kiev decided to make friends with the Byzantines of Constantinople instead. Underline Kiev in brown.

7. Ivan the Great and Ivan the Terrible lived in the capital of Russia, the city of Moscow. Draw a green star over Moscow to show that it was the capital.

COLORING PAGE   Ivan the Great ran the country of Russia from his palace inside the Kremlin.
(Student Page 93)

―――――――――――――――――― **PROJECTS** ――――――――――――――――――

ACTIVITY PROJECT **Practicing the Bread-and-Salt Greeting**

During the old days in Russia, salt was very precious and was seen as a luxury. In Moscow, there is a street called Salt Street or Solyanka where the salt was kept in a very strong storehouse. The traditional greeting for guests was to offer a fresh loaf of bread on a beautifully embroidered linen towel, given by the host's youngest daughter. On top of the loaf sat a small dish of salt. The guest would pinch off a chunk of bread and dip it in the salt and then eat it. Try this at home as you welcome each other to the study of the Rus!

CRAFT PROJECT — Maiden's Kokoshnic

Made from red velvet and embroidered with sleek golden thread, the Kokoshnic was the Russian women's head adornment for centuries. All wore this simple hat except for the women of royal birth. Along with the hat, the Russian peasants wore a sleeveless dress called a sarafan, which reached their toes and went over a rubakha, or shirt. These jumper-like dresses were decorated according to each tribe or district.

Materials:
- Kokoshnic pattern *(Student Page 94)*
- Red posterboard
- Tracing paper and pencil
- Glitterglue in gold
- Red wide ribbon, 1½ yards long
- Stapler

Optional: Glue or glue-gun
Optional: Strip of multi-colored or gold sequins (at fabric store)
Optional: Strip of hanging pearl or gold craft beads (at fabric store in ribbon section or in packets)
Optional: Medium-sized pearl or gold loose craft beads

Directions:
1. Test pattern by placing it on the center of the head so it faces you. If it is too small, cut pattern until it fits. If too large, trace the pattern adding some thickness to the opening. Trace pattern onto posterboard.
2. Using the Glitterglue, make a flowery design onto the posterboard. You may use the pattern on the guide and trace it onto the posterboard or you may make your own. This pattern was taken from an authentic Kokoshnic.
3. Cut ribbon in half, making two long strips. Using the stapler, staple the ribbon on the bottom edges to make the tie so the Kokoshnic will sit secure.
4. Optional: Decorate top edge of the Kokoshnic with the strip of sequins and the bottom edge with the hanging beads. Glue loose beads evenly around the open spaces of the Kokoshnic face.
5. When dry, place hat on center of head and tie on the back bottom of head to secure. This is the style worn by young and unmarried girls. The married women's Kokoshnic was closed and kept their hair tucked up and not visible.

COOKING PROJECT — Borscht and Bread

Borscht is still a national dish in Kiev. Made from beets and potatoes grown all around the Kievan area, now known as the Ukraine, this rich soup has fed the Russians for centuries. The Ukrainians also have several sweet breads for festivals and many dark rye and wheat breads for every day. See *Joy of Cooking*, by Irma Rombauer, for one of these traditional recipes, or pick up a dark rye loaf at the grocery store. Try this recipe, along with your loaf, for an authentic Kievan-Rus lunch or dinner in honor of the people in Russia.

Ingredients for Borscht:

2 tablespoons of beef bouillon	1 tablespoon parsley
4 beets	1 small can of tomato paste
12 cups of water	1 teaspoon lemon juice
2 carrots, peeled and sliced	Salt and pepper
1½ onion, peeled	Sour cream
4 medium potatoes, peeled and quartered	Dried dill
1 cup cabbage cut up (or buy in bag already sliced)	

Directions for Borscht:

1. In a saucepan, place beets and fill with water until it is one inch over the beets. Cook until soft, about 1 hour. With a slotted spoon, put beets in a bowl to cool and save the water (for Batik Design below). When beets are cool, peel them and cut beets up in small bite-size pieces.

2. In the large pot, put 12 cups of water with bouillon and boil.

3. Put potatoes, carrots and onions, parsley and salt in and cook for 20 minutes.

4. Add tomato paste and cabbage, and cook another 10 minutes.

5. Add beets to soup and cook for 8 minutes. Do not over cook because the beets will lose their color.

6. Add lemon juice just before serving, stirring the pot once it is added.

7. Serve in large bowl with a dollop of sour cream in the top and a sprinkle of dried dill on top of that.

CRAFT PROJECT **Russian Batik Design**

Using the natural color from your beet water above, you can create a wax picture using techniques similar to those used long ago in Russia, Asia and India.

Materials:
- ☐ White piece of paper
- ☐ Black marker and pencil
- ☐ Beet juice water
- ☐ Paraffin wax, used for canning (grocery store)
- ☐ Eye dropper (drug store)
- ☐ Clean, large can and sauce pan
- ☐ 1 square of white, cotton fabric, such as muslin, the size you would like your picture to be (suggested size: 8½ × 11)
- ☐ Large cooking pot
- ☐ Newspaper
- ☐ Thin dowel rod 2 inches longer than your picture's width

Directions:
1. Create your design on a white piece of paper. Use a story from this chapter or make the brown bear, a national symbol for Russia. Keep it simple if this is your first time. Trace your pencil design with a thick black marker.

2. Fill the saucepan with water ¼ of the way and place pan on stove. Put the can in the center of it and place chunks of the paraffin wax in it. Turn heat to medium and slowly melt the wax. You only need about ½ of a brick of wax to begin.

3. Cover working space with newspaper. Place your black outlined piece of paper under your fabric. Make sure your picture is visible so you can use it as a guide.

4. Using the eyedropper, suck up some of the wax and then "draw" your design with the wax on to the fabric. Continue this step until design is on the fabric with wax. Let design cool.

5. Place beet juice in the large cooking pot. Carefully place the fabric into the beet-water. Let it soak for 30 minutes. Wring the picture out and carefully lay on newspaper in your bathtub (or someplace safe for the drying time). Allow it to dry overnight.

6. Carefully pick off the wax. To finish your picture, iron your dry fabric picture and fray the edges on the bottom and sides only. Glue the top edge to the back side of the thin dowel rod. When dry, you can hang up your Russian Batik design.

CRAFT PROJECT **Architectural Eggs**

Russian Orthodoxy has a rich heritage which includes many religious festivals. A week before Easter, for example, is egg decorating time. Some blow out the insides of a raw egg and paint a beautiful scene on the delicate shell. Or the eggs are boiled with onion skins. The next time you make hard-boiled eggs, boil them in a pot of water filled with onion skins. What happens?

Here's another way to enjoy two artistic expressions from Russia. Blow out an egg and paint it black! Why black? This technique is rooted in the Ural Mountains, which Ivan the Terrible gained during his reign. There they would paint a picture with a black background so that it stands out dramatically. During Catherine the Great's reign, this art form appeared on metal trays, which she had several of! Today, the Russians make beautiful paper-mache lacquer boxes using this same Ural Mountain technique.

Materials:
- 5 eggs
- 5 wooden skewers
- Black acrylic paint
- Craft paint brush
- Architectural Pictures *(Student Page 95)*
- Colored pencils in rich colors (metallic needed)
- 1 meat packaging foam dish or a block of Styrofoam from the craft store
- Glue
- Hairdryer
- Polyurethane finishing spray
- Matches
- Gold or white thread

Directions:
1. Blow the insides of the egg out by piercing both ends with a needle and blowing out from one side, gently. Have a small bowl under you to catch the contents. If egg doesn't come out easily, make the holes slightly bigger. Carefully rinse the egg in a gentle stream of water in the sink. Shake out any water inside. Dry off outside with a paper towel.

2. Make an egg-painting center by breaking a skewer in half and sticking it upright in the meat dish. Place the cleaned egg on to the other end of the skewer and you're ready to paint. If you need to turn the egg around, you can turn the skewer and keep your fingers free from black paint.

3. Paint all of the egg black. Let it dry or speed dry it with the hairdryer.

4. Color your architectural Moscow buildings and cut them out. Optional: You may want to paint the onion domes on the Ivan the Great Tower and the top of Saint Basil's Cathedral with gold metallic paint to add a very Russian touch to your eggs. See pictures of these buildings for details.

5. Glue them onto one side of the egg. Smooth each picture on carefully to keep air bubbles from your work. When glue is dry, spray egg outdoors with the polyurethane spray to make it shiny and to secure the edges.

6. When eggs are dry, lift them carefully off the skewer. Cut 5 strands of thread about 8 inches long. Secure both ends onto a match. Slip the match into the top of the egg. The match will shift sideways and keep the loop available. Hang your Russian architectural eggs where everyone can see them and be ready to tell about each building!

Russian Beeswax Candle

Grain, furs, honey and beeswax were some of the cargos loaded onto Kievan ships and sold to Scandinavia and to the Byzantine or Persian empires. The Kievan princes who collected a tribute, which was like a tax, protected these trade routes. These nobles gained great wealth from the items they sold and from this tribute while the peasants did the work of harvesting the grain, hunting the furs, and keeping the bees. If possible, find a local beekeeper who can show you all the work and excitement involved in raising bees!

Materials: ☐ Sheet of beeswax, any color (at craft store)
☐ Thin wick (no wire wick because candle will burn too quickly; at craft store)
☐ Scissors

Directions: 1. Cut a wick the length of the sheet of beeswax plus an inch.

2. Lay the wax down on a table. Press the wick gently along the edge, making sure a small wick is sticking out on the top.

3. Roll the edge over gently so that it is just covering the wick. As you continue to roll it carefully, make sure to press out any air bubbles all the way to the end. Trim wick.

Russian Gingerbread Tradition

In Russian cities the gingerbread was usually baked in carved wooden molds for special occasions and holidays. If you have a cookie dough mold at home, use it with the recipe below.

Materials: ☐ Gingerbread Dough (recipe below)
☐ Cookie dough molds (optional)
☐ Your imagination

Directions: 1. Use your imagination or a cookie mold and design a gingerbread character like the Russian children did! When finished with the gingerbread character, bake at 350 degrees until done (at least 10 minutes depending on size).

Gingerbread Recipe

Ingredients: ¾ cup solid shortening
¾ cup brown sugar
¾ cup dark molasses
¼ cup cold water
1 teaspoon vanilla

4½ cups all-purpose flour
2 teaspoons ground cinnamon
½ teaspoon ground ginger
½ teaspoon ground nutmeg
¾ teaspoon salt

Directions: 1. Beat together shortening, sugar, molasses and water.

2. In a separate bowl, mix flour, spices and salt. Add dry ingredients to the shortening mix and blend together.

3. Take out of the bowl and form a ball. If you are making this ahead of time, put a teaspoon of flour into a zip lock bag and shake. Put the dough in and set in refrigerator up to four days.

CRAFT PROJECT **You Are a Noble, You Are a Peasant**

The life of a peasant was difficult, but the life of a noble had its own challenges. Which life would you choose? Under Ivan the Terrible, the nobles were brutally attacked. But the peasants were never allowed to move and rarely permitted to change jobs. So, which would you choose: the life of a rich noble or the calm life of a peasant? Make costume cut-outs of both. You can stand behind each one and take a picture of yourself as either a noble or a peasant!

Materials:
- ☐ Plastic rectangle tablecloth, any color (inexpensive at party or craft store)
- ☐ Black marker (test to see if it shows up on plastic tablecloth)
- ☐ 1 volunteer
- ☐ Acrylic paints
- ☐ Craft brushes
- ☐ Hairdryer
- ☐ Doorway
- ☐ *DK's Eyewitness Book on Russia*, by Kathleen Berton Murrell (Dorling Kindersley, 2000) for costume ideas

Directions:
1. Measure the distance of your chosen doorway. Fold the tablecloth in half, width-wise, and make sure each half will cover the doorway.

2. Stretch out the plastic tablecloth onto a floor surface. First child must lie down in the center of the tablecloth. Trace the body onto the tablecloth with a black marker.

3. Lie down on the other tablecloth half. Trace body onto the tablecloth with black marker.

4. Using the DK Russia book, or any book on Russian costumes and historical dress, design the dress for the first figure. If you are making a tsar costume, don't forget the pointed-cone crown with the sable-fur trimming along the bottom to make it comfortable. Their robes were also fur-lined as a symbol of wealth. If you're making the male peasant, don't forget the long, belted tunic shirts, the blousy pants, and the leather boots. Female peasants wore kokoshnic hats and long jumpers over the tunic shirts.

    Once you get an idea of what kind of costume your first and second character will have, paint the clothes on the bodies you have traced onto the tablecloth halves. Use a hairdryer if you want the paint to dry faster. DO NOT PAINT THE FACE.

5. Once the clothes and hats (and hair?) are all on your "bodies" and the paint has dried, cut out the face.

6. Secure your figures onto a doorway. Put your face in it and take a picture! You are a tsar! Now you are a Russian peasant!

The Ottoman Empire

CHAPTER **24**

Encyclopedia Cross-References

UBWH 142–143, UILE 252–253, 298–299
KIHW 302–303, 358–359, KHE 101, 182–183, 266

THE OTTOMAN TURKS ATTACK

REVIEW QUESTIONS

Where did the Ottoman Turks come from? *They were nomads from central Asia.*

What religion did the Ottoman Turks follow? *They followed Islam. OR They became Muslims.*

Where did these nomads settle down? *They settled on the edge of the Byzantine Empire.*

What did they do when they settled down? *They grew crops, became shepherds, and traveled around telling stories and singing songs.*

In the story of the thirsty shepherd, what did Allah turn the shepherd and his sheep into? *He turned them into rocks.*

Who were *ghazi*? *They were warriors who conquered unbelievers and spread Islam.*

Who was the Sultan? *He was the king of the Ottoman Turks.*

What was the only city in the Byzantine Empire that resisted the attacks of the Ottoman Turks? *Constantinople resisted them.*

According to the people of Constantinople, when would their city fall? *It would fall when the moon turned dark.*

NARRATION EXERCISE

"The Ottoman Turks started out as nomads in central Asia. They became Muslims and settled down to become shepherds and farmers. Then they began to expand their empire. They conquered many parts of the Byzantine Empire. Only Constantinople managed to resist their attacks." OR

"The Ottoman Turks told the story of the Sheep-Rocks. A shepherd climbed a mountain with his flock of sheep and became thirsty. He asked Allah for water and promised to sacrifice seven of his sheep. Allah sent him water, but the shepherd killed seven bugs instead of seven sheep. So the shepherd and his sheep were turned into rocks."

THE CAPTURE OF CONSTANTINOPLE

REVIEW QUESTIONS

As the Ottoman Empire grew, what happened to the Byzantine Empire? *It began to shrink.*

How did Mehmed the Conqueror behave towards the Byzantine emperor at first? *He pretended to be friends and sent friendly messages.*

What weapons did Mehmed the Conqueror use to attack Constantinople? *He used gunpowder and cannons.*

What is a mercenary? *A mercenary is a paid soldier from another country.*

What is a harbor? *A harbor is a deep quiet body of water where ships can anchor.*

How did Mehmed get by the Byzantine ships to attack the northern wall? *He dragged his warships across dry land.*

What sign of disaster led the Turks and the Byzantine defenders to believe that Constantinople would fall? *The moon turned dark. OR An eclipse happened.*

What did the emperor do just before the last battle against the Turks? *He went to the last Christian service in the Hagia Sophia.*

What did Mehmed and his men do to the Hagia Sophia? *They made it into a mosque.*

What was the new name of the city? *Constantinople became known as Istanbul.*

Because the last remnants of the old Roman Empire were destroyed by the conquest of Constantinople, the conquest is sometimes called "The End of" what? *It is called "The End of the Middle Ages."*

Narration Exercise

"The Ottoman Turks attacked the city of Constantinople. Mehmed the Conqueror shot cannonballs at the city and even ordered his warships to be dragged across dry land. The city was eventually conquered by the Turks. The cathedral, Hagia Sophia, was turned into a mosque, and Constantinople was called Istanbul. Now the last bit of the old Roman Empire was destroyed." OR

"The conquest of Constantinople is sometimes called the End of the Middle Ages because the old Roman Empire was now truly gone. The Ottoman Turks took the city after an eclipse made everyone think that disaster was coming. Mehmed the Conqueror became the new ruler. He renamed Constantinople Istanbul and made its cathedral into a mosque."

SULEIMAN THE LAWGIVER

Review Questions

What did the Ottoman Turks do to improve their new city, Istanbul? *They repaired the broken walls and the streets, dug new wells, and opened the harbors.*

Who was the greatest sultan of the Turks? *Suleiman was the greatest sultan.*

Like Justinian, what did Suleiman do to unite his kingdom and make sure all his people were treated fairly? *He made one set of laws for everyone to follow.*

How could Suleiman tell whether or not his people liked him? *He had spies tell him if his people prayed for him to have a long life. He also traveled around his empire in disguise.*

Who was the Caliph? *He was the head of all the Muslims.*

What three cities did Suleiman's empire include? *His empire included Mecca, Medina, and Jerusalem.*

Suleiman had a dream where two huge lions snarled at him. What did he think that God was telling him to do through this dream? *He thought God was telling him to rebuild the walls surrounding Jerusalem OR protect Jerusalem.*

Suleiman's title had five different parts! Can you remember at least three of those parts? *Suleiman called himself "Slave of God, Master of the World, Shah of Baghdad and Iraq, Caesar of all the land of Rome, and the Sultan of Egypt."*

Was Suleiman's son a good ruler? *No, he was called The Drunkard.*

What happened to the Ottoman Empire after Suleiman died? *It began to shrink and become less powerful.*

"Suleiman the Magnificent was the greatest emperor of the Ottoman Empire. He made one set of laws for everyone to follow and he rebuilt the walls around Jerusalem. He expanded the empire until it was the largest empire in the world. After he died, it began to shrink." OR

"The Ottoman Empire was most powerful when it was ruled by Suleiman the Magnificent. He made one set of laws for his people to follow, he chose governors to watch over different parts of his empire, he had spies tell him if he were popular, and he rebuilt Jerusalem so that the holy city would be protected against invaders."

Additional History Reading

Daily Life in Ancient and Modern Istanbul, by Robert Bator, illus. Chris Rothero (Lerner Publications, 2000). Written on an advanced fourth-grade level, this guide to Istanbul illustrates the city's historical past and includes photographs of its present. (RA 1–4, IR 4–5)

The Ottoman Empire: Cultures of the Past, by Adriane Ruggiero (Benchmark Books, 2002). Written on a fourth-grade level, this is one of the few guides to the Ottoman Empire targeted at young students; too long for a read-aloud, but you can use selected sections. (RA 1–3, IR 4–5)

The Siege of Constantinople: April 6–May 29, 1453, by Tim McNeese (Chelsea House, 2003). Although written for older students, this account of the battle is one of the few available (and does include pictures of the Turkish attack on the city). (RA 1–4, IR 5)

Suleyman the Magnificent and the Ottoman Empire, by Miriam Greenblatt (Benchmark Books, 2002). Part of the "Rulers and Their Times" series, this book is written for slightly older students, but no lower-grade biography of Suleiman is currently available. Use selections as read-alouds. (RA 1–4, IR 4–5)

Turkey: Enchantment of the World, by Tamra Orr (Children's Press, 2003). This heavily photographed guide to Turkey is written on an advanced fourth-grade level, but the chapters about Turkey's history could serve as read-alouds for younger students. (RA 1–4, IR 4–5)

Turkey: Festivals of the World, by Maria O'Shea and Fiona Conboy (Gareth Stevens, 1999). An easy-reader guide to the customs of the Turkish people, much simpler than the Orr volume listed above. (RA 1, IR 2–4)

Corresponding Literature Suggestions

The Girl Who Lost Her Smile, by Karim Alrawi, illus. Stefan Czernecki (Winslow Press, 2000). This picture-book retelling of a legend from Baghdad has very bright color illustrations. (RA 1, IR 2–4)

The Golden Sandal: A Middle Eastern Cinderella Story, by Rebecca Hickox, illus. Will Hillenbrand (Holiday House, 1999). This retelling of the Cinderella story is based on a version coming from Iraq. (RA 1, IR 2–4)

The Legend of the Persian Carpet, by Tomie DePaola, illus. Claire Ewart (G. P. Putnam's Sons, 1993). The story of an Ottoman-era king whose most precious possession is stolen by a thief. (RA 1, IR 2–4)

——————————— **MAP WORK** ———————————

The Ottoman Empire *(Student Page 96, answer 259)*

1. Mehmed the Conqueror took the city of Constantinople for his own and renamed it Istanbul. Circle the city of Istanbul in yellow. Then draw one yellow line through the name "Constantinople."

2. Istanbul is located next to the Black Sea. Color the Black Sea black. (Note: Try not to color over the name, "Black Sea," so you can still read it.)

3. The Ottoman Empire was very large; it included land west and south of the Black Sea, as well as land in Egypt and Arabia. Color the Ottoman Empire green.

COLORING PAGES

The Turks overtaking Constantinople *(Student Page 97)*

Suleiman, great emperor and sultan *(Student Page 98)*

PROJECTS

CRAFT PROJECT **Byzantine Icon**

Special thanks to Father John Matusiak of the OCA Communications Office for the suggestion and directions for this activity.

Icons are special pictures used by Orthodox Christians to help them in worship. Though they do not believe in worshiping the picture, they see its beauty as an aid in both public and private devotional times, reminding the believer of those who have lived well and of what was done for them in the past.

Materials:
- Precut square wooden craft board (available at any craft store)
- Wood stain and sponge brushes
- Spray glue or contact cement
- Spray varnish
- Icon *(Student Page 99)* colored or painted, using gold around the figure and on the halo

Directions:
1. Stain the wood with the sponge brushes. Let dry.
2. Spray the picture with glue and carefully press it onto the wooden board. Smooth the paper to eliminate air bubbles. Let it dry.
3. Spray several coats of varnish on, letting each coat dry before applying the next. Spray varnish prevents smearing. But you may use regular clear (paint-on) varnish for the picture.

COOKING PROJECT **Edible Byzantine Cross, Painted with Egg Tempera**

Icon artists during the Byzantine era worked with paint that was made out of the yolk of an egg. The egg worked to bind the powdered pigments together to form a spectacular and colorful medium that has lasted through the centuries. This form of painting is still practiced today.

Materials:
- Egg yolk
- Food coloring paste (blue, yellow, red and green)
- Sugar cookie dough (your favorite recipe or a pre-mixed roll)
- Flour
- Toothpicks
- Clean, small paint brush
- Cross pattern *(Student Page 100)*
- Cardboard or poster board

Directions:
1. Cut out cross pattern and trace onto cardboard. Cut that out and set aside.
2. Roll out dough, using flour to keep the dough from sticking.

3. Place cardboard pattern of the cross onto the dough and cut around it with a table knife. Repeat until you have several crosses.

4. Egg Tempera recipe: Mix the egg yolk and 1 teaspoon of water together in a small bowl. Make sure no egg white gets in the mixture or it will dry too quickly and colors will not be as vibrant. Using a teaspoon, place a spoon full of the yolk mixture into a bowl. Dip a toothpick into the food coloring paste container and swirl it into a bowl of egg yolk mix until the bright color is throughout the mix. Repeat with each color. (It is fine to use the grocery store food coloring tubes, though colors will not be as vibrant.)

5. Using the small paint brush, create a design using the different colors to decorate your Byzantine cross.

6. Bake according to the cookie directions. Enjoy!

CRAFT PROJECT   **The Circles of Islam**

Geometric designs were used by Islamic artists to decorate walls, floors, book covers, pages, lamps and decorative pots. Geometric designs were popular probably because of the warning Muhammad gave against idol worship. The interpretation was understood as a commandment against drawing anything in a human or animal form. The geometric designs were also said to express the unchanging laws of God, which can be seen in the repeating patterns. The patterned art is purposely two-dimensional to focus the observer on the ideal of the life after rather than illuminating the three-dimensional physical life that surrounds us.

Materials:
- Seven chenille wires, white
- 231 plastic beads, either all one color or several different colors (each circle uses 33)
- Parchment paper
- Straight edge (like a ruler)
- Pencil
- Cookie sheet
- 12 inches of fishing line or clear plastic thread
- Oven set at 350 degrees

Directions:

1. String the seven wires with 33 beads each. Make a circle with the ends twisted to secure the beads.

2. Pull out enough parchment paper to cover the cookie sheet. Draw a straight line down the middle with the pencil.

3. Lay your circles together like the illustration. Try to connect them if it is possible. If not, make sure they are lying securely. The plastic beads will melt and lock together in the oven.

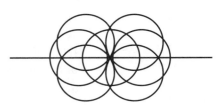

4. Place cookie sheet in the oven. After 10 minutes, use a table knife and pat down gently the beads that are sticking up. Let cook for five more minutes.

5. After 15 minutes, take the cookie sheet out and place outside to cool or in a well ventilated place, like the garage.

6. When it is cool, clip off any ends of the wires that may be visible.

7. You can loop the plastic thread at the top to hang the Islamic circle design.

CRAFT PROJECT **Build Your Own Cannon**

The Ottoman Turks used cannons to crack the walls and crumble the towers of Constantinop[...]
own cannon that fires Ping-Pong balls.

Materials:
- 2 toilet paper tubes
- Plastic wrap
- Tape
- 4 paperclips
- Scissors
- 2 rubber bands
- Ping-Pong ball

Directions:
1. Cut one toilet paper tube lengthwise. Retape the tube so that it is slightly smaller and able to fit inside the other tube.
2. Cover one end of the narrow tube with plastic wrap. Secure with tape.
3. Clip the two paperclips to the open end of the narrow tube. Attach the two paperclips directly across from one another.
4. Clip two paperclips to one end of the uncut tube. Again, place the paperclips directly across from one another.
5. Slide the narrow tube inside the wider tube. The plastic-covered end of the narrow tube should be sliding toward the paperclips at end of the wider tube.
6. Attach a rubber band to a paperclip on the outer (wider) tube. Attach the other end to a paperclip on the inner (narrow) tube. Repeat this step with the other two paperclips.

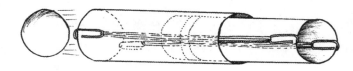

7. Pull the inner tube halfway out of the outer tube. Place the Ping-Pong ball inside the paper-clipped end of the outer tube so it rests against the plastic-wrap covering.
8. Slide the inner tube out so it pulls on the rubber bands. Aim and fire your cannon!

CRAFT PROJECT **Make Turkish Dancing Bears**

At first, the Ottoman Turks were just a ragged band of nomads. Some Turks were shepherds, others were entertainers with trained dancing bears. Make your own Turkish dancing bear. When you're finished, put on a show like the Turks used to do. Turn on some music and make the bear dance!

Materials:
- Dancing Bear template (Student Page 101)
- 4 2" pieces of yarn
- Glue
- Crayons and markers
- Scissors

Directions:
1. Color the dancing bear template. Cut out the front and back body of the bear, and the fronts and backs of its four paws.
2. Glue the four pieces of yarn to the blank side of the front body to make two arms and two legs.
3. Glue the free ends of the yarn to the blank sides of the front bear paws.
4. Glue the back body of the bear to the front body of the bear. The blank sides should be facing each other.
5. Glue the paws together. The blank sides should be facing each other.
6. Let dry.

Make Lion Heads to Guard Your Home

Suleiman had a dream in which two giant lions appeared from behind the city walls of Jerusalem and attacked him. He thought the dream had come from God, so he had the walls around Jerusalem rebuilt. He also commanded that a gate be built with a carved lion on either side, as a reminder of his dream. Make some lion heads to guard the entrance to your home or room.

Materials:
- ☐ 2 white paper plates
- ☐ Crayons, markers, or paint
- ☐ Scissors
- ☐ Brown, red, or orange construction paper
- ☐ Tape or glue

Directions:
1. Decorate the front side of the two paper plates to look like two lion heads.
2. Cut the construction paper into strips. Make snips partway through the strips to make fringe.
3. Tape the fringe along the back side of the plates to make the lions' manes.

GAME ACTIVITY **Play the Sheep-Rock Game**

This game is perfect to play with a group of six or more!

Directions:
1. The players all stand in a circle. One player walks around the outside. He is the shepherd.
2. He approaches one person in the circle. This person is the villager. Here is what they say to one another:

    Shepherd: Good morning, villager.

    Villager: Good morning, shepherd.

    Shepherd: Have you seen my sheep?

    Villager: How is it dressed?

    Shepherd: (Describes what a person near the villager is wearing).
3. As soon as the "sheep" recognizes himself, he starts running around the circle. The shepherd chases after him.
4. If the shepherd tags the sheep before the sheep is able to get back to his original spot, the sheep turns into a rock. He must sit in the center of the circle.
5. If a shepherd doesn't tag the sheep, a sheep-rock is freed from the center of the circle.
6. The villager becomes the next shepherd.

The End of the World

CHAPTER 25

Encyclopedia Cross-References

UBWH 104, UILE 342
KIHW 290–291, 298–299, 308–309, KHE 178–179

THE PLAGUE

REVIEW QUESTIONS

What symptoms did people with the mysterious illness have? *They had headaches and fever; they coughed and sneezed; they had pains in their arms and legs; they had swollen lumps under their arms.*

When people in the villages along the Black Sea grew sick, who did they blame for bringing the sickness? *They blamed the foreigners OR the Italian merchants.*

How did the attackers get the sickness inside the city of Caffa? *They threw dead bodies into the city with catapults.*

By what name did people call this terrible, unstoppable sickness? *They called it the Black Death.*

Giovanni Boccaccio described the Black Death in his book, the *Decameron*. What happened to the pigs he wrote about? *They died after sniffing the clothes of a beggar.*

Boccaccio says that people reacted to the plague in two ways. What were the two ways? *Some people shut themselves in their houses and wouldn't come out. Others pretended nothing was wrong.*

What is the real name for the Black Death? *The Black Death was bubonic plague.*

Years later, what did scientists determine was the real source of the plague? *Fleas on rats spread the disease.*

What were some of the reasons that people of the Middle Ages gave for the plague? *They thought it was caused by God's judgment, earthquakes, evil spirits, and bad food.*

NARRATION EXERCISE

"The Black Death spread all over Europe, Africa, and China. No one knew how the disease was spreading or how to stop it. So many people died that it seemed like the end of the world. Scientists later discovered that the disease was carried by fleas on rats." OR

"A terrible disease called the Black Death caused millions of people to die. It started near the Black Sea. People there thought that Italian traders had caused it. Other people thought that it was a judgment of God. And others thought it was because of evil spirits. The Black Death was really caused by the fleas on rats, and rats were everywhere during the Middle Ages."

A NEW WAY OF LIVING

REVIEW QUESTIONS

What happened to farms during the Black Death? *Fields grew weedy, grain wasn't harvested, animals turned wild or died.*

Why did the peasants and farmers become wealthier after the plague? *Because so many peasants died, workers and farmers were in high demand. They could demand higher wages for their work.*

Why did the noblemen become poorer after the plague? *They couldn't afford to have all their land farmed because the peasants demanded higher wages. So the estates of the noblemen shrank.*

Because so many of the country villages were wiped out, where did the survivors go to live? (Hint: This move is called urbanization.) *They went to cities.*

How did the Black Death change the land itself? *Forests grew up because there weren't enough people to farm the fields.*

What happened to the empty houses in the country? *Peasants moved into some of them and became the new owners.*

How did apprenticeship change after the Black Death? *An apprentice didn't have to study as long to become a craftsman.*

Narration Exercise

"The Black Death changed many things about the Middle Ages. The peasants became wealthier, the noblemen became poorer, and people moved from the country to the city. It was easier to become a craftsman. Woods grew up over land that used to be farmed." OR

"Many people died from the Black Death. There weren't enough farmers to work on the noblemen's land. So the farmers demanded higher wages, and the noblemen could not afford to keep such large farms. People began to move to the cities, and many farms began to grow up into forests. We call the move to the city urbanization."

Additional History Reading

The Black Death, by Tracee de Hahn (Chelsea House, 2001). Written for slightly older students, this book provides details about the plague for those who want to discover more. (RA 1–4, IR 5)

Blacksmith: People of the Middle Ages, by Melinda Lilly (Rourke Book Company 2002). Covers the routine of a rural medieval artisan in easy-to-read text. (RA 1, IR 2–5)

Eyewitness: Medieval Life, by Andrew Langley, illus. Geoff Dann and Geoff Brightling (Dorling Kindersley, 2002). Many photographs and brief paragraphs of text, covering many different aspects of medieval life, including rural and city life and a double-page spread on the plague. (RA 1–3, IR 4–5)

Kids in the Middle Ages, by Lisa A. Wroble (Powerkids Press, 1998). A very simple introduction to daily life in medieval times; large type and nice illustrations. Includes a brief discussion of the Black Death. (IR 1–4)

Medieval Times: Art and Civilization, by Giovanni Di Pasquale (Peter Bedrick Books, 2001). This innovative picture-book covers farm and city life through an examination of famous paintings. (RA 1, IR 2–5)

The Middle Ages, by Jane Shuter (Heinemann Library, 2001). Written on an advanced second-grade level, this simple guide to the Middle Ages discusses both rural and city life and the ways in which both changed in the late medieval period. (RA 1–2, IR 2–5)

Plague, by Katie Roden, illus. Richard Rockwoord (Copper Beech Books, 1996). This briefer, simpler guide to the plague also discusses other epidemics. (RA 1–3, IR 4–5)

Plagues: Natural Disasters, by Victor Gentle (Gareth Stevens, 2001). An illustrated, easy-to-read discussion of various plagues in the ancient and medieval world. (RA 1–2, IR 3–5)

Corresponding Literature Suggestions

The Duchess Bakes a Cake, by Virginia Kahl (Purple House Press, 2002). Okay, this only has a peripheral relationship to the chapter, but there aren't too many good picture books about the Black Death, and this classic rhyming story about a duchess is (at least) set in the Middle Ages (and will give everyone a good laugh). (RA 1, IR 2–4)

Little Johnny Buttermilk: After an Old English Folktale, by Jan Wahl, illus. Jennifer Mazzucco (August House Publishing, 1999). A retelling of an old English tale about country-dwellers. (RA 1, IR 2–4)

The Time Trekkers Visit the Middle Ages, by Kate Needham, illus. Sheena Vickers and Dave Burroughs (Copper Beech Books, 1996). A very easy chapter-book account of time travelers visiting the medieval world. (RA 1, IR 2–4)

The Toy Brother, by William Steig (HarperCollins, 1998). Also has nothing to do with the Black Death, but it's set in the Middle Ages. In this witty picture book, an English alchemist warns his sons not to venture into the laboratory—but his oldest son does and accidentally shrinks himself to the size of a mouse, and the younger son becomes the "big brother." (RA 1, IR 2–5)

MAP WORK

Europe at the Time of the Black Death *(Student Page 102, answer 260)*

1. Color the key:
   a. Find the key and color box 1 blue.
   b. Color box 2 green.
   c. Color box 3 yellow.
   d. Color box 4 orange.
   e. Color box 5 red.

2. Now color the path of the plague:
   a. The areas labeled "1" got the plague in 1347. Color those areas blue.
   b. The areas labeled "2" got the plague in 1348. Color those areas green.
   c. The areas labeled "3" got the plague in 1349. Color those areas yellow.
   d. The areas labeled "4" got the plague in 1350. Color those areas orange.
   e. The areas labeled "5" got the plague in 1351. Color those areas red.

COLORING PAGE   People thought costumes like this kept the Black Death away. *(Student Page 103)*

PROJECTS

CRAFT ACTIVITY   ### Make a Cycle of the Plague Wheel

Materials:
- Photocopy of the Cycle of the Plague Wheel *(Student Page 104)*
- Colored pencils or markers
- Scissors
- Brass plated fastener
- Paper

Directions:
1. Color the pictures on the plague wheel.
2. Lay another sheet of paper on top of the wheel and trace the circle and one of the five wedge shapes.

3. Cut out the wedge shape from the circle you traced. Do not cut past the smaller inner circle. This is the top of your plague wheel.

4. Put the two pieces together and push the brass plated fastener through the middle and fasten.

5. Turn your plague wheel to see the different stages of the Black Plague.

CRAFT PROJECT **Make Black Rat Mask**

Materials:
- Egg carton—cardboard type
- Black pom pom or button for nose
- Round elastic cord
- Black craft wire or fishing line for whiskers
- Scissors
- Black paint
- Glue

Directions:
1. Look at the inside of the egg carton. The two end egg cups will be the rat's eyeholes and the part that sticks up between will be the rat's nose. Cut this part out.

2. Once the mask is free from the rest of the egg carton, cut out the inside of the 2 cups, forming the eye slots.

3. Paint the mask black.

4. Glue on the pom pom or button for the rat's nose.

5. For whiskers, poke the wire through the nose close to the end and bend then glue to secure. Hot glue works well for this purpose. Or, use a needle and fishing line to make your whiskers.

6. Attach the elastic cord to the sides to hold the mask on your face.

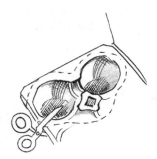

CRAFT PROJECT **Make a Plague Doctor Mask**

Materials:
- Black Flexi-foam craft foam (or black construction paper)
- Scissors
- Hot glue (or tape)
- Round elastic cord
- Beak template *(Student Page 105)*
- Mask template *(Student Page 106)*

Directions:
1. Trace the mask and the beak template onto the foam or construction paper. Cut out mask. Cut out the eye holes and mouth hole.

2. Cut out the beak pieces. Glue (or tape) the two pieces of the top beak together joining edge to edge. Glue a small portion at a time waiting until each piece is dry before gluing the next portion. Use glue sparingly.

3. Glue the bottom beak to the top beak starting at one end and working all the way around to the other end. It may be necessary to trim a little off the tip and end pieces. Glue a small portion at a time waiting until each piece is dry before gluing the next portion. Use glue sparingly.

4. Put the beak through the mouth hole in the mask leaving a very small edge sticking out on the inside of the mask. Glue the beak to the mask along the small edge. Glue a small portion at a time waiting until each piece is dry before gluing the next portion. Use glue sparingly.

5. Attach elastic cord on sides so mask will fit securely on face.

A black, hooded sweatshirt with the hood strings pulled tight so no skin or hair shows and a hat will complete the Plague Doctor suit. Or use your monk's robe from chapter 3.

ACTIVITY PROJECT   Get Rid of the Fleas!

The plague was an infection carried by fleas on rats. Go on a hunt to get rid of the fleas!

Materials: □ Plastic Easter eggs
□ "Fleas" (raisins, chocolate chips, marbles, or M&Ms)

Directions: 1. Put several "fleas" in an Easter egg. Fill as many eggs as you wish.

2. Have your parent hide the eggs in a room of the house.

3. Try to find all the flea eggs. See how fast you can get rid of the fleas. (*Note:* This game is also fun to play with someone else. Who can find more fleas?)

CRAFT PROJECT   Make a "Ward Off the Plague" Necklace

Some people believed they could ward off the plague by wearing or carrying flowers and scented herbs. They thought the scent would keep the plague away. Create your own necklace of herbs and flowers.

Materials: □ Fresh herbs and flower petals
□ Needle and thread
OR
□ 1 teaspoon dried herbs
□ 4" diameter circle of tulle or cloth
□ String

Directions for the fresh herb necklace:

1. Measure a length of string that can slip easily over your head. Cut double that length of thread. (*Note:* Parents may need to assist with steps 2 and 3)

2. Thread the needle. Tie the two ends of the thread together in a secure knot. Push the needle to the middle of the loop so the needle is at the top and the thread is at the bottom.

3. Thread herb leaves and petals on to the necklace.

4. When finished, tie the necklace together with a knot.

Directions for dried herb necklace:

1. Put one teaspoon of dried herbs in the center of the cloth.

2. Gather the sides of the cloth to create a pouch. Tie it off with string.

3. Cut a length of string for the necklace. Tie the pouch to it.

Wear the necklace all day. Remember to smell it frequently to "ward off" sickness!

France and England at War

CHAPTER 26

Encyclopedia Cross-References

UBWH 108 (one reference), UILE 219, 233
KIHW 286–287, 304–305, KHE 176–177

HENRY V AND THE BATTLE OF AGINCOURT

REVIEW QUESTIONS

What two countries quarreled for over one hundred years? *England and France fought the Hundred Years' War.*

What two things did Henry V demand from the king of France? *The land and the king's daughter's hand in marriage.*

Why wouldn't the French king, Charles VI, give Henry V the land? *If he had given Henry the land, he would have been admitting that Henry should have France for himself.*

What did the prince of France (the Dauphin) send to Henry V to insultingly show that Henry V was acting childishly? *The Dauphin sent Henry tennis balls.*

What happened when Henry's army landed in France? *His soldiers got sick, their shoes wore out, and winter came.*

Who won the Battle of Agincourt and the right to rule France—Henry V or the prince of France (the Dauphin)? *Henry V won the battle.*

Did Henry V get to be king of France? *No, he died before the king of France died.*

Who became king of England and France after Henry V and Charles VI both died? *Henry V's son, Henry VI, became king of both countries when he was a year old.*

NARRATION EXERCISE

"England and France had been at war for nearly one hundred years. Then Henry V became king of England, and he wanted to rule France as well. He demanded land in France and the princess of France for his wife. When the king of France wouldn't give Henry what he wanted, Henry invaded France. He won his battle against France at Agincourt." OR

"King Henry V of England wanted to be the king of France as well. He invaded France, defeated the prince, and married the princess of France. He won the right to be king of France after the French king died. But Henry died first. His little boy became king of France and England."

JOAN OF ARC

REVIEW QUESTIONS

Why were the people of France fighting one another? *Some people wanted the Dauphin to be king; others wanted Henry VI to be king.*

What were the French people who wanted Henry VI to be king called? (Hint: They followed the Duke of Burgundy.) *They were called Burgundians.*

What is a civil war? *A civil war is when the people of a country fight against each other.*

What were the two sides of the French civil war? *The French who wanted the Dauphin to rule fought against the Burgundians and the English.*

What city were the two sides fighting over? *They were fighting over Orleans.*

Joan of Arc claimed that God had sent her a vision telling her to do what? *She said that she had to lead the French into battle against the Dauphin's enemies.*

What test did the Dauphin use to see if Joan really was sent by God? *He gave his crown and robe to a friend and hid in the crowd. If Joan were sent by God, she would recognize him even without his royal clothes.*

How did Joan of Arc and her army do at the Battle of Orleans? *They won.*

What was Joan's nickname after this battle? *She was called "Joan, the Maid of Orleans."*

When Joan was captured by the Burgundians, what did Charles VII (formerly the Dauphin) do? *He did nothing!*

What happened to Joan when the English and the Burgundians tried her for witchcraft? *She was found guilty and burned to death.*

After Joan's death, who won the civil war? *Charles VII and his men defeated the Burgundians and the English.*

What happened to Joan twenty-five years after her death? *She was declared to be innocent.*

NARRATION EXERCISE

"Joan of Arc had visions of saints and angels who told her to lead the army of the Dauphin against the Burgundians. She drove back his enemies and he became king of France. But when she was captured by enemies, the king did nothing to help her. She was burned to death. After her death, the king of France defeated his enemies, and finally Joan was declared innocent." OR

"The people of France were fighting against each other over who should be king, Henry VI or the Dauphin. The English and the Burgundians wanted Henry VI to be king of France. Joan of Arc approached the prince of France and told him she was sent by God to lead his army into battle against the Burgundians and the English. Joan was victorious and the prince became king. But when Joan was captured by the Burgundians, he didn't help her."

Additional History Reading

Don't Know Much About the Kings and Queens of England, by Kenneth C. Davis, illus. S. D. Schindler (Harper-Collins, 2002). Two-page spreads give very brief information about British rulers, including Henry V and his son Henry VI. **Out of print.** (RA 1–2, IR 3–5)

Great Events that Changed the World: History As Immediate As the Present, by Brian Delf and Richard Platt (Dorling Kindersley, 1997). This oversized book tells the stories of great events in a running series of illustrations; includes a good clear account of the Hundred Years' War, from the initial sea battles in 1340 to Joan of Arc's execution and the final defeat of the English under Charles VII. (RA 1–3, IR 4–5)

Joan of Arc, by Josephine Poole, illus. Angela Barrett (Random House, 1998). Lovely colored-pencil pictures and interesting text; halfway between Hodges and Stanley (below) in difficulty. (RA 1–2, IR 3–5)

Joan of Arc, by Nancy Wilson Ross (Random House, 1981). This simple biography is good for slightly older readers—probably too long for a comfortable read-aloud, but excellent for third grade and up. (RA 1–2, IR 3–5)

Joan of Arc, by Diane Stanley (Morrow Junior Books, 1988). Beautiful full-page illustrations, but more difficult text than most picture books; better for older readers. (RA 1–3, IR 4–5)

Joan of Arc: The Lily Maid, by Margaret Hodges (Holiday House, 1999). A very brief, picture-book biography of Joan of Arc. (RA 1–2, IR 3–5)

Journey to the Past: Medieval Paris, by Anna Cazzini Tartaglino and Nanda Torcellan (Raintree Steck-Vaughn, 2001). A slightly wordy journey through the famous places and different classes of medieval Paris, but with colorful and engaging pictures; worth looking at the pictures and reading selected text. (RA 1–4, IR 5)

Women in Medieval Times, by Fiona Macdonald (Peter Bedrick Books, 2000). Covers a number of different topics (work, family, dress, sickness, the law) and their relationship to women; some text will be too difficult for young children, but pick and choose those pages which have simpler and larger text. (RA 1–3, IR 4–5)

Corresponding Literature Suggestions

Adventures of Tom Thumb, by David Cutts, illus. Fuka Hervert (Troll, 1989). A simple retelling of this classic English story about a brave (but tiny) young man. (RA 1, IR 2–5)

Henry V, directed by Kenneth Branagh, (MGM/UA 1989). Rated PG-13 for realistic medieval battle scenes. Film adaptation of Shakespeare's play. Preview first; may be inappropriate for some students.

Medieval Tales That Kids Can Read and Tell, by Lorna MacDonald Czarnota (August House Publishers, 2000). Very brief tales along with historical background and tips for kids who want to tell them out loud; includes tales of Joan of Arc. (RA 2, IR 3–5)

Red Balloon, Albert Lamorisse (Doubleday, 1967). A young French boy takes his red balloon on his day in Paris. (RA 1, IR 2–5)

Three Sacks of Truth: A Story from France, by Eric A. Kimmel, illus. Robert Rayevsky (Holiday House, 1993). Hero Petit Jean tends the royal rabbit herd—all ten thousand bunnies! (RA 1, IR 2–5)

————————————————— **MAP WORK** —————————————————

England and France *(Student Page 107, answer 260)*

1. Henry V was king of England. Color England red.
2. Henry V invaded France. Draw a red arrow from England to Agincourt, the location of the major battle between the English and the French.
3. Henry V was the victor at the Battle of Agincourt. Circle Agincourt in red.
4. Trace the Loire River in purple. The Loire divided the territory of the Dauphin (to the south) and the territory of the Burgundians (to the north).
5. Color the territory of the Burgundians dark red (burgundy).
6. Color the territory loyal to the Dauphin blue.
7. Joan of Arc led the Dauphin's army at the Battle of Orleans. Put a blue box around Orleans.

Coloring Page   Joan of Arc was determined to take the Dauphin to the great cathedral at Rheims so he could be crowned king *(Student Page 108)*

CRAFT PROJECT | **Joan of Arc Paper Dolls**

Materials:
- ☐ Joan of Arc Paper Dolls *(Student Pages 109 and 110)*
- ☐ Double-sided tape (optional)
- ☐ Heavy cardstock or lightweight cardboard
- ☐ Coloring supplies
- ☐ Glue, scissors

Directions:
1. Color Joan of Arc figure and clothing.
2. Cut page in half so that figure and armor are on two different half pages.
3. Now glue Joan of Arc figure to cardstock or cardboard. Let dry.
4. Cut out.
5. Cut out clothing and armor. Use double-sided tape to attach clothes to figure. If desired, cut paper tabs on clothing to attach dress without tape.

ART PROJECT | **Sandpaper Print Battle Flag**

The Dauphin's soldiers fought under a battle flag. Design your own flag for battle. You can draw it on a piece of paper or do a fun sandpaper print.

Materials:
- ☐ Scratch paper
- ☐ Sandpaper (150 fine)
- ☐ Crayons
- ☐ Construction paper
- ☐ Paper towels
- ☐ Glue
- ☐ Iron

Directions:
1. Select a design for your battle flag. The simpler the better. Try to pick a symbol that tells something about you and your army (for example, a lion for bravery, a star for beauty, an owl for wisdom, a dog for loyalty, or a rabbit for speed). Work it out on scratch paper first.
2. Copy your design onto the gritty side of the sandpaper. Press very hard with the crayon so that your design is very dark. Try to cover the sandpaper completely.
3. Place a light color of construction paper on top of the gritty side of the sandpaper. Place 2 sheets of paper towel over the construction paper.
4. Iron over the paper towels. Lift the construction to check and see if the iron is too hot (colors blur together) or too cold (not enough color transfer). Iron very quickly—constantly move the iron. (*Note:* Have an adult do this step.)
5. Remove the construction paper. Trim the edges so only the colored parts show. Glue the print onto a piece of colored construction paper.

GAME ACTIVITY | **Bowl for the Crown**

The Dauphin of France sent Henry V a rude insult: tennis balls. The Dauphin said to Henry, "You're acting like a child. Stop running around threatening France, and go play some tennis instead to burn off all that extra energy." Henry was furious! He replied, "Tell the prince that when I have hit these balls with my racquet, I will hit his father's crown right out of bounds!"

Play a game of Bowl for the Crown and have fun knocking over French crowns!

Materials: ☐ Tennis ball   ☐ Tape or glue
            ☐ 12 empty soda cans   ☐ Markers
            ☐ Paper (12 sheets cut to 5 × 8 inches)

Directions: 1. Draw a crown on each of the sheets of paper. The crown should be drawn along the long side of the paper. The paper will be taped around the soda can, so draw an "open" crown (or a line of crown, if you will).

2. Tape or glue the crowns around the soda cans.

3. Set the soda cans in the shape of a pyramid like bowling pins (one can in the front line, two cans in the second line, three in the third line, and four in the fourth line). Set them up outside or at the end of a long hallway.

4. Stand at least ten feet from the crowns, and roll your tennis ball toward the pins. Try to knock down as many as you can. Play a game with someone else. Each player gets two rolls to try to knock down as many pins as they can. At the end of two rolls, record the number of pins that were knocked down. Then reset the pins for the next player. Each player gets 10 turns of two rolls each. The player who knocked down the most pins wins.

ACTIVITY PROJECT The Coronation of Charles VII

Joan of Arc escorted the Dauphin from Orleans to the cathedral at Rheims, where he was crowned Charles VII of France. The crowning, or *coronation,* was a long elaborate process. Act out the coronation with your siblings, friends, or stuffed animals!

Materials: ☐ Siblings, friends, or stuffed animals
            ☐ A pillow
            ☐ The Battle Flag from this chapter, or a white pillowcase to use in its place.
            ☐ A small bottle or jar with vegetable or olive oil in it (you could use water instead)
            ☐ A hat or baseball cap
            ☐ Another hat to serve as a crown, or the crown from the Chapter Thirteen activity
            ☐ One or more brooms or mops
            ☐ A paper towel or wrapping paper tube. Write the word "JOYEUSE" along the length of the tube with a black marker

Directions: 1. Appoint a sibling, friend, parent, or stuffed animal to be Charles VII. Choose a room to be the cathedral at Rheims. Place a pillow in the middle of the floor. "Charles VII" should kneel down (or be placed) on the pillow.

2. Joan of Arc was given a place of honor at the Dauphin's side. Appoint another sibling, friend, parent, or stuffed animal to play Joan of Arc. "Joan" can hold the Battle Flag made in this chapter—or, if you haven't made the Battle Flag, a pillowcase will do!

3. Charles VII took an oath. The medieval French coronation oath was very long and complicated, so you will use a simple "oath" instead. Have your Charles VII repeat, "I will follow all the laws of this country, I will protect my people, and I will protect the Church." (If your Charles VII is a stuffed animal, you will have to repeat the oath for him!)

4. Charles VII received an insignia of chivalry, golden spurs, and a sword from the Archbishop of Rheims. Traditionally, French kings received the sword of the great king Charlemagne at their coronations. But this sword, Joyeuse, was kept at the abbey of St. Denis—and the abbey was in the hands of the English and the Burgundians! So the Archbishop had to substitute another sword. The paper tube is your "substitute sword." Now you will be the Archbishop of Rheims. Take the paper tube, go out of the room, put on your hat (to show that you are now the Archbishop), and come back in. Give the paper tube to Charles VII.

5. The Dauphin had to be anointed with special oil, kept in a crystal bottle at a nearby monastery called St. Remi Abbey. According to legend, this oil had appeared from heaven when Clovis, the king of the Franks, was baptized. Here is the medieval account:

> As Clovis knelt down, a dove, white as snow, descended bearing in his beak a tiny bottle of holy oil. A delicious odor rose from the oil and filled those nearby with joy. The holy bishop took the tiny bottle, and suddenly the dove vanished. Amazed by the sight of this miracle, the King renounced evil and demanded to be baptized!

> You will pretend that your little bottle of oil is this legendary oil, which was called the Sacred Ampoule. The Abbot of St. Remi walked into the cathedral carrying this bottle, surrounded by four carefully chosen noblemen called the "Hostages of the Sacred Ampoule" who rode beside the Abbot from the abbey to the cathedral to protect the sacred oil. They even rode their horses right into the cathedral beside him! You are the Abbot. Go out of the room, put on your hat (to show that you are now the abbot), and walk into the room carrying your Sacred Ampoule. If you have friends or siblings helping you, have one or more "ride" broomsticks beside you to represent the Hostages of the Sacred Ampoule! Now "anoint" your Charles VII. Put a little oil on your finger and touch the top of his head, his chest, his back, both elbows, and both wrists.

6. Now it is time to crown your king. Put the hat or crown on Charles VII's head. Now the Dauphin has become Charles VII of France!

ACTIVITY PROJECT **Find the Dauphin**

The Dauphin disguised himself as a way of testing Joan. If she were really sent by God, she would be able to pick him out of the crowd even if he were not wearing his royal robe and crown. Test your parent or sibling. Can they pick Charles VII out of a crowd?

Materials: Stuffed animals or action figures

Directions:
1. Set up your stuffed animals and action figures in a crowded group in your room. Select which one is going to be the Dauphin. Don't tell anyone.

2. Invite your parent or sibling into the room. Pretend to be a courtier in the room. Announce, "Joan the Maid to see the Dauphin." Have the person guess which one is the Dauphin. Remember: DON'T LOOK AT THE DAUPHIN! You might give him away!

3. For a variation of the game, the person is allowed to ask three yes or no questions before they guess. For example (if you are playing with stuffed animals), "Does the Dauphin have whiskers?" or "Is the Dauphin a bear of some kind?"

War for the English Throne

CHAPTER 27

Encyclopedia Cross-References

UBWH not included, UILE 248–249
KIHW 316, KHE not included

THE WARS OF THE ROSES

REVIEW QUESTIONS

What were the civil wars for the English throne called? *They were called the Wars of the Roses.*

What were the two sides in the civil war called? *They were the Lancastrians and the Yorks.*

Why wasn't Henry VI, the baby son of Henry V, able to rule England when he grew up? *He was more interested in reading and praying than in ruling. When he was older, he went mad.*

When Henry went mad, who did his family ask to become Protector, or substitute king? *They asked the duke of York to become Protector.*

What happened when Henry got better? *The duke didn't want to give up the throne, so Henry VI had to fight to get it back.*

Who attacked Henry VI next? *The duke of York's son, Edward, attacked Henry's forces.*

Who won this battle for the throne? *Edward won and became Edward IV.*

What did Edward IV do that upset the English nobles so much that they put Henry VI back on the throne? *Edward married a woman (Elizabeth Woodville) and gave too much power to her family.*

What did Edward IV do when Henry VI became king again? *He raised an army and took Henry prisoner and then had him killed.*

When Edward's twelve-year-old son, Edward V, became king, why didn't he remain king for long? *His uncle, Richard III, took over and declared himself king of England.*

What happened to Edward V and his little brother? *They mysteriously disappeared.*

What did Henry Tudor do, two years after Richard III became king? *He gathered yet another army and fought against Henry.*

Why didn't King Richard III run away from the Battle of Bosworth Field when he saw that he was losing? *He wanted to die king of England.*

NARRATION EXERCISE

"When Henry VI went mad, the duke of York ruled England for him. The duke didn't want to give up the throne. Henry VI and the duke's son fought over the throne. Then the duke's son, Edward IV, became king. Edward's son became king next. But because he was so little, his uncle Richard took the throne away. Then Henry Tudor took the throne from Richard. These were the Wars of the Roses." OR

"The Wars of the Roses were English civil wars between two sides of the royal family. The two sides were called the Lancastrians and the Yorks. They each wanted a king from their side of the family. The wars finally ended when Henry Tudor became king of England."

REVIEW QUESTIONS

Who were the two sons of Edward IV and Elizabeth Woodville? *The two boys were Edward and Richard.*

Where did little Edward live? *He lived in the country with tutors and a governor to look after his schoolwork.*

When Edward IV died, who did he appoint Protector for his son? *He made his brother Richard the Protector.*

Why did young Edward V's mother and mother's family want him to be crowned king right away? *Because they didn't want his uncle Richard acting as a substitute king. They wanted to help young Edward rule!*

How did Richard find out that young Edward was about to be crowned? *A friend sent him a message.*

What did the queen do when she found out that Richard had taken control of young Edward? *She hid in a church with her other son (Edward's brother).*

Where did Richard insist that young King Edward stay so that he would be safe in London? *He put the young king in the Tower of London.*

Why did Richard's soldiers surround the church where Edward's mother and brother were hiding? What did they want? *They wanted to take Edward's brother to live with Edward in the Tower of London.*

Who soon became king of England? *Richard III.*

So what happened to Edward and his brother? *Nobody knows! OR They were killed.*

NARRATION EXERCISE

"When young Edward V became king of England, his uncle Richard insisted on helping him rule. But Richard really wanted to be king himself! So he put Edward and his younger brother in the Tower of London and surrounded it with armed guards. Then Richard declared himself to be the king. No one knows what happened to Edward and his brother." OR

"After Edward IV died, his son Edward V became king of England. His mother wanted to help him rule, but so did his uncle Richard. Richard took Edward to London and locked him in the Tower with his brother. Then Richard declared himself to be the king of England. The two princes mysteriously disappeared!"

Additional History Reading

Don't Know Much About the Kings and Queens of England, by Kenneth C. Davis, illus. S. D. Schindler (Harper-Collins, 2002). Two-page spreads give very brief information about British rulers, including Henry VI, Henry VII, and the wars they fought. **Out of print,** but available at most libraries. (RA 1–2, IR 3–5)

The Little Princes in the Tower: Mysterious Deaths, by William W. Lace (Lucent Books, 1997). This book, which tells the story of the princes and their disappearance, invites the reader to solve the mystery; it is intended for older readers but can be adapted as a read-aloud. (RA 2–4, IR 5)

Corresponding Literature Suggestions

Bravo, Mr. William Shakespeare! by Marcia Williams (Candlewick Press. 1998). Shakespeare's *Richard III* (among others) in a highly entertaining frame-by-frame retelling, using colorful illustrations with characters speaking lines from the plays; cartoons of Elizabethans commenting on the action enliven the margins. (RA 2–3, IR 3–5)

Music From the Time of Richard III, by "The York Waits: Renaissance Town Band" (Saydisc, 1995). This CD offers twenty-three dances and airs from the days of the Yorks and Lancasters; listen while you read!

―――――――――――――――――――――― **MAP WORK** ――――――――――――――――――――――

England During the Time of the Wars of the Roses *(Student Page 111, answer 260)*

1. Using red, outline the island of Britain (not Ireland) which contains England, Scotland, and Wales. This is where the Wars of the Roses took place.

2. Henry VI's wife ordered that the duke of York's head be put up on the city walls of York. As an added insult, a paper crown was placed upon his head. Underline York in blue. If you want, you can draw a blue crown on top of the city.

3. When Edward IV died, his son Edward V left his home in Mortimer's Cross to go to London and be crowned king. Underline Mortimer's Cross in yellow. Then draw a yellow line from Mortimer's Cross to London to represent young Edward's journey.

4. Richard III imprisoned Edward V and his younger brother in the Tower of London. London is the capital city and the home of the king of England. Put a green star on the city of London.

5. Richard III died defending his crown at the Battle of Bosworth Field. Circle Bosworth in green and draw the Roman numeral "III" overtop of it to show that Richard III met his end there. That was the end of the Wars of the Roses.

COLORING PAGES

Edward V inherited the throne when he was 12 years old *(Student Page 112)*

Richard III had been made Protector, or "substitute king," for Edward V when the king died *(Student Page 113)*

―――――――――――――――――――――― **PROJECTS** ――――――――――――――――――――――

CRAFT PROJECT   Make Banners for the Yorks and Lancastrians

The Yorks had a white rose on their banner and the Lancastrians had a red rose on their banner. Pretend you are creating banners for each family—draw or paint them. For a rose template, see *Student Page 114.*

GAME ACTIVITY   York and Lancaster Checkers

Who will win the English crown: the Yorks or the Lancastrians? Play a game of checkers to determine the victor. If you like, you can tape roses to the tops of the checkers *(see Student Page 115).*

Materials: ☐ Checkers
           ☐ Checkers game board
           ☐ 24 copies of rose checker top *(optional: Student Page 115)*;
              color half red, leave other half white

Directions for Playing Checkers:

Checkers is a board game played between two players. The players take turns moving. When one player can no longer move because all of his pieces are gone or blocked, he loses.

The **board** is square, with 64 smaller squares on it. The squares alternate between light and dark. Play checkers on the dark squares only.

The *pieces* are light and dark (red and white, black and white, or red and black). Place your pieces on the black squares of the board. Each player's pieces should take up three rows.

Moving: Every checker can move one square forward—but only on the dark squares (moving diagonally). You can only move your checker onto a vacant square—unless you plan on jumping your opponent.

Jumping: Capture a checker of the opposite color by jumping over it, diagonally, to the square beyond it. The three squares must be lined up diagonally! An ordinary checker can only jump forward, never backwards, and can only jump one other checker at a time. However, a checker can make successive jumps (jumping one opponent and landing in a blank space, then jumping over another opponent and landing on another blank space, and so forth). When you jump your opponent's piece, take it off the board. Here are several rules to remember: Never jump the same piece twice, in the same move. Never jump your own checkers! If your checker *can* jump, you must take that move! But, if more than one jump is open to you, you can choose whichever jump you please.

Kinging: When a piece reaches the last row of the opposite side of the board (the King Row), it becomes a king. A second checker is placed under that one by the opponent. When a checker is "kinged," its turn is over until the next move. Unlike an ordinary checker, a king can move backwards as well as forwards (but still must move diagonally on black spaces only). A king can also jump backwards as well as forwards. An ordinary checker *can* jump and capture a king.

Red (Lancaster) moves first. Now begin playing! Alternate turns, moving one checker per turn. If you can't move, you have lost the game (and the war!).

CRAFT PROJECT   **Build a Pop-Out Tower of London Card**

Materials:
- ☐ 1 (8½" × 11") sheet of thin cardboard or heavy construction paper
- ☐ 1 (approx. 5" × 8") sheet of thin cardboard or heavy construction paper
- ☐ Markers or crayons
- ☐ Tower of London Template *(Student Page 116)*

Directions:
1. Fold the larger sheet of construction paper in half and open it again.
2. Cut out the Tower of London template in the Student Pages. Color it. Glue it onto the smaller piece of construction paper (the tabs should overhang a little on the short side).
3. Fold the fused Tower in half along the middle turret so it is symmetrical. Fold back the tabs on each side of the Tower toward the blank back side.
4. Glue the tabs to the larger sheet of paper (approximately in the middle of each open side—see diagram).
5. Decorate the inside of the card with trees and grass. Write "The Tower of London" on the inside of the card.
6. On the front side of the card, write the question, "Where did Richard III put young King Edward V?" Now open the card. Watch the Tower of London pop out!

The Princes in the Tower Game

The princes in the tower are surrounded by Richard's men! Can they escape? Play the game and see. This game requires two players: one to be the princes and the other to be Richard's guards.

Materials:
- ☐ Princes in the Tower Game Board *(Student Page 117)*
- ☐ 24 pennies
- ☐ 2 dimes

Directions:
1. Pick who will be the princes and who will be the guards.

2. The princes are represented by two dimes. The guards are the 24 pennies.

3. The princes are placed on any of the points inside the Tower of London (the area marked off by the square). The guard pieces are placed on the empty spaces outside the tower.

4. Guards may move in straight or diagonal lines *toward* the fortress (they can never move backwards). Princes may move in *any direction along the lines* and may eliminate the guards by jumping over them onto an empty space. For each player, one move is one turn. If a prince misses a chance to capture a guard, the prince is taken off the board.

5. Winning the game: Guards win by trapping the princes anywhere on the board, holding every spot in the tower, or removing both princes (see rule 4). Princes win by taking the guards one by one until there are too few left to defend themselves.

The Kingdoms of Spain and Portugal CHAPTER 28

Encyclopedia Cross-References

UBWH 122, 143, UILE 259, 288
KIHW 306–307, 328–329, KHE 109, 174–175, 200–201

FERDINAND AND ISABELLA UNITE SPAIN

REVIEW QUESTIONS

Spain had three kingdoms in it—two large kingdoms and a small kingdom. Can you remember their names? *The two large kingdoms were Aragon and Castile, and the small kingdom was Portugal.*

In exchange for plenty of soldiers, what did King Enrique of Castile promise Pedro Giron? *He promised Giron the king's sister, Isabella, in marriage.*

Was Isabella pleased? *No, she was horrified.*

What happened to Pedro Giron? *He died on his way to the wedding.*

When her brother decided that she should marry the old, fat king of Portugal, what did Isabella do? *She sent a message to Prince Ferdinand of Aragon, asking him to marry her instead.*

When Isabella, queen of Castile, and Ferdinand, king of Aragon, united their two kingdoms, what was their new, large kingdom called? *It was called Spain.*

What was Granada? *Granada was the last part of Spain under Muslim rule.*

How long did Ferdinand and Isabella fight against Granada? *It took them ten years to win.*

What did Ferdinand and Isabella declare Spain to be? *They declared it a Christian kingdom.*

What happened to the Jews who lived in Spain? *They were forced to leave.*

NARRATION EXERCISE

"The king of Castile wanted his sister Isabella to marry a powerful man. But Isabella did not like any of her brother's choices! So she asked Prince Ferdinand to marry her. Eventually they combined their kingdoms into one large kingdom, Spain. They made Spain a Christian kingdom and forced the Jews to leave." OR

"Princess Isabella of Castile decided she would choose her own husband. She married Prince Ferdinand of Aragon. They combined their kingdoms into one, called Spain, and drove out anyone who was not a Christian. They fought for ten years to conquer the last Muslim part of Spain, a fortress called Granada."

HENRY THE NAVIGATOR, PRINCE OF PORTUGAL

REVIEW QUESTIONS

What small country kept its independence from Spain? *Portugal remained independent.*

What foods were the Portuguese known for? *They were known for olives, grapes, and tripe.*

Why was it easy for the Portuguese to build boats and sail them? *Portugal had a long coastline.*

What was the goal of Prince Henry of Portugal? *He wanted to make the Portuguese into great sailors and explorers. OR to have the Portuguese sail farther than anyone else in the world. OR to have the Portuguese sail down the coast of Africa and over to India.*

The Portuguese could get gold, silver, ivory and salt from Africa. What did the Portuguese want to get from India? *They wanted spices such as pepper, cloves, and nutmeg.*

Why was pepper so important? *Spices like pepper covered up bad tastes!*

Why did Muslim traders avoid their trading city in North Africa after Henry and his brothers captured it? *The traders knew that the Portuguese were Christians who had driven the Muslims out of their country.*

When Henry realized that it would be difficult for the Portuguese to trade in North Africa, what did he plan for the Portuguese to do instead? *He planned for them to sail down the African coast and trade directly with the West African tribes.*

What is navigation? *Navigation is following a map to a certain destination.*

What instruments did Henry's sailors learn to use? We read about three. Can you remember at least two? *An astrolabe measured how far the sun or North Star lay above the horizon. A compass had a magnetic needle that always pointed north. A rope with knots helped them to measure the speed of a ship.*

What nickname did Prince Henry earn because of his love for sea exploration? *Henry the Navigator.*

What did Henry's sailors think the waters down south were like? *They thought that the Sea of Darkness was in the south; they thought the waters were shallow; they thought that the seawater boiled; they were afraid that currents would pull them off into nowhere.*

What did Gil Eannes do? *He was the first explorer to venture into the Sea of Darkness.*

Did Henry's ships find their way to India? *No, they never made it all the way around Africa.*

Narration Exercise

"Prince Henry of Portugal wanted the Portuguese to sail to Africa and India. But nobody had ever sailed that far before! They were afraid of the waters down south. Henry trained sailors to navigate and to sail long distances. After many attempts, the Portuguese finally got to West Africa. Prince Henry was called Henry the Navigator." OR

"Henry the Navigator tried to trade in North Africa, but he wasn't successful. He thought if his ships could sail to Africa and India, they could trade for gold, ivory, and spices. So he started a school for sailors, where they could learn how to use compasses and astrolabes. Finally, the Portuguese ships made it to the coast of Africa. But they never got to India."

Additional History Reading

Henry the Navigator: Famous Explorers, by Claude Hurwicz (PowerKids Press, 2001). An easy-reader guide to Henry and the art of navigation. (RA 2, IR 3–5)

Lives of Extraordinary Women: Rulers, Rebels, and What the Neighbors Thought, by Kathleen Krull, illus. Kathryn Hewitt (Harcourt Brace, 2000). Very brief (3–4 pages) and interesting biographies, including Isabella of Castile. (RA 2–3, IR 4–5)

Outrageous Women of the Renaissance, by Vicki Leon (John Wiley and Sons, 1999). Brief, interesting biographies (5–6 pages) of fifteen Renaissance women from ten different countries; readable by advanced third grade and above. Includes Isabella of Castile. (RA 2–3, IR 3–5)

Ten Queens: Portraits of Women of Power, by Milton Meltzer, illus. Bethanne Andersen (Dutton Children's Books, 1998). Ten interesting biographies for reading aloud; each is 8–14 pages, with color illustrations. Includes Isabella, here called Isabel of Spain. (Mentions the Inquisition and some of the punishments inflicted by the inquisitors.) (RA 2–4, IR 5)

Corresponding Literature Suggestions

Bernal and Florinda: A Spanish Tale, by Eric A. Kimmel, illus. Robert Rayevsky (Holiday House, 1994). A poor man courts a beautiful girl in medieval Spain and has to convince her father that he is worthy of her love. **Out of print.** (RA 1–2, IR 3–5)

Three Swords for Granada, by Walter Dean Myers, illus John Speirs (Holiday House, 2002). This chapter book features three cat friends who unite in 1492 to keep Granada free from treacherous rats and invading Spanish dogs; too long to read at one sitting, but a worthwhile read-aloud project for several weeks (RA 1–3, IR 4–5)

——————————— **MAP WORK** ———————————

Spain and Portugal *(Student Page 118, answer 260)*

1. Isabella was from the kingdom of Castile. Underline Castile in purple.
2. Ferdinand was from the kingdom of Aragon. Underline Aragon in red.
3. When Isabella and Ferdinand united their kingdoms, the new kingdom of Spain was created. Color Spain (the kingdoms of Castile and Aragon) yellow.
4. Ferdinand and Isabella now wanted the Islamic kingdom of Granada for themselves. Outline Granada in brown.
5. Ferdinand and Isabella conquered Granada. Color the inside of Granada yellow. Now Spain was complete.
6. The other country on the peninsula is Portugal. Color Portugal orange.
7. Prince Henry the Navigator built a fleet of ships to sail south to Africa and trade for gold, ivory, and salt. Draw the path the Portuguese sailors took to get to Africa. Starting at the dot in Portugal, use orange to connect the dots and trace the southern path of the Portuguese ships.

COLORING PAGE   An explorer using an astrolabe to measure how far the sun or North Star lay above the horizon
(Student Page 119)

——————————— **PROJECTS** ———————————

CRAFT PROJECT **Isabella and Ferdinand Paper Dolls**

Isabella and Ferdinand's marriage was like a fairy tale! But Isabella wasn't a helpless fairy tale princess. Even though she was a woman, she insisted on inheriting the crown. And she and Ferdinand made decisions together.

Materials: □ Colored pencils
□ Scissors
□ Scotch Removable Double-Stick Tape
□ Photocopy of the paper dolls *(Student Page 120)* on card stock
□ Paper doll clothes *(Student Pages 121 and 122)*

Directions: 1. Color the paper dolls and their clothes. Some portraits of the couple show them with dark hair while others show them with reddish-brown hair.

2. Cut them all out.

3. Use the removable double-stick tape to keep the outfits on your dolls.

CRAFT PROJECT **Isabella's Crown Jewels**

Later in their reign, Isabella made a very important investment. Since the war to remove the Moors from Spain had emptied their royal treasury, Isabella gave her jewels to a persuasive explorer who convinced her that he knew a short cut to the spices of India. Do you know this famous explorer's name and what he really found? (For help, look ahead to chapter 31!)

Materials: □ Craft wire
            □ Wire cutters or scissors
            □ Plastic beads of any color (use 8mm or larger)
            □ Plastic pearls

Directions: 1. Wrap a piece of craft wire around your head to get the size. Add one hand's length to one of the ends. Cut that amount off the spool.

2. Find the center of the wire by folding it gently in half. Bend the wire so that you make a triangle at the center point like the diagram.

3. Slip the beads through in the pattern of your choice. Secure the end by wrapping the wire around a bead at the end.

4. Bend the ends to make a hook to secure the crown on your head.

5. For more jewels, refer to Chapter 4 in this activity book. Make some earrings to match your new crown!

ACTIVITY PROJECT **Make Your Own Prince Henry Compass!**

Prince Henry the Navigator had a goal. He realized that if the Portuguese wanted to trade for the gold and ivory of West Africa, they'd have to sail into the unknown. His school of navigational methods used tools that we use today, though they might look a little different! Make a working compass.

Materials: □ A glass or bowl of water
            □ A sewing needle
            □ Small circle of paper
            □ A magnet (Refrigerator magnets may work. If not, try a bar magnet from hardware store.)

Directions: 1. Draw and cut out a small paper circle the size of the illustration.

2. Put the small paper circle on the water in the center of the bowl or glass.

3. Holding the eye of the needle, wipe the magnet down the body of the needle in the same direction. Make 60 swipes over the needle. This magnetizes the needle.

4. Place the needle gently on the floating circle of paper. Twirl the paper and make sure it stays in the center. When it stops, the needle should point to the magnetic north. *Note:* Obviously, one end of the needle points north and the other end points south. To figure out which way is north, stand facing either direction the needle is pointing. Think to yourself: does the sun rise on my right and set on my left? If so, you are facing north. If not, you're facing south; turn around and face north.

You may wonder what makes a magnetized compass needle face north. The earth itself acts like a magnet—it has a magnetic north and south pole. No one knows exactly why the earth has a magnetic pull, but some people believe it is caused by the molten iron (extremely hot liquid iron) deep in the earth.

ACTIVITY PROJECT | Find the North Star

Before any of Prince Henry's navigators could use their navigational instruments, they had to be able to find the North Star! Use your new compass and find the North Star out of your window tonight.

Materials:
- ☐ Your Prince Henry Compass or any compass
- ☐ Piece of paper and pen
- ☐ Dark, clear, night sky, preferably far from street lights (but not necessary)

Directions:
1. Using your Prince Henry Compass, find the northern direction and use a window or stand outside looking into the northern sky.

2. Look for the star constellation called The Big Dipper. It looks like a dipper you might use in an old well. The end two stars in the bowl of the dipper (opposite the handle) are called the "pointers" because they point to the North Star. Follow the pointer stars and draw a mental line from them until you come to a bright star. That is the North Star.

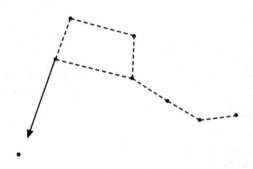

3. Draw a picture of the sky you see from this position. Try again on a clear night the following week and see where the North Star is. Has it changed places?

Note: If you live close to the ocean or a big lake, you may find classes in simple navigational skills taught by retired Coast Guard servicemen. These are often a delight!

African Kingdoms

CHAPTER 29

Encyclopedia Cross-References

UBWH 82,122, UILE 260–263
KIHW 192–193, 264–265, 344–345, KHE 117, 208

GOLD, SALT, AND GHANA

REVIEW QUESTIONS

Why was it difficult to travel down into the south of Africa? *The Sahara Desert blocked the way.*

Why was Africa called the Dark Continent? *Almost no one had traveled down into Africa.*

What part of Africa did the people live in kingdoms with houses, roads, palaces, and schools? *The African kingdoms in West Africa.*

What was the land of Ghana called by Europeans? *It was called the Land of Gold.*

What did Arab traders give in exchange for the gold? *They traded salt.*

Can you describe Taghaza, the city of salt mines? What was the water and food like? What were the houses made out of? *It was hot and dry. Everything was salty. The water and food had salt in them. Trees and plants had died. The houses were made out of salt blocks covered with camel skins.*

How did Ghana become rich from gold and salt when they didn't have any gold and salt of their own? *They taxed the gold and salt that went through their country.*

Can you remember any part of the description of the king of Ghana given by Al-Bakri? *He had horses draped in gold cloth; he wore gold necklaces and bracelets and a gold cap; he had ten pages; his noblemen had gold braided into their hair; officials sat at his feet; he was guarded by dogs with gold and silver collars.*

Why did African Muslims attack the cities of Ghana? *Ghana's king would not convert to Islam.*

NARRATION EXERCISE

"Gold was mined south of Ghana. Salt was mined in northern Africa. Ghana, which was located in the middle of Africa, became a very rich kingdom because the king collected money from every pound of salt and gold that passed though its borders. Ghana had an enormous army and a big capital city, and the king dressed in gold." OR

"Ghana was one of the richest kingdoms in Africa. The king charged a toll for every pound of gold and salt that passed through the kingdom. Since Ghana was located in the middle of those two trades, it made a lot of money! It grew until it went all the way to the coast. But then African Muslims began to attack it."

MANSA MUSA OF MALI

REVIEW QUESTIONS

When Ghana began to crumble, what kingdom took over the gold and salt trade? *Mali took over the gold and salt trade.*

What religion did the people of Mali follow? *They followed Islam.*

Who brought Islam into West Africa? *Muslim traders who brought salt from the north also brought Islam.*

What did the kings of Mali build? *They built schools, universities, and libraries.*

According to Ibn Battuta, how did the people of Mali show respect for their kings? *They groveled in front of them; they wore dirty clothes, rolled up their trousers, and put their elbows, turbans, and hats on the ground; they would throw dust on themselves when the king spoke to them.*

What was the name of the most famous king of Mali? *Mansa Musa was the most famous king of Mali.*

Because Mansa Musa was a good Muslim, what was he determined to do (even though it would take two years)? *He was determined to travel to Mecca. OR make a pilgrimage OR make a hajj.*

Who went with Mansa Musa on his journey to Mecca? *Mansa Musa took his wife, children, sisters, brothers, cousins, nieces, uncles, cooks, servants, bodyguards, palace advisors, soldiers, and holy men—sixty thousand people!*

What did Mansa Musa give away on his way to Mecca? *He gave away gold.*

Mansa Musa did four things when he arrived in Mecca. Can you remember three of them? *He washed himself, put on a white robe (took off his royal robes and gold), prayed in the holy city, and gave away alms.*

How did maps change after Mansa Musa's journey? *Maps began to show the kingdom of Mali; Europeans now knew about the country.*

Narration Exercise

"After Ghana crumbled, Mali grew larger. It was an Islamic kingdom. The people respected their king so much that they threw dust on themselves when he spoke! The greatest king of Mali was Mansa Musa. He made a pilgrimage to Mecca." OR

"Mansa Musa was the most famous king of Mali. He was a Muslim and he made a pilgrimage to Mecca with sixty thousand people. He gave away huge amounts of gold. When he got to Mecca, he prayed in the holy city and gave away alms. After that, Mali started to be shown on maps."

THE SONGHAY EMPIRE

Review Questions

Ghana was famous for its salt and gold. Mali was famous for its kings. What was Songhay known for? *Songhay was known for its large size.*

What was Songhay's best-known city? *The best-known city of Songhay was Timbuktu.*

What was the name of the traveler who wrote a book about his travels in Africa and the Songhay Empire? (Hint: His last name sounds like the continent where he traveled.) *Leo Africanus wrote a book about his travels.*

Where was Leo Africanus born, and why did he leave his country? *He was born in Granada. He had to leave when Ferdinand and Isabella conquered the country and added it to their Christian kingdom.*

Can you remember two things that Leo Africanus describes in his book? *He describes clay houses and stone temples; the food eaten by the people (grain, milk, butter, melons, cucumbers, meat, pumpkins, rice); a gold bar that weighs a thousand pounds; the king's leadership in battle (he and the soldiers ride horses, the servants ride camels; they shoot poisoned arrows); priests, judges, and scholars; the value of books; singing and dancing in the streets.*

As a result of Leo Africanus's book, what happened to the Songhay Empire? *It was invaded. The sultan of Morocco wanted the gold and salt mines for himself.*

"Songhay grew powerful after Ghana and Mali. The people of Songhay liked books and learning, so they had many schools. The largest city was Timbuktu. The army rode into battle on horses and camels and shot poisoned arrows. Songhay was invaded by the sultan of Morocco because he wanted gold mines." OR

"Leo Africanus was born in Portugal, but he went to North Africa with his parents. He traveled to Songhay and wrote a book about it. He described the city of Timbuktu and wrote that the people liked to sing and dance in the streets. After he wrote his book, more people knew about West Africa. The sultan of Morocco invaded Songhay and won because his soldiers had guns and cannons."

Additional History Reading

Ancient West African Kingdoms, by Jane Shuter (Heinemann, 2002). One of the History Opens Windows series, this introduction to West African kingdoms includes the three countries studied in this chapter along with others. (RA 1–3, IR 3–5)

Ancient West African Kingdoms: Ghana, Mali, & Songhai, by Mary Quigley (Heinemann, 2002). Written on a fourth-grade level, this text covers the history of each of these countries; selected sections would work well as read-alouds. (RA 1–3, IR 4–5)

Ghana: Countries of the World, by Lucile Davis (Bridgestone Books, 1999). An easy-reader introduction to the culture of this African country. (IR 1–4)

Heroes: Great Men Through the Ages, by Rebecca Hazell (Abbeville Press, 1997). Twelve interesting read-aloud biographies, including that of Mansa Musa. (RA 2–3, IR 4–5)

Kings and Queens of West Africa, by Sylvaine Diouf (Franklin Watts, 2000). A number of sections on different kingdoms and rulers; fairly simple reading, so you can select one section for a child to read. (RA 1–2, IR 3–4)

Sundiata: Lion King of Mali, by David Wisniewski (Houghton-Mifflin 1999). A picture-book account of the great thirteenth-century Mali king who grew from a weak child into a strong warrior. (RA 1–2, IR 2–5)

Corresponding Literature Suggestions

Africa Calling, Nighttime Falling, by Daniel Adlerman, illus. Kimberly M. Adlerman (Whispering Coyote Press, 1996). The animals of the African desert at nighttime, in a picture book for beginning readers. (IR 1–2)

Ashley Bryan's African Tales, Uh-Huh, by Ashley Bryan (Atheneum, 1998). This collection of African tales is illustrated with woodcuts, but is intended for oral telling; the stories are fairly lengthy. (RA 2–3, IR 4–5)

Mansa Musa: The Lion of Mali, by Khephra Burns, illus. Leo and Diane Dillon (Harcourt Brace, 2001). A detailed picture-book account of the mythical boyhood of Mansa Musa; written on a third-grade level. (RA 1–2, IR 3–5)

Traveling Man: The Journey of Ibn Battuta, 1325–1354, by James Rumford (Houghton Mifflin, 2001). A simple, lyrical retelling of Ibn Battuta's journal, describing his travels to Africa, India, and Persia; lovely illustrations and maps, with Arabic script surrounding many of the pages. (RA 2, IR 3–5)

West African Kingdoms (Student Page 123, answer 261)

Note: Parent may need to assist the child with this activity.

The three African kingdoms all occupied the same land, one after another. Outline the border of each kingdom:

1. Using the key, find the empire of Ghana.
2. Now outline the border of the empire of Ghana in red.
3. Using the key, find the empire of Mali.
4. Now outline the border of the Mali empire in green.
5. Using the key, find the Songhay empire.
6. Now outline the border of the Songhay empire in blue.

COLORING PAGE   The greatest king of Mali was Mansa Musa. *(Student Page 124)*

PROJECTS

CRAFT PROJECT   **Make Salt Blocks**

Salt was a valuable trade item for northern Africa. Salt was cut into blocks in the mine, making it easy to carry, measure, and transport. There was so much salt in northern Africa, that some buildings were made of salt blocks and covered with camel skins. Make your own salt blocks. If you want, make a building out of the blocks (though you would need two ice cube trays full of salt to do this).

Note: Save your salt blocks for use in the Fast Tax Game (at the end of this chapter). You will also use them in a Chapter 42 activity.

Materials: □ Salt
　　　　　　□ Ice cube tray (in a pinch, use a Styrofoam egg carton)
　　　　　　□ Water

Directions: 1. Fill the ice cube tray with salt. Pour a very small amount of water into each cube—just enough to dampen the salt.
　　　　　　2. Leave the ice cube tray in a sunny spot (for a couple of days) until the water has evaporated.
　　　　　　3. Pop out the mini salt blocks.

CRAFT PROJECT   **Make an African Spear**

Spears were used for hunting and fighting and sometimes in ceremonies and festivals. Make your own African spear. Lean your spear next to your chair at mealtime and against your bed at night. What if a gazelle wanders by? You need to have your spear ready!

Materials: □ 3 or more paper towel tubes　　　　　□ Markers
　　　　　　□ Colored construction paper　　　　　□ Sharpened pencil
　　　　　　□ Lightweight cardboard (like a cereal box)　　□ Scissors
　　　　　　□ Strong tape (like clear packing tape or duct tape)　□ String

Directions: 1. Cut a triangle for the spear's point from the cardboard. It should be about 3 inches at the base.
　　　　　　2. Cut two short slits opposite each other at the end of one of the paper towel tubes.

3. Slide the spear point into the slits. Secure with tape if necessary.

4. Draw feathers on colored paper and cut them out. Make as many as you like.

5. At the top of each feather, make a hole with the pencil point.

6. Tape the paper towel tubes together to make a spear of desired length. The spear tip should be at the top end.

7. Tie the feathers to the spear with the string. Secure the string with tape.

CRAFT PROJECT **Make Your Own Gold Nuggets**

Southern Africa was filled with gold. The traders traveled north through the African kingdom of Mali. Make your own gold nuggets.

Note: Save your nuggets for the Fast Tax game in this chapter. You will also use them again in a Chapter 42 activity.

Materials: □ 12 small rocks
□ Glue
□ Gold glitter

Directions: 1. Rub glue on the rocks. Roll the rocks in glitter.

CRAFT PROJECT **Make an African Mask**

Masks are often worn in rituals that bring in the change of seasons, protect crops, heal the sick, or guide a dying person to the next world. Make an African ritual mask.

Materials: □ Paper grocery bag   □ Glue
□ Paint or marker   □ Scissors
□ Dried beans (optional) □ Stapler
□ Raffia or yarn

Directions: 1. Cut the bottom of the paper bag so that it rests on top of the head and falls slightly below the chin.

2. Cut a pair of eyeholes and a mouth hole.

3. Paint the mask. It can be painted to look like the face of a human or the face of an animal. Don't try to use realistic colors. You can paint a blue lion or an orange-striped face. You can also decorate your mask by gluing dried beans to it.

4. Cut the raffia or yarn into lengths of about 6 inches. Gather a small bunch of it and knot one end. Staple the knotted end to the top of the bag to make a tassel.

5. Staple raffia or yarn to the underside of the bottom of the bag. The raffia should drape down the neck, brushing the shoulders. (See illustration.)

GAME ACTIVITY **Hunt the Rhino**

This game needs seven or more players, so it is ideal for a large family or co-op. For centuries children have played this game to learn hunting skills. The rhinoceros is an animal found in Africa. It was hunted for its valuable horn, but today it is protected by the government because there aren't very many rhinos left.

Materials:
- ☐ 2 scarves or bandannas
- ☐ Watch or timer

Directions:
1. Choose one player to be the hunter and one player to be the rhinoceros. Everyone else stands in a circle around the two players.
2. Blindfold the hunter and the rhino with the scarves and spin them around. Let go; the hunter and the rhino are allowed to move anywhere within the circle. The object of the game is for the hunter to tag the rhino. The players in the circle are not allowed to touch the hunter or the rhino, but they are allowed to make animal noises to distract them.
3. If the hunter catches the rhino, two new players take over. If the rhino manages to avoid the hunter for a set period of time (30 seconds to 1 minute), the rhino wins and a new hunter is chosen.

ACTIVITY PROJECT **Gold and Salt: The Fast Tax Game**

The West African kingdoms became rich from the gold and salt trade. Although they had little gold and salt of their own, they taxed traders that passed through their kingdoms. The path through these kingdoms was the quickest route from northern to southern Africa. Play the Fast Tax game and see whether it is better to pay a tax or take the long way around.

Materials:
- ☐ Timer
- ☐ 12 pieces of gold (gold nuggets from chapter project or you can use pennies or gold foil candy like Werther's Originals)
- ☐ 12 salt blocks (from chapter project or you can use sugar cubes or Legos)
- ☐ 2 bowls

Directions:

Set Up: Place the 12 pieces of gold in a bowl at one end of the house. Place the 12 salt blocks in a bowl at the other end of the house (as far apart as possible—consider using an upstairs and a downstairs). Have a parent stand halfway between the two locations with a timer.

Object of the Game: The goal of the game is to have the fewest points. Points are subtracted by successfully transporting blocks of salt and nuggets of gold.

Scoring: You start with an automatic 20 points. For every gold nugget you successfully place in the salt bowl, subtract 1 point. For every salt nugget you place in the gold bowl, subtract 1 point. For every 20 seconds of time you take, add 2 points.

Rules: You are only allowed to carry two salt blocks or gold nuggets at one time. If you decide to take the direct route from the gold bowl to the salt bowl, you must pay the tax. Give one nugget or salt block to your parent as you pass him/her. If you want to avoid the tax, you must run all the way around the house once before you are allowed to go to your destination.

How to Play: Start at the salt bowl. Your parent yells "go" and starts the timer. Take two blocks of salt and go to the gold bowl. If you take the direct route, give your parent one salt block as you pass by. If you take the long route, circle the house but don't pay the tax when you pass your parent. Drop the salt blocks in the gold bowl. Now grab two gold nuggets and take them to the salt bowl. You can take the direct route and pay the tax or you can take the longer, tax-free route. Continue playing the game until you have placed all the gold nuggets in the salt bowl and all the salt nuggets in the gold bowl. When you have finished, yell "stop" so your parent knows when to stop the timer. Tally your points.

Play the game several times: Play one time using only the direct, taxed route every time. What is your score? How much gold and salt does your parent get? Play one time using only the long, tax-free route every time. Which way has the better score? Play a game where you use a combination of the tax-free and the taxed routes. Can you improve your score?

India Under the Moghuls

CHAPTER 30

Encyclopedia Cross-References

UBWH 152, UILE 264–265, 300–301
KIHW 321, 360–361, KHE 218–219, 234–235, 265

THE MOGHUL DYNASTY

REVIEW QUESTIONS

Do you remember which Indian king brought the small kingdoms of India together into one empire? *Chandragupta united the small kingdoms of India.*

Who brought the Gupta empire to an end? *The Huns invaded India.*

After the Hun invasion, what was India like? *It had many different small kingdoms.*

Why were the people of India suffering? *India had had floods, famines, and disease.*

What empire did Babur the Tiger come from? *He came from the old Ottoman Empire.*

Who was he descended from? *He was a descendent of Genghis Khan.*

What Indian city did Babur invade? *He invaded Delhi.*

How did he defeat the Sultan's elephants? *His men rode horses that were quicker than the elephants, and his men also had muskets.*

Why were the Hindu kingdoms especially frightened of Babur's rule? *They thought that Babur would be cruel to Hindus because he was Muslim.*

How did Babur treat the people under his reign? *He allowed Hindus to practice their religion; he made sure that the laws were obeyed; he made sure children learned how to read and write.*

What did Babur do to remind himself of his homeland? *He planted a beautiful garden by the river.*

Name one thing that Babur did in his garden. *He built water wheels pulled by buffalo; he planted flowers, cypress trees, and fruit trees; he put marble benches in his garden.*

What did he call his garden in Agra? *He called it the Garden of Scattered Flowers.*

What is the name of the Indian dynasty that Babur the Tiger began? *He began the Moghul dynasty.*

NARRATION EXERCISE

"Babur the Tiger was an Ottoman Turk who decided to take the kingdom of India for himself. He united India under his dynasty, the Moghul dynasty. He was a fair and just ruler. But he missed his homeland, so he planted a beautiful garden to remind him of it. He called it the Garden of Scattered Flowers." OR

"Babur the Tiger invaded India and united all the kingdoms again. He was a descendent of Genghis Khan, and he had been driven out of his own kingdom. When he ruled India, he allowed people to worship in their own way, and he made sure that laws were followed. But he didn't like India very much. He thought that it was hot and dry, so he planted a garden with water wheels, flowers, and trees in it."

REVIEW QUESTIONS

How did Babur's oldest son, Humayan, die? *He fell and hit his head on the steps of his library.*

What was the name of Babur's grandson, the famous ruler of India who is the subject of so many stories? *He was called Akbar.*

How large was his empire? *It covered half of India.*

How did Akbar remain popular with his Hindu subjects? *He married a Hindu princess and allowed Hindu worship to continue.*

In the story, what did everyone think of Gulshan the servant? *They thought he was bad luck.*

How did Akbar plan to prove to his servants that Gulshan was indeed not bad luck? *Akbar would make Gulshan his servant for a day. Then when nothing bad happened, it would prove to everyone that Gulshan was not bad luck.*

Can you remember two of the bad things that happened to Akbar while Gulshan was waiting on him? *He had a hair in his bread; he was bitten by a sand fly; the peasants in the north rioted; there were maggots in the meat; his favorite horse went lame; his son fell and cut his arm.*

The minister Birbal freed Gulshan from his death sentence by proving that someone caused more bad luck than Gulshan. Who was that person? *The emperor Akbar caused bad luck for Gulshan by sentencing him to death!*

NARRATION EXERCISE

"Babur's son was a weak emperor who died when he hit his head on the library steps. But his grandson Akbar made the empire huge and strong. He was a fair ruler who married a Hindu princess and let Hindus worship. Many stories were told about Akbar and his Hindu minister Birbal. One was 'The Bad-Luck Servant.'" OR

"Gulshan was a servant in the emperor Akbar's palace. Everyone thought he was bad luck, so Akbar decided to prove that he wasn't. Gulshan came to wait on Akbar, but then all sorts of bad things happened! So Akbar agreed that Gulshan was bad luck. He sentenced him to death. But then his minister, Birbal, said that Akbar had brought even worse luck to Gulshan—because now Gulshan was about to be executed! So Akbar decided to let Gulshan go free."

Additional History Reading

Count Your Way through India, by Jim Haskins, illus. Liz Brenner Dodson (Carolrhoda Books, 1990). Each page of this simple guide to the history and culture of India has two–three paragraphs of text written on an advanced second-grade level, along with both Arabic and Indian numerals. (RA 1–2, IR 2–4)

India (Countries of the World), by Michael S. Dahl (Bridgestone, 1997). Focuses on the modern culture of India, with occasional glances back at the past. (RA)

India: Let's Investigate Nations, by Adele Richardson (Creative Education, 2001). A heavily photographed walk through the subcontinent of India, with many pictures of landscape, animals, and ancient sites; clear read-aloud text. (RA 1–2, IR 3–5)

Corresponding Literature Suggestions

The Foolish Men of Agra and Other Tales of Mogul India, by Rina Singh, illus. Farida Zaman (Key Porter Books, 1998). A lively and enjoyable retelling of ten folktales about Akbar, the Moghul king of India. (RA 1–2, IR 3–4, although most children will need help with the unfamiliar Indian names)

Premlata and the Festival of Lights, by Rumer Godden (Greenwillow Books, 1996). This chapter book for slightly older readers tells the story of a young Indian girl attending the festival of the goddess Kali. (IR 4–5)

The Rumor: A Jataka Tale from India, by Jan Thornhill (Maple Tree Books, 2002). A hare thinks that the sky is falling, but a wise lion explains that she has only heard a mango falling from a nearby tree. Beautiful illustrations and fairy-tale text in this traditional Indian tale. (RA 1, IR 2–5)

Savitri: A Tale of Ancient India, by Aaron Shepard, illus. Vera Rosenberry (Albert Whitman & Co., 1992). This story of a princess who saves her husband is taken from the Mahabharata, an ancient Indian epic. (RA 1–2, IR 3–5)

Stories from India, by Vayu Naidu (Raintree/Steck Vaughn, 2000). A read-aloud collection of tales from ancient and medieval India. (RA 1–3, IR 3–5)

―――――――――――――― **MAP WORK** ――――――――――――――

The Moghul Dynasty in India *(Student Page 125, answer 261)*

1. India borders three bodies of water: the Bay of Bengal to the east, the Indian Ocean to the south, and the Arabian Sea to the west. Outline the coast of India in dark blue. Begin where the Ganges River meets the Bay of Bengal and end where the Indus River meets the Arabian Sea.

2. Circle the name "Bay of Bengal" in yellow. Do the same for "Indian Ocean" and "Arabian Sea." Then fill in the three circles with yellow.

3. Color all the surrounding water in light blue (outside of the yellow circles).

4. Babur the Tiger conquered the city of Delhi and named himself its emperor. Delhi, now called New Delhi, is also the capital of India today. Put a red box around the city of Delhi and draw a red star above it.

5. The capital city of Moghul India was Agra. Babur the Tiger built a beautiful garden there. To signify the breathtaking garden in Agra, circle the city in green and color it in. (If you want, you can also draw flowers around the city, because Babur called his garden the Garden of the Scattered Flowers.)

6. Babur came to India from the Mongol lands in the north. Beginning at the top right-hand side of your map, draw a red arrow from the top (north) border of the map, down across the Ganges, and point the end of the arrow at Delhi.

COLORING PAGES

Moghul King: Akbar's empire covered half of India. *(Student Page 126)*

Babur's garden: The remains of the garden of Ram Bagh are found today in Agra, India. In this picture of Babur's Garden, drawn from a medieval tapestry, Babur is directing his men to make another garden in the dry ground. *(Student Page 127)*

COOKING PROJECT **Indian Dal**

Dal is the Indian word for lentils. It is cooked almost daily in every Indian home. As a result, there are many different ways to prepare dal. Try this dal and rice dish—use red lentils, also known as Indian lentils, to make the dish more authentic.

Ingredients:
1 tablespoon olive oil
1 large onion, thinly sliced
1–2 cloves garlic, minced
1 cup brown rice, uncooked
1 tablespoon curry powder

2 teaspoon mustard seeds
1 teaspoon salt
½ teaspoon black pepper
1 cup lentils
4 cups water

1 (14 ounce) can of diced tomatoes or 3–4 fresh tomatoes, diced
½ cup chopped cilantro (optional)

Directions:
1. Sauté the onions and garlic in olive oil until the onions are soft.
2. Add rice, curry, mustard seeds, salt, and pepper. Sauté one minute.
3. Add water and lentils; bring to a boil.
4. Simmer 40 minutes. Add tomatoes and simmer an additional 20 minutes.
5. Remove from heat. Stir in cilantro. If desired, top each serving with a dollop of sour cream.

GAME ACTIVITY **Elephants and Horses**

You need six or more players to play this game, so it is ideal for a large family or co-op. The Sultan of Delhi had a huge army of a hundred thousand men and a thousand war elephants. Babur the Tiger had only twelve thousand men, but they were mounted on quick horses. Play a game to see who will win: Babur's horses or the Sultan's elephants.

Materials: ☐ 6 scarves or bandanas (or as many scarves as you have players)

Directions:
1. Choose two players to be the horses. The other four players are the elephants. (*Note:* If you are playing with a group larger than six people, there should be twice as many elephants as there are horses).
2. Have everyone tuck a scarf in their back pocket or back waistband. The horses are allowed to run normally, but the elephants must hop on one foot. The elephants must also put their left hand on their right shoulder (or vice versa). They may only try to catch a scarf with their free hand.
3. The object of the game is to remove the scarves of all the elephants or all the horses. Once all the scarves of either the elephant or the horse team are removed, the other team wins. Play the game. Is it better to be slow and numerous like the elephants or few and quick like the horses?

CRAFT PROJECT **Make Babur's Garden of Scattered Flowers**

Babur planted a beautiful garden on the banks of the river in his capital city, Agra. The garden reminded him of his homeland. Build your own garden of Ram Bagh (or, as Babur called it, the Garden of Scattered Flowers). You can do it all on a plate!

Materials:
- Plate (paper plate would work)
- Sand
- Potting compost
- Pebbles
- Sticks
- Dried flowers and moss
- Leaves and flowers
- Modeling clay

Directions:
1. Place a layer of sand on the plate and cover with a layer of compost.
2. Use small pebbles to lay a path.
3. Make some bean poles from twigs tied with thread and press them firmly into the earth.
4. Use some moss to create a hedge.
5. The garden is now ready for the vegetables to be "planted."
6. A small-leaved plant stem can be wound around the bean pole and a larger leaved plant stem can be laid on the earth.
7. Clay models of leaves can be laid among the leaves.
8. Clay models of flowers or small dried flowers can also be used in the garden.

ACTIVITY PROJECT **Gulshan for a Day**

Gulshan was a servant in the palace of the emperor Akbar. What would it be like to be Gulshan for a day? You would have to do nice things for the emperor: serve him breakfast, get him his morning slippers, and open the door for him. Pretend you are Gulshan and that your parent is the emperor or empress of India. Every time your parent asks you to do something, say "Yes, Your Majesty!" and do it right away. Try to think of nice things to do for your parent that would make his or her life easier.

Exploring New Worlds

CHAPTER 31

Encyclopedia Cross-References

UBWH 140–141, UILE 289, 296–297
KIHW 340–341, KHE 207

CHRISTOPHER COLUMBUS

REVIEW QUESTIONS

Why was trade with Africa easier once the Portuguese began sailing down the West African coast? *They could carry goods by sea rather than taking them through the hot dry desert.*

What hazards did merchants traveling to India face? *It was a long rough journey; they had to fight off bandits and war bands; they had to face hostile Ottoman Turks.*

How did Christopher Columbus plan on getting to India? *He thought he could reach India by traveling west into the Atlantic Ocean.*

What shape did he believe the world to be? *He believed the world was round.*

What did Columbus need to get from the king of Portugal or Ferdinand and Isabella before he could go on the expedition? *He needed money to pay for the ships.*

Why did the king of Portugal refuse to buy ships for Columbus? *He thought that Columbus would run out of food and water on the long journey.*

Why did Isabella decide to help Columbus? *She knew that the journey could make Spain very rich.*

What were Columbus's three ships called? *They were called the Nina, the Pinta, and the Santa Maria.*

What did Columbus pass on his way out of the Spanish harbor? *He passed ships loaded with Jews leaving Spain.*

What happened to the sailors after they had been sailing for a long time? *Many of them got scurvy because they hadn't eaten fresh fruit or vegetables.*

When Columbus landed on the islands off the coast of Florida, why did he call the people there "Indians"? *He thought he had landed on islands off the coast of India.*

What gifts did these "Indians" bring to Columbus? *They brought him balls of cotton thread, parrots, sweet potatoes, and green peppers.*

What two land masses lay between Columbus and India? *North and South America were in the way.*

What explorer finally sailed around Africa and reached India? *Vasco da Gama made it all the way around Africa.*

NARRATION EXERCISE

"Christopher Columbus believed the world was round and that he could find a route to India by sailing west. King Ferdinand and Queen Isabella gave him money for three ships. He never found India, but he did find a whole new continent! Five years later, Vasco da Gama sailed around Africa and reached India." OR

"Christopher Columbus sailed across the Atlantic Ocean hoping to find a new route to India. He did not find it, because a new continent was in the way. He bumped into North America! He called the people Indians, because he thought he had reached India. But others realized that he had found a new continent."

VESPUCCI AND MAGELLAN

REVIEW QUESTIONS

Which explorer first realized that Columbus's new land was not India or Asia, but a whole new continent? *Amerigo Vespucci realized that North America was a new land.*

Where did Amerigo Vespucci sail? *He sailed down South America and up the coast of North America.*

Why did more people read about Amerigo's voyages? *He wrote and published many accounts of his travels.*

The new land was named after Amerigo Vespucci. What was it called? *It was called America.*

What journey did Ferdinand Magellan hope to complete? *He wanted to sail past the Americas to get to India.*

How did Magellan plan to get through South America? *He thought he could find a river that cut all the way across it.*

How did Magellan finally get through South America? *He found a river in South America that allowed him to cut through the continent to the other side. OR He passed through the Straits of Magellan.*

What did he call the ocean on the other side of South America? *He called it the Pacific because it was so calm.*

What do we call the river that cuts through the southern tip of South America? *We call it the Straits of Magellan.*

Magellan reached two groups of islands before his ship got to India. Can you remember the name of one group? *Magellan reached the Marianas and the Philippines.*

Did Magellan's ship ever reach India? *Yes, but Magellan was killed in the Philippines.*

NARRATION EXERCISE

"Amerigo Vespucci realized that the land that Columbus's ship had found was not Asia, but a new continent. The land was called 'America,' after Amerigo. Then Ferdinand Magellan found a way to India by passing through South America and across the Pacific Ocean. He died before he reached India, but one of his ships and thirty-five men got there." OR

"Amerigo Vespucci sailed up and down the coasts of North and South America. He realized it was not Asia, but a new continent. Ferdinand Magellan set out to sail to India by cutting through South America and sailing further west. He went through the Straits of Magellan and then kept sailing west until he got to the Philippines. He died there, but his ship sailed around the whole world!"

Additional History Reading

Christopher Columbus and the Discovery of the New World, by Carol Gallagher (Chelsea House Publishers, 2000). An excellent longer biography of Columbus, written for advanced third-grade or fourth-grade readers. (RA 2–3, IR 3–5)

Christopher Columbus: First Biographies, by Jan Gleiter and Kathleen Thompson, illus. Rick Whipple (Raintree Steck-Vaughn, 1995). The story of Columbus's thirteen-year-old son Fernando, who went with his father on his fourth attempt to find a route to the Indies. Simple and interesting. (RA 1, IR 2–4)

Columbus, by Ingri and Edgar Parin D'Aulaire (Doubleday & Co., 1955). A classic in its own right, this D'Aulaire picture book describes each of Columbus's journeys. (RA 1–3, IR 4–5)

The Discovery of the Americas, by Betsy and Giulio Maestro (Lothrop, Lee & Shepard, 1991). Begins with an account of early America and then describes the different journeys of exploration, from the Vikings to Magellan. Simple and interesting reading. (RA 2, IR 3–5)

Explora-a-Maze, by Robert Snedden (The Millbrook Press, 1998). Brief accounts of the voyages of Leif Eriksson, Marco Polo, Columbus, Vasco da Gama, Magellan, and later explorers—each with its own maze! (RA 2, IR 3–5)

Ferdinand Magellan, by Jon Noonan (Crestwood House, 1993). This biography of Magellan is written on a third–fourth grade level but could be a worthwhile read-aloud over several days. (RA 1–2, IR 3–5)

Ferdinand Magellan and the First Voyage Around the World, by Jim Gallagher (Chelsea House Publishers, 2000). A slightly longer biography which begins with a brief discussion of the spice trade and Marco Polo's journeys to the east. (RA 2–3, IR 4–5)

Follow the Dream: The Story of Christopher Columbus, by Peter Sís (Alfred A. Knopf, 1991). Simple and beautifully illustrated story of Columbus's wish to explore, with one–three lines of text per page. (RA 1–2, IR 2–4)

Forgotten Voyager: The Story of Amerigo Vespucci, by Ann Fitzpatrick Alder (Carolrhoda Books, Inc., 1991). Written for slightly older readers, this book on Vespucci explains why he thought Columbus had discovered a new continent; Chapter Four would make a good stand-alone read-aloud. (RA 2–3, IR 4–5)

A Long and Uncertain Journey: 27,000-Mile Voyage of Vasco da Gama, by Joan Elizabeth Goodman (Mikaya Press, 2001). A detailed picture-book account of da Gama's voyage, with a fold-out map. (RA 2–3, IR 3–5)

Magellan: Ferdinand Magellan and the First Trip Around the World (Exploring the World), by Michael Burgan (Compass Point Books, 2002). Briefer and more highly illustrated than the Noonan biography listed above, this biography focuses less on Magellan's life and more on the trip around the world. (RA 2, IR 3–5)

Meet Christopher Columbus, by James T. de Kay (Random House, 2001). A Landmark Books biography; clear and interesting, written for third-graders. (RA 2, IR 3–5)

A Picture Book of Christopher Columbus, by David A. Adler, illus. John & Alexandra Wallner (Holiday House, 1991). A simple retelling of the life of Columbus, from his childhood through his voyages to America. (RA 1, IR 2–4)

Three Ships for Columbus, by Eve Spencer (Raintree Steck-Vaughn, 1993). An easy-reader account of Columbus's first voyage. (IR 1–3)

Vasco da Gama, by Tanya Larkin (PowerKids Press, 2001). This brief biography is written for young children; large print without much detail, but the background paper is distracting. (RA 1–2, IR 3–4)

Vasco da Gama and the Portuguese Explorers, by Jim Gallagher (Chelsea House Publishers, 2000). This longer, more difficult, and more interesting biography tells both of da Gama's voyage and of earlier Portuguese attempts to sail around Africa. (RA 2–3, IR 4–5)

Who Really Discovered America? by Avery Hart (Williamson Publishing, 2001). Gives the evidence for each "discoverer" of America and challenges the reader to decide who should be awarded the title of "first." (RA 2–3, IR 4–5)

Young Christopher Columbus: Discoverer of New Worlds, by Eric Carpenter (Troll Associates, 1992). A very simple Troll First-Start Biography about Columbus's boyhood and first voyage. (IR 1–3)

Corresponding Literature Suggestions

Brendan the Navigator: A History Mystery about the Discovery of America, by Jean Fritz (Paper Star, 1999). This easy-to-read story recounts the tale of St. Brendan, an Irish monk who was rumored to have sailed to America long before Columbus. (RA 2–3, IR 4–5)

Follow the Dream: The Story of Christopher Columbus, by Peter Sís (Knopf, 1991). A particularly good biography of Columbus, which presents both fact and legend (distinguishing the two) along with lov illustrations that show Columbus's imaginings about the ocean to the west. A New York Times Best Illus trated Book of the Year. (RA 1–2, IR 3–5)

The Four Voyages of Christopher Columbus, by Christopher Columbus, trans. J. M. Cohen (Penguin, 1992). This is the Penguin classic edition of Columbus's own journal; although it is intended for adults, children will enjoy hearing actual sections of Columbus's diary read aloud in his own words. (RA 2–5)

To the Edge of the World, by Michele Torrey (Knopf, 2003). In this chapter book, intended for slightly older students, a Spanish orphan joins Magellan's crew and travels to the Spice Islands. Entertaining and interesting; a good family read-aloud. (RA 1–4, IR 5)

Where Do You Think You're Going, Christopher Columbus? by Jean Fritz, illus. Margot Tomes (Putnam, 1980). Another story-like biography, longer and more detailed than the Sis biography listed above; a modern classic in its own right. (RA 1–3, IR 4–5)

Who in the World Was the Forgotten Explorer? The Story of Amerigo Vespucci, by Lorene Lambert (Peace Hill Press, 2005). Follows Vespucci from his childhood in Italy to his discovery of new lands for Spain and Portugal. (RA 1–2, IR 3–4)

―――――――――――――――― **MAP WORK** ――――――――――――――――

Routes of the Great Explorers *(Student Page 128, answer 261)*

Trace the journeys of Christopher Columbus, Vasco da Gama, and Ferdinand Magellan.

1. Christopher Columbus tried to find a new western trade route to India. Underline India in green.

2. Trace the path of Columbus's journey. Using green, begin at the Iberian Peninsula, where Spain and Portugal are located. Follow the dotted line across the Atlantic Ocean. Columbus thought he had reached India, but he had really landed off the coast of Florida.

3. Trace the path of Vasco da Gama in blue. Da Gama found a new trade route to India by sailing around the tip of Africa. Begin again at the Iberian peninsula. Then follow the dotted line along the coast of Africa.

4. Ferdinand Magellan sailed all the way around the world. Trace his journey around the world in red. Begin at the Iberian peninsula and follow the line down to the tip of South America. Then continue to the middle of the Pacific Ocean (the ocean that Magellan named!). Now because this is only a flat map and the world is actually round, move your crayon or marker to the right hand side of the page. Continue to the islands to the south of China.

COLORING PAGE   One of Columbus's three ships was the *Santa Maria. (Student Page 129)*

―――――――――――――――― **PROJECTS** ――――――――――――――――

CRAFT PROJECT **Make a Hydro-Jet Boat**

The wind pushed the big sails of Columbus's ships, propelling them forward. Build a boat that propels forward because of a different method. When you mix baking soda and vinegar, a gas is produced. The gas flows out the straw in the rear of this boat, pushing the boat forward.

Materials:
- 1 plastic 16 ounce soda bottle with cap
- ¼ cup vinegar
- 1 tablespoon baking soda
- Plastic straw
- White glue

1. Poke a hole in the bottom edge of the plastic bottle.

2. Insert the straw into the hole leaving one inch hanging out.

3. Seal the air cracks around the straw with white glue. Let the glue completely dry before continuing. Apply a second layer of glue if necessary.

4. Pour the vinegar into the bottle. Add baking soda and quickly put the cap back on the bottle.

5. Place the hydro-jet boat in a tub of water and watch it go!

   Note: You can put blue and/or green food coloring in the water to make it look like the boat is in the ocean!

COOKING PROJECT **Sweet Potatoes**

Columbus and his men claimed the islands for Spain. But he was puzzled. He saw no gold, no pepper, no nutmeg, no riches. Instead, the people of the islands brought him balls of cotton thread, green and yellow parrots, and strange foods—sweet potatoes and green peppers.

Ingredients: Sweet potatoes (as many as you like)

Directions:
1. Poke holes in the potatoes and then wrap the potatoes in aluminum foil.

2. Bake at 420°F for one hour (more or less, depending on the size of the potato. A potato is done when a knife slides easily through the center of the potato.)

3. Once the potatoes are finished, cut them length-wise in half and put your favorite topping on them: butter, cinnamon, maple syrup, cheddar cheese, brown sugar, or pecans.

ACTIVITY PROJECT **Explorer Scramble**

The explorers are all scrambled and they need your help! Unscramble the answers to these questions and print them neatly in the blanks. *(Student Page 130)*

ACTIVITY PROJECT **Are the Natives Friendly?**

When explorers returned home, they reported on what they had found. They talked about how they discovered this new land, what it looked like, what the native people were like, what you could eat there, and more. Take an exploration of your own. Visit a "new land" and then report back to the king or queen (your parent) who sent you.

Visit the house of a neighbor or family friend. Take some things with you that you might need on your journey. Here are some things you may want to include: a water bottle, a snack, a map, a peace offering for the natives (flowers or brownies or a card), and a notebook and pencil for taking down your observations. When you reach the new land, jot down your observations in the notebook: What does the home look like? How many people are there? What is the weather like?

Then interview a native of this new land. Ask them about where and how they live. What do they eat? Where do they get their food? Are there any animals in this new land? What type of clothes do they wear? Do they have any special traditions for holidays? How long have they been in this land? Have they ever traveled to a distant land?

When you return home from your journey, report back to the king and queen. Tell them all that you saw and found. Use your notes as your guide. If you want, you can write up the report and present it to the king and queen.

The American Kingdoms

CHAPTER 32

Encyclopedia Cross-References

UBWH 81, 125–127, 138–139 UILE 180–181, 199, 278–283
KIHW 80, 150–151, 208–209, 268, 278–279, 301, 322–323, 326–327, 335 KHE 32, 86–87, 128–129, 196–199

THE MAYANS OF CENTRAL AMERICA

REVIEW QUESTIONS

Why do we sometimes still call Native Americans "Indians"? *Columbus named them "Indians" because he thought he had reached India.*

What is the bridge of land that links North and South America called? *It is called Central America.*

What was the name of the first great empire of Central America? *The first great empire was called the Mayan Empire.*

What peninsula did the Mayans live on? *They lived on the Yucatan Peninsula.*

Who lived in the Mayan cities? *Kings, noblemen, and governors lived in the cities. Farmers and craftsmen lived in the jungles.*

Name one way the Mayan kings looked "godlike." *They filed their teeth into fangs and painted their faces. They had pointed heads and eyes that were crossed.*

How much power did the Mayan kings have? *They were allowed to have complete power.*

What unpleasant duty did the king have before a battle? *He had to shed some of his own blood.*

What happened to the losers of the Mayan ball game? *Their heads were cut off.*

Name two reasons the Mayan cities crumbled away into the jungle. *The cities grew so big that the ground around them couldn't grow enough food to support all the city people; hurricanes and earthquakes toppled buildings; people were tired of the cruel kings; the Aztecs were attacking.*

NARRATION EXERCISE

"The Mayan Empire was a large empire in Central America. The Mayans thought that their kings were gods. The kings had pointed heads and crossed eyes and were extremely powerful. The empire lasted for hundreds of years before it crumbled from earthquakes and attacks from other tribes." OR

"The Mayans of Central America built great pyramids and large cities. One of their favorite sports was a ball game where the winner was given gold necklaces and the losers had their heads cut off."

THE MARVELOUS CITY OF TENOCHTITLAN

REVIEW QUESTIONS

Why did the Aztecs decide to build Tenochtitlan in the middle of a lake? *The priests saw an eagle sitting on a cactus with a snake in its talons. OR They received a message from the gods.*

Can you name two of the three ways that the Aztecs made the island dry enough to build houses on? *They hauled basketfuls of earth and stone from the land around the lake and dumped them on the beaches; they pulled basketfuls of mud from the lake bottom and filled in the swamps; they cut poles, drove them into the bottom of the lake, attached reed mats to the poles to make fences, and filled the fences with dirt.*

What were the streets of Tenochtitlan like? *They were canals.*

How did the Aztecs of Tenochtitlan get food? *They bought food from people living around the lake and grew crops on the lake itself.*

How did the Aztecs grow crops on the lake? *They covered the lake with mats with dirt on top. Then the plants grew on the mats and their roots stretched down into the lake water.*

What did the Aztecs eat? *They ate vegetables, but also water lizards, fish, salamanders, frogs, fish-eggs, algae pressed into cakes, ducks, birds, deer, rabbits, and fermented cactus juice.*

What brand-new food from cacao plants did the Aztecs learn how to make? *They learned how to make chocolate.*

How could the Aztecs keep people from crossing over the earthen roads into their city? *They built moats filled with logs. When they rolled the logs away, no one could come in.*

Were the Aztecs well-liked by the neighboring tribes? *No, they were disliked for their cruelty.*

NARRATION EXERCISE

"The Aztecs were a warlike tribe who often fought with the neighboring tribes. They built the city Tenochtitlan on a swampy lake by filling the wet places with dirt. They learned to grow crops on the water and often traveled through their city by canoe. They also learned to make chocolate." OR

"The Aztecs received a message from the gods telling them to build a city on a marshy lake. The Aztecs were able to grow crops on the lake. One of the crops, cacao trees, was used to make chocolate. The Aztecs were very powerful, but the tribes around them hated them because the Aztecs kidnapped their men, women, and children for sacrifices."

THE INCAS

REVIEW QUESTIONS

Where did the Incas live? *They lived in the mountains on the western coast of South America.*

What do we call this area today? *We call it Peru.*

Why did the Incan god Inti send his son and daughter to the earth? *He sent them to teach people to build cities, wear clothes, and live in peace.* OR *He sent them because the people on earth were living like animals.*

According to legend, how did Manco Capac know where to build the city Cuzco? *His gold staff leapt from his hand and stuck in the ground.*

Can you repeat one part of the description of the city of Cuzco? *Cuzco had straight streets, paved with cobblestones; it had stone houses built without mortar; the houses had small doors and no windows because of the cold; the city was laid out in the shape of a puma.*

What did the Incan king Huayna Capac build that made trade and travel easy within the empire? *He built good, wide roads.*

Can you remember two kinds of goods traded by the Incas? *They traded cloth made from llama wool and sheep wool, pottery jars made in the shape of animals and men's heads, and gold and turquoise jewelry.*

How did Huayna Capac's city governors send messages to one another? *They tied complicated knots in ropes that messengers carried from one city to another.*

Why was the Incan empire so weak when the Spanish explorers arrived? *The empire had been divided by Huayna Capac and his two sons were fighting with one another. The two kingdoms became weaker and poorer.*

Narration Exercise

"The Incan empire of South America had a legend saying that the son of the sun god chose the site of their capital city of Cuzco. Cuzco was shaped like a puma. The great Incan king Huayna Capac made the Incas into a huge empire and built good, wide roads for traders and messengers. But after he died, the empire became poor and weak." OR

"Huayna Capac was a great king of the Incan empire of South America. He lived in the capital city, Cuzco. Cuzco was made out of stones without mortar and was shaped like a puma. The Incas traded cloth and jewelry and traveled all through their empire on wide roads. But when the king died, he divided the kingdom between his two sons. They fought with each other and made the empire weak. So when the Spanish arrived, they were able to destroy the Incan empire."

Additional History Reading

The Aztecs, by Peter Chrisp (Raintree/Steck Vaughn, 2000). Using both photographs of ancient objects and drawings, this book describes the culture of the Aztecs and the complications of exploring it beneath the foundations of Mexico City. (RA 1–3, IR 4–5)

Explore a Tropical Forest: A National Geographic Action Book, by Barbara Gibson (National Geographic Society, 1989). This complicated, absorbing pop-up book leads the reader through a Central American tropical forest. The text is on an advanced second-grade level. (RA 1–2, IR 2–5)

Hands of the Maya: Villagers at Work and Play, by Rachel Crandell (Henry Holt, 2002). A simple, photographic picture book about modern Mayan Indians and their daily lives. (RA 1, IR 2–5)

Inca Town, by Fiona MacDonald, illus. Mark Bergin (Franklin Watts, 1999). A detailed exploration of the city of Cuzco, with beautiful color drawings of temples, forts, houses, workshops, and more. Cutaway illustrations show what happens inside each building! (RA 1–3, IR 4–5)

Machu Picchu: The Story of the Amazing Incas and Their City in the Clouds, by Elizabeth Mann, illus. Amy Crehore (Mikaya Press, 2000). This beautifully illustrated advanced picture book describes not only the ancient Inca city, but also the roads that connected the different parts of the empire, burial customs, fine Inca weaving, and much more. (RA 1–3, IR 4–5)

The Maya: First Reports, by Petra Press (Compass Point Books, 2001). A simple guide to ancient Mayan civilization, written on a second-grade level. (RA 1–2, IR 2–4)

Tikal: The Center of the Maya World, by Elizabeth Mann, illus. Tom McNeely (Mikaya Press, 2002). Part of the same series as the Machu Picchu volume recommended above, this beautiful book describes Mayan history, religion, life, and more. Includes a fold-out illustration of the city. (RA 1–3, IR 4–5)

Corresponding Literature Suggestions

Cuckoo (Cucú), by Lois Ehlert (Harcourt Brace, 1997). A Mayan tale retold, with Spanish and English on facing pages. (RA 1, IR 2–5)

Fiesta Femenina: Celebrating Women in Mexican Folktale, by Mary-Joan Gerson, illus. Maya Christina Gonzalez (Barefoot Books, 2001). These retellings of Central American folktales include stories from the Aztec,

Mayan, and Zapotec traditions; generous use of Spanish words, with a glossary and pronunciation guide supplied. (RA 2–3, IR 4–5)

Mario's Mayan Journey, by Michelle McCunney (Mondo Publishing, 1997). A young boy falls asleep and then wakes up to discover himself in the country of the ancient Mayans. (RA 1, IR 2–4)

Moon Rope (Un lazo a la luna), by Lois Ehlert (Harcourt Brace, 1992). A Peruvian story retold, with Spanish and English on facing pages. (RA 1, IR 2–5)

Musicians of the Sun, by Gerald McDermott (Simon & Schuster, 1997). An Aztec tale, brightly illustrated and very simply retold. (IR 2–3)

My Song Is a Piece of Jade: Poems of Ancient Mexico in English and Spanish, by Toni de Gerez, illus. William Stark (Little, Brown & Co., 1984). This bilingual book reprints ancient poems handed down in the Toltec culture of central Mexico, just north of Tenochtitlan. (RA 1–2, IR 3–5)

Rain Player, by David Wisniewski (Clarion Books, 1995). A young Mayan boy plays a game against the rain god to bring rain in a drought. (RA 1, IR 2–4)

So Say the Little Monkeys, by Nancy Van Laan, illus. Yumi Heo (Atheneum, 1998). A Brazilian folktale retold for beginning readers. (IR 1–2)

MAP WORK

The Mayan, Aztec, and Incan Empires *(Student Page 131, answer 261)*

First, let's outline North, Central, and South America:

1. Outline the continent of North America (the part that is on your map) in blue. (**Note:** Stop outlining once you reach the Mayan empire.) Underline the words "North America" in blue.

2. Outline the continent of South America in green. (**Note:** Stop outlining where the narrow strip of land pinches off next to Central America.) Underline the words "South America" in green.

3. Outline the strip of land that connects the continents of North and South America in pink. We call this land Central America. (**Note:** Don't forget to include the edges of the Mayan empire!)

Now color the great American kingdoms:

4. Color the Aztec empire orange.

5. The capital of the Aztec empire was Tenochtitlan. Circle the city of Tenochtitlan in red.

6. Color the Mayan empire brown.

7. Color the Incan empire yellow.

8. The capital of the Incan empire was Cuzco. Circle the city of Cuzco in red.

COLORING PAGE   Mayan carvings *(Student Page 132)*

PROJECTS

ACTIVITY PROJECT **Mayan Numbers**

Our number system is based on 10, perhaps because we have ten fingers. The Mayan number system is based on 20 (maybe because 10 fingers + 10 toes = 20). The Mayan number system is considered one of their greatest achievements because any whole number could be expressed using place notation. This system allowed the Mayans to write numbers in the millions using the place value and just three symbols. (For an excellent and brief explanation of the Mayan number system, see Steven Fought's article, available online at: http://mathforum.org/k12/mayan.math/.)

Mayan numbers are written from top to bottom. Fill in the missing numbers on the Mayan Numbers pages *(Student Pages 133 and 134)*.

MATH ACTIVITY Mayan Mathematics

Now use your chart to do the Mayan Math Page! *(Student Page 135)*

ACTIVITY PROJECT Grinding Maize

Maize was the main food of the Mayans and the Aztecs and is still a very important crop today. The women would grind the maize into meal or flour every morning using a metate (may-TAH-tay). The metate consisted of a flat stone called a metlatl and a long cylindrical stone, like the rolling pins we use today, called a metlapil, which means "son of the metate." The women put the maize on the metlatl and rolled the metlapil over it until it was like flour. The flour was used to make tortillas. After the Spanish came to Mexico, they started using metates. They called the top part "mano" which means hand. Metates are still used today.

Materials:
- ☐ Popcorn kernels
- ☐ 2 large rocks or one rock and pavement

Directions:
1. Get a handful of popcorn kernels to use as maize.
2. Find one large flat rock to grind the maize on or use a sidewalk or driveway.
3. Find a large rock you can hold in your hand or with both hands.
4. Try to grind the popcorn until it looks like flour. Be careful not to smash your fingers!

ART PROJECT Make an Aztec Jaguar Mask

The jaguar was feared and respected by both the Aztecs and the Mayans. When a warrior proved he was very brave, he was rewarded by getting to wear the jaguar mask and robe.

Materials:
- ☐ Brown sack
- ☐ White paper or card stock
- ☐ Scissors
- ☐ Orange and brown paint
- ☐ Black, brown and orange markers

Directions:
1. Cut jaguar ears in the bottom of the sack and fold up (see example).
2. Cut eye and mouth holes.
3. Mix a little brown paint with orange to make a jaguar color and paint the entire sack and let dry.
4. Use the paper or card stock to make jaguar teeth and glue those to the inside of the sack so they show through the open mouth.
5. Draw a jaguar nose and whiskers using a black marker.
6. Make jaguar spots using black, brown and orange markers.

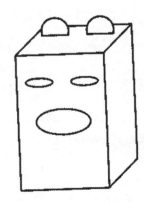

Make a Mayan Codex

The Aztec and Mayan people used books called codices for keeping records. Making the paper for a codex was very hard work because it was made from the bark of fig trees. The handmade paper was folded accordion style and painted on both sides using natural colors. Everything was outlined in black, and then the codex was covered with a protective coating of paste.

The Mayans printed their records using a kind of picture writing called "glyphs." Some glyphs, like a picture of a tree, represented a word. Other glyphs represented a thought, like a shield and knife for war. The Spanish destroyed most of the Mayan books because they didn't understand the glyphs and thought they were evil.

Pretend you are a Mayan and plan the story you want to tell on your codex. Think about the pictures that you will need to tell your story. If you want to tell about a bountiful crop of maize, you will need to show the planting, growing, and harvesting stages. Maybe you had to fight the crows to keep them from eating your maize. Use Mayan numbers from the provided chart to show how much maize you planted, how many days before it sprouted, how many days before it was ripe and the amount of maize you harvested. Or you might want to tell about a battle!

Materials:
- Brown wrapping paper or grocery sack
- Scissors
- Colored pencils or markers
- Mayan number chart (*Student Pages 133 and 134*)

Directions:
1. Cut a strip of brown wrapping paper approximately 8½" wide and 20" long.
2. Put the 8½" ends together and fold in the middle. Then fold the ends back to make an accordion with four sections.
3. Use your markers and colored pencils to make your codex.

COOKING PROJECT **Aztec Hot Chocolate**

The Mayans and Aztecs often used cocoa as a sacred drink. Cortez first tasted chcolati when Montezuma served it at a feast for the conquistadors in the early 1500s. Chcolati means "cacao and water." The Aztecs often put spices in their cocoa mixture, and sometimes even added chili peppers and mushrooms! Spanish explorers and traders took cocoa beans back to Spain. The Spaniards thought it tasted bitter, so they added cane sugar. Soon the wealthy families in Spain enjoyed "Chocolate." They often added vanilla or cinnamon and found it tasted best served hot.

Aztec Hot Chcolati (Chocolate)

Ingredients:
1 cup hot water	½ teaspoon ground cinnamon
3 tablespoons honey	3 cups hot milk
⅛ teaspoon salt	Cinnamon bark sticks

2 ounces unsweetened chocolate bar (baking chocolate) or Mexican-style chocolate bars

Directions:
1. Start heating the water slowly in one pan and the milk in a separate pan.
2. Chop up the chocolate and add it to the water as it heats. Stir until all the chocolate is melted.
3. Add the honey to the mixture.
4. Add the salt and ground cinnamon.
5. Slowly add the heated milk to the chocolate mixture, stirring constantly.
6. Serve in mugs and add a cinnamon stick. Let cool slightly and enjoy!

Keeping Track with Incan Quipu

The Incas were able to keep track of the number of people in the empire, the number of births and deaths each year, the amount of stored food they had, and much more—without writing it down! They invented a method of recording called quipu (KEY-poo) which used knots in colored string. Keep track of your own life for a week using quipu.

Materials:
- ☐ Scissors
- ☐ 6 different colors of yarn (cut 24 inches in length)
- ☐ Ruler
- ☐ Pencil
- ☐ Lightweight cardboard (like a cereal box or file folder)
- ☐ Tape

Directions:
1. Draw a 2 × 11-inch rectangle on the lightweight cardboard. Cut it out.
2. Tape the pieces of yarn to the cardboard. Tape each piece of yarn separately—space the pieces out so they don't touch.
3. Over each piece of yarn write something you would like to keep track of. Here are some examples:

   Books I Read

   Times I Was Nice to My Brother/Sister

   Vegetables I Ate

   Made My Bed

   Rode My Bike

   Played a Game

   Watched TV/Movie

   Walked My Dog

   Fed My Cat

4. Each time you do one of the activities on your list, tie a knot in the corresponding piece of yarn. Start tying knots at the top of the yarn, and work your way down.
5. At the end of the week, tally your results. Count the number of knots in each yarn strand and write it down. What did you do the most? What did you do the least? What should you do more? What should you do less often?

Spain, Portugal, and the New World

CHAPTER 33

Encyclopedia Cross-References

UBWH 140–141, 151, UILE 279, 283, 324–325
KIHW 252–251, 352, 362–364, KHE 212–213, 270–272

THE SLAVE TRADE

REVIEW QUESTIONS

Why did Ferdinand and Isabella pay for explorers to go to the New World? *They wanted to make money and find treasure.*

Which two European countries claimed land in Central and South America as their own? *Spain and Portugal both claimed land in the New World.*

What do we call the islands just off South America? *We call them the West Indies.*

Who were *conquistadores*? *They were Spanish and Portuguese soldiers.*

Who did Spain and Portugal have to fight to take the land in the New World? *They had to fight the native tribes OR the Aztecs, the Mayans, and the Incas.*

What deal did Spain and Portugal make? *They decided to divide the land.*

How did the Spanish and Portuguese treat the people of Central and South America? *They marched into their cities and villages and killed them; they destroyed temples, houses and palaces; they claimed the land for themselves.*

How did the Spanish and the Portuguese settlers in the New World first get people to grow crops and mine gold for them? *They brought slaves from Africa over to the New World.*

Where did they get slaves at first? *They bought slaves from Muslim traders.*

Where did the Muslim traders get slaves? *They bought them from the West African empires.*

What did the Spanish and Portuguese do when they couldn't get enough slaves from the Muslim traders? *They kidnapped West Africans.*

What do we call the long journey from West Africa to the West Indies and Central and South America? *We call it the Middle Passage.*

NARRATION EXERCISE

"The Spanish and the Portuguese wanted to build colonies in the New World, so they marched into villages and cities and took them over. They needed workers, so they bought slaves from Muslim traders. When they needed more, they kidnapped people from West Africa. They took them to the New World. We call this journey the Middle Passage." OR

"Slaves were people forced to work for someone without pay for the rest of their lives. The Spanish and Portuguese in the New World needed workers to build cities, mine gold, and grow crops. So they kidnapped people from Africa and forced the native tribes of the Americas to work as slaves. These slaves could never be free."

Review Questions

When the Spanish came to Central America, what kingdom did they find? *They found the kingdom of the Aztecs.*

What was Cortes looking for in Central America that he had heard rumors about? *He was looking for a city with streets of gold and walls of jewels.*

Why did the Aztecs think that Cortes and his men were two-headed, six-legged monsters? *The Aztecs had never seen horses before. They though each horse and rider were one terrifying monster!*

How did the Aztecs welcome Cortes and his men? *They brought Cortes and his men gold wheels, gold shields, and buckets full of gold dust.*

Who did Montezuma, king of the Aztecs, think Cortes was? *He thought Cortes was a god (Quetzalcoatl) coming to claim his throne.*

How did the fight between Cortes's men and the Aztecs begin? *Cortes's men got bored and argued with the Aztec priests, and a fight broke out.*

After the first fight, Cortes and his men looked out from their hideout and saw empty streets. Where were the Aztecs? *They were waiting in canoes to launch a surprise attack.*

What happened to the Spaniards who fell into Lake Texcoco? *They drowned because they were so weighed down with gold.*

What did Cortes do once he escaped from Tenochtitlan? *He gathered a fresh army, including fighters from villages around the Aztec empire, and marched back to the city. He launched a fleet of warships and besieged the city.*

Who ultimately gained control of the great city of Tenochtitlan? *The Spanish OR Cortes took over the city.*

Narration Exercise

"Cortes and his men landed on the shores of Central America hoping to find a city made of gold and jewels. The Aztecs thought these visitors were the gods coming to rule their city and welcomed them into their capital city, Tenochtitlan. But when the Aztecs figured out that Cortes was not a god, they fought. Cortes was driven off, but then he returned and captured the city." OR

"Cortes was welcomed into the Aztec city of Tenochtitlan because the Aztecs thought he was a god. But when the people realized he was only interested in the gold and jewels of the city, they began to fight. Cortes and his men hid in Montezuma's palace until they thought the Aztecs had gone away, but it was a trap. The Aztecs were waiting for them! Cortes escaped and then returned with a large army and warships. He defeated the Aztecs."

Additional History Reading

Cortes: Conqueror of Mexico, by William Jay Jacobs (Franklin Watts, 1994). Seven brief chapters describing the arrival of Cortes and his battles with the Aztecs; too long for a single-sitting read-aloud, but good for a longer project. (RA 2–3, IR 4–5)

Great Events That Changed the World: History As Immediate As the Present, by Brian Delf and Richard Platt (Dorling Kindersley, 1997). This oversized book tells the stories of great events in a running series of illustrations; includes the fall of the Aztec empire led by Cortes and his soldiers. (RA 1–3, IR 4–5)

Hernando Cortes and the Conquest of Mexico, by Gina de Angelis (Chelsea House Publishers, 2000). A clear and interesting biography, written on an advanced third- to fourth-grade level; too long for a single-sitting read-aloud, but good for a longer project. (RA 2–3, IR 3–5)

Lives of Extraordinary Women: Rulers, Rebels, and What the Neighbors Thought, by Kathleen Krull, illus. Kathryn Hewitt (Harcourt Brace, 2000). Very brief (3–4 pages) and interesting biographies, including the West African queen Nzingha, who fought against the Portuguese invasion of her country. (RA 2–3, IR 4–5)

The Middle Passage, by Tom Feelings (Dial Books, 1995). This wordless book of powerful black-and-white paintings tells the story of the Middle Passage; excellent, but some of the paintings are extremely disturbing (preview first). (IR 3–5, may be inappropriate for some children)

Outrageous Women of the Renaissance, by Vicki Leon (John Wiley and Sons, 1999). Brief, interesting biographies (5–6 pages) of fifteen Renaissance women from ten different countries; readable by advanced third grade and above. Includes Malinali of Mexico, a sixteenth-century Mayan woman who became a translator for Cortes and his expedition. (RA 2–3, IR 3–5)

Treasures from Spain, by David and Patricia Armentrout (Rourke Book Company, 2001). This brief survey of Spanish history focuses on Spain's acquisition of treasure and on modern attempts to salvage sunken Spanish treasure ships. Selected chapters will be of interest. (RA 2–3, IR 4–5)

Corresponding Literature Suggestions

Jackal's Flying Lesson: A Khoikhoi Tale, by Verna Aardema, illus. Dale Gottlieb (Alfred A. Knopf, 1995). A tale from southwest Africa about evil and justice. (IR 2–4)

Koi and the Kola Nuts, by Verna Aardema, illus. Joe Cepeda (Atheneum, 1999). A younger son triumphs in this traditional African tale. (IR 2–4)

Mufaro's Beautiful Daughters: An African Tale, by John Steptoe (Lothrop, Lee & Shepard, 1987). A gorgeously illustrated tale of love and loyalty from southern Africa; an African version of the Cinderella story. (RA 2, IR 3–4)

The Spirit of the Maasai Man, by Laura Berkeley (Barefoot Books, 2000). A picture-book parable about slavery and freedom. (IR 2–4)

―――――――――――――――――――― **MAP WORK** ――――――――――――――――――――

The Empires of Spain and Portugal *(Student Page 136, answer 262)*

Trace the path of the slave trade to the Americas:

1. Spanish and Portuguese ships sailed to West Africa to get slaves. Draw a red line from Portugal to the "W" in West Africa. (Remember to stay in the Atlantic Ocean as much as possible; this was a sea journey.)

2. Once the ships were loaded up with slaves, they would travel across the Atlantic Ocean to the New World. This journey was known as the Middle Passage. Slaves could go to the West Indies, Central America, or South America. Draw a red line from the "W" on West Africa to the dot in the West Indies. Then, trace the line labeled "The Middle Passage" in red.

3. Using red, trace the second line from Africa to South America. Now extend the first line (that came from West Africa to the West Indies) all the way to Tenochtitlan (in Central America). Slaves might also travel one of these routes.

COLORING PAGE — Spanish and Portuguese soldiers, called *conquistadores*, were fighting with the Aztecs, the Mayans, and the Incas who lived in Central and South America. *(Student Page 137)*

ACTIVITY PROJECT **Treasure Hunting**

Cortes hoped to find his fortune in the Spanish Colonies, but you can find a fortune of fun by playing this hide and seek game with your family or with friends.

Materials:
- ☐ Shoebox, coffee can, large jar or large plastic bag
- ☐ Treasure*
- ☐ 10 strips of paper and a pen

Directions: (These can be followed by student or by parent!)

1. Place your treasure in the box or can and find a place to hide it. Try to find a place to bury it outside in your yard. Make sure no one who is playing the Treasure Hunt game is watching. Mark the spot carefully.

2. Write messages of directions on the strips of paper that will lead the players to the treasure. Try to send them to 10 messages before they find the treasure. It may be helpful to write the messages in backwards order. For example, you buried the treasure under the back willow tree. Mark an "X" on the covered-up spot and then write a message that says, "Go to the back willow tree and dig at the X." Place that message in the dryer. Your next message would say something like, "Find the machine that dries what's wet and get your next message." Then tape that note under the dining room table. Your next message may say, "Eat, eat, that's all I do! Find the next message under where I do that." That message might be taped behind the bedroom door, and so on.

3. Take turns being the treasure hunter and the treasure hider!

   *Note: Treasure can come in many forms. You can make your own: paint small stones with jewel acrylic paint or in gold and silver. For the adventurous, check out gum or chocolate coins wrapped in gold paper.

CRAFT PROJECT **Conquistador's Mask**

Materials:
- ☐ Photocopy the Conquistador mask template onto white cardstock paper (Student Page 138) (enlarge to fit if necessary*)
- ☐ Stapler or tape
- ☐ Colors, markers or colored pencils
- ☐ Large red feather (found in craft stores)—optional

Directions:

1. Color the helmet and cheek guards silver, the face a Mediterranean flesh color and the hair a blackish-brown. Cut out the eyes and mouth part only at the shaded parts. Cut out the mask.

2. Make two strips of paper the length and width of a ruler. Staple them (or tape them) to the mask just above the ears of the one who will wear the mask. Test the length and secure the two strips together at the point where the mask fits snugly.

3. Add the feather by taping it to the top of the helmet.

   *Note: If the mask is too small, enlarge it on 11" × 14" paper at 10% increments until you find the right size. Make the final copy on cardstock.

Shrinkable Shield Suncatchers

Cortes and his men proved to Montezuma that they were not Aztec gods—by fighting! In the battle, both Aztecs and Spaniards relied on their shields for defense.

Materials:
☐ Photocopy of the stencil template *(Student Page 139)*
☐ Hole punch
☐ Colored pencils
☐ Sandpaper
☐ White thread
☐ Suction cup hooks for windows
☐ Deli plastic containers, #6 recyclable, flat sides cut out (or use "Rough and Ready" plastic shrinkable sheets found at a craft store)

Directions:
1. Cut up a deli plastic container, freeing the useable top and bottom. Sand one side of the plastic until it is cloudy and you can feel the roughness on every part of it (delete this step if using the "Rough and Ready" shrinkable sheets). This is so that the color will stick.

2. Lay the plastic on top of the shield stencil pattern. Trace it onto the plastic, making sure you are working on the scratched side.

3. Fill in the shield with the colored pencils. You can use markers as well, but the pencils seem to work best. The centers of both shields are empty so that you can decide what you want them to represent. In Spain, the shields represented the lord you served or the family you represented. Pick an animal or symbol that represents your family and draw that in the center of your conquistador shield. The Aztecs would paint pictures on their shields of animals that represented the strength they believe they gained from these animals. What animal would you like to be like and why? Draw that animal in the center of your Aztec shield.

4. Punch a hole at the top to hang the shield. Cut the shield out and place on a cookie sheet.

5. Bake at 250 degrees for about 15 minutes and check often. Take out when the shields are lying flat and are thicker. As they shrink, the color will intensify. Be careful—burning plastic is not good for you to breathe.

6. Thread the cooled shields and hang on the suction cup hook at a sunny window.

Battle for Gold Game!

The battle between the Spanish conquistadores and the Aztec Indians was fierce. The Spanish were fighting for wealth—but the Aztecs were fighting for their whole way of life. Test your memory!

Materials:
- *Story of the World, Volume 2*
- Game board *(Student Page 140)*
- Game pieces, beans, coins, buttons or small plastic toys to serve as player markers
- One die or two, depending on how fast you want it to go
- Clear contact paper (optional)

Directions:
1. Before the game:
   a. Enlarge the game board to fit on an 11" × 14" sheet of paper.
   b. Color the board and the designs around it.
   c. Glue game board onto cardboard or posterboard to add strength. (optional)
   d. Cover with clear contact paper. (optional)
   e. Select game pieces, one for each player.

2. To play:
   a. All players begin at the place marked "Start".
   b. Roll the dice. The lowest number gets to be first. Go clock-wise from the first player.
   c. Follow the pathway to the end.
   d. If you land on a shaded square, answer the question in the box and follow the instructions.
   e. The first one to the end who can answer the last question correctly wins the game.

Martin Luther's New Ideas

CHAPTER 34

Encyclopedia Cross-References

UBWH 134–135, UILE 302–303
KIHW 350–351, 354–355, KHE 210–211, 214–215

MARTIN LUTHER'S LIST

REVIEW QUESTIONS

Can you remember one of the two names that we use for the time when countries began planting colonies and new settlements? *We call this the Age of Discovery* OR *the Age of Exploration.*

Martin Luther's parents wanted him to be a lawyer, but what did he become instead? *He became a monk.*

Martin Luther went on a pilgrimage to Rome, prayed in front of the relics of the saints, and crawled on his hands while reciting the Lord's Prayer because he was afraid of something. What was it? *He was afraid that God would punish him for his sin OR that God would be angry with him unless he did those things.*

When Martin Luther studied the book of Romans, how did his way of thinking change? *He realized that God already loved him and would give him the power to be good.*

What Catholic church practice greatly upset Martin Luther? *He was upset by the selling of indulgences OR paying money to the Church to get out of doing penance for sin.*

What did Martin Luther preach about God's forgiveness? *He preached that God would forgive any sinner who believed in Jesus Christ.*

What were the "Ninety-five Theses"? *It was a list written by Martin Luther of ninety-five reasons why indulgences were wrong.*

Where did he put this list up? *He nailed it to the church door at Wittenberg.*

NARRATION EXERCISE

"Martin Luther was a monk who did all kinds of things to earn God's love. When he studied the Bible, it seemed to him that God's love for him did not depend on what he did. He questioned the way the Catholic church thought about God. For the first time, people began to say out loud that the church might not always be right." OR

"Martin Luther disagreed with the Catholic church over the forgiveness of sin. The church said you had to do penance or buy an indulgence. Martin Luther said that anyone who believed in Jesus would be forgiven. He wrote out his ideas in a list called the Ninety-five Theses and nailed it to a church door. Then people began to talk about his ideas all over Germany."

HENRY VIII'S PROBLEM

REVIEW QUESTIONS

Why was Henry VII so anxious to make sure that his son and grandson and great-grandson would inherit the English throne? *He had already fought one war for the throne, and he didn't want another war to start after he died.*

Who did Henry VII arrange for his son, Arthur, to marry? *He arranged for him to marry Catherine, the daughter of the king of Spain.*

How old were the bride and groom? *The bride was three and the groom was two!*

What happened to Prince Arthur, six months after his wedding? *He died.*

Who married Catherine, Arthur's young wife? *Arthur's younger brother Harry married Catherine.*

When Harry became king, what did his name become? *He became King Henry VIII.*

Why was Henry VIII dissatisfied with his first wife, Catherine? *Because she couldn't give him a son and heir to his throne.*

What did Henry VIII ask the pope to do? *He wanted the pope to say that Henry's marriage to Catherine didn't count because Catherine had been married to Arthur. That way, Henry would be free to marry another woman.*

When the pope declared that Henry had to stay married to Catherine, what did Henry do? *He declared that nobody in England could follow the pope anymore. He started a new church and made himself in charge of it. Then he gave himself permission to marry again.*

What new church did Henry start? *He started the Church of England.*

How did Henry end his marriage with his second wife, Anne Boleyn? *He had her head chopped off.*

How many wives did Henry VIII have in all? *He had six wives.*

Did he ever have a son? *Yes, he had a son, Edward (by Jane Seymour).*

Narration Exercise

"Henry VIII was upset because his wife could not give him a son to be his heir. He asked the pope to declare that his marriage wasn't real, so that he could marry someone else. The pope refused. So Henry started his own church in England and made himself the head of it. He called it the Church of England." OR

"Henry VIII married Catherine, his brother's wife. She didn't have a son to be the next king, so he started his own church and gave himself permission to divorce her. He married Anne Boleyn, but he still didn't have a son. So he got married six times! If he wasn't happy with a wife, he divorced her or had her head chopped off. Finally he had a son, Edward."

Additional History Reading

King Henry VIII, by Robert Green (Franklin Watts, 1998). An excellent, clear, five-chapter biography of Henry VIII, written on a fourth-grade level; selected chapters would also work as a read-aloud for younger children. Includes full-color contemporary portraits of all of Henry's wives. **Out of print**, but easy to find at most libraries. (RA 1–3, IR 4–5)

Martin Luther: The Great Reformer, by Edwin P. Booth and Dan Harmon (Chelsea House, 1998). Although this volume in the "Heroes of the Faith" series is intended for older readers, there are no beginner biographies of Martin Luther currently available; this would be good for older readers or for a family read-aloud. (RA 1–4, IR 5)

A Medieval Cathedral, by Fiona MacDonald (Peter Bedrick Books, 1991). A guide to the construction of the medieval cathedrals built across Europe and (after the Norman invasion) in England as well; also discusses the culture of the medieval church, including daily life for priests and monks, church doctrines, and the use of miracle plays. **Out of print**, but relatively easy to find. (RA 2–4, IR 5)

The Middle Ages: A Watts Guide for Children, edited by William Chester Jordan (Franklin Watts, 2000). This illustrated encyclopedia features brief entries with simple text; look up "papacy," "church," and "monastery" to learn more about Martin Luther's world. (RA 1–2, IR 3–5)

Corresponding Literature Suggestions

Courage and Conviction: Chronicles of the Reformation Church, by Brandon and Mindy Withrow (Christian Focus, 2007). From the History Lives series, this book is the third volume and includes a section on Martin Luther. (RA 2–3, IR 4–6)

Francis: The Poor Man of Assisi, by Tomie De Paola (Holiday House, 1990). This picture book about St. Francis also introduces children to the life of a monk. (RA 1, IR 2–5)

A Medieval Monk, by Giovanni Caselli (Peter Bedrick Books, 1986). Young Pierre enters the monastery of Cluny, learns to live as a monk, and solves a mystery. **Out of print** (RA 1–2, IR 3–5)

———— MAP WORK ————

Europe at the Time of Martin Luther and Henry VIII *(Student Page 141, answer 262)*

1. Martin Luther was a monk in Germany. Underline Germany in green.
2. Martin Luther nailed the Ninety-five Theses to a church in Wittenberg, Germany. Circle Wittenberg in orange.
3. The head of the Catholic church, the pope, lived in Rome. Put a red box around the city of Rome in Italy.
4. England was a Catholic country. Outline England in red to show its relationship with Rome and the Catholic church.
5. Henry VIII, king of England, lived in London. Draw a dark blue star over London.
6. Henry VIII decided that the people of England would no longer follow the Catholic church. Instead, he formed the Church of England and ordered his subjects to be part of it. Color England light blue.

COLORING PAGES

Martin Luther nailed a copy of the Ninety-five Theses to a church door in Wittenberg. *(Student Page 142)*

Henry VIII, king of England *(Student Page 143)*

———— PROJECTS ————

ACTIVITY PROJECT   Take a Vow of Silence

Martin Luther was an Augustinian monk. The Augustinians took vows of poverty, celibacy, and obedience, but not of silence. Other orders, like the Trappists, do not require vows of silence, though they will generally only speak when absolutely necessary. Most meals are taken in contemplative silence.

Take a vow of silence. See how long you can go without speaking. Take a notepad and pencil around with you to communicate if you like.

ART PROJECT   **Illuminate the Book of Common Prayer**

The Book of Common Prayer is a collection of prayers used in the Church of England. Illuminate the prayer of thanksgiving.

Materials:
- ☐ Illuminated "A" *(Student Page 144)*
- ☐ Scissors
- ☐ Glue
- ☐ Pens, markers, crayons (metallic gel pens are fantastic for this activity)
- ☐ Paper

Directions:
1. Color the illuminated capital "A" from the student page. Clip it out.
2. Glue the A to the top left corner of a piece of paper.
3. Copy the following prayer with your best penmanship, leaving out the first A:

    Almighty God, Father of all mercies, we thine unworthy servants do give thee most humble and hearty thanks for all thy goodness and loving-kindness to us, and to all men.

4. Decorate the paper.

ACTIVITY PROJECT   **Smuggle Out the Monks' Treasure**

When Henry VIII formed the Church of England, he closed all the Catholic monasteries in England and took their treasure for himself. Many of the monks buried the treasure in secret places rather than have it fall into the hands of Henry VIII and the Church of England. Although some of the treasure was recovered by the monks, many of the monks were driven out of the country and were unable to retrieve the valuables. Play a game with your parent or older sibling: Can you smuggle out the buried treasure in time?

Materials:
- ☐ 3 or 4 "treasure" items—like a book (for an illuminated manuscript), a candlestick, or a cup (for a gold communion chalice). *Note:* Don't hide anything that you would be really upset if you lost. Much of the monks' treasure was never found.
- ☐ Timer

Directions:
1. Pick a room in the house. You are the monk. Have Henry VIII (your parent) go out of the room. Hide the 3 or 4 treasure items in the most difficult-to-find places in the room.
2. Invite Henry VIII back in. Set the timer for 30 minutes. You now have to smuggle out the pieces of treasure without Henry VIII seeing you! If the monk is spotted with the treasure, he must give the item to Henry VIII. How much treasure can you escape with undetected?

The Tudor Family Tree

The Tudor family tree has many names. Henry VIII had seven brothers and sisters and he also had six wives! Draw the Tudor family tree, using the template on *Student Page 145.*

Materials: ☐ Tudor Tree Template *(Student Page 145)*
☐ Markers, crayons, or colored pencils

Directions: 1. First fill in Henry VII and his wife Elizabeth of York at the top of the page.

2. On the next row, fill in their children in the order in which they were born: Arthur, Margaret, Henry VIII, Elizabeth, Mary, Edmund, Edward, Catherine

3. On the next row down, fill in all six of Henry VIII's wives. They should be in order from first to last. Use your book to find the names of the wives and to put them in the right order.

4. Fill in Henry's children. Use your book to help you find the names of Henry's children. Make sure the right child is placed under the right mother!

Key for Parents:

Henry VII marries Elizabeth of York

Children: Arthur, Margaret, Henry VIII, Elizabeth, Mary, Edmund, Edward, Catherine

Henry VIII marries:

1. Catherine of Aragon—has Mary from that marriage

2. Anne Boleyn—has Elizabeth from that marriage

3. Jane Seymour—has Edward from that marriage

4. Anne of Cleves

5. Catherine Howard

6. Catherine Parr

The Renaissance

CHAPTER 35

Encyclopedia Cross-References

UBWH 130–133, UILE 284–287
KIHW 260, 312–313, 324–325, 330–337, KHE 202–203, 234–239

A NEW WAY OF THINKING

REVIEW QUESTIONS

What happened to reading, writing, and learning after the fall of the Roman Empire? *People were too busy staying alive to read, write, and learn.*

Since the people of countries with strong armies (like England and Spain) didn't have to worry about invasion, what did they spend their time doing? *They could spend time thinking, reading, and studying.*

When the Ottoman Turks conquered Constantinople, what did many of the Eastern Orthodox Christian scholars take with them when they left the city? *They took scrolls written in Greek (and/or the Bible).*

What did Eastern Orthodox scholars teach other men and women to do? *They taught others how to read Greek writings.*

What do we call the time in history when the older Greek and Roman ideas were "reborn"? (Hint: The word means "rebirth" and it starts with the same letter, too.) *We call it the Renaissance.*

How did art change during the Renaissance? *Art became more realistic.*

How did the Renaissance change the way that people thought about the world? *People began to make new theories about what the world was like.*

During the Renaissance, how did men and women begin to believe that they could find out truth? *They believed that they could find truth by looking at the world and figuring out how it worked.*

When you observe something and try to draw conclusions from your observations, what kind of thinking is this? *This is scientific thinking.*

NARRATION EXERCISE

"After Rome fell, people were too busy staying alive to read and think. But when strong countries like England and Spain began to make their kingdoms more peaceful, more people started to be interested in books. They read Greek and Roman books, thought about Greek and Roman ideas, and copied Greek and Roman art. We call this time the Renaissance." OR

"After Constantinople fell, Eastern Orthodox scholars settled in other parts of the world. They taught people to read Greek. More and more people got interested in books from ancient times. Many of the ideas in those books were reborn. We call this time in history the Renaissance. During the Renaissance, scientific thinking became important."

REVIEW QUESTIONS

What invention did the most to change the world during the time of the Renaissance? *The printing press OR A machine that printed books changed the world.*

Who invented the printing press? *(Johannes) Gutenberg invented the printing press.*

Before the printing press, how were books made? *Books were written out by hand on animal skins (parchment).*

How did the Chinese make paper? *They soaked bark, straw, or rags in water and pressed it into sheets.*

How did books help scientists? *They could read about what other scientists had discovered instead of having to figure out everything on their own.*

How did books help Christians who wanted to find out what the Bible says? *They could read their own Bible instead of having to ask a priest.*

Can you list two of the three kinds of books printed by William Caxton? *Caxton printed history books, poetry books, and a book about how to play chess.*

NARRATION EXERCISE

"The invention of the printing press changed the world. Books were now easier to make and cheaper to buy. Scientists and explorers could read about other people's discoveries, and Christians could read their own Bibles in their own languages." OR

"In the Middle Ages, books were written by hand. Then Johannes Gutenberg invented the printing press, a machine that could make books quickly. He also made ink and used paper instead of parchment. Now more people could buy and read books. Scientists, explorers, and ordinary people could find out what others were doing and thinking."

Additional History Reading

Fine Print: A Story about Johann Gutenberg, by Joann Johansen Burch, illus. Kent Alan Aldrich (Carolrhoda Books, 1991). For advanced readers, a good chapter-book biography of the great printer. (IR 4–5)

Getting to Know the World's Greatest Artists series, by Mike Venezia (Children's Press). This series, which includes the titles *Pieter Bruegel, Leonardo da Vinci, Michelangelo,* and *Rembrandt,* reproduces color paintings and describes both artistic techniques and the lives of the artists in simple prose. A good easy alternative to the *What Makes A...* series described below. (IR 2–5)

Heroes: Great Men Through the Ages, by Rebecca Hazell (Abbeville Press, 1997). Twelve interesting read-aloud biographies, including that of Leonardo Da Vinci. (RA 2–3, IR 4–5)

How a Book Is Made, by Aliki (Thomas Crowell, 1986). A group of animals get together to write a book, typeset and illustrate it, send it to the printing press, bind it, and distribute it. A clear and heavily illustrated guide to the modern printing press and the world of books. (RA 1, IR 2–5)

Introducing Michelangelo, by Robin Richmond (Little, Brown & Co., 1991). This introduction to Michelangelo's life includes information on Renaissance Florence; good illustrations and text on a fourth-grade level, but the sections on the Sistine Chapel are well worth reading aloud. (RA 2–3, IR 4–5)

Lives of the Artists: Masterpieces, Messes (and What the Neighbors Thought), by Kathleen Krull, illus. Kathryn Hewitt (Harcourt Brace, 1995). Brief (three page), engaging biographical sketches of great artists from Da Vinci to Andy Warhol; the first five are Renaissance-era and include the female Italian Renaissance painter Sofonisba Anguissola. (RA 2, IR 3–5)

Leonardo Da Vinci (Tell Me About...), by John Malam (Carolrhoda Books, 1999). An easy-reader guide to the life of this Renaissance genius. (RA 1, IR 2–4)

Leonardo Da Vinci (The Life and Work of...), by Sean Connolly (Heinemann Library, 2000). The simplest Leonardo biography, with large print and color illustrations. (IR 1–3)

Leonardo Da Vinci, by Diane Stanley (Morrow Junior Books, 1996). Picture-book format, but more difficult text and more attention to Da Vinci's scientific work. (RA 2–3, IR 4–5)

Michelangelo, by Diane Stanley (HarperCollins, 2000). Gorgeous picture-book illustrations with text for slightly older students; a wonderful account of this Renaissance artist's life. (IR 4–5)

Outrageous Women of the Renaissance, by Vicki Leon (John Wiley and Sons, 1999). Brief, interesting biographies (5–6 pages) of fifteen Renaissance women from ten different countries; readable by advanced third grade and above. (RA 2–3, IR 3–5)

The Printing Press: A Breakthrough in Communication, by Richard Tames (Heinemann Library, 2001). A more advanced guide to the printing process, beginning with medieval scribes, moving through Caxton and Gutenberg, and ending with modern printing processes. A little long for a read-aloud, but good for a family reading project or for older students. (RA 1–3, IR 4–5)

Renaissance: Eyewitness Books, by Alison Cole (Dorling Kindersley, 1994). With many illustrations and "snippets" of text ranging from third to sixth grade in reading difficulty, this book provides an overview of Renaissance art over three centuries. (RA 2–4, IR 5)

What Makes a Rembrandt a Rembrandt? and *What Makes a Bruegel a Bruegel?* and *What Makes a Raphael a Raphael?* by Richard Muhlberger (The Metropolitan Museum of Art). This series reproduces famous paintings and points out the unique aspects of each artist's technique. A little too much text for younger students, but older students or younger children particularly interested in art will benefit. (RA 2–4, IR 4–5)

Corresponding Literature Suggestions

Katie and the Mona Lisa, by James Mayhew (Orchard Books, 1999). On a magical museum trip, little Katie convinces the Mona Lisa to climb out of her frame and go on a tour of famous Renaissance paintings. Beautiful color illustrations of the paintings and an engaging story. (RA 1, IR 2–4)

Leonardo and the Flying Boy, by Laurence Anholt (Barron's, 2000). A little boy who works in Leonardo's workshop gets to see the first trial of a new flying machine. (RA 1, IR 2–4)

Leonardo's Horse, by Jean Fritz, illus. by Hudson Talbott (G. P. Putnam's Sons, 2001). A beautiful picture-book retelling of the twentieth-century attempt to recreate Leonardo's favorite incomplete sculpture. (RA 1–3, IR 3–5)

Who in the World Was the Secretive Printer? The Story of Johannes Gutenberg, by Robert Beckham (Peace Hill Press, 2005). The story of Gutenberg from his childhood to his development of movable type and the printing press. (RA 1–2, IR 3–4)

Europe at the Time of the Renaissance *(Student Page 146, answer 262)*

1. The monks in Constantinople copied hundreds of scrolls. Circle Constantinople in yellow.

2. Many of the scrolls were written in Latin and Greek. Latin was used in the old Roman Empire. Underline Rome in red. The Greek language was used in Greece. Underline Greece in green.

3. The first printing press was created by Johannes Gutenberg in Germany. Underline Germany twice in purple.

COLORING PAGE During the Middle Ages, merchants trading with China learned how to make paper from the Chinese. *(Student Page 147)*

--------- PROJECTS ---------

CRAFT PROJECT **What's Your Name in Greek?**

When the Ottoman Turks conquered the city of Constantinople and turned its great cathedral into a Muslim mosque, hundreds of Eastern Orthodox Christian scholars left the city and traveled west into Europe. They brought with them scrolls written in Greek. When the Eastern Orthodox scholars settled down in Europe, they taught others to read Greek writings. Try writing your name or initials in Greek letters.

A	a	alpha	a	☒	☒	nu	v
B	☒	beta	b	☒	☒	xi	ks
☒	☒	gamma	g	☒	☒	omikron	o
☒	☒	delta	d	☒	☒	pi	p
☒	☒	epsilon	e	☒	☒	rho	r
☒	☒	zêta	z	☒	☒, ☒	sigma	s
☒	☒	êta	ê	☒	☒	tau	t
☒	☒	thêta	th	☒	☒	upsilon	u
☒	☒	iota	i	☒	☒	phi	f
☒	☒	kappa	k	☒	☒	chi	ch
☒	☒	lambda	l	☒	☒	psi	ps
☒	☒	mu	m	☒	☒	omega	ô

ACTIVITY PROJECT **The Scientific Method: Observation**

Prepare a Meal

For the next meal you eat, watch your parent make the meal. Notice what the ingredients look like before anything is done to them. What colors are they? What do they smell like? What do they taste like? What do they sound like? What do they feel like? Watch what your parent does to make your meal. Does he cook the ingredients? Does he mix multiple ingredients together? Do you hear anything that you did not hear when the ingredients were by themselves? Once your meal is made, look at your plate of food. Do the ingredients look, smell, taste, sound, and feel different now that they have been made into a meal? Talk about these questions with your parent while you enjoy your meal!

Alternate activity: Make Playdough

Ingredients: 4 cups flour   1 to 1½ cups cold water
               1 cup salt   Food coloring
               2 tablespoons cooking oil   Magnifying glass (optional)

Directions: 1. Separate all measured ingredients.

              2. Feel the oil. How does it feel? Feel the water. Do they feel the same? How are they different? Pour the water and the oil into the big bowl. Do they mix completely? What happens to the oil?

              3. Look at the food coloring. What color does it look like? Put several drops in the bowl (that now has water and oil in it). What color does it look like now? Is it lighter or darker? Without stirring the bowl, how does the food coloring spread? What does it look like?

              4. Put your hand in the salt. How does it feel? Taste a little bit. How does it taste ?

              5. Put your hand in the flour. How does it feel? How does it taste?

              6. Look at the salt as you pour it into the big bowl. Listen to it. Look at the flour as you pour it into the big bowl. Listen to it. Do they pour the same? Do they sound the same as they pour? Why do you think they pour differently?

              7. Mix all of the ingredients together with your hands. What is happening to the salt and flour part as you mix them? Can you see the salt part or the flour part?

              8. How does the playdough feel? Like the salt part? Like the flour part?

              9. Do you think it would be easy to take out the salt from the playdough? the flour? the water?

             10. If you have a magnifying glass, look at the playdough. What does it look like close up?

             11. When you are finished observing (and playing), store the playdough in a plastic bag in the refrigerator.

CRAFT PROJECT   **Potato Printing**

When we pick up a book we hardly think of the time it took to make it. In fact, although handwritten books took an enormous amount of time, early printed texts took quite a bit of time as well! When Gutenberg set up his press, he had to set up every metal letter for each word in each page. Try this craft to get a feel of the work it took.

Materials: ☐ One large baking potato for two stamps you want to make.
             ☐ Metal cookie cutters in different shapes that would fit in the space on a potato*
             ☐ Paring knife
             ☐ Paper, any color
             ☐ Acrylic paint in different colors that would be complementary to your paper choice
             ☐ Craft paint brushes

Directions: 1. Wash and dry the potatoes. Choose which cookie cutter you are going to use first. Slice the potato in half the direction that would allow the cookie cutter to fit best.

             2. Press the cookie cutter deep into the flesh of the sliced potato. Leave it in and cut away on the outside of the cookie cutter. When Gutenberg made his metal letters he poured the hot metal into molds that held their shape as the metal cooled. The cutter will guard the stamp part inside as you chip away the outside of the potato. Cut away all of the potato on the outside of the cookie cutter.

3. Once you reach the end of the cutter on the bottom, stop cutting away the outside of the potato and gently slip off the cutter from the stamp part inside.

4. Brush some acrylic paint on to your potato stamp and decorate your paper! Use this method to create your own wrapping paper. Simply stamp butcher block or newsprint paper sheets with your potato-printing stamp.

Note: To give an even greater Gutenberg-feel to this craft, consider investing in Alphabet cookie cutters which would allow you to print words using the potato printing method. These are available at cooking stores.

Recreate the Frankfurt Book Fair

The printing press was a hit! But many that went into the printing business went out of business very soon after. Why? The books were being printed, but the means to get them to the people had not been developed yet. Distribution and advertising didn't exist for books at that time. Frankfurt, Germany, however, was one of the first towns to begin to solve the problem. They had their own book fair. Other kinds of fairs had been pulled together so that the people in a town could show off and sell their wares. Frankfurt had a book fair that pulled together the writers, publishers and buying public.

Recreate your own Frankfurt Book Fair. Gather together the books you no longer use. Ask your friends to do the same. You can set up tables to display and sell the items to each other, or you can trade books with one another.

You could also donate the books from your book fair to a local children's hospital. Do it in the name of the clever people of Frankfurt!

Be a Renaissance Architect

The architects during the Renaissance used Greek and Roman elements in their buildings—especially Greek columns. There are three types of Greek columns: Corinthian, Ionic, and Doric.

Materials:
- Greek Columns *(Student Page 148)*
- Markers, crayons, or colored pencils
- Playdough (optional—you can use what you made in the earlier activity)

Directions:
1. Color the columns on the student page.
2. If you want, pick your favorite column and sculpt it out of playdough.

Reformation and Counter Reformation CHAPTER 36

Encyclopedia Cross-References

UBWH 134–135, UILE 302–303
KIHW 354–355, 364–365, 368–369, KHE 214–215

THE SPREAD OF THE REFORMATION

REVIEW QUESTIONS

If a medieval Christian did penance, what was he trying to show? *He was trying to show that he was sorry for his sins.*

If you bought an indulgence, what did that do for you? *It meant that you didn't have to do penance.*

When Martin Luther criticized indulgences, what was he really saying about the Catholic church? *He was saying that the Catholic church didn't always know what God wanted.*

Did Martin Luther teach that Christians needed a priest to tell them what God was saying? *No, they did not need a priest.*

According to Martin Luther, how could Christians find out what God was saying to them? *They could read their own Bibles and figure it out for themselves.*

Why did this worry the Catholic church? *The church thought that the Christian church would splinter into many different pieces and no one would know what the truth really was.*

Why was the Church worried about the different translations of the Bible? *The church was afraid that some of the translations would be wrong.*

People like Martin Luther wanted the Catholic church to change. What were these people called? (Hint: Another word for "change" is "reform.") *They were called Reformers OR Protestants.*

What is a heretic? *A heretic no longer followed the truth about God.*

What is another name for a statement of faith? *A statement of faith is also called a Confession.*

After the Reformation, what two groups did the church divide into? *The church divided into Catholics and Protestants.*

Why did kings of other countries, like Henry VIII, think that the Reformation was a good idea? *Kings of other countries didn't like an Italian pope telling them what to do.*

Were Catholics and Protestants friendly with each other? *Usually they argued with each other, and sometimes these arguments turned into wars.*

NARRATION EXERCISE

"Martin Luther taught that people could read the Bible and figure it out for themselves without the help of the church. The people who followed him were called Reformers or Protestants. The church was afraid that people would get wrong ideas about God if they did this. They called the Reformers heretics. Many people liked Martin Luther's ideas because during the Renaissance, people wanted to figure things out for themselves." OR

"Protestants split apart from the Catholic church during the Reformation. Protestants thought that they didn't need a priest or a pope to tell them about God. They could teach themselves by reading the Bible. Catholics believed that the pope and the priests of the Catholic church needed to teach them about God. Catholics and Protestants are still different today."

THE COUNCIL OF TRENT

REVIEW QUESTIONS

Why did the pope call for a council to meet at Trent? *He wanted the leaders of the Catholic church to talk about what the Catholic church believed.*

Did this meeting take eighteen days, eighteen months, or eighteen years? *It took eighteen years!*

Besides preaching and taking care of spiritual needs, what else did some bishops and priests do during the Middle Ages? (Hint: it has to do with owning land.) *They acted like landlords and mayors.*

How did some rich men get to be bishops? *They paid archbishops so that they could become bishops or priests.*

After the Council of Trent reformed the Catholic church, what did men have to do before they could become priests? *They had to go to special schools called seminaries.*

What do we call the years after the Council of Trent? *We call them the Counter Reformation.*

Did the Counter Reformation bring peace between Protestants and Catholics? *No, they still fought with each other.*

NARRATION EXERCISE

"The leaders of the Catholic church got together and discussed what the church taught about every area of belief. This meeting was called the Council of Trent, and it took eighteen years! During this meeting, the Catholic church decided that priests would have to go to special schools called seminaries. They couldn't pay to become bishops any more." OR

"The bishops of the Catholic Church met together for the Council of Trent. They wrote down exactly what the church taught about the Bible, the pope, and many other things. We call the time after the Council of Trent the Counter Reformation. But Catholics and Protestants still fought with each other."

Additional History Reading

Come Worship With Me: A Journey Through the Church Year, by Ruth L. Boling and Tracey Dahle Carrier (Geneva Press, 2001). Published by a Presbyterian company, this guide to the Protestant church year (including many traditions still shared by Catholics) is conducted by a church mouse and geared towards young children. (RA 1, IR 2–5)

I Am Lutheran, by Erica Bradley (Powerkids Press, 1999). A very simple guide to the distinctives of Lutheran practice. (IR 2–3)

I Am Roman Catholic, by Philemon D. Sevastiades (Rosen Publishing Group, 1997). A very simple guide to basic Catholic doctrine and practice. (IR 2–3)

Places of Worship: Christian Church, by Angela Wood (Gareth Stevens Publishing, 2000). This very basic guide to Christian practice describes both Catholic and Protestant places of worship and customs. (IR)

The Reformation, by Fiona MacDonald (Raintree/Steck Vaughn, 2002). Written on an advanced fourth-grade level, this more difficult book traces the causes and results of the Reformation. (RA 1–4, IR 4–5)

Corresponding Literature Suggestions

Child's Guide to the Mass, by Sue Stanton, illus. H. M. Alan (Paulist Press, 2001). Watercolors illustrate this picture book, in which a little girl named Sarah goes to Mass and describes everything that happens in simple language; published by a Catholic press. (RA 1, IR 2–5)

Cathedral Mouse, by Kay Chorao (E. P. Dutton, 1988). A mouse explores an enormous cathedral and finally finds a hole of his own in this picture book. **Out of print** (RA 1, IR 2–4)

MAP WORK

The Reformation and Counter Reformation *(Student Page 149, answer 262)*

In 1560, after the Reformation and the Council of Trent, not all of Europe was Roman Catholic anymore. Color the map of Europe to show which areas were Catholic and which areas were Protestant.

1. The purpose of the Council of Trent was to write a statement telling everyone exactly what the church taught about every important belief. This took eighteen years! Circle the city of Trent in red.

2. The following areas were officially Lutheran, a form of Protestantism. Draw a light blue box around all the Lutheran areas. Include Germany, Denmark, Prussia, and the Scandinavian peninsula (Norway and Sweden).

3. The following areas were officially Calvinist (or Reformed), another type of Protestantism. Put a purple circle around each of the Calvinist areas. This includes Switzerland, Netherlands, and Scotland.

4. England and Wales followed the Church of England. (Remember when Henry VIII decided to start his own church?) Underline England and Wales in green.

5. Catholicism was still very widespread in Europe. Draw a yellow C next to the Catholic areas, which includes Italy, the islands of the Mediterranean, Spain, Portugal, France, Austria, Hungary, Poland, and Ireland.

COLORING PAGES Color in these pictures of stained glass. Use bright colors to simulate how the glass would look when light shines through it. *(Student Pages 150 and 151)*

PROJECTS

CRAFT PROJECT ### Make a Priest or Minister's Hat

During the Reformation and Counter Reformation, Catholic priests and Protestant ministers would have worn different types of hats. Make one or both of these hats!

Catholic Priest's Hat

Materials: ☐ Felt (a dark color)   ☐ Neddle and thread
☐ Pom pom for top of hat

Directions: 1. Cut a piece of felt into a rectangle approximately 8 inches wide and 20 inches long. (*Note:* this amount of felt will be too big for most children's heads so you may have to cut it down to fit your child well.)

2. Put the felt around the child's head and get it snug. Once you have a good fit, sew the ends of the felt together.

3. The felt should now be rather tall when it is on the child's head. Gather the felt in the center and run a bit of thread through it to sew it together.

4. Sew the pom pom on top of where the felt was gathered at the center.

Protestant Minister's Hat

Materials:
☐ Paper plate
☐ Glue or tape
☐ Black and white construction paper
☐ Black paint, brush
☐ Scissors

Directions:
1. Paint the paper plate black. Once the paint is dry, cut out the center of the paper plate. Leave the outside rim about 2 inches thick.

2. Cut a piece of black construction paper to approximately 8 inches by 8 inches. Glue or tape this into the circle you cut out of the paper plate so as much as possible sticks out through the hole in the plate.

3. Place the cut-out center of the paper plate on top of the black construction paper to form the top of the hat. Glue or tape it into place.

ACTIVITY PROJECT ## Reading Genesis in Other Languages

The invention of the printing press made books more available to everyone. Bibles were translated into many different languages—now Christians could read the Bible for themselves. Here is Genesis 1:1 is several different languages. Can you recognize any of the words? (Remember, English took words from many different languages.) If you like, you can copy the English translation and another translation onto the same paper.

English:
In the beginning God created the heaven and the earth.

Latin:
In principio creavit Deus caelum et terram.

French:
Au commencement, Dieu crea le ciel et la terre.

German:
Im Anfang schuf Gott die Himmel und die Erd.

Italian:
In principio Dio creo il cielo e la terra.

Spanish:
En el principio crio Dios el cielo y la terra.

ART PROJECT ## "Hot Off the Press! Bishop Yanks Beard at Council of Trent!"

Pretend you have just read a newspaper article updating the public on the Council of Trent. The author of the article recorded the story of the two bishops who got into such a heated debate that one bishop pulled the other's beard! Draw a picture to go along with that newspaper article.

ART PROJECT ## Make Stained Glass

Most people during medieval times were poor and uneducated—many could not even read. Bibles were rare and expensive. And even if a person had a Bible, he probably wouldn't be able to read it. So how could people learn about the Bible? One way was by looking at the beautiful stained glass windows inside the cathedrals and churches. The pictures on the glass showed scenes from the Bible.

Glass is made by mixing ash and sand together. Metals and pigments are added to the mixture to color the glass. The mixture is heated until it melts, and then cooled until it hardens into glass. The small pieces of glass are then connected to one another using strips of soft lead. Then the leaded glass is painted to add small details (such as faces and writing) to the pictures.

Easy Shrinky-Dink Simulated Stained Glass

Materials:
- ☐ Stained glass coloring pages (*Student Pages 150, 151*)
- ☐ Hole punch
- ☐ Stained glass paint (comes in a strip of several colors for under $2.00, available in craft stores) or markers, colored pencils or water color pencils
- ☐ Small paint brush if using paints
- ☐ Sandpaper
- ☐ Scissors
- ☐ Fishing line to hang
- ☐ Deli plastic containers, #6 recyclable, top and bottom circles cut out (or "Print & Shrink" oven-bake crafts sheets)

Directions:
1. Cut up a deli plastic container, freeing the useable top and bottom. Sand one side of the plastic until it is cloudy and you can feel the roughness on every part of it. This is so the color will stick. (Or if Print & Shrink sheets are used and you have a scanner, scan the stained glass coloring pages and print onto the sheets, then color as directed in step 2.)
2. Using the Stained Glass Coloring Page as a template, lay the plastic on top of the pattern. Trace the pattern on the plastic using a black marker. Make sure you are working on the scratched side. Then paint the picture using the stained glass paint or color with markers or colored pencils. Let the picture dry thoroughly.
3. Use the hole punch to make a hole in the top
4. Once you are finished, cut the picture out and place on a cookie sheet. Bake at 250 degrees for about 10 to 15 minutes (large projects will need to be baked at a lower temp). Check often. Burning plastic is not good for you to breathe. Take out when the items are lying flat and are thicker. Your item will shrink and the colors will intensify.
5. Use fishing line to hang your stained glass. These make beautiful Christmas ornaments.

Simulated Stained Glass on Plastic

Materials:
- ☐ Stained glass coloring pages (*Student Pages 150, 151*)
- ☐ Plastic craft sheets
- ☐ Stained glass paint (comes in a strip of several colors for under $2.00—available at craft stores) or markers
- ☐ Small paint brush if using paints
- ☐ Liquid leading (this takes a strong, steady hand and will be too difficult for young children) or Instant lead lines (works best when used with the stained glass coloring page)
- ☐ Fishing line for hanging

Directions: 1. Put template under plastic and trace it with black marker or with the liquid lines. If using the instant lead lines, cut and stick those onto the plastic.

2. When the leading is dry, use black glass paint or makers to fill in the black details. Then color or paint the rest of the picture.

3. Make a small hole in the top and hang your stained glass in a window using the fishing line.

Simulated Stained Glass on Glass

Materials: ☐ Stained glass coloring pages *(Student Pages 150, 151)*
      ☐ Clear glass (glass from an inexpensive picture frame works well)
      ☐ Tape
      ☐ Stained glass paint (comes in a strip of several colors for under $2.00—available at craft stores)
      ☐ Small paint brush
      ☐ Liquid leading (this takes a strong, steady hand and will be too difficult for young children) or Instant lead lines (works best when used with the stained glass coloring page)

Directions: 1. Tape all edges of the glass for safety.

2. Put template under glass and trace it the liquid lead. If you are using instant lead lines, cut and stick them on the glass.

3. Paint the glass with stained glass paint and let it dry thoroughly.

4. Glue the glass into a frame using hot glue and hang it in a window.

Simulated Stained Glass on Your Window

Materials: ☐ Stained glass coloring pages *(Student Pages 150, 151)*
      ☐ Window
      ☐ Washable markers
      ☐ Tape

Directions: 1. Tape the template outside your window.

2. Using the template as a guide, color on the window with the washable markers.

3. Let dry and enjoy. When ready to remove, the marker should come off easily with window cleaner.

The New Universe

CHAPTER 37

Encyclopedia Cross-References

UBWH 133, UILE 314
KIHW 332, 372–373, 446–447, KHE 203, 239, 269, 286

THE REVOLUTION OF COPERNICUS

REVIEW QUESTIONS

Do you remember where Nicholas Copernicus grew up? *He grew up in the part of Europe we now call Poland.*

What is the name for the science of the stars? *It is called astronomy.*

What does a star map show? *It shows where each star is at different times during the year.*

During Copernicus's time, what did most people believe was at the center of the universe? *They believed that the earth was at the center of the universe.*

According to this idea, what was the earth surrounded by? *It was surrounded by clear spheres with planets and stars attached to them.*

This idea was based on the theories of Ptolemy. But when Copernicus began to make measurements, what did he find out about Ptolemy's theories? *They were sometimes wrong!*

According to Copernicus's theory, the stars and planets didn't revolve around the earth. What did the earth and all the other planets revolve around? *They revolved around the sun.*

Why was Copernicus afraid to publish his theory? *Because he was a Catholic. The Catholic church taught that the earth was the center of the universe (or creation), and Copernicus was afraid to disagree.*

Why do we call Copernicus the "Father of Astronomy"? *He was the first to explain the movement of the planets and stars in a way that made sense.*

NARRATION EXERCISE

"Nicholas Copernicus realized that the earth was not at the center of the universe. In fact, the earth and all the other planets revolved around the sun. But he was afraid to write about this, because the Catholic church taught that the earth had to be at the center of God's creation." OR

"Many people in the Middle Ages believed that the earth was at the center of the universe. The planets and stars were on spheres all around the earth. But Copernicus thought this was wrong. He said that the planets went around the sun, not the earth. We call him the Father of Astronomy because of this."

GALILEO'S STRANGE NOTIONS

REVIEW QUESTIONS

What country was Galileo born in? *He was born in Italy.*

Why did his teachers call him "The Arguer"? *He spent a lot of time disagreeing with them!*

Name one thing that Galileo observed that led him to conclude that a downward force must pull on objects. *He saw a chandelier slowly stop swinging. OR He dropped two weights off a tower and noticed that they hit the ground at the same time.*

What do we call this downward force? *We call it gravity.*

Can you remember two of the experiments Galileo did to find out how things worked? *He threw balls; he swung pendulums; he moved objects with levers; he shot cannonballs; he dripped water from one cup into another.*

What instrument did Galileo invent when he was thirty-two? (Remember, he didn't *invent* the telescope—he just made it better.) *He invented the thermometer.*

Why do we consider Galileo to be one of the first *modern* scientists? *He tested his theories by performing experiments.*

What object did Galileo improve that enabled him to see hundreds of new stars and show that Copernicus's theories may have been right? *He improved the telescope.*

What book did Galileo write about his discoveries? *He wrote* The Starry Messenger.

How did the Catholic church react to Galileo's theories about the earth, sun, and stars? *They didn't like his theories and ordered Galileo to say that he was wrong.*

What do we call the study of why objects behave as they do? *We call this study* physics.

NARRATION EXERCISE

"Galileo was one of the first modern scientists. He tested his ideas by performing experiments. He also improved the telescope, which proved that Copernicus's theories could be true. He showed his telescope to the pope, but the Catholic church still did not accept his new ideas about the universe." OR

"Galileo was interested in the way things worked. He did many experiments and also made theories about gravity. When he saw many stars through his telescope, he could see that moons go around Jupiter. This showed that Copernicus could be right! Sometimes he is called the Father of Modern Physics."

Additional History Reading

Copernicus: Founder of Modern Astronomy, by Catherine M. Andronik (Enslow, 2002). This biography, written on an advanced fourth-grade level, covers both Copernicus's life and the theories believed in his day. (RA 2–4, IR 4–5)

Galileo: Astronomer and Physicist, by Paul Hightower (Enslow, 1997). A longish but easy-to-follow biography of Galileo, with clear descriptions of his scientific discoveries. Too long for an easy read-aloud, but a good family reading project. (RA 2, IR 3–5)

Galileo: Groundbreakers, by Paul Mason (Heinemann Library, 2001). A detailed but simply written biography of Galileo which includes diagrams of his universe and an account of the Catholic church's position on scientific discovery during the Renaissance. (IR 4–5)

Galileo: What's Their Story? by Jacqueline Mitton (Oxford University Press, 1997). A colorful 32–page biography of Galileo; good for a long read-aloud or a short independent reading assignment for an advanced third-grade reader. (RA 2–3, IR 3–5)

The Planets, by Gail Gibbons (Holiday House, 1994). This beginner's guide to the solar system features excellent illustrations of the planets and their orbits. (RA 1, IR 2–5)

Renaissance: Eyewitness Books, by Andrew Langley (Knopf, 1999). This Eyewitness guide to the Renaissance is a different title than the one listed for Chapter 35; it contains two-page spreads on anatomy, astronomy, and inventions during the Renaissance. **Out of print,** but worth finding at your local library. (RA 2–4, IR 5)

Corresponding Literature Suggestions

Children of the Sun, by Arthur John L'Hommedieu (Child's Play, 1994). Explore the solar system from the sun's point of view with this creative paper-engineered book! (IR 1–5)

The Genius of Leonardo, by Guido Visconti, illus. Bimba Landmann (Barefoot Books, 2000). Leonardo Da Vinci's new apprentice, Giacomo, gets off to a bad start with his new master—but learns to listen and watch and appreciate Da Vinci's genius. With quotes from Leonardo's own manuscripts. (RA 2–3, IR 4–5)

The Magic School Bus: Lost in the Solar System, by Joanna Cole, illus. Bruce Degen (Scholastic, 1992). Investigate the planets in their orbits around the sun with Ms. Frizzle and her class. (RA 1–2, IR 3–5)

Starry Messenger, by Peter Sis (Farrar, Straus & Giroux, 1996). An innovative and fascinating book telling Galileo's discoveries in plain simple language, with more complex cursive text and illustrations showing Galileo's own documentation of his ideas. (RA 1–2, IR 3–4)

Uh-oh, Leonardo! The Adventures of Providence Traveler, by Robert Sabuda (Atheneum, 2003). A little girl finds a mysterious design in a book about Leonardo—and is magically sent back to Florence during Leonardo's lifetime. (RA 1–2, IR 3–5)

MAP WORK

Poland and Italy *(Student Page 152, answer 263)*

1. Nicholas Copernicus grew up in the part of Europe we now call Poland. Underline Poland in green.
2. Copernicus studied science at a university in the city of Cracow. Put a purple box around Cracow. If you want, you can put some purple stars around the city, because Copernicus studied astronomy, the science of the stars.
3. Copernicus was a devout Roman Catholic, and he worried that the church would not approve of his theory. Underline Rome, the center of the Catholic church, in red.
4. Galileo Galilei was born in Italy. Color the "boot" of Italy yellow.
5. Galileo dropped objects from the Leaning Tower of Pisa. Put a blue box around the city of Pisa. If you want, you can draw a small "leaning tower" overtop of the city of Pisa.

COLORING PAGES

Today we call Nicholas Copernicus the *Father of Astronomy* because he was the first to explain the movement of the planets and stars in a way that made sense. *(Student Page 153)*

Our solar system *(Student Page 154)*

PROJECTS

CRAFT PROJECT   The Universe Hangs from My Ceiling!

(Note: This project has been edited to reflect Pluto's re-classification from planet to dwarf-planet in 2006.)

Below is a picture of the Copernican Universe. Now look at the coloring page for this chapter (this depicts what we think our solar system looks like today) and notice the differences between the two. How many planets are there in each diagram? Do the orbits of the planets look the same?

For this project you can make either Copernicus's universe or our solar system as we know it today.

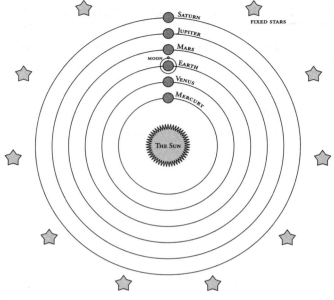

Note: If you would prefer a simpler non-hanging universe, skip the string and the buttons and just glue the Styrofoam balls directly onto the posterboard. OR If you don't want to go through the hassle of trying to attach something to your ceiling, consider using a large cardboard box. Lay an open box on its side. If you were to lie down with your head in the box you would be looking at the "ceiling" of the box. Cut the posterboard to the size of that ceiling. Attach the hanging universe to the ceiling of the box. Now you can climb inside the universe!)

Materials:
- One piece of black posterboard
- Eight (or ten if you are representing the modern solar system) Styrofoam balls of various sizes for the planets, sun, and moon
- Paint for the Styrofoam balls, including white paint for the orbits of the planets around the sun and the moon around the earth. (*Note:* Glow-in-the-dark paint is great for this activity—substitute it for the white.)
- Light gel pens (that will show up on black)
- Fishing line
- Small paperclips
- Buttons
- Scissors
- Sharpened pencil
- Tiny ceiling hooks (from which to hang posterboard)
- Optional: Tiny Christmas lights
- Tape for lights (clear masking tape is best)

Directions:
1. Mark a spot on the posterboard where you will eventually put the sun. This ought to be near the center of the poster because it will represent the center of the solar system.

2. Using a pencil, draw the orbits of the planets around the sun and the orbit of the moon around Earth. If you are drawing what we now know of the solar system, remember to make eight orbits for planets (Mercury, Venus, Earth, Mars, Jupiter, Saturn, Uranus, Neptune) and one orbit around Earth for its moon. If you are representing Copernicus's solar system you will need six orbits for planets and one orbit around Earth for its moon. Remember to make the orbits in the appropriate shape (circle or oval).

3. Paint the orbits white so they can be seen clearly on the black poster board (white, yellow, or glow-in-the-dark). You may also dot the poster board with white for stars. (*Note:* If you decide to do the Christmas lights, just mark with a pencil where you plan on putting the stars.)

4. While the orbits are drying, paint the Styrofoam balls for the planets, sun, and moon.

216

5. When all of the paint has dried, open a paperclip so it looks like a square and stick the open ends into the top of each Styrofoam ball. This should create a secure loop. Tie a piece of fishing line to the loop. The length of the line depends on how far down you want the planets to hang.

6. Place a dot on the posterboard where each of the planets, sun, and moon will be located. Pierce those dots with the end of a sharpened pencil.

7. Thread the line of the planets (and sun and moon) through the correct hole. The styrofoam balls should hang from the painted side of the posterboard. Tie the line to a button on the blank side of the posterboard.

8. Once all of the balls are attached, label each planet (and sun and moon) on the posterboard with the gel pen.

9. If you want to use the Christmas lights, pierce holes into the posterboard where you want the stars to go. Punch the Christmas lights through from the back of the holes so only the lighted portion shows on the front. Secure the strand of lights to the back of the posterboard with tape. Plug in the lights to see the stars shine!

10. Hang your universe. You can use the ceiling hooks (with more buttons and fishing line) to suspend your universe from the ceiling. This method is recommended if you use the lights. Or you can attach your universe to the ceiling with tape.

`ACTIVITY PROJECT` **Do the Pisa Drop!**

Pretend that you are the scientist Galileo dropping objects from the Leaning Tower of Pisa. See what happens when you drop things of different weights.

Materials: ☐ One golf ball*
            ☐ One Ping Pong ball*
(*Note:* You can use other items as long as they are similarly shaped but have different weights.)

Directions: 1. Have one of your parents go to an upstairs window, the top of a set of stairs (off of which you can drop the balls straight down instead of just onto other steps), a balcony, or some other place where you can drop the balls straight down. It would be best to be at least nine or ten feet from the ground.

2. Stand near where the balls will land so you can see when they drop. Which object do you think will touch the ground first? If you were alive in Galileo's time, everyone would think the heavier object would touch first.

3. Have your parent drop the balls. Notice when they touch the ground. Do they touch the ground at about the same time? They should!
(*Note:* The balls may not touch the ground at *exactly* the same time due to air resistance.)

`ACTIVITY PROJECT` **Star Light, Star Bright, Explore the Stars in the Sky Tonight**

Go outside at night and look at the stars. Do you know any constellations? See if you can find the Big Dipper. It looks like a giant spoon. In the fall it is right-side up but in the spring it is upside down. Do you see the pair of stars that are on the edge of the spoon furthest from the handle? These are known as the "Pointer Stars" because they point to Polaris, the North Star. Draw an imaginary line between the two stars, starting at the star at the base of the spoon and going up through the star at the top of the spoon. Continue drawing this imaginary line about five times as far as the distance between the Pointer Stars. Follow the curve of the sky just slightly and you will reach Polaris. (See page 165 of this guide for a diagram of the Big Dipper.)

Although the stars appear to rotate slowly in the night sky, Polaris stays in the same place. That is why it is called the North Star—if you are facing it, you are always facing north.

Polaris is in a constellation of its own—the Little Dipper. The stars of the Little Dipper are not as bright as the Big Dipper stars, so you will need a dark, clear night to see it well. Polaris is at the end of the dipper handle of the Little Dipper.

Find the Big Dipper again and draw an imaginary line through the Pointer Stars again, this time turning left (a right angle). Follow this line about four times the distance between the Pointer Stars and you will come to the three bright stars of Orion's belt. (The constellation of Orion the Hunter is best viewed around January in the middle to northern latitudes.)

There are many other constellations in the night sky, and every month certain constellations are in better view. Consider getting a constellation guide. You can also put your favorite constellations on your bedroom ceiling using glow-in-the-dark stars.

ACTIVITY PROJECT   Make a Bubble Telescope

Galileo improved the telescope—a device that used lenses to make far away objects seem very close. Make your own pretend telescope. You can imagine that you are Galileo peering at the night sky, seeing stars, planets, and moons. (Although Galileo would never have done this, you can also use your telescope to make bubbles!)

Materials:
- 3–4 (6 ounce) empty frozen juice containers, ends removed
- Masking tape
- Paint
- Bubble formula (optional: recipe below)

Directions:
1. Tape the juice containers end to end to make one long tube.
2. Paint tube the color you want the telescope to be.

Bubble Formula Recipe

Ingredients:
4½ cups water
½ cup hand dishwashing detergent
½ cup corn syrup or glycerin (optional: but it makes stronger bubbles)

Directions:
1. Combine and stir (but do not shake).
2. For best results, make 2–3 days ahead. When ready to use, pour into a pan. Dip one end of the telescope into the liquid for 2–3 seconds. Don't slosh it around—this creates foam which will burst your bubble. Gently blow on the other end of your telescope. Turn your telescope gently to close off the bubble.

England's Greatest Queen

Encyclopedia Cross-References

UBWH 146–147, UILE 304–305
KIHW 374–376, KHE 211

THE QUEEN WHO ALMOST WASN'T

REVIEW QUESTIONS

How old was Edward VI when he became king? *He was only nine years old.*

What happened to Edward? *He became sick and died.*

After the sickly Edward VI died, who became the ruler of England? *Mary, Henry's oldest daughter, became queen.*

Why was Elizabeth frightened when her sister Mary first became queen? *Elizabeth knew that Mary didn't like her very much. OR Elizabeth had been favored by their father when she was little. She worried that Mary might still resent her for it.*

Before Elizabeth was born, Mary was Princess of Wales. Can you name two special ways in which she was treated? *She had her own coat of arms, her own private apartments, and 160 servants. She rode in a velvet litter and ate her meals beneath a velvet canopy.*

As soon as Elizabeth was born, what did the herald announce? *He announced that Elizabeth, not Mary, was Princess of Wales.*

What happened to Mary's coat of arms and her 160 servants? *She lost them all.*

What happened to Elizabeth when Prince Edward was born? *The same thing—she lost her special servants, coat of arms, litter, and place to eat.*

When Mary became queen, what terrible thing did she do to her sister, Elizabeth? *She arrested her and put her in prison. OR She accused Elizabeth of plotting against her and had her imprisoned in the Tower of London.*

After Elizabeth was released from the Tower of London, where was she sent to live? *She was sent to a small house in the country.*

When Mary died, who became the next ruler of England? *Elizabeth became the next ruler.*

NARRATION EXERCISE

"When Henry VIII died, his son Edward became king. But then Edward died, and Mary became queen of England. She had her younger sister Elizabeth put in prison. She was afraid that Elizabeth would plot against her. But when Mary died, Elizabeth became the next queen." OR

"When Elizabeth was born, Mary lost her right to be the Princess of Wales. Then, when Edward was born, Elizabeth lost *her* right to be Princess of Wales! Elizabeth was nervous when her older sister Mary became queen of England. She thought that Mary didn't like her, and she was right! But when Mary died, Elizabeth became the new queen of England."

Review Questions

What did Mary do as queen that made her very unpopular? (Hint: She tried to undo something that her father Henry VIII had done.) *She forced people to return to the Catholic faith. If they refused, they were put to death.*

Why was she called "Bloody Mary"? *Some people called her Bloody Mary because of her cruelty.*

Do you remember three things that Elizabeth wore at her coronation when she was crowned Queen? *She wore a gold gown, a velvet cape with ermine fur, a ruby and pearl necklace, and a heavy gold crown.*

How long did Elizabeth reign? *She ruled for 45 years.*

What do we call the years of her reign? *We call them the "Elizabethan Age."*

Queen Elizabeth declared England to be a Protestant country again. Did she force her people to swear that they were Protestants? *No, she did not force them to swear.*

What did her people, her advisors, and especially the Parliament expect Elizabeth to do as soon as she became queen? *They expected her to get married.*

Why didn't Queen Elizabeth want to marry? *She knew that if she married, her husband would be the real ruler of England. OR She didn't want to give up her power to a husband.*

Who sent Parliament a letter offering to marry Queen Elizabeth and "relieve her of those labors which are only for men"? *Prince Philip of Spain OR Mary's husband, Philip, offered to marry Elizabeth.*

To what did Elizabeth claim to be married? *She said that she was married to England.*

What affectionate nickname did the people of England give to Queen Elizabeth? *They called her Good Queen Bess.*

Narration Exercise

"Elizabeth was crowned Queen of England in a huge ceremony and was given a golden crown. When Elizabeth became queen, everyone expected her to get married right away so a man could rule England. Mary's husband Philip offered to marry her! But Queen Elizabeth did not get married because she wanted to rule England all by herself. She was the best ruler England ever had." OR

"Mary wanted England to be Catholic, so she punished people who refused to worship in the Catholic church. Her people called her Bloody Mary. When Elizabeth became Queen, she made England Protestant. But she didn't force people to worship in the Protestant church. Queen Elizabeth was such a good ruler that her people called her Good Queen Bess. She made alliances with other countries, defended her country from invasion, and sent out explorers to claim land for England."

Additional History Reading

Elizabeth I and Tudor England, by Miriam Greenblatt (Benchmark Books, 2002). This biography, which covers both Elizabeth's life and everyday life in England under her rule, is for slightly older children. However, the chapters are very brief and selected chapters ("A Religious Compromise," "The Question of Marriage," and "The Spanish Armada" in particular) would make good read-alouds. (RA 1–3, IR 4–5)

Elizabeth the First, Queen of England: A Rookie Biography, by Carol Greene (Children's Press, 1990). Written for beginners, this biography still covers all the important events of Elizabeth's life. Illustrated with contemporary portraits; highly recommended. (RA 1, IR 2–4)

Good Queen Bess: The Story of Elizabeth I of England, by Diane Stanley and Peter Vennema. (Four Winds Press, 1990). A detailed picture-book with beautiful pictures and longish (but interesting) paragraphs of text on each page; covers the religious wars of England with tact. (RA 1–2, IR 3–5)

Queen Elizabeth I, by Kate Havelin (Lerner Publishing, 2002). For older students, an engaging biography which gives detailed attention to Elizabeth's sponsorship of explorers and her war with Spain. (IR 4–5)

Ten Queens: Portraits of Women of Power, by Milton Meltzer, illus. Bethanne Andersen (Dutton Children's Books, 1998). Ten interesting biographies for reading aloud; each is 8–14 pages, with color illustrations. Includes Queen Elizabeth and Eleanor of Aquitaine, a fascinating French princess who married into the English royal line and became the mother of John and Richard. (Mentions King Henry's mistresses and affairs.) (RA 2–4, IR 5)

Corresponding Literature Suggestions

Elizabeth I: Red Rose of the House of Tudor, England, 1544, by Kathryn Lasky (Scholastic, 1999). In this chapter book designed for slightly older students (part of the "Royal Diaries" series), Princess Elizabeth keeps her journal and records her fears about her future. Good for older readers or as a family read-aloud. (RA 1–4, IR 5)

She Was Nice to Mice: The Other Side of Elizabeth I's Character Never Before Revealed by Previous Historians, by Alexandra Elizabeth Sheedy (McGraw Hill, 1975). The mice of Queen Elizabeth's court dance, play, and watch Elizabeth's reign in this classic picture book. **Out of print.** (RA 1–2, IR 2–5)

———————————— MAP WORK ————————————

Elizabeth's England *(Student Page 155, answer 263)*

1. Elizabeth spent much of her childhood in the Old Palace in Hertfordshire. It was here that she was told that she was queen. Circle Hertfordshire in blue.

2. Both Mary and Elizabeth were each declared to be "Princess of Wales." Put an orange box around Wales. Wales is part of Britain; the heir to the British throne is always called the "Prince" or "Princess of Wales."

3. When Mary became queen, she worried that her sister Elizabeth would plot against her. So she had Elizabeth imprisoned in the Tower of London. Put a green box around London.

4. Windsor Castle in Berkshire was one of Queen Elizabeth's principle residences (a queen can't be expected to live in just one castle!). It is still a royal residence today. Circle Berkshire in yellow.

COLORING PAGE
Queen Elizabeth was the best ruler England ever had. Her people loved her and gave her the nickname Good Queen Bess. *(Student Page 156)*

———————————— PROJECTS ————————————

CRAFT PROJECT Make Elizabethan Clothing

Styles of dress were very different in the time of Queen Elizabeth than they are today. Women (and sometimes men) often wore large ruffles around their necks called "ruffs." Men also adopted a fashion called "slashing" where tailors cut slashes in a garment to be worn over another garment of a contrasting color to have the color of the garment underneath show through.

Make a Woman's Ruff

Materials:
- ☐ One long piece of paper or several short pieces of paper, taped together.
- ☐ Tape

Directions:
1. Fold the paper accordion style, with the folds parallel to the short side.
2. Put the paper gently around your neck. Tape the ends together. Now you look like the Queen of England!

Make a Man's "Slashed" Shirt

Materials:
- ☐ Old shirt with long sleeves
- ☐ Newer shirt of a contrasting color, also with long sleeves
- ☐ Scissors

Directions:
1. Using scissors, cut three long slits (running from about six inches below the shoulder to about six inches above the cuff) an equal distance apart in each sleeve. Make two long cuts in the front of the shirt and two in the back as well.
2. Put the shirt on over the contrasting color. When you walk or move your arms, the cuts should gape open to show the shirt beneath!

ACTIVITY PROJECT ## Design an Elizabethan E-Shaped Building

In the days of Queen Elizabeth, many architects constructed buildings that were in the shape of an "E" to honor the queen. What is the first letter of your first name? Would it be easy to design a building in that shape? Now try making a building in the shape of an "E."

Materials:
- ☐ Cereal box
- ☐ Two additional sheets of thin cardboard
- ☐ Scissors
- ☐ Glue or tape
- ☐ Paint (optional)

Directions:
1. On the cereal box, draw a large block letter E that uses up the entire box. (So the long side of the box should be the spine of the E.)
2. Cut away the parts of the box that are not part of the E. (You are making a 3-dimensional E, so the only parts you are cutting are two long, thin rectangles.)
3. Use the extra cardboard to close the parts of the E that are still open. Glue or tape into place.
4. Paint the building with a solid color or with designs if you choose. Draw doors and windows. Elizabethans often planted gardens between the legs of the E. You can plant a garden too! Put the building on a larger piece of paper and tape or glue silk, dried, or fresh flowers and leaves to the paper.

COOKING PROJECT ## Take a Renaissance Cure

When Edward VI became sick, his physicians tried every cure they knew. One cure was to put leeches on the young king to suck out some of his blood. Another was to have him swallow a live spider covered in molasses! But none of these cures worked. Is it any wonder? Take a Renaissance cure yourself.

Swallow a Spider to Rejuvenate the Body

Ingredients: Gummi spider or cooked spaghetti noodles cut into 2 inch strips
Molasses or honey

Directions: 1. Cover your spider with molasses or honey.

2. Chew it up and swallow it. Do you feel a boost of energy?

Make a Salve to Cure Sores

Ingredients: Egg yolk
Rose petals (or any flower petals)
Vinegar

Directions: 1. Combine all the above ingredients. Stir well.

2. Smear on the skin to treat sores.

Brew Lettuce Tea to Help You Sleep

Ingredients: Lettuce (a mug full of torn lettuce, any type)
Hot water
Chicken bouillon cube (optional)

Directions: 1. Fill a mug with torn bits of lettuce.

2. Pour very hot water over the lettuce. Add a chicken bouillion cube if desired. Stir until the lettuce is wilted and the bouillon cube is dissolved. Drink—are you getting sleepy?

Make an Emerald and Ruby Powder to Relieve Sore Limbs

Ingredients: Red and green hard candy (like Lifesavers or Jolly Ranchers)

Directions: 1. Put hard candy in a zip-close plastic bag. Seal the bag. Crush candy with a mallet, wooden spoon, or hammer.

2. Apply the powder to a sore limb.

Swallow a Handful of Spider Webs to Relieve a Cough

Ingredients: Cotton candy

Directions: 1. Eat a handful of cotton candy. Did that cure your cough? If not, try the next cure.

Boil Cherry Bark to Relieve a Cough

Ingredients: Cinnamon sticks (about 8 inches worth of stick)
1½ cups water
1 tablespoon maple syrup

Directions: 1. Place the cinnamon sticks and water in a sauce pan. Heat until boiling. Cover; lower heat until it simmers. Let simmer for 15 minutes.

2. Pour into a mug (leave in the cinnamon sticks, although you will not eat these). Add the maple syrup. Stir; drink when cool enough.

Cow Manure Poultice to Draw Out Poison from Inflamed Limbs

Ingredients: Playdough (preferably brown)
OR
Cocoa Oat Treats (no bake; recipe below)

Directions: 1. Apply a small amount of poultice to your arm. Let sit for a few minutes. Rinse off.

Cocoa Oat Treat Recipe

Ingredients:

3 cups rolled oats	½ cup (1 stick) butter or margarine
⅔ cup peanut butter	½ cup milk
½ cup peanuts, chopped (optional)	⅓ cup unsweetened cocoa powder
2 cups sugar	2 teaspoons vanilla extract

Directions:

1. Line cookie sheets with waxed paper.

2. Combine oats, peanut butter, and peanuts in a bowl. Set aside.

3. In a saucepan, add sugar, butter, milk, cocoa. Heat until mixture boils, stirring constantly.

4. Remove from heat. Add vanilla and oat mixture. Stir quickly and mix well.

5. Immediately drop mixture by spoonfuls onto waxed paper. (Reserve a couple spoonfuls for poultice.) Cool. Store in an airtight container. Makes 4 dozen treats.

ACTIVITY PROJECT   The Queen's Coronation Parade

Elizabeth planned a great ceremony in which she would be crowned queen. There was a grand and elaborate coronation parade that led to the site of the coronation ceremony, Westminster Abbey. Reenact the coronation parade. Have a parent or sibling play Elizabeth (if you want, you can do it twice with you playing Queen Elizabeth the second time). You will wait on her majesty and organize the parade stops.

Materials:

- ☐ Paper
- ☐ Pencil
- ☐ Chair
- ☐ Cape or twin flat-sheet
- ☐ Classical instrumental or choral music
- ☐ Gold lamé fabric, yellow/gold colored fabric, or a sheet
- ☐ Necklaces (costume jewelry pearls or jewels)
- ☐ Fur stole (don't have one? Use faux-fur fabric or a floppy stuffed animal)
- ☐ Circlet (use a necklace or follow the directions for a fairy halo in the next activity)
- ☐ Flower petals, silk flowers, or bits of construction paper
- ☐ 4 knights (4 action figures, dolls, or stuffed animals)
- ☐ Assorted dolls and stuffed animals
- ☐ Safety pins
- ☐ Towels, sheets, or rugs
- ☐ CD or tape player
- ☐ Bowl

Directions: **Set Up**

1. Wherever Elizabeth traveled on the parade, blue cloth was placed over the route. Lay out a parade route using the towels, rugs, or sheets. It does not need to be long. You can lay the path around one room, or travel to several rooms near one another. Place the dolls and stuffed animals around the path. They will be the cheering crowds.

2. Queen Elizabeth rode a chariot. Four knights walked alongside the chariot, carrying a golden canopy that sheltered Elizabeth from sun or rain. Unless you are allowed to have horses inside the house, your Queen Elizabeth will have to walk from stop to stop. But you can't allow a queen to stand all that time! Place a chair on the beginning of the path. At every stop you will have to fetch the chair for her. After all, your job is to wait on the queen.

3. *Set up stop 1:* Elizabeth traveled through the streets of London, stopping at several neighborhoods. People lined the streets, cheering for the new queen. Some threw flower petals, some played music, others recited speeches. At stop 1 on this coronation parade, Elizabeth will receive a showering of rose petals (or silk flowers or torn bits of construction paper). Place a bowl of petals at the beginning of the path, near the chair. This will be stop 1.

4. *Set up stop 2:* This will be the music stop. Put the classical music in the CD or tape player and plug it in. Cue up the music so you only have to press the "play" button to get it going.

5. *Set up stop 3:* People gave speeches telling Elizabeth how glad they were that she was queen, how they fondly remembered the reign of her father, King Henry VIII, how they hoped she lived a long and healthy life, and how glad they were to have a Protestant ruler again. Write a short speech to give to Queen Elizabeth. Begin it with "Your Royal Majesty Queen Elizabeth." Set this at stop 3.

Prepare Queen Elizabeth for Her Coronation

1. Have the queen sit down in another room. Make sure she is comfortable. Ask her, "Are you comfortable, Your Majesty?" Does she need a glass of water to quench her thirst or perhaps a pillow to cushion her? Once she is ready, prepare her for the ceremony.

2. If your Queen Elizabeth has long hair, have her wear it down. That is how the young queen wore her hair on coronation day.

3. Place the necklace(s) around her neck. Queen Elizabeth had a heavy necklace of rubies and pearls that she wore.

4. Place the circlet on her head. Elizabeth wore the gold circlet during the parade. The circlet was replaced with the crown during the ceremony at Westminster Abbey.

5. Ask the queen to stand. Drape her with the gold or yellow fabric (the queen wore a gown made of gold cloth). Secure the fabric with safety pins to make it stay in place.

6. Place the cape (or twin sheet) around her shoulders. Secure it with a safety pin or brooch. Queen Elizabeth wore a cape of velvet, trimmed with fur. Place the fur stole around her neck.

   She is now ready for her coronation.

The Parade

1. *Escort the queen to her chariot (the chair) at stop 1.* Set the four knights around her. Grab the bowl of petals. Walk around the queen, tossing petals into the air and saying, "Long live the queen! Long live Queen Elizabeth!" The queen may nod and wave to you, but she would not smile. This is a very serious occasion.

2. *Escort the queen to stop 2.* Fetch the chair for her, and replace the knights around her. Say to the queen, "In your honor, we shall play music." Play the music on the player. Play only one song (the queen's time is precious).

3. ***Escort the queen to stop 3.*** Again, fetch the chair and knights for her. Read the speech you prepared. It is said that when Queen Elizabeth heard a speech, she smiled (so your queen may smile too). Present her with the written speech when you are through.

4. ***Escort the queen to the end of her path.*** The parade is over; she must now go on to Westminster Abbey. Send her off with cries of "Long live the queen!"

Be Elizabeth, the Fairy Queen

Renaissance writers had a special name for Elizabeth. They called her "Gloriana" because she was so glorious! In his long poem "The Faerie Queene," the poet Edmund Spenser, who lived during Elizabeth's reign, wrote about a beautiful, shining royal court, ruled over by a powerful Fairy Queen. This "Queen" stood for Elizabeth I!

Fairy Wings

Materials:
- Posterboard (large size)
- Pencil
- Scissors
- Lacy fabric pieces, paper doilies, markers, glitter, or aluminum foil
- Hole punch
- Ribbon (1 yard)
- Glue stick

Directions:
1. Fold the piece of posterboard in half crosswise. Sketch one half of a heart on one side of the folded posterboard (or half of a butterfly's wing, depending on the style of wing you would like to make). Make sure that the straight edge of the heart half is along the folded edge of the posterboard.

2. Cut out your half-heart. Unfolded, you should have one large heart. Punch one hole on each side of the heart. Each hole should be about 3–4 inches from the center crease, and in line horizontally with the other hole. The holes should be in the middle to upper portion of the heart.

3. Decorate the wings however you choose: glue lacy fabric or paper doilies to make lacy wings, glue on glitter to make sparkly wings, glue on aluminum foil to make shiny wings.

4. Set the wings down so they are open like a book would open. Thread the ribbon from the underside of one hole, up over the crease, and down through the other hole. You should have two strands of equal length hanging from the underside of the wings. Now put the left strand of ribbon under the left arm of the child. Put the right strand under the right arm. Loop the strands over the respective shoulders and tie them in a bow behind the child's neck.

Fairy Halo

Materials:
- Aluminum foil or 6–10 chenille wires
- Scissors
- Tape

Directions:
1. If using aluminum foil, measure a length of foil 1½ times the circumference of the child's head. Twist the aluminum foil into a strand. Twist the ends together and secure with tape. The shiny halo should rest on the child's head.

2. If using the chenille wires, twist two contrasting colors together. When you reach the ends, twist on the next set of chenille wires. Keep twisting and attaching until you have a halo that will rest on the child's head. You may have to snip the pipe cleaners to get them to fit.

Fairy Wand

Materials:
- Thin wooden dowel (about 1½ feet in length) or two unused pencils taped securely together with clear packing tape
- Tape
- Stapler
- Thin cardboard or cardstock
- Aluminum foil or glitter
- Glue stick
- Ribbon (several strands about 1½ feet in length)

Directions:
1. Draw a star (or trace a cookie cutter) onto the cardboard. Cut it out. Trace the cut-out star onto another piece of cardboard and cut that out. You should have two identical stars.
2. Cover the stars with aluminum foil or decorate them with glue and glitter. Let dry if necessary.
3. Gather the ribbon lengths into a bunch. Tie them (as one) to the top of the dowel (or pencils).
4. Place the stars on either side of the ribbon knot, decorated sides facing out. Try to line the star edges up exactly. The strands of ribbon should dangle beneath the stars, down the length of the dowel. Staple the sides of the stars as close as possible to the dowel (try to staple some of the ribbons in there too—to secure them). Secure the bottom inside of the stars to the dowel with glue or tape.

England's Greatest Playwright

CHAPTER 39

Encyclopedia Cross-References

UBWH 146–147, UILE 304
KIHW 375, KHE 211, 234

WILLIAM SHAKESPEARE

REVIEW QUESTIONS

Can you remember two of the ways in which Queen Elizabeth entertained herself? *She kept a choir and an orchestra, she sang to herself and played the lyre, she read and wrote poetry, and she saw plays.*

When Shakespeare was young, he belonged to a traveling company. What did this company do? *It went from town to town and performed plays in wooden theatres and the courtyards of inns.*

What is a comedy? *A comedy is a funny play.*

What is a tragedy? *A tragedy is a sad play.*

What is a play based on the lives of famous men and women of the past? *It is a historical play.*

Name at least one play that Shakespeare wrote. *He wrote Macbeth, The Taming of the Shrew, A Midsummer Night's Dream, Hamlet, Romeo and Juliet, Richard III, Henry V, Henry IV, Othello.* (These are the plays listed in the text.)

Do you remember one of the famous phrases from Shakespeare's plays? *Something is rotten in the state of Denmark; to be or not to be—that is the question; a horse, a horse, my kingdom for a horse; you're going to eat me out of house and home; the green-eyed monster.*

What was King Duncan afraid of, at the beginning of the story? *He was afraid that rebels would throw him from his throne.*

Why did King Duncan give Macbeth the title "Thane of Cawdor"? *He gave Macbeth the title because Macbeth fought bravely for him.*

How did Macbeth *first* hear that he would be Thane of Cawdor and King of Scotland? *Three weird women told him.*

How did Macbeth and his wife plan to make Macbeth king? *They planned to murder the king (King Duncan).*

Who was more willing to kill the king—Macbeth or Lady Macbeth? *Lady Macbeth was more willing.*

Why did Lady Macbeth say that no one would suspect them of the crime? *They would be weeping over Duncan's death!*

NARRATION EXERCISE

"William Shakespeare is a famous English playwright. He wrote many plays including *Macbeth*. In that story, three weird women tell Macbeth that he will be the next king of Scotland. He and his wife decide to kill the king, King Duncan." OR

"*Macbeth* is a play written by William Shakespeare. It is about a man named Macbeth who meets three weird women who tell him that he will be king. He tells his wife about their message. The two of them decide to kill the king of Scotland. When the king comes to visit them, they make their plans."

REVIEW QUESTIONS

Why doesn't Banquo want to put out his candle? *He is restless and thinks that something terrible may happen.*

How did Lady Macbeth get rid of Duncan's guards? *She gave them drugged wine that made them sleep.*

Why wasn't Lady Macbeth able to kill King Duncan? *She thought he looked like her father, so she lost her nerve.*

What does Macbeth think that he sees, hanging in the air? *He thinks he sees a dagger.*

After Macbeth murdered King Duncan, what did he tell his wife he would never be able to do again? *He says that he will never sleep.*

After Macbeth became King of Scotland, what did he do to Banquo? *He hired three murderers to kill him.*

Macbeth and Lady Macbeth both suffered from terrible guilt over what they had done. Name one way that the guilt showed itself. *They both had nightmares. Macbeth saw Banquo's ghost. Lady Macbeth started walking in her sleep and rubbing her hands as if she were washing them. Eventually Lady Macbeth died of a guilty conscience.*

Macbeth went back to the weird women to ask them how long he would be king. What did the women say? *He would be king until the forest walked up to his castle.*

How did the approaching army manage to look like a forest? *Each soldier held a tree branch in front of his body.*

NARRATION EXERCISE

"Macbeth became king of Scotland after he murdered the former king. He and his wife felt very guilty about the murder. She walked in her sleep, and he said that he would never sleep again. He asked the weird women how long he would be king. They said he would rule until a forest attacked his castle. But then soldiers carrying branches attacked and defeated him!" OR

"Macbeth murdered the king of Scotland and was made the new king. Once he was king, Macbeth felt uneasy about what he had done. He worried that someone might now kill him for the crown. He even had his friend Banquo killed. His wife died because she felt so guilty! Eventually Macbeth was killed by relatives of the former king. He came to a bad end because he plotted treason!"

Additional History Reading

The Bard of Avon: The Story of William Shakespeare, by Diane Stanley (William Morrow & Company, 1992). This beautifully illustrated picture-book with advanced third-grade text tells about Shakespeare's life and work and even covers his effect on the English language. (RA 1–3, IR 3–5)

Heroes: Great Men Through the Ages, by Rebecca Hazell (Abbeville Press, 1997). Twelve interesting read-aloud biographies, including that of William Shakespeare. (RA 2–3, IR 4–5)

Welcome to the Globe: The Story of Shakespeare's Theater, by Peter Chrisp (Dorling Kindersley, 2000). Using the voices of Richard Burbage, a stage apprentice, and other characters, Chrisp describes the Globe, Shakespeare's plays, and life in Elizabethan London. Nice large font, beautiful pictures. (RA 1–2, IR 3–5)

William Shakespeare and the Globe, by Aliki (Harpercollins, 1999). A wonderful picture-book that begins with Shakespeare's childhood, covers his founding of his own theater company and the building of the Globe, and ends with the collection of Shakespeare's works, the rediscovery of the Globe's foundations in the twentieth century, and its rebuilding. (RA 1–2, IR 3–5)

William Shakespeare: What's Their Story? by Haydn Middleton (Oxford University Press, 1997). An interesting and simple biography of Shakespeare, from his beginnings as a playwright through his involvement with the Globe and his death at 52; on an advanced third-grade level. (RA 2–3, IR 3–5)

Corresponding Literature Suggestions

Bravo, Mr. William Shakespeare! by Marcia Williams (Candlewick Press, 1998). These highly entertaining tales are retold, frame by frame, using colorful illustrations with characters speaking lines from the plays; cartoons of Elizabethans commenting on the actions enliven the margins. Includes *As You Like It, Richard III, Antony and Cleopatra, Twelfth Night, King Lear, The Merchant of Venice,* and *Much Ado About Nothing.* (RA 2–3, IR 3–5)

Hamlet: From Shakespeare Stories by Leon Garfield, read by Simon Russell Beale (Chivers North America, 1999). An audiobook presentation of the retold tale. (IR 2–5)

A Midsummer Night's Dream: From Shakespeare Stories by Leon Garfield, read by Clare Higgins (Chivers North America, 1999). An audiobook presentation of the retold tale. (IR 2–5)

A Midsummer Night's Dream, retold by Bruce Coville, illus. Dennis Nolan (Dial Books, 1996). An entertaining and lavishly illustrated picture-book version of the Shakespeare play, with relatively lengthy text. (RA 1–2, IR 3–5)

Shakespeare Can Be Fun! series, by Lois Burdett (Firefly Books). This series, which includes *Hamlet, Macbeth, Romeo and Juliet, The Tempest,* and *A Midsummer Night's Dream,* is retold in rhyme (using some original quotes) and illustrated by the author's second- and third-grade classes. Includes photos of the children performing the plays and suggestions for projects and activities; a wonderful resource for introducing Shakespeare. (RA 2–3, IR 4–5)

Tales from Shakespeare, by Marcia Williams (Candlewick Press, 1998). These highly entertaining tales are retold, frame by frame, using colorful illustrations with characters speaking lines from the plays; cartoons of Elizabethans commenting on the actions enliven the margins. Includes *Romeo and Juliet, Hamlet, A Midsummer Night's Dream, Macbeth, The Winter's Tale, Julius Caesar,* and *The Tempest.* (RA 2–3, IR 3–5)

―――――――――――――― **MAP WORK** ――――――――――――――

England *(Student Page 157, answer 263)*

1. William Shakespeare was born in Stratford-upon-Avon. Underline Stratford-upon-Avon twice in red.
2. He traveled to London to make a living as a writer and a playwright. Draw a red line from Stratford-upon-Avon to London.
3. Shakespeare's famous theater, the Globe, put on productions of many of his plays including *Macbeth.* The Globe Theater is located in London. Draw an orange box around London.
4. Macbeth killed Duncan so that Macbeth could be King of Scotland. Color Scotland yellow.
5. King Duncan made Macbeth Thane of Cawdor as a reward for defeating the rebels. Circle Cawdor in brown.

COLORING PAGE   William Shakespeare, England's greatest playwright *(Student Page 158)*

ART PROJECT | Draw a Picture of Macbeth

Draw a picture of Macbeth visiting the weird women or the feast with Banquo's ghost.

COOKING PROJECT | Make Eye-of-Newt Soup

The three weird women concoct spells in their bubbling cauldron. Make your own eye-of-newt soup. As you go, read the following adaptation from *Macbeth* (Act 4, Scene 1). Add the ingredients at the appropriate time. (*Note:* Do not add the "baboon's blood"—that is to be drunk at the end of the poem.) It is really fun to put the ingredients in glass jars and label them with their fictitious names (i.e., "eye of newt," "tooth of wolf").

Ingredients: Fingers—tootsie rolls
Eye of newt—chocolate chips
Tongue of dog—red licorice
Lizard's leg—pretzel sticks

Owlet's wing—mini marshmallows
Scale of dragon—smarties
Tooth of wolf—candy corn
Gall of goat—raisins

Also:
A cup of baboon's blood—Grape juice or cranberry juice

Directions: Read the poem. When you get to each ingredient, put it in a big pot and stir the soup with a big wooden spoon!

> Double, double toil and trouble;
> Fire burn, and cauldron bubble.
> Round about the cauldron go;
> In the **severed fingers** throw.
> Fillet of a fenny snake,
> In the cauldron boil and bake;
> **Eye of newt** and toe of frog,
> Wool of bat and **tongue of dog,**
> Adder's fork and blind-worm's sting,
> **Lizard's leg** and **owlet's wing,**
> For a charm of powerful trouble,
> Like a hot broth boil and bubble.
>
> Double, double toil and trouble;
> Fire burn and cauldron bubble.
> **Scale of dragon, tooth of wolf,**
> Witches' mummy, maw and gulf
> Of the ravined salt-sea shark,
> **Gall of goat** removed in the dark.
>
> Now drink a cup of baboon's blood,
> Then the charm is firm and good.

The actors of Shakespeare's day played scenes of battle and war almost every night! When they dueled with each other, though, they weren't really fighting. They were "stage fighting." When they punched and slashed, they did so in a way that looked real to the audience—but wasn't dangerous. And when someone was "killed," they used props such as false blood to make the death look realistic. You can pretend that you are a Shakespearean actor, playing in *Macbeth,* preparing for the big duel at the end of the play!

Materials:
- ☐ Corn syrup
- ☐ Red and blue food coloring
- ☐ Water
- ☐ A small plastic bag (such as a sandwich bag)
- ☐ Four cardboard tubes, two slightly smaller in diameter than the other two (for example, Two wrapping paper tubes and two smaller tubes from a paper towel or plastic wrap roll; two paper towel tubes and two toilet paper tubes; etc.)

Directions:

1. Mix one-half cup of corn syrup, six drops of red food coloring, five drops of blue food coloring, and one teaspoon of water. Put this gooey mixture into your plastic bag, and seal or twist-tie it closed.

2. Prepare your "swords." Slide the smaller tubes into the larger tubes so that they overlap by 2–3 inches. If the smaller tube keeps falling out or slipping all the way into the larger tube, use a single piece of tape to attach the tubes to each other.

3. Practice "sword fighting" with a friend, parent, or sibling. Here are a few principles of stage combat for you to remember:

   a. Never be close enough to actually hit each other with the swords. Stage fighters stay safe by remaining out of each other's reach! Your swords should touch, but when you extend your arm with your sword in it, you should not be able to touch each other. Stage fighting is exciting because the swords clank against each other a lot, not because the fighters actually hit each other's bodies.

   b. Whenever you thrust your sword at your opponent, aim for the left or right of your opponent's body, NOT at his chest or stomach. Remember that the audience will be sitting to the side of your fight. They won't be able to tell whether or not you're actually aiming at your opponent's body!

   c. Stage fighting is done slowly, so that the audience can follow each move. Each swing of your sword should be slightly slower than you feel like it should be. Fast movements are dangerous and are hard for the audience to see properly.

   d. Stage fights aren't really fights at all. Every move and sword swing is planned ahead of time. Try walking through the following set of moves. (This is a very well-known sequence of stage sword-fighting moves, used in many productions.) Your opponent should always parry so that the two swords form an X shape when they meet. Do these moves very slowly and practice them a number of times. Once you know them, be sure to look at your opponent, rather than at your opponent's sword—otherwise, the fight will look "staged"!

      i. Raise your sword over your head and chop downwards as though you were intending to cut your opponent in half down the middle. Remember, your sword should be OUT of range of your opponent's body! Your opponent should parry by bringing his own sword upwards from the ground so that the two swords meet in front of his chest.

ii. Now swing your sword sideways (parallel to the ground), aiming at your opponent's left shoulder (remember, this would be *your* right). Your opponent should parry by moving his sword to the left with the sword tip pointing up.

iii. Now swing your sword at your opponent's right shoulder. Your opponent should parry by moving his sword to the right with the sword tip pointing up.

iv. Now swing your sword at your opponent's left leg, with your sword pointing down at a 45 degree angle. Your opponent should parry by moving his sword left with the tip of the sword pointing *down.* (He will have to rotate his hand downwards.)

v. Now swing your sword at your opponent's right leg, with your sword pointing down at a 45 degree angle. Your opponent should parry by moving his sword right with the tip of the sword still pointing down.

vi. Now thrust forward at your opponent's chest. Remember: he should not be within range of your sword! He should parry by bringing his sword up and knocking your thrust up and away.

4. Once you feel very comfortable with this series of moves, you can change the last move so that your opponent dies—just as Macbeth does in the last scenes of Shakespeare's play. Your opponent should hold the plastic bag of goo in his left hand, or safety-pin it to the inside of his shirt at the level of his chest. (You will want to wear old clothes for this—the blood can stain!) Then unseal the bag. On the last move of the duel, move close enough to your opponent so that the end of your paper tube bumps his chest. When he feels the tube touch him, he should lean forward so that the smaller tube is pushed back into the larger tube. This should squish the "blood" out of the plastic bag. Or, if he is holding the bag in his left hand, he can clap his hand over the "wound" and let the blood run out through his fingers.

5. Now switch places, so that you can play Macbeth and lose the duel!

MEMORY PROJECT | **Memorize Macbeth's Famous Speech**

When Macbeth realizes that he is about to lose his battle with Duncan's relatives, he makes a famous speech about the ending of his life. In a paraphrase, here's what Macbeth is saying:

"Day after day will come and go, until time ends—and the purpose of all of those days is to bring foolish men to their deaths! All that a day is good for is to lure a foolish man onwards to the next day—until he dies. His life is as brief as a candle, blown out by the wind. Life is like an actor who comes out and pretends to be doing something important—but actually doesn't do anything real at all. Life is like a story told in nonsense words!"

Here is how Shakespeare writes these words:

Tomorrow, and tomorrow, and tomorrow
Creeps in this petty pace from day to day
To the last syllable of recorded time;
And all our yesterdays have lighted fools
The way to dusty death. Out, out, brief candle!
Life's but a walking shadow, a poor player
That struts and frets his hour upon the stage
And then is heard no more. It is a tale
Told by an idiot, full of sound and fury,
Signifying nothing.

Directions: 1. Memorize this speech. For three days, read the first five and a half lines (to "dusty death") out loud in front of a mirror, five times in the morning and five times in the evening. For three more days, read the entire speech out loud in front of a mirror, five times in the morning and five times in the evening. On the seventh day, you'll know the speech by heart!

2. Now recite the speech twice from memory. Ask your mother, father, or siblings to play the part of an Elizabethan audience. The first time you recite the speech, the "audience" will be the well-to-do Elizabethan theater-goers who paid for tickets and sat in the seats. The "audience" should sit on a chair about ten feet away from you, listen to your speech carefully, and applaud and shout loud "Hurrahs!" at the end. The second time you recite, have your "audience" pretend to be the "groundlings"—the poor people who got in for a reduced rate and who didn't get seats. Instead, they stood on the ground right in front of the stage. Your "groundlings" should stand two feet away from you. While you recite your speech, they should talk loudly with each other and throw things at you. Would you have enjoyed being an Elizabethan actor?

ACTIVITY PROJECT   **Shakespearean "Camouflage"**

Soldiers who fight in modern wars often paint their faces and wear clothes that will blend into the background. Soldiers in Shakespeare's day did the same thing! When Macbeth sees the forest moving towards his castle, he sees the soldiers who are fighting for Duncan's family, camouflaging themselves with branches. Dress up like one of the army fighting for Duncan's family!

Materials: ☐ Old hat or baseball cap
  ☐ Large, thick rubber band
  ☐ Old belt that fits around your waist and buckles fairly tightly
  ☐ Small branches or twigs, preferably with leaves
  ☐ Larger branches (three or four)

Directions: 1. Put on the old hat. Stretch the rubber band around your head, on top of the hat. Poke the small branches and twigs into the rubber band so that the top of your head looks like the top of a tree.

2. Buckle the belt around your waist. Push two of the larger branches into the belt at your front, and two more into the belt at your back.

3. Now you're camouflaged like one of Macbeth's enemies! Go outside and try to sneak through the back yard without anyone seeing you. If they see you move, they'll know you're not really a tree. You'll have to tiptoe very slowly! Before you can fight, what will you have to do?

New Ventures to the Americas

CHAPTER 40

Encyclopedia Cross-References

UBWH 146, 148, UILE 304, 321
KIHW not included, KHE 248

WALTER RALEIGH AND THE NEW WORLD

REVIEW QUESTIONS

Why didn't Queen Elizabeth want the Spanish to take over North and South America? *If they did, Spain would become the largest empire in the world.*

Elizabeth planned two ways to keep Spain from becoming more powerful. Can you remember one of them? *She allowed pirates to attack Spanish ships, and she planned English journeys to North America.*

Who did Queen Elizabeth put in charge of the English attempt to explore North America? *She put Sir Walter Raleigh in charge.*

Why did the Queen like Sir Walter Raleigh so much? *He was charming, handsome, poetic, and once laid his cloak down in a puddle so that she could cross.*

What did she promise Raleigh in exchange for his work? *She promised him land in North America.*

Raleigh had already tried to get to the New World. What stopped him? *First a Spanish fleet attacked him; then a storm drove him back to land.*

Did he go to North America? *No, Elizabeth ordered him to stay in England.*

Did Raleigh send colonists to the New World as his very first act? *No, he sent sailors to explore the coast and find a place for the colony.*

Name two things that the English ships brought back from the east coast of North America. *They brought pearls, animal skins, potatoes, and tobacco.*

Why did Raleigh's servant dump water on his head? *The servant thought Raleigh was on fire when he was smoking!*

What did Walter Raleigh name the English colony in the New World? (Hint: The name was in honor of Elizabeth, the Virgin Queen.) *He named it Virginia.*

Why did the colonists want to come home? Name one reason. *They were cold; they had very little food; the Indians were hostile.*

Why did Queen Elizabeth arrest Sir Walter Raleigh? *She found out that he was married to one of her maids of honor.*

How did Sir Walter Raleigh die? *He was beheaded because he could not bring gold back from South America.*

NARRATION EXERCISE

"Spain had a huge empire, but Elizabeth wanted England to be just as powerful. She wanted English colonies in the New World. So she put her favorite knight Sir Walter Raleigh in charge of explorations in North America. He sent several ships to the New World, and named the new colony 'Virginia.' But then Elizabeth sent Raleigh away from court because he married one of her maids." OR

"Sir Walter Raleigh was put in charge of establishing an English colony in the New World. The colony only lasted a year. The winters were too cold and the Indians weren't very friendly so the settlers returned to England. However, they had brought new plants such as tobacco and potatoes to England. When he was older, Walter Raleigh was put in jail by the king who came after Elizabeth. Finally he was beheaded."

THE LOST COLONY

REVIEW QUESTIONS

Where did the first colonists sent by Raleigh settle? *They settled on Roanoke Island.*

Roanoke Island turned out to be a bad place to settle. Why? *Storms blew across it, and the Native Americans were unfriendly.*

Who stayed behind when the colonists went back to England? *Fifteen soldiers stayed behind.*

When the second band of colonists went to pick up the fifteen soldiers left in the first colony, what did they find? *Nothing. OR The settlement was empty. Only the skeleton of one soldier was found.*

Why didn't the second band of colonists go on and settle near the Chesapeake Bay like they had planned? *The commander of the ships left them on Roanoke Island.*

Who was the first English baby born in the New World? *Virginia Dare was born on Roanoke Island.*

Why did the Indians stop helping the colonists? *The colonists attacked a group of friendly Indians by mistake.*

Why did John White return to England? *He needed to get food, supplies, and more ships.*

Why didn't he go back to Roanoke at once? *War with Spain kept him from going back OR Elizabeth took his ship and used it to fight Spain.*

When John White finally managed to return to Roanoke Island, what was the only thing he found? *He found a carved tree. OR The word "Croatoan" carved into a tree.*

What had happened to the houses of the colony? *They had been moved somewhere else.*

What happened to the colonists? *No one knows. They might have been killed, or they might have gone to live with the Native Americans nearby.*

NARRATION EXERCISE

"A band of colonists led by John White settled on Roanoke Island. They needed more food and supplies, so they sent John White back to England to ask for help. Then war with Spain began, and John White could not get back to Roanoke. By the time John White returned to the settlement, nothing was left. He found the word 'Croatoan' on a tree, but he never found the colonists." OR

"English settlers tried to start another colony in North America. They meant to settle in a good place, but instead they ended up on Roanoke Island. The colonists ran out of food and sent their leader John White back to England to gather more supplies. But when he returned the colonists were nowhere to be found. No one knows what happened to them."

Additional History Reading

Maps and Mapping, by Barbara Taylor (Kingfisher, 1993). This chapter covers one of the first voyages to the New World based on maps made by previous explorers; this book describes how maps represent terrain and objects, covers map distortion, map reading, and map making, and suggests projects. (RA 2–3, IR 4–5)

Roanoke: The Lost Colony, by Bob Italia (ABDO Publishing Company, 2001). Explains the problems that both colonies on Roanoke Island faced. (RA 1–2, IR 3–4)

Sir Walter Raleigh, by Susan Korman (Chelsea House, 2001). This six-chapter biography of Raleigh is simple to read, but may be too long for very young children. Chapter Three, "Keeping Secrets from the Queen," describes Raleigh's marriage and the disappearance of the Roanoke colony and would make a good stand-alone story for reading out loud. (RA 1–3, IR 4–5; a good third-grade reader would also be able to read this independently)

Sir Walter Raleigh and the Search for El Dorado, by Neil Chippendale (Chelsea House Publishers, 2002). This interesting six-chapter biography begins with the tale of the Lost Colony, covers Raleigh's career at court, and ends with Raleigh's disgrace and execution. Single chapters would also make good read-alouds. (RA 2–3, IR 4–5)

Sir Walter Raleigh: Famous Explorers, by Tanya Larkin (PowerKids Press, 2001). This simpler biography also discusses the Lost Colony but ends before Raleigh's execution; many illustrations and large print, but the background paper is distracting. (RA 2, IR 3–4)

The Whole World in Your Hands: Looking at Maps, by Melvin and Gilda Berger, illus. Robert Quackenbush (Ideals Children's Books, 1993). This chapter covers one of the first voyages to the New World based on maps made by previous explorers; this book describes the process of map-making for young children. (IR 2–4)

Corresponding Literature Suggestions

The Lyon's Roar, by M. L. Stainer, illus. James Melvin (Chicken Soup Press, 1997). In this chapter book, designed for slightly older students, a young girl in the Roanoke colony watches the colonists struggle to survive. The first of a popular five-volume series; good for strong readers or as a family read-aloud. (RA 1–4, IR 5)

—————————————— **MAP WORK** ——————————————

English Settlements in North America *(Student Page 159, answer 263)*

1. Queen Elizabeth was worried that the Spanish empire would become too powerful if it controlled North America. Color Spain purple.
2. The Spanish already had a colony in North America, located in what we now call Florida. Underline the words "Spanish colony" in purple.
3. Colonists would sail to the Florida colony from Spain. Draw a purple line from Spain to the Spanish colony.
4. Queen Elizabeth wanted England to have its own North American colony. Color England green.
5. Sir Walter Raleigh sent colonists to North America to start a colony (today, the island on which the English settled is a part of North Carolina). Draw a green line from England to the English colony to represent the sea journey needed to get there.

COLORING PAGES

No one has ever solved the mystery of the "Lost Colony." *(Student Page 160)*

Sir Walter Raleigh was put in charge of establishing an English colony in the New World. *(Student Page 161)*

CRAFT PROJECT **The Poet Raleigh**

Walter Raleigh was an explorer, a poet—and a historian! While imprisoned in the Tower of London, he used his time to write a book on the history of the world. This quote, from the book's preface, says that only history and eternity have triumphed over time. What does Raleigh mean? He means that time passes and no one can stop it—except for God, and except for the historian, who is able to "stop" time by making us "live" in the past.

Materials:
- Raleigh Quote page *(Student Page 162)*
  (You can photocopy this quote onto cardstock if desired)
- Colored pencils or markers
- Craft magnet

Directions:
1. Color a design around the frame of the poem.
2. Stick a craft magnet on the back and hang it where you can see it and be reminded of the great opportunities learning history gives us.

CRAFT PROJECT **Be Raleigh's Cartographer**

When the ships of the first explorers came back from the North American coast, Walter Raleigh hired map makers to make maps, based on the descriptions given by the sailors who had sailed along the coast. There were no cameras, so the map makers (or cartographers) had to rely on these descriptions alone! The best cartographers were also gifted artists who could help travelers to imagine the new land. Try your hand at the art of cartography!

Materials:
- Making a Map page *(Student Page 163)*
  (You may want to photocopy this to use more than once)
- Pencil
- Watercolor paints or colored pencils
- Black pen
- Gold paint (optional)

Directions:
1. Pick a place to map. Your back yard, your street, a nearby field or park, or even the downstairs of your house would do. Visit this place. Make notes of all the special things (places, trees, flowers, rocks, etc.) that could appear on a map. Make a list of these things.
2. Cartographers use symbols to represent trees, houses, rivers, rocks, etc. Make up symbols for some of the special things on your map. (For example, a straight line with small branches might represent a forest; a circle might represent a playground with a merry-go-round in it; wavy lines might represent a pond.)
3. Fill in your "key." A key is a box that tells the reader what your symbols mean. Draw each symbol in the "key" box, and then write out what the symbol means.
4. Using your map page, draw out a map of your place in pencil. Try to help someone who has never seen the place before "see" it through your map! Include the locations of some of the special things on your map. Be sure to use your symbols!
5. In the older maps of Raleigh's day, little boxes on the top of maps often gave descriptions, or explained why the map had been made. Fill in the scroll box on the side of the map with the reason why this place is special to you.

6. Color your map with the colored pencils or use watercolor paint to make the colors mo vivid. Go back over the areas you have named and write them in with a black pen.

7. At the top left corner of your map there is a crest symbol. Paint it gold. Draw a symbol that represents your family inside. This can be your "crest"!

ACTIVITY PROJECT **Leaving a Trace**

John White had made a pact with the settlers he left: If they had to move to a new place, they were to make a sign of the cross above the name of the destination. When he did find a name scrawled on a tree trunk, no cross was above it. We will never know why the colonists didn't follow the agreement to help others find them. What would you have done?

Grab a friend or family member and try this in your back yard:

1. Have one person stay in the house without watching the second person in the back yard.

2. Look outside for something you can write with, like a piece of black, charred wood from a fire, or a red, clay rock. (You can also use a stick to write in the dirt.)

3. Find a stone or thick tree stump to write on with your natural writing tool. Leave a message for the other person, telling him where you will go. (For example, if you are going to hide in the lawnmower shed, you might write, "Cut grass." If you are going to go hide on the front porch, you might write, "Sit and rock.") Now go and hide. See if the other person can find it and can understand the message!

Encyclopedia Cross-References

UBWH 150, UILE 213, 289, 296, 321
KIHW 340–341, 408–411, KHE 248

THE NEW-FOUND LAND

REVIEW QUESTIONS

What do we call the three parts of the American continents? *We call them North America, Central America, and South America.*

What two countries settled in Central and South America? *Spain and Portugal took control of these two areas.*

Where did the English try to settle? *They tried to settle in Virginia.*

What was the name of the *new* North American colony that was filled with settlers from all different nations? *It was called Newfoundland.*

What explorer first reached Newfoundland? *John Cabot reached Newfoundland.*

When John Cabot first reached Newfoundland, what did he find that, according to him, could "feed the whole country"? *He found fish, so many that they jumped into the baskets his men lowered over the sides of the ship.*

For what country did Cabot claim Newfoundland? *He claimed it for England.*

John Cabot had landed off the coast of North America, but he didn't realize that. Where did he think he had landed? *He thought he had landed on the coast of Asia.*

What happened to Cabot? *He took five ships to find Asia, but then he disappeared along with four of his ships.*

Who settled on Newfoundland then? What country were they from? *Fishermen from many different countries settled in Newfoundland.*

What is a flake? *A flake is a wooden platform for salting and drying fish.*

What did the new colony become known as? *It was called St. John's.*

Did the Newfoundland fisherman stay in the colony all year long? *No, they stayed only in the summer.*

NARRATION EXERCISE

"The English explorer John Cabot found Newfoundland, an island surrounded by waters full of fish. Settlers from many countries came to live on Newfoundland. They fished, dried the fish, and took the fish back to their home countries. Shops and villages were built on the island. But the colonists only stayed on Newfoundland in the summer. The winters were too cold for people to live there year-round." OR

"John Cabot thought he had landed off the coast of Asia, but he really found Newfoundland, an island off the coast of North America. He claimed it for England. Newfoundland soon became a summer fishing settlement called St. John's. Settlers from many nations would stay there during the summer, but not during the cold winter!"

REVIEW QUESTIONS

When Spain, Portugal and England built their colonies in the Americas, what country wanted its own colonies? *France wanted to build colonies as well.*

In addition to claiming new land for France in North America, what else did Jacques Cartier hope to do on his sea journey? *He wanted to find a new route to China. OR find a river in North America that would take him across the continent and out the other side so that he could sail to China.*

Why did Cartier decide to befriend the Micmac Indians? *He needed to sail down the St. Lawrence River and he didn't want the Micmacs to attack him when he went ashore.*

What is a wigwam? *A wigwam is a cone-shaped hut made of animal skins stretched over wooden timbers.*

Where did the Micmacs move their wigwams during the winter? *They took them into the deep woods.*

What did Cartier name the vast expanse of North American land before him? (Hint: The land still goes by that name today.) *He named it Canada.*

What tribe did Cartier meet next? *He met the Hurons.*

Who did Cartier take with him back to France for the winter? *He took Donnacona's two sons. OR The chief's two sons.*

How did Donnacona try to keep Cartier from sailing further down the St. Lawrence River? *His medicine men dressed up like devils and tried to frighten Cartier.*

How did Cartier respond? *He ignored Donnacona and the medicine men.*

Did the St. Lawrence River lead Cartier to China? *No, it did not.*

Why did Cartier take Donnacona back to France? *He wanted Donnacona to tell the French king stories of treasure.*

Did Cartier find treasure in Canada? *No; he found quartz!*

NARRATION EXERCISE

"Jacques Cartier wanted to follow a river through North America and get to China. He made friends with the Micmacs and the Hurons, and he tried to sail down the St. Lawrence River. But the river ended right in front of him. Then he hoped to get rich, so he took the chief of the Hurons back to France to tell the French king about treasure. But there was no treasure, and Cartier never did get rich." OR

"Jacques Cartier set off to claim new land for France. He sailed into Canada, down the St. Lawrence River. He had hoped the river would lead him to China, but it didn't. Then he thought that he might find jewels in Canada, but he didn't. So he never went back to Canada. But other explorers and traders went to Canada and started a colony there."

Additional History Reading

Famous Explorers: Jacques Cartier, by Jeff Donaldson-Forbes (Powerkids Press, 2002). An easy-reader biography of Cartier, written on an advanced second-grade level. (RA 2, IR 2–5)

Famous Explorers: John Cabot, by Tanya Larkin (PowerKids Press, 2001). An easy-reader biography of John Cabot, with a brief description of his voyage. (RA 2, IR 3–5)

Jacques Cartier in Search of the Northwest Passage, by Jean F. Blashfield (Compass Point Books, 2001). Covers Cartier's journeys in a simple and heavily illustrated picture-book format. (RA 2, IR 3–5)

John Cabot and the Rediscovery of North America, by Charles J. Shields (Chelsea House Publishers, 2002). A six-chapter book about Cabot's voyages, on an advanced third-grade reading level. (RA 2–3, IR 3–5)

Newfoundland & Labrador: Hello Canada, by Lawrence Jackson (Fitzhenry & Whiteside, 1999). This heavily photographed guide, with simple text, is an excellent introduction to the island. Other titles in this valuable *Hello Canada* series include *Alberta, British Columbia, Manitoba, New Brunswick, Northwest Territories, Nova Scotia, Nunavut, Ontario, Prince Edward Island, Quebec, Saskatchewan,* and *Yukon* (by various authors). (RA 1–2, IR 3–5)

Corresponding Literature Suggestions

The Huron Carol, by Jean De Brebeuf, illus. Frances Tyrrell (Dutton, 1992). The words of the carol, which make up the text of this picture book, tell the story of Christmas and are written in French, English, and Huron. (RA 1, IR 2–4)

Kayuktuk: An Arctic Quest, by Brian Heinz, illus. Jon van Zyle (Chronicle Books, 1996). An Inupiat boy in the cold North successfully completes his quest. (RA 2, IR 3–4)

Rough-Face Girl, by Rafe Marin, illus. David Shannon (Philomel Books, 1992). This powerful Cinderella story, told by the Algonquin Indians of southern Canada, also bears resemblances to the Greek legend of Psyche. (RA 1–2, IR 3–5)

—————————————————— **MAP WORK** ——————————————————

Newfoundland *(Student Page 164, answer 264)*

1. John Cabot sailed from England to Newfoundland. Color the island of Newfoundland pink.
2. The fishing settlement on Newfoundland was the first European colony in the country we now call Canada. Circle the fishing settlement, called St. John's, in red.
3. Jacques Cartier sailed past the island of Newfoundland and into the Gulf of St. Lawrence. Color the Gulf of St. Lawrence green.
4. Cartier befriended the Micmacs, a Native American tribe. Circle the Micmac territory in orange.
5. Cartier also befriended the Hurons. Circle the Huron territory in blue.
6. Cartier sailed from the Gulf of St. Lawrence down the St. Lawrence River, a river he hoped would go all the way to China. Trace the St. Lawrence River in green. It starts at the Gulf of St. Lawrence and ends at the Great Lakes.

Coloring Pages

The English explorer John Cabot found Newfoundland, an island surrounded by waters full of fish. This statue of Cabot is located at Bristol Harbor. *(Student Page 165)*

Here is a picture of Jacques Cartier. *(Student Page 166)*

GAME ACTIVITY **The Fish Flake Puzzle**

The fishermen on the island of Newfoundland built wooden platforms called flakes where they salted and dried the fish so that their catch wouldn't spoil. Build your own fish flake that doubles as a puzzle.

Materials:
- Contact paper
- 10 tongue depressors/craft sticks *or* 16–20 clean Popsicle sticks (use more for a more complicated puzzle)
- Marker

Directions:
1. Lay out a sheet of contact paper, sticky side up. (Secure the edges with paperweights if they roll.)
2. Lay the tongue depressors side by side (the sides should touch) on the contact paper. This helps to keep the sticks in place while you color.
3. Draw fish on the tongue depressors with magic markers. They are lying on the flake.
4. Peel the sticks off the contact paper. Now mix up the sticks. Try to reassemble them in the right order on the table. Can you solve your puzzle? Can your parent?
5. For some more fun, lay some gummi fish on your assembled fish flake puzzle. Don't eat them right away! They need to be salted and dried first!

ACTIVITY PROJECT **Make Cartier's "Fool's Jewels"**

Jacques Cartier found a river in Canada lined with sparkling stones. He was sure that he had discovered the land of jewels. But when he arrived back in France with his boatload of "treasure," the French laughed at him. The stones were worthless, common quartz! Make your own "fool's jewels"—crystals made out of sugar! They take a while to form, but they taste great!

Materials:
- 1 cup boiling water
- 5 cups sugar
- 3 paperclips
- 1 clean glass jar (pint size or slightly smaller)
- 3 strands of clean string (each about 8 inches in length)
- Saucepan
- Pencil

Directions:
1. Wash the paperclips and glass jar in warm water. Dry. Tie the ends of the three pieces of string to the pencil. Tie the paperclips to the other ends of the string, one paperclip per strand.
2. Lay the pencil horizontal on the top of the glass jar. The paperclips should dangle into the glass jar, not quite touching the bottom. Make adjustments to the string length as needed. Remove the pencil and paperclips.
3. Have a parent help you with this step. Bring the water to a boil in a saucepan. Once the water is boiling, add the sugar. Stir until the sugar is completely dissolved and the water is "crystal" clear.
4. Set the glass jar in the sink. Then pour the hot water-sugar mixture into the jar. Reset the pencil and paperclips.
5. Now be patient. Crystals will start to form in a few hours, but let them sit in the water at least a week. DO NOT SHAKE OR MOVE THE JAR! Remove the crystals from the water and let dry. They make a tasty treat.

Note: Food coloring may be added to the water to make colored sugar crystals.

Wake Up in Newfoundland

No one tried to stay all winter on the island of Newfoundland. Icy winds would blow across St. John's, and snow would cover the houses, the flakes, and the merchant's shops. Pretend that you decided to brave the winter on the island of Newfoundland. It would be so cold! Grow some salt crystals on your window sill to look like ice.

Materials:
- 4 tablespoons Epsom salt
- 1 cup stale beer
- Bowl
- White facial tissue

Directions:
1. Mix the salt and stale beer in a bowl until the salt is pretty much dissolved.
2. Dip a piece of facial tissue in the beer, and wet the windowpane with it.
3. Dip a tissue in the liquid and lay it flat on the windowpane. The tissue should be completely moist. Repeat with as many tissues as you desire.
4. As the mixture dries, "icy" crystals will form. The crystals will continue to grow for 24 hours. When you are ready to remove them, wash the window with a cloth and warm water.

Go Fish

Newfoundland was an amazing fishing spot. John Cabot said, "There are so many fish in the water that England's fishermen could feed the whole country." Make a bowl of fish and go fishing!

Materials:
- Colored construction paper
- Scissors
- Markers
- 13 Paperclips
- 2 Pencils
- String
- Tape
- Pie plate

Directions:
1. Draw the outline of a fish onto the construction paper (the fish should be 3–4 inches long).
2. Cut out the fish. Trace that fish onto 10 other pieces of construction paper; cut them out. You should now have eleven fish.
3. Fasten a paperclip to the mouth of the fish. Make sure the smaller loop of the paperclip is on top. Bend up the smaller loop of the paperclip in its middle (the trick is to make sure the paperclip still attaches securely *and* that a loop sticks up perpendicular to the fish).
4. Bend two new paperclips into the shape of a hook. The hook should have a loop at the top. Tie a foot-long piece of string to each loop.
5. Tie the other end of each string to a pencil. You now have two fishing poles.
6. Put all of the fish in the pie plate, bent paperclips sticking up. See how fast you can hook all the fish and lift them out of the bowl (only using your fishing pole). You can also play a game against someone else. Start at the same time. Who can hook more fish?

Sleep in a Wigwam

The Micmacs had learned to survive the cold northern winters. They lived in wigwams, cone-shaped huts made of animal skins stretched over wooden timbers. These wigwams could be taken apart and moved. So, during the warm summer, the Micmacs moved their village to the coast, where they could fish and swim in the waters. In the fall, when the wind began to grow cold, the Micmacs took their wigwams apart and journeyed back into the deep woods away from the ocean. Here, the trees would protect them from the cold northern winds. Make your own wigwam—pull a sleeping bag into the wigwam and sleep there tonight.

Materials:
- Several broom sticks or mops (or similar building materials)
- Rope or thick twine
- Blankets

Directions:
1. Assemble the broom sticks with the broom part at the top. They should form a tee-pee-like structure. Tie a piece of rope around the broom necks to secure them.
2. Drape blankets along the side of the wigwam. Climb inside and enjoy your home!

Empires Collide

CHAPTER 42

Encyclopedia Cross-References

UBWH 136–137, 144, 146, UILE 305, 308
KIHW 374–376, KHE 223

SPAIN AND ENGLAND'S WAR

REVIEW QUESTIONS

What country had an empire so large that it was called "Mistress of the World and Queen of the Ocean"? *Spain had this empire!*

What problem did Spain have? *The English kept getting in Spain's way.*

Spain's king, Philip, was also the king of England for two years. How did he get to be king of England for a short time? *He married Mary, Elizabeth's sister.*

What did Philip threaten to do if English ships didn't stay out of Spanish waters? *He threatened to declare war on England.*

What was the name of the Spanish fleet of ships? *It was called the Spanish Armada.*

Name one reason that King Philip of Spain ordered his Spanish Armada to attack England. *English ships were sailing into Spanish waters and robbing Spanish ships. OR He wanted to prove that Spain, not England, was the most powerful country in the world. OR He wanted to make England a Catholic country again.*

How did Philip plan to defeat England? *He planned to crush the English navy and then to unload his soldiers on England's shores.*

What was the name of the experienced sailor who was second in command over England's navy? *Sir Francis Drake was second in command.*

What did Sir Francis Drake and Sir Howard tell the messenger who came to announce that the Spanish were in sight? *They said they had time to finish their game!*

Where did the battle with the Spanish Armada take place? *In the English Channel. OR In the waters off the coast of England.*

The Spanish ships were huge and filled with soldiers. How did the English manage to win the battle? *They shot the Spanish ships full of holes.*

NARRATION EXERCISE

"King Philip of Spain decided to attack England and make it a Catholic country again. He built a huge fleet of ships called the Spanish Armada to conquer England in a sea battle. Queen Elizabeth put Sir Francis Drake and her cousin in command of the English. Then the English fleet fought the Spanish Armada and won." OR

"Spain had a huge empire and was called the 'Mistress of the World.' But the English ships kept attacking Spanish ships, and English explorers kept coming into Spanish territory. Elizabeth promised that the English would leave the Spanish alone—but they didn't! So Spain attacked England with a huge fleet of ships called the Spanish Armada. After the English fleet defeated the Spanish Armada, Spain was never as powerful again."

REVIEW QUESTIONS

You don't need a flying carpet to travel around the world any more. What do you need? *You need a fast sailing ship.*

What does the merchant ship hope to get from the Native Americans of Canada? *It hopes to get thick, soft skins.*

Why are the Spanish galleons leaking? *The English shot them full of holes!*

What did the English, Spanish, or Portuguese ships take from Africa? *They took gold, ivory, and African captives.*

After you round the Cape of Good Hope at the tip of Africa, what country do you come to next? *You come to the Arabian peninsula.*

What is the name of the empire that rules over the city of Istanbul (formerly Constantinople) and much of Arabia? *The Ottoman Empire rules Istanbul.*

Were foreigners welcome in China during the Ming dynasty? *No, they were not allowed to visit!*

What are the warriors of Japan called? *They are called samurai.*

What ruins do you see when you pass South America? *You see ruins of Incan temples and Incan roads.*

What do you see when you pass Roanoke Island? *You see ruined fences and an old garden—the remains of the Lost Colony.*

What are the settlers doing off the coast of Newfoundland? *They are fishing.*

NARRATION EXERCISE

"I sailed around the world at the end of the sixteenth century. The English had just defeated the Spanish Armada, European ships are taking gold, ivory and slaves from Africa, and the Ottoman Empire is ruling over Istanbul and Arabia. India is ruled peacefully by the Moghuls, China is keeping to itself during the Ming dynasty, and Europeans are establishing settlements in the New World."

NARRATION EXERCISE (Alternative Option)

Instructions: Tell me your favorite story from one of the chapters of this book. Here are some choices:

The story of Beowulf	Joan of Arc
Muhammad's vision	The Princes in the Tower
Yang Chien Unites North and South China	Ferdinand and Isabella Unite Spain
Charles the Hammer drives back the Muslims	Mansa Musa of Mali
Eric the Red discovers Greenland	Christopher Columbus and his new discovery
Richard the Lionhearted and his faithful friend Blondel	Martin Luther's list
Ivan the Terrible	Gutenberg invents the printing press
The Ottoman Turks capture Constantinople	Elizabeth becomes queen of England
Henry V and the Battle of Agincourt	The story of Macbeth
	The defeat of the Spanish Armada

Additional History Reading

See Inside a Galleon, by Jonathan Rutland (Franklin Watts, 1978). Although **out of print,** this book is worth finding at your local library for a look at the detailed illustrations of Spanish galleons. (RA 1–2, IR 3–5)

Sir Francis Drake, by Tanya Larkin (Powerkids Press, 2001). This brief beginner biography of Drake, part of the Famous Explorers series, should be an independent read for all but beginners. (RA 1, IR 1–3)

Sir Francis Drake, by Neil Champion (Heinemann Library, 2001). Part of the "Groundbreakers" series of biographies, this detailed but brief biography is written on an advanced third-grade level. (RA 3, IR 3–5)

Sir Francis Drake and the Struggle for an Ocean Empire, by Alice Smith Duncan (Chelsea House Publishers, 1993). Written on a slightly more difficult level, this lengthy account of Drake's life focuses on his sea explorations and his leadership in the battle against the Armada. Too long for a read-aloud, although selected sections may be useful. (RA 3, IR 4–5)

Sir Francis Drake, Navigator and Pirate, by E. Rice, Jr. (Benchmark Books, 2003). This 80-page exploration of Drake's deeds is written on an advanced fourth-grade level and covers some of Drake's piratical acts against the Spanish; sections will be useful as a read-aloud. (RA 3–4, IR 4–5)

Corresponding Literature Suggestions

Do Pirates Take Baths? by Kathy Tucker, illus. Nadine Bernard Westcott (Albert Whitman & Co., 1997). Follow up on the description of English piracy with this silly picture book about pirates for young children. (IR 1–3)

Pirates, by Dina Anastasio, illus. Donald Book (Grosset & Dunlap, 1997). In this lovely picture book, readers meet famous pirates and follow the exploits of a fictional one—an Englishman determined to rob a Spanish treasure ship. (RA 1, IR 2–5)

The Queen's Progress, by Celeste Davidson Mannis, illus. Bagram Ibatoulline (Viking, 2003). In this rhymed picture book (illustrated with rich painted illustrations), Queen Elizabeth makes a fictional journey through England's countryside and faces the threat of murder from her enemies! (RA 1, IR 2–4)

———————————— MAP WORK ————————————

Spain and England *(Student Page 167, answer 264)*

1. Spain was so huge and powerful that it was called "Mistress of the World and Queen of the Ocean." Color Spain orange.

2. English ships were sailing in Spanish waters and sometimes robbing Spanish ships. King Philip II of Spain decided to attack England. Color England light blue (just up to the line; don't color Scotland).

3. The English fleet was anchored in Plymouth Harbor. Sir Howard and Sir Francis Drake were lawn bowling on a grassy field in Plymouth when they heard the Spanish Armada was approaching. Circle the English port city of Plymouth in green.

4. The battle between the English fleet and the Spanish Armada took place in the English Channel, the waterway between England and France. Color the English Channel yellow.

COLORING PAGES

King Philip assembled over 130 ships into a great floating army called the Spanish Armada. *(Student Page 168)*

Spanish fighting ships *(Student Page 169)*

ACTIVITY PROJECT **Buccaneers! The Game**

There were so many great explorers during the sixteenth century that we couldn't study them all in *The Story of the World!* But let's use the life of one, Sir Francis Drake, to review the accomplishments described in Chapter 42. His life's motto was *Sic Parvis Magna,* "Greatness from small beginnings." Sir Francis Drake rose from the family of a poor Protestant preacher to become *El Draque,* "The Dragon," to the Spanish. But to Queen Elizabeth, Francis Drake was just "My deare pyrat." Put together the game following the instructions and travel through the life of Sir Francis Drake on his great ship, *The Golden Hind,* while reviewing all that happened in Chapter 42.

Materials:
- □ *Story of the World, Volume 2,* chapter 42
- □ Game board *(Student Page 170)*
- □ Question, Answer, Win! cards *(Student Page 171)*
- □ Treasure! cards *(Student Page 172)*
- □ Rough Waters! cards *(Student Page 173)*
- □ Game pieces: beans, coins, buttons or small plastic toys to serve as player markers
- □ Two dice or one, depending on how fast you want it to go
- □ **TREASURE!** (maybe a bag of M&Ms for each player, or Skittles or some other treat you are fond of. For the adventurous or for those who want to keep in the spirit of the game, include a bag of golden foil-wrapped gum or chocolate coins.)

Directions:
1. Before the game:
    a. Enlarge the game board to fit on an 11" × 14" sheet of cardstock paper. (optional)
    b. Color the board and the designs on it.
    c. Glue game board onto cardboard or posterboard to add strength. (optional)
    d. Cover with clear contact paper. (optional)
    e. Select game pieces, one for each player.
    f. Cut out the cards. Or, photocopy the three decks of cards onto three different colors of cardstock paper. Enlarge the cards so that they fit on a sheet of 11" × 14" cardstock. Cut them out and place at the side of the board.

2. To play:
    a. All players begin at the place marked "Start."
    b. Each player gets five treasure pieces at the beginning of the game. Remind each other not to eat the treasure until the game is over (see 3. TO WIN!)
    c. Roll the dice and the lowest number goes first (remember, "Greatness from small beginnings.") Go clock-wise from the first player.
    d. Follow the pathway of squares to the end.
    e. If you land on a square with a symbol on it then draw a card from the corresponding deck and follow the instructions. Place the used card at the bottom of the pile when your turn is over.

    📖 **Question, Answer, Win! Cards**

    These cards will be a review of chapter 42. Use your book only if you need to.

Treasure! Cards

Tales from the life of Sir Francis Drake! Want to know more? See Albert Marrin's book, *The Sea King, Sir Francis Drake and His Times*, (Atheneum, 1995). Land on these and gain treasure.

Rough Waters! Cards

The dark side of the struggles of those who fought for England against Spain as seen in the life of Sir Francis Drake, his cousin, John Hawkins, Queen Elizabeth, and King Philip II. Land on these and lose treasure.

3. **TO WIN!** Once a player has landed at the finish, all of the players count their treasure pieces. The one with the most treasure, wins!

ACTIVITY PROJECT ## Battle in Your Bathtub: The Spanish Armada Attacks

The English ships sailed into the English Channel and waited for the Spanish Armada. When the Spanish ships arrived, they found the English navy ready to fight. The battle for England began! The Spanish ships were huge and filled with soldiers, while the English ships were small and quick. Stage your own battle in your bathtub. You can use your own toy boats or make boats. Who will win the battle?

Materials:
- ☐ Paper Boat Diagram (below)
- ☐ Spanish and English fleet flags *(Student Page 174)*
- ☐ Crayons
- ☐ Glue
- ☐ 10 sheets of computer, typing, or photo paper, or 10 sheets of aluminum foil (approximately 8½" × 11" paper size)

  (*Note:* Computer or photo paper has a slight sheen to it, making it water resistant; foil is obviously the waterproof choice, so the boats will last for more than one bath.)

Directions:
1. Fold your 10 sheets of paper or foil in half crosswise (so you have 5½" × 8" folded rectangles). Follow the diagram for folding the boats. You should have ten boats when finished.

2. Color the Spanish and English fleet flags with your crayons. The English flag (the Cross of St. George) is a red cross on a white background and the Spanish flag (the Cross of St. Andrew) is a white cross on a red background. Once all flags are colored, cut them out.

3. Glue the five Spanish flags to five of the ships (inside the ships). Glue the English flags to the other five boats. Let dry.

4. Fill up your bathtub and pretend it is the English Channel. The Spanish fleet should sail up to the English ships. Have the English dart quickly around the Spanish fleet, shooting the Spanish ships full of holes until they sink. Perhaps a Spanish ship will be able to pull up along side an English ship, throw hooks over the edge, and pull the ships side by side. Then the Spanish soldiers can climb onto the English ship and take over.

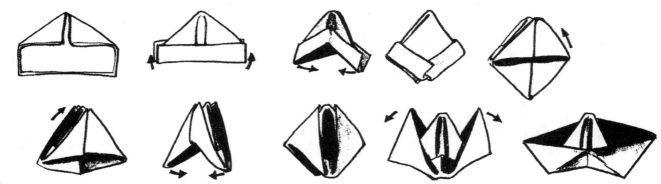

Lawn Bowling

Sir Howard and Sir Francis Drake were having a friendly game of lawn bowling when they heard the news that the Spanish Armada was approaching. Sir Francis Drake heard the news and kept playing his game. "Don't worry," he said, "there is plenty of time to finish the game and beat the Spaniards too." Play a version of lawn bowling. What do you think? Would you want to put a battle on hold to finish a game?

Materials:
- ☐ Tennis balls (for 2 players, 3 balls each; for 3 players, 2 balls each; for 4 or more players, 1 or 2 balls each)
- ☐ Markers
- ☐ 1 golf ball or croquet ball

Directions:
1. With a marker, have each player mark their tennis balls with a brand or mark (perhaps player 1 puts a red "X" on the ball and player 2 puts a blue "X").
2. Go outside to a clear area of grass. Throw the golf ball about 10–30 feet away.
3. The youngest player goes first—he or she is player 1. Player 1 tosses or rolls a tennis ball as close as he can to the golf ball. (*Note:* The tennis ball's position is where it stops, not where it lands.)
4. Now it is player 2's turn. He tosses it as close to the golf ball as he can. He can knock player 1's ball out of the way if he wants.
5. The players alternate turns until no tennis balls remain. The player who has *the closest tennis ball to the golf ball* gets the game point. There is one point each round. (*Note:* If player 1 has one ball touching the golf ball and the rest are far away, and player 2 has three balls near but not touching the golf ball, player 1 gets the point.)
6. Play five rounds of lawn bowling. The player with the most points wins the game.

ACTIVITY PROJECT **Sail Around the World**

Take a trip around the house and pretend you are sailing around the world at the end of the sixteenth century.

Materials:
- ☐ World/house map (*Student Page 175*)
- ☐ Crayon or colored pencil
- ☐ Potatoes
- ☐ Basket, tote bag, or backpack
- ☐ Silver (tin foil, silverware)
- ☐ Salt (table salt or the salt blocks from Chapter 29)
- ☐ Gold (gold foil candy like Werther's Originals or the gold nuggets from Chapter 29)
- ☐ Gummi fish or paper fish (that you cut out yourself or use the fish from the Go Fish game in Chapter 41)
- ☐ Nutmeg and/or cloves
- ☐ Pepper
- ☐ Paper
- ☐ Pen

Directions: **Set Up: (*Do it yourself or have a parent do it*)**

1. Using the world/house map, write a location in the house in the blank box next to each stop. (For example, India—hall closet; Africa—garage.)
2. Make signs for each of the stops: England, Newfoundland, North America, South America, Japan, China, Spice Islands, India, and Africa. Also make two signs that say "Do Not Enter."
3. Set the following items (and their signs) at the appropriate stops:

England—tote bag, labeled map, and crayon or colored pencil

Newfoundland—paper fish

North America—potatoes

South America—silver, half of gold

Japan—"Do Not Enter" sign

China—"Do Not Enter" sign

Spice Islands—nutmeg and/or cloves

India—pepper

Africa—salt and other half of gold

The Trip:

1. Start in England (stop 1). Queen Elizabeth is sending you on an around-the-world trading expedition. Gather your map, your crayon or pencil, and your bag. You will need to gather items at each stop.

2. On your map, draw a line from England (stop 1) to Newfoundland (stop 2). Travel there. You see a busy fishing settlement on its shores. Fishing ships circle the island, dragging fishing nets behind them. Smoke rises up from the chimneys of dozens of small houses. Drying fish lie on stands all along the shore. It's the height of the fishing season in Newfoundland, and the colony of St. John's is busy! By fall, the ships will be gone and the island will be empty. Pick up some fish there.

3. Draw a line from Newfoundland to North America (stop 3). Journey there. You glimpse a hunting party of Native Americans, silently stalking a herd of deer, but when they see your ship they disappear into the forest. As you reach the middle of the continent, you sail past a windswept island a little off the coast. When you squint, you can see the ruins of a fence, with deer grazing contently on the watermelons that grow in an old garden, overgrown with weeds. These are the remains of the Lost Colony on Roanoke Island. Stop at a settlement and gather some potatoes, a crop that grows very well here in North America.

4. Draw a line from North America to South America (stop 4). Go there. You see the ruins of Incan temples and broad Incan roads, high on the mountains that rise up from South America's beaches. Stop at a Spanish settlement and pick up some silver and gold.

5. Draw a line from the east coast of South America, down around the tip of the continent. Keep drawing west (to the left-hand side of the page). Now pick up your pencil and put it on the far right-hand side of the page (remember, the world is round but the map is flat). Continue drawing the line to Japan (stop 5). Journey there. You see the four islands of Japan, where the samurai are fighting with each other for control of their country. The emperor isn't strong enough to stop them. No one there is interested in trading with you. Do you see the "Do Not Enter" sign?

6. Draw a line from Japan to China (stop 6). Travel there. Once China had its own ships and traded with the outside world. Traders would travel the Silk Road, the road from Europe to China, to get gold, ivory, exotic plants and animals, and especially silk. But now the Ming dynasty rules over China. The Ming emperors have forbidden sailors to set out into the ocean and trade with other countries. You'd like to land your ship and explore China—but you're afraid that you won't be welcome! There is a "Do Not Enter" sign for that country.

7. Draw a line from China to the Spice Islands (stop 7). Go there. The Spice Islands are a tiny cluster of islands that are frequented by foreign traders. There you pick up spices such as nutmeg and cloves.

8. Draw a line from the Spice Islands to India (stop 8). Journey there. There are many trading ships docked here, hoping to trade for Indian spices such as pepper. India, ruled by a strong Moghul emperor, is at peace; Hindus and Muslims live side by side, and the whole country prospers because of trade with Europe. Pick up your pepper and go on.

9. Draw a line from India to Africa (stop 9). Travel there. The southern African coast is thick, green, and mysterious. Past the coast, deep in the heart of the African continent, tribes roam the grassland and the jungles, hunting and fishing. You don't know anything more about these tribes; the rest of the world hasn't yet explored into the center of Africa! You round the tip of Africa, the Cape of Good Hope, and start north. As you sail up the coast of Africa, you see Portuguese, Spanish, and other English ships, anchored at ports. Some ships are loading up gold. Some are filling their holds with ivory and salt. But you also hear the wails and cries of African captives being herded onto slave ships headed for the New World. You are not interested in carrying slaves; you gather the gold and salt and head back home to England.

10. Draw a line from Africa back to England (stop 10). Go back there. Show Queen Elizabeth your map (have a parent be the queen). Tell her about the places you went, and show her what you brought back from each stop.

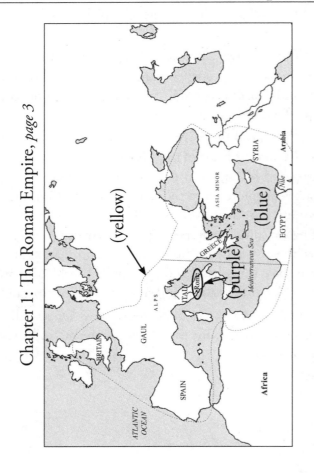

Chapter 1: The Roman Empire, *page 3*

Chapter 2:
Barbarians Come to Britain, *page 8*

Chapter 3:
From Rome to Canterbury, *page 13*

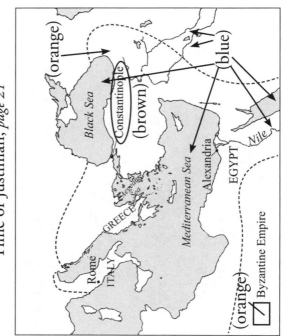

Chapter 4: The Byzantine Empire at the Time of Justinian, *page 21*

Map Work Answers

Chapter 5: The Gupta Empire, *page 27*

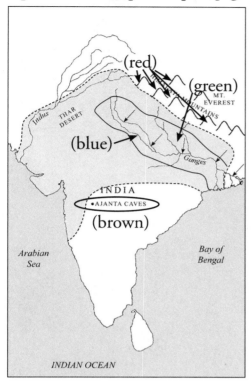

(red)

(green)

MT. EVEREST

MOUNTAINS

Indus

THAR DESERT

(blue)

Ganges

INDIA

• AJANTA CAVES

(brown)

Arabian Sea

Bay of Bengal

INDIAN OCEAN

Chapter 6: The Birthplace of Islam, *page 32*

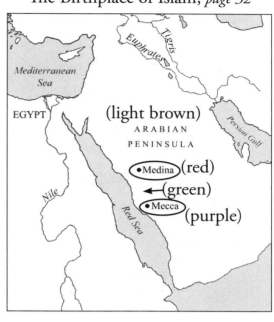

Mediterranean Sea

Euphrates

Tigris

EGYPT

(light brown)

ARABIAN PENINSULA

Persian Gulf

Nile

• Medina (red)

(green)

Red Sea

• Mecca

(purple)

Chapter 7: The Spread of Islam, *page 37*

INDIA

(light brown)

Arabian Sea

Caspian Sea

(orange)

Persian Gulf

☆ Baghdad

Tigris

Euphrates

ARABIAN PENINSULA

• Medina

• Mecca

Red Sea

(light brown)

Black Sea

Constantinople

Mediterranean Sea

EGYPT

Nile

(light brown)

Africa

Chapter 8: China and the Grand Canal, *page 43*

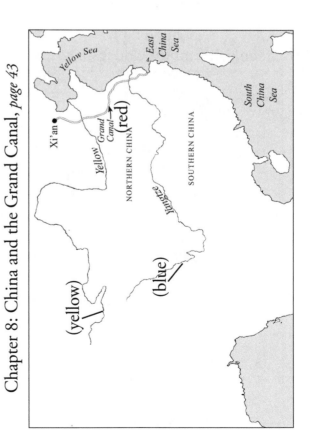

Yellow Sea

East China Sea

South China Sea

Xi'an •

Grand Canal (red)

Yellow

NORTHERN CHINA

SOUTHERN CHINA

Yangtze

(yellow)

(blue)

Chapter 9:
Korea, China, and Japan, *page 48*

(pink) CHINA
.1
(orange) KOREA
.2
(dark blue) Sea of Japan
(light blue)
JAPAN
.3
Yellow Sea
(light blue)
(yellow)
East China Sea
(light blue)
PACIFIC OCEAN

Chapter 10: Australia and New Zealand, *page 56*

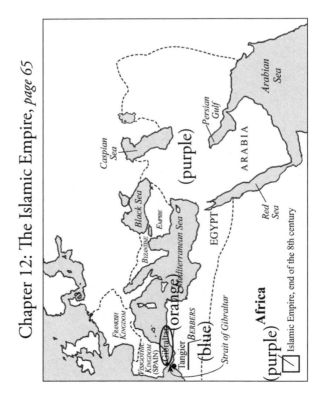

PACIFIC OCEAN
TE-IKA-A-MAUI
(bright orange)
NEW ZEALAND
(blue)
AUSTRALIA (green)
SOUTHERN OCEAN

Chapter 11:
The Frankish Empire Under Clovis, *page 60*

North Sea
(blue)
Baltic Sea
(blue)
(light blue)
(pink)
(yellow)
FRANKS
BURGUNDIANS
ALEMANNI
•Lutetia Parisiorium (*Paris*)
(dark blue)
ATLANTIC OCEAN
FRANKISH KINGDOM
(blue)
Mediterranean Sea

Chapter 12: The Islamic Empire, *page 65*

Caspian Sea
Arabian Sea
Persian Gulf
(purple)
Black Sea
BYZANTINE EMPIRE
ARABIA
Mediterranean Sea
EGYPT
Red Sea
FRANKISH KINGDOM
BERBERS
(orange)
Tangier
Gibraltar
VISIGOTHIC KINGDOM (SPAIN)
Strait of Gibraltar
(blue)
Africa
(purple)
(purple)
◹ Islamic Empire, end of the 8th century

Chapter 13:
The Empire of Charlemagne, *page 71*

Note: The edge of the
Frankish Empire should be purple)

Chapter 14: Viking Lands, *page 78*

Chapter 15:
England and Normandy, *page 84*

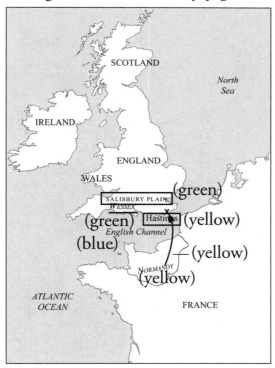

Chapter 16:
England After the Conquest, *page 92*

Chapter 17:
From England to Japan, *page 98*

Chapter 18:
The World at the Time of the Crusades, *page 104*

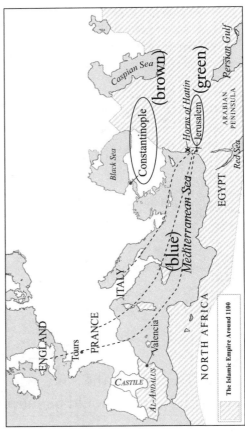

Chapter 19: Richard and the Crusades, *page 109*

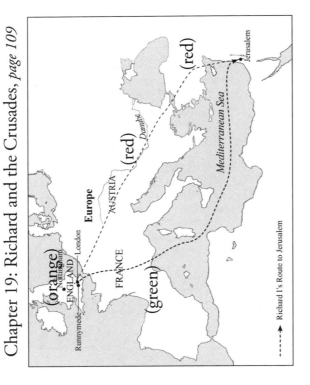

Chapter 20: The Scattering of the Jews, *page 115*

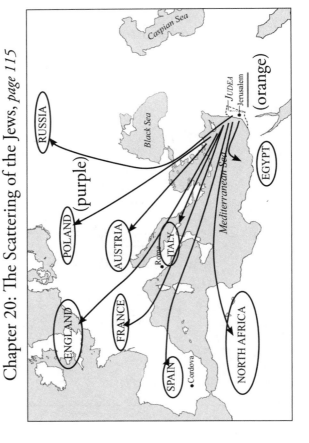

Map Work Answers

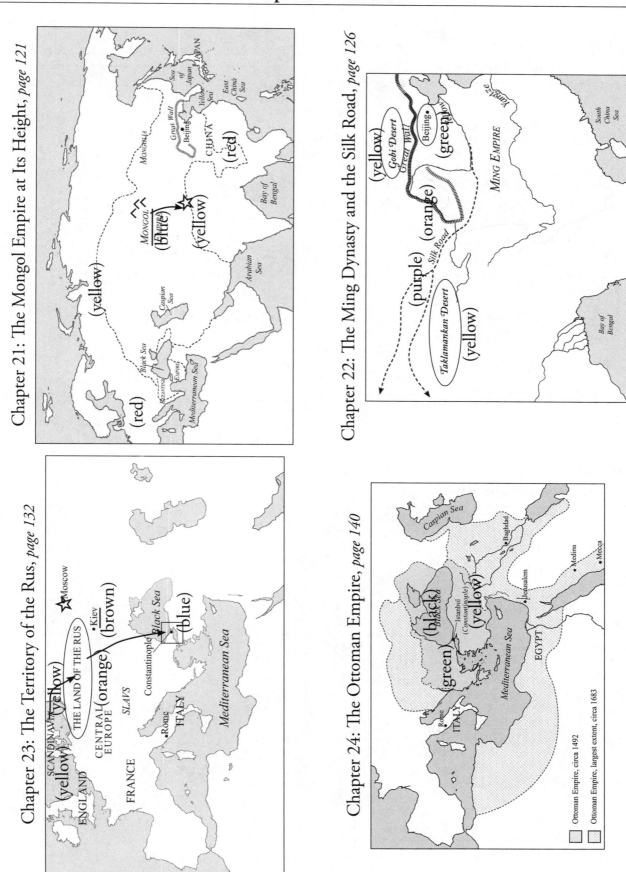

Chapter 21: The Mongol Empire at Its Height, *page 121*

JAPAN

Sea of Japan

East China Sea

Yellow Sea

Great Wall

Beijing

MONGOLIA

CHINA

(red)

MONGOL (blue)

(yellow)

Bay of Bengal

Arabian Sea

Caspian Sea

Black Sea

BYZANTINE

Mediterranean Sea

(red)

Chapter 22: The Ming Dynasty and the Silk Road, *page 126*

Yangtze

Yellow

South China Sea

(yellow)

Gobi Desert

Great Wall

Beijing

(green)

MING EMPIRE

(orange)

(purple)

Silk Road

Taklamakan Desert

(yellow)

Bay of Bengal

Chapter 23: The Territory of the Rus, *page 132*

Moscow

Kiev

Black Sea (blue)

THE LAND OF THE RUS

(brown)

SCANDINAVIA (yellow)

(yellow)

CENTRAL EUROPE (orange)

SLAVS

Constantinople

Rome

ITALY

Mediterranean Sea

FRANCE

ENGLAND

Chapter 24: The Ottoman Empire, *page 140*

Caspian Sea

Baghdad

Medina

Mecca

Jerusalem

(black)

Black Sea

Istanbul (Constantinople)

(yellow)

(green)

Mediterranean Sea

EGYPT

Rome

ITALY

Ottoman Empire, circa 1492

Ottoman Empire, largest extent, circa 1683

259

Map Work Answers

Chapter 25: Europe at the Time of the Black Death, *page 147*

KEY
1 the year 1347 (blue)
2 the year 1348 (green)
3 the year 1349 (yellow)
4 the year 1350 (orange)
5 the year 1351 (red)

Chapter 26: England and France, *page 152*

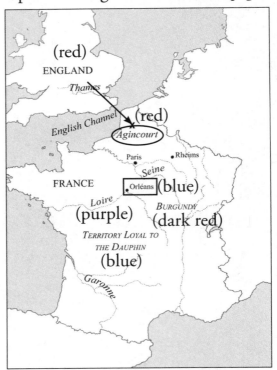

Chapter 27: England During the Time of The Wars of the Roses, *page 158*

Chapter 28: Spain and Portugal, *page 163*

Map Work Answers

Chapter 29: West African Kingdoms, *page 169*

Chapter 30: The Moghul Dynasty in India, *page 175*

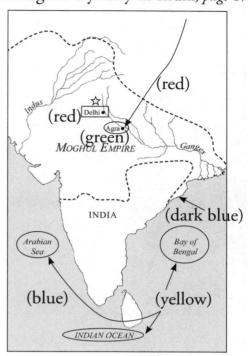

Chapter 31: Routes of the Great Explorers, *page 181*

Chapter 32: The Mayan, Aztec, and Incan Empires, *page 186*

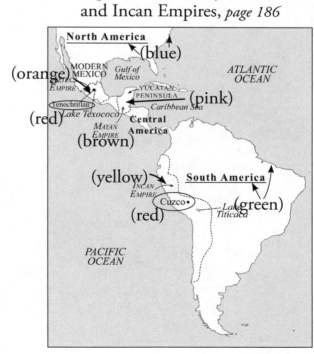

Chapter 33: The Empires of Spain and Portugal, *page 192*

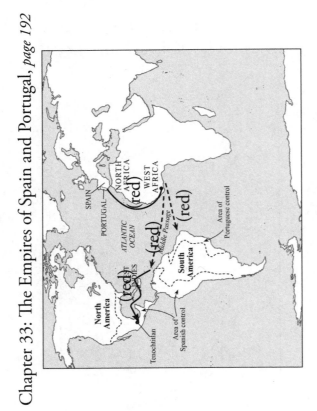

Chapter 34: Europe at the Time of Martin Luther and Henry VIII, *page 198*

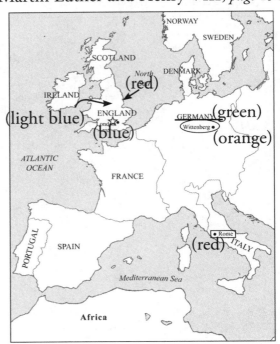

Chapter 35: Europe at the Time of the Renaissance, *page 204*

Chapter 36: The Reformation and Counter Reformation, *page 209*

Map Work Answers

Chapter 37: Poland and Italy, *page 215*

Chapter 38: Elizabeth's England, *page 221*

Chapter 39: England, *page 230*

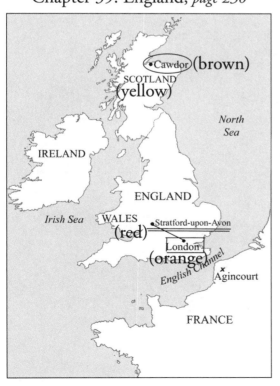

Chapter 40: English Settlements in North America, *page 237*

Chapter 41: Newfoundland, *page 242*

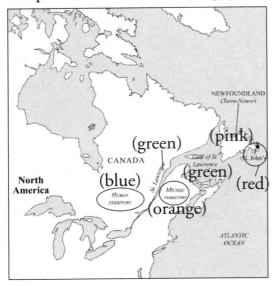

Chapter 42: Spain and England, *page 248*

The Story of the World
Activity Book, Volume Two

Student Pages

Peace Hill Press
www.peacehillpress.com

$11.95

ISBN 978-1-933339-16-0

51195>

9 781933 339160

PHOTOCOPYING AND DISTRIBUTION POLICY

The illustrations, reading lists, and all other content in this Activity Book are copyrighted material owned by Peace Hill Press. Please do not reproduce reading lists, etc. on e-mail lists or websites.

For families: You may make as many photocopies of the maps and other Student Pages as you need for use WITHIN YOUR OWN FAMILY ONLY.

Schools and co-ops MAY NOT PHOTOCOPY any portion of the Activity Book. Smaller schools usually find that purchasing a set of the pre-copied Student Pages for each student is the best option. Other schools may purchase a licensing fee ($100 per volume, per year) that allows unlimited school and co-op duplication. For more information, please contact Peace Hill Press: e-mail info@peacehillpress.com; phone 1.877.322.3445.

Chapter 1: The Roman Empire

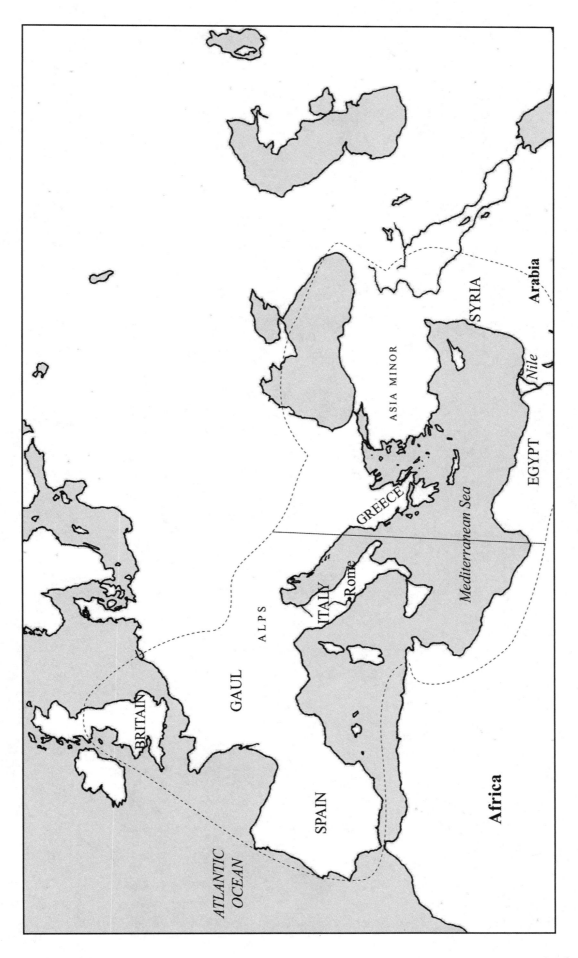

BRITAIN

ATLANTIC OCEAN

GAUL

ALPS

SPAIN

ITALY

Rome

GREECE

Mediterranean Sea

ASIA MINOR

SYRIA

Nile

Arabia

EGYPT

Africa

A Barbarian

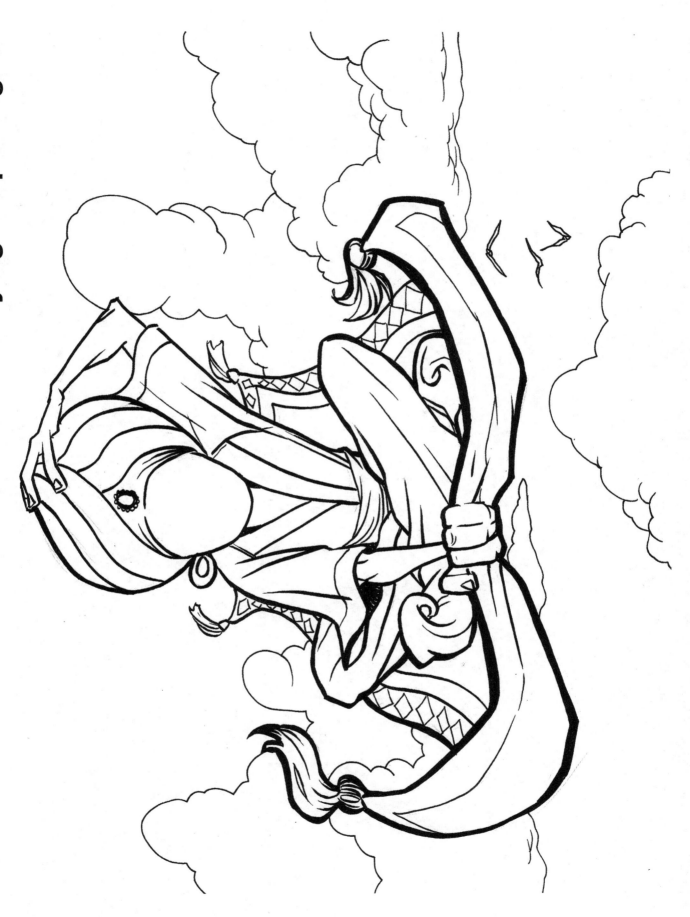

Chapter 2: Barbarians Come to Britain

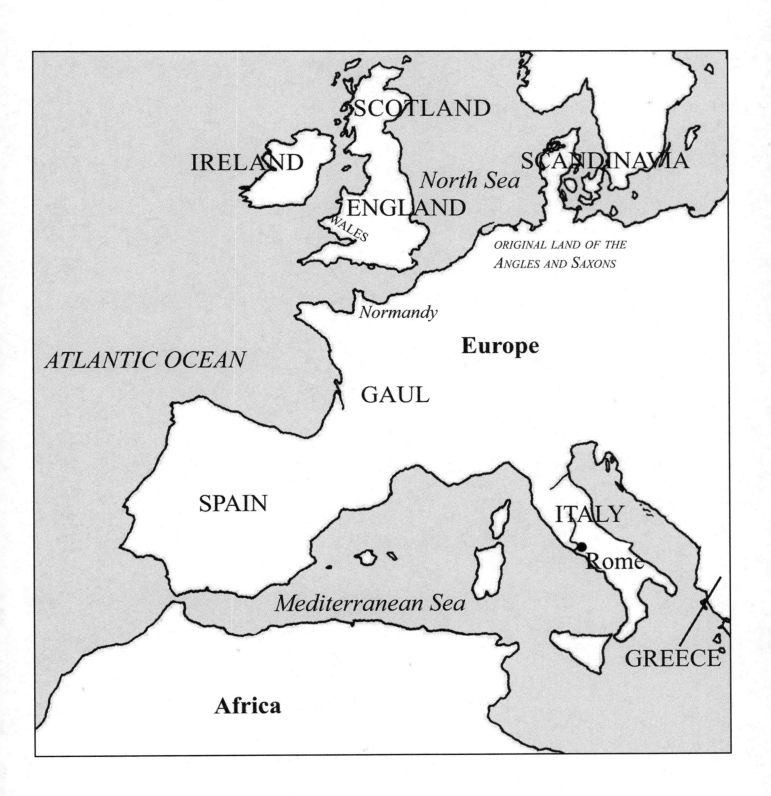

Beowulf

Axe Blade Pattern

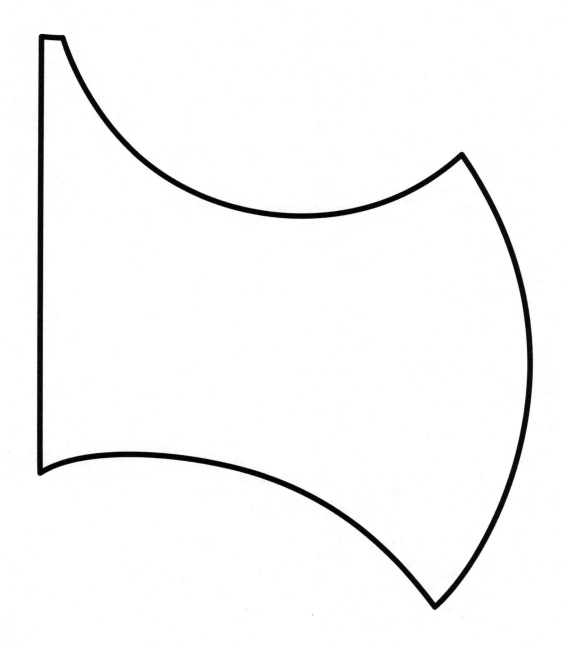

Dragon Brooch Pattern

Chapter 3: From Rome to Canterbury

Three Slave Boys

Medieval Manuscript

abcdefghijk
lmnopqr st
ux ç ƶ

Illumination Pattern

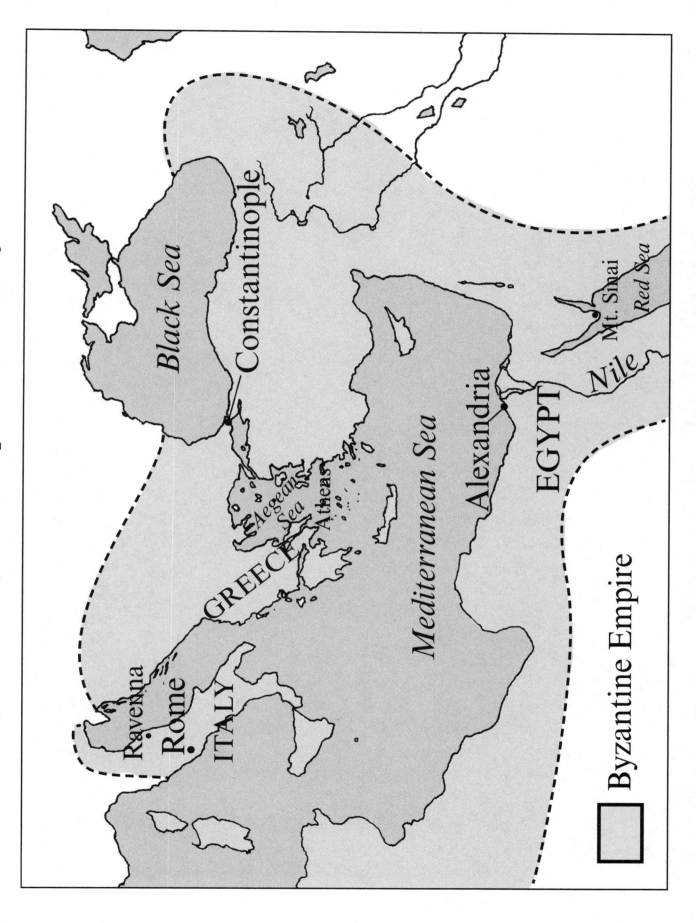

Black Sea

Constantinople

Ravenna

Rome

ITALY

GREECE

Aegean Sea

Athens

Mediterranean Sea

Alexandria

EGYPT

Nile

Mt. Sinai

Red Sea

Byzantine Empire

Chapter Four Advanced Map Work

Hagia Sophia, Constantinople's jewel! Find Constantinople on your map. Color Hagia Sophia and place it close to the capital city.

Ravenna is called the "capital of mosaics." Ravenna's Byzantine church is the **Basilica of San Vitale.** Can you find Ravenna on the map? A bishop of the Ostrogoths began to build the octagonal (eight-sided) church, but before it was finished, Justinian conquered the town and finished building the church. This church has a famous mosaic of Justinian and Theodora bringing gifts to the altar of the Lord. Ravenna became the home of Byzantine power in Italy.

Saint Catherine Monastery, tucked high in what is known as the mountain of Moses, is a fortress and shrine on the traditional site of the Burning Bush. On the wood roof of the entrance of the chapel, an inscription of honor says: "Our most pious Emperor (Justinian), and his late Empress" (Theodora). To find Mount Sinai, look for the Nile River down on the bottom of your map. Next to it you'll find the tips of the Red Sea. In between the two tips, down close to the water, is the location of Mount Sinai. Color this picture of Saint Catherine's and cut it out. Then paste it on the location of Mount Sinai.

Ayioi Theodoroi is located in Athens, Greece. Justinian did not build it; a Byzantine official named Nicolaos Kalomaos built it five centuries after Justinian. Byzantine style had changed, but some things were the same. Can you see similarities in the architecture? Find Athens on your map. Color Ayioi Theodoroi and paste it on to the map close to Athens.

Theodora

Hagia Sophia

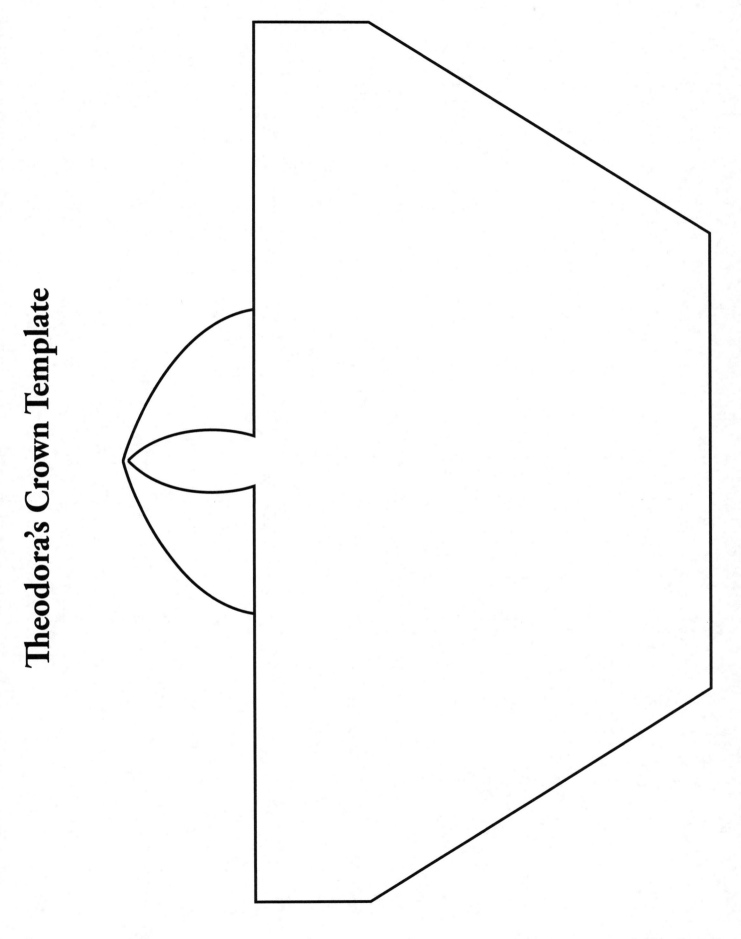

Theodora's Crown Template

Theodora and Justinian Paper Dolls

Paper Dolls

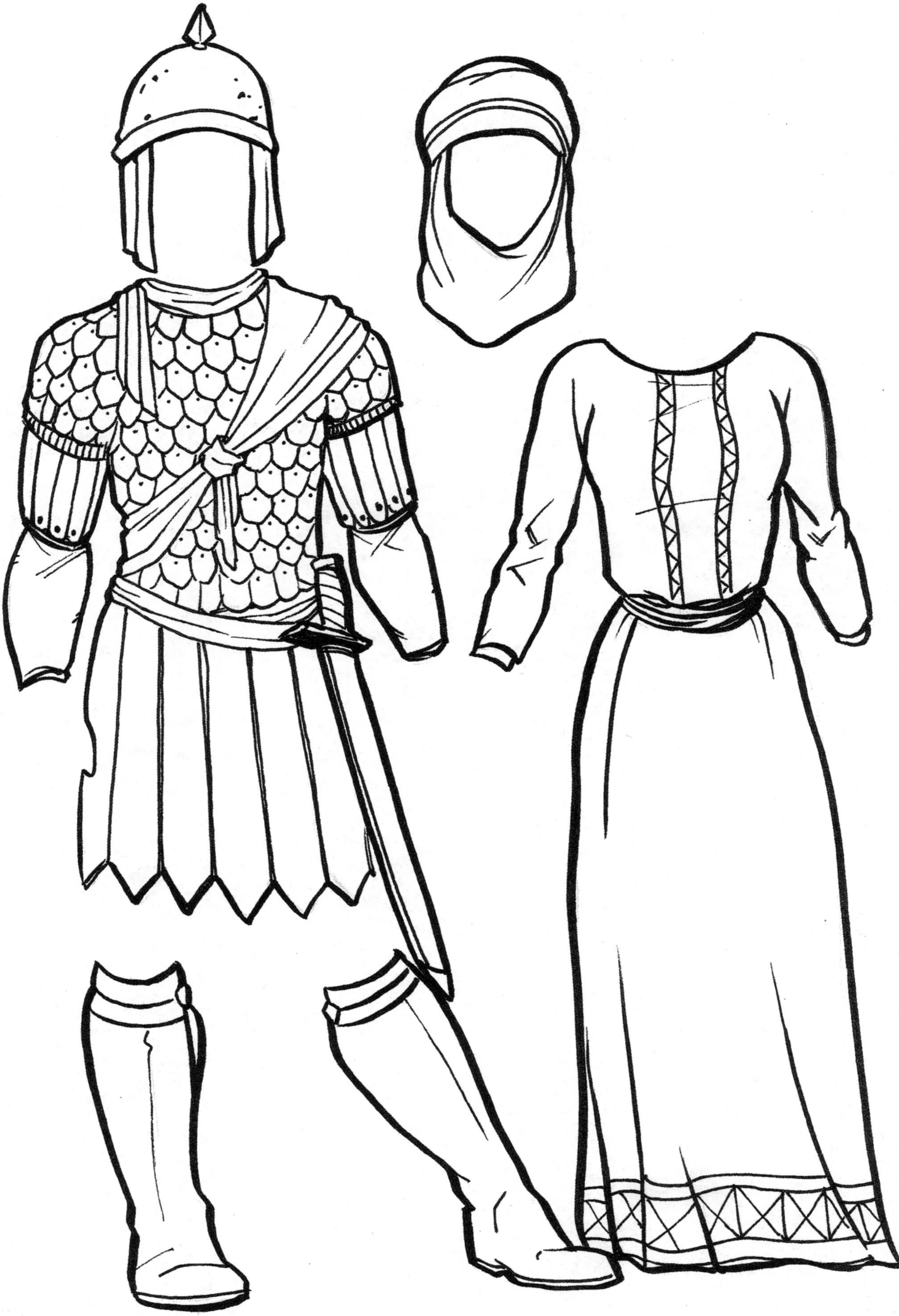

Chapter 5: The Gupta Empire

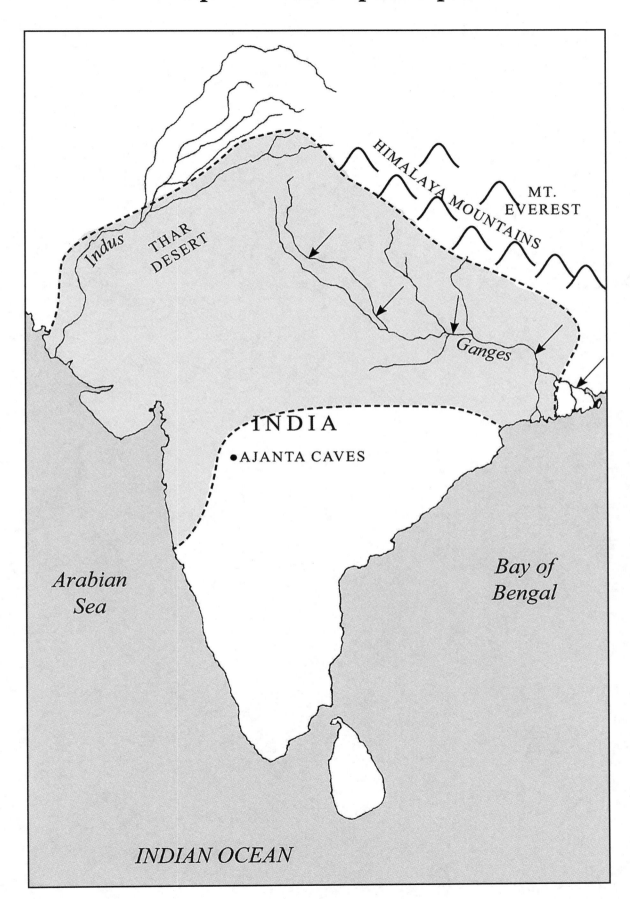

The Gupta Dynasty

Chapter 6: The Birthplace of Islam

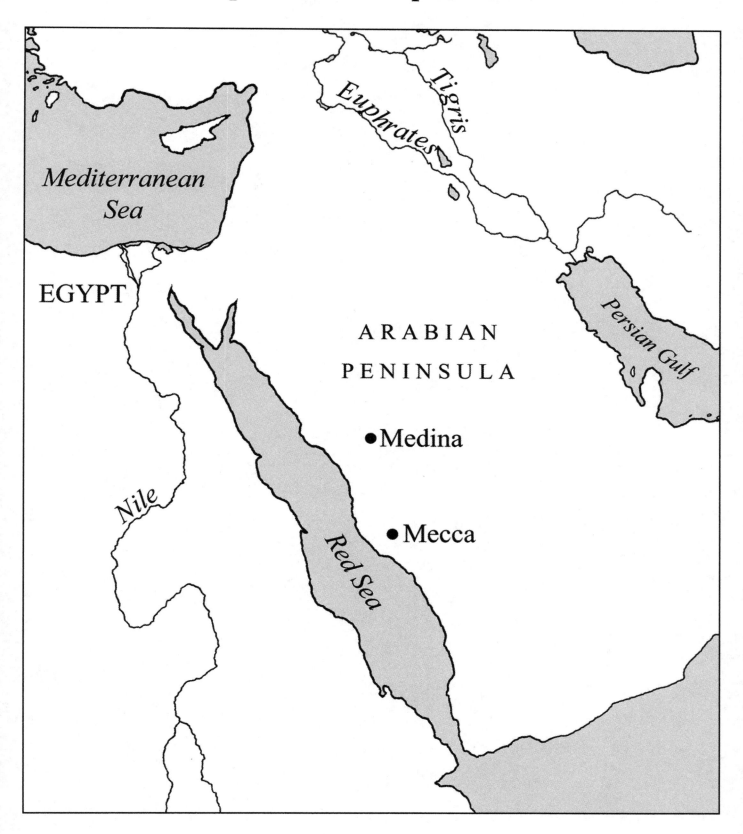

Bedouin and His Camel

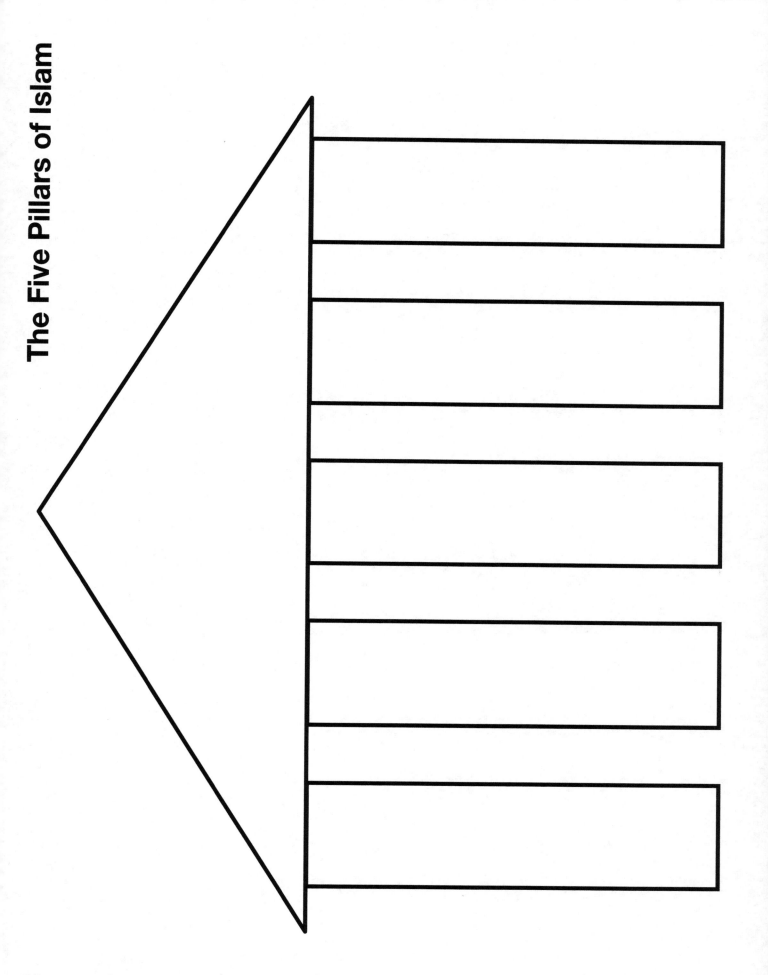

The Five Pillars of Islam

An Islamic Shahadah

There is no god but Allah
and
Muhammad is his prophet.

Chapter 7: The Spread of Islam

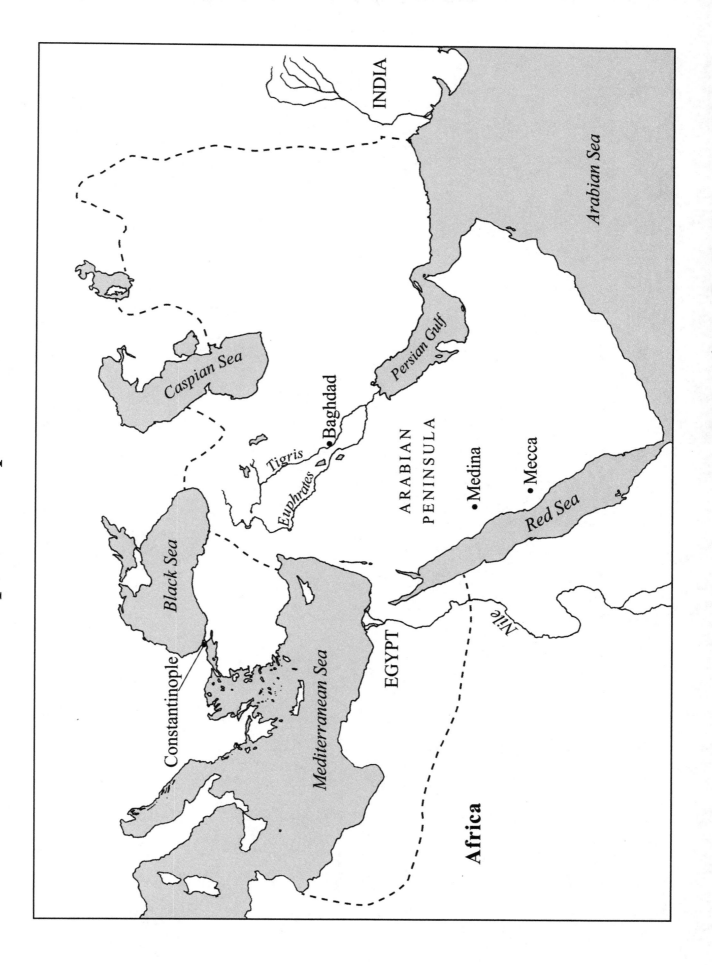

Sinbad

FROM MECCA TO THE WORLD

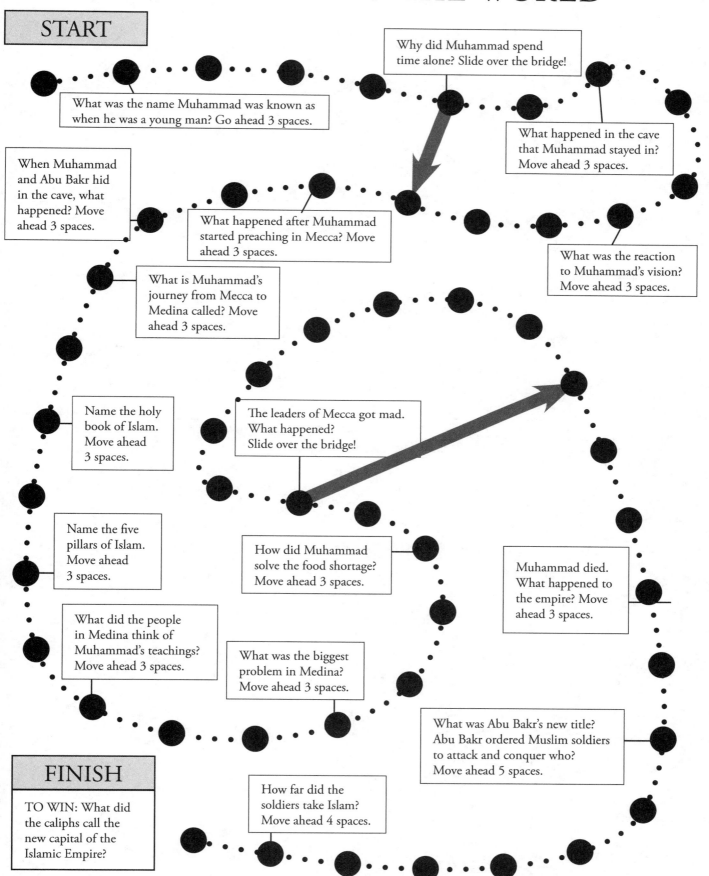

START

Why did Muhammad spend time alone? Slide over the bridge!

What was the name Muhammad was known as when he was a young man? Go ahead 3 spaces.

What happened in the cave that Muhammad stayed in? Move ahead 3 spaces.

When Muhammad and Abu Bakr hid in the cave, what happened? Move ahead 3 spaces.

What happened after Muhammad started preaching in Mecca? Move ahead 3 spaces.

What was the reaction to Muhammad's vision? Move ahead 3 spaces.

What is Muhammad's journey from Mecca to Medina called? Move ahead 3 spaces.

Name the holy book of Islam. Move ahead 3 spaces.

The leaders of Mecca got mad. What happened? Slide over the bridge!

Muhammad died. What happened to the empire? Move ahead 3 spaces.

Name the five pillars of Islam. Move ahead 3 spaces.

How did Muhammad solve the food shortage? Move ahead 3 spaces.

What did the people in Medina think of Muhammad's teachings? Move ahead 3 spaces.

What was the biggest problem in Medina? Move ahead 3 spaces.

What was Abu Bakr's new title? Abu Bakr ordered Muslim soldiers to attack and conquer who? Move ahead 5 spaces.

FINISH

TO WIN: What did the caliphs call the new capital of the Islamic Empire?

How far did the soldiers take Islam? Move ahead 4 spaces.

Sinbad Spoon Puppets

Scimitar

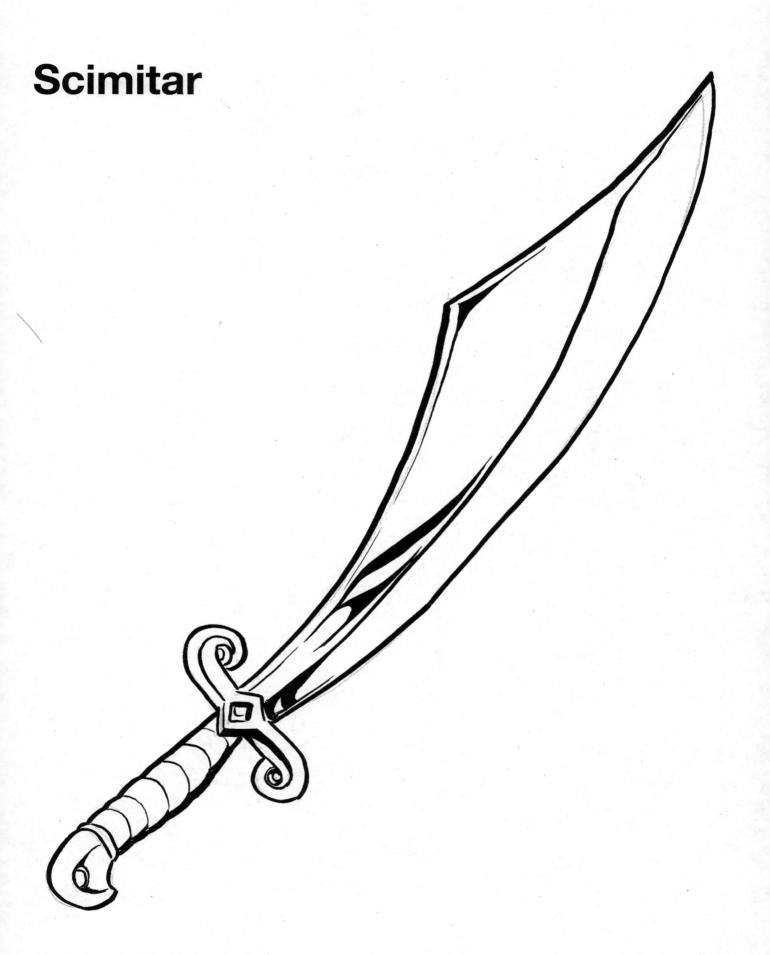

Chapter 8: China and the Grand Canal

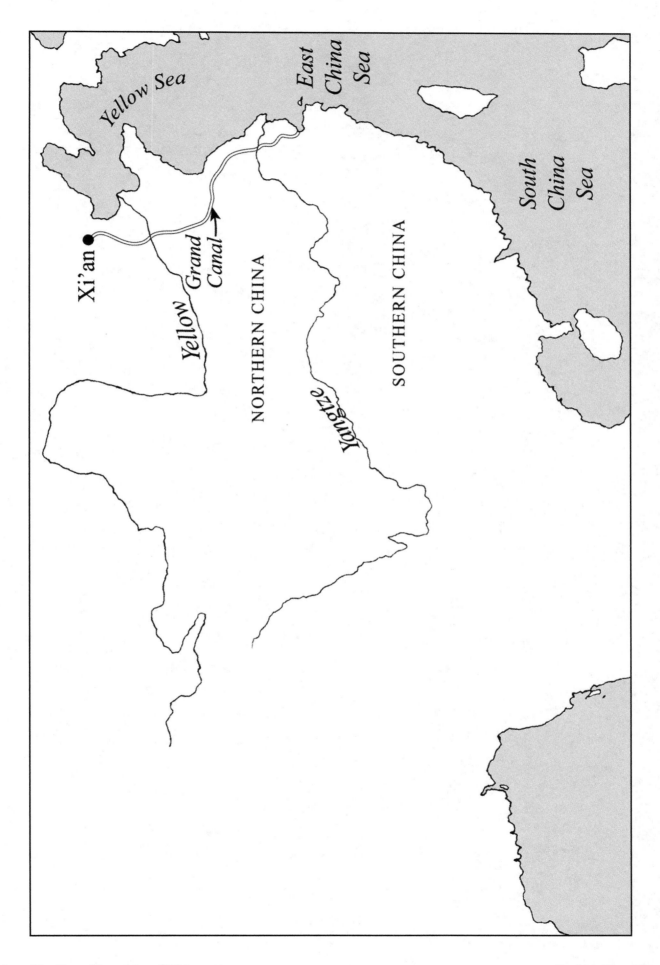

Statue of a Tang Warrior

Chapter 9: Korea, China, and Japan

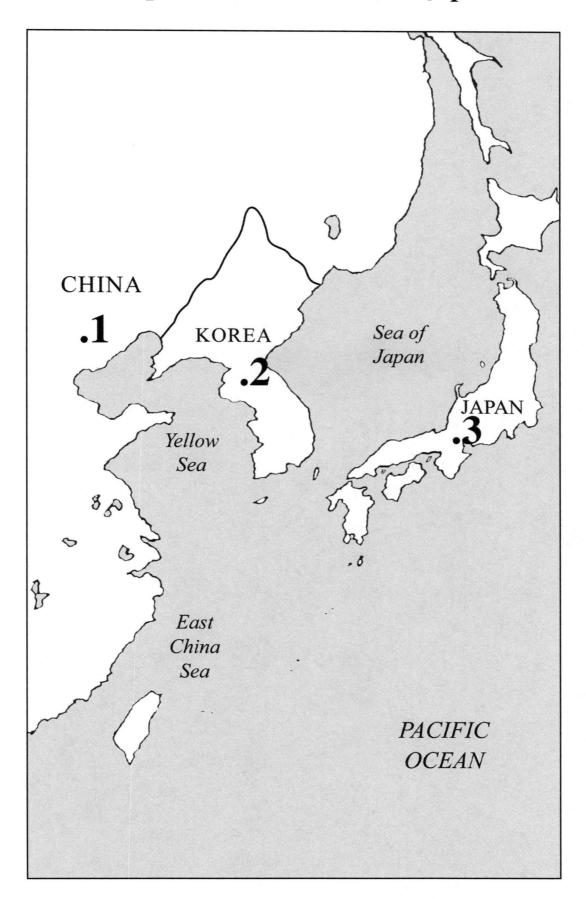

Susano

Chapter 10: Australia and New Zealand

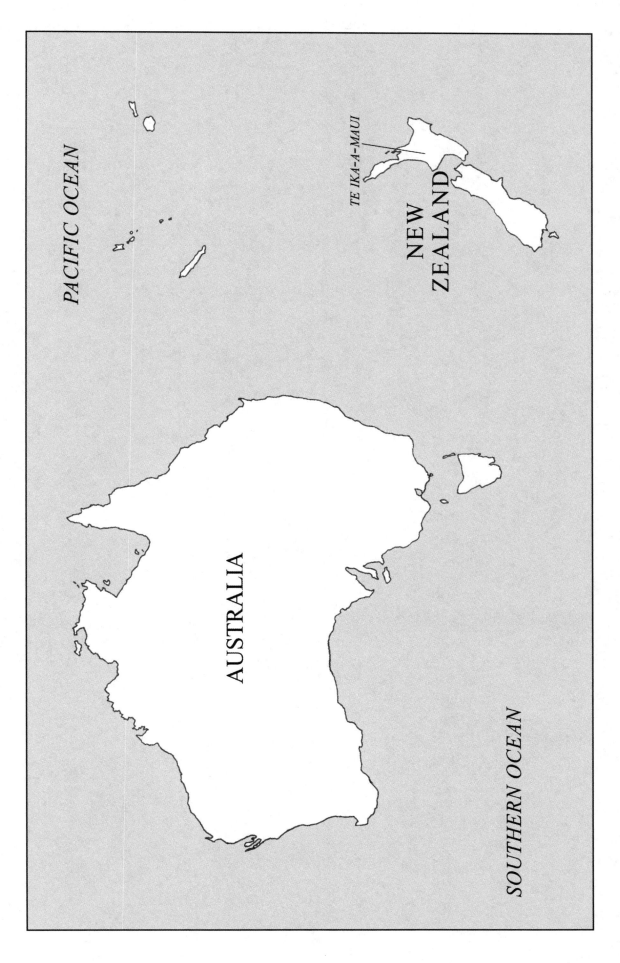

PACIFIC OCEAN

TE IKA-A-MAUI

NEW ZEALAND

AUSTRALIA

SOUTHERN OCEAN

A Maori Warrior

Chapter 11: The Frankish Empire Under Clovis

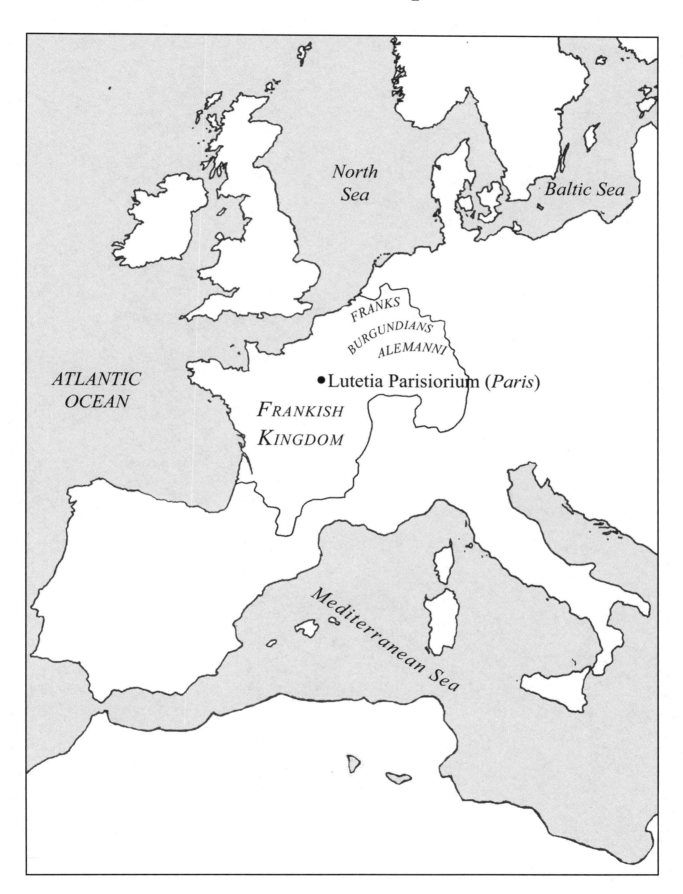

North Sea

Baltic Sea

FRANKS

BURGUNDIANS

ALEMANNI

●Lutetia Parisiorium (*Paris*)

ATLANTIC OCEAN

FRANKISH KINGDOM

Mediterranean Sea

Clovis

Fleur-de-lis Pattern

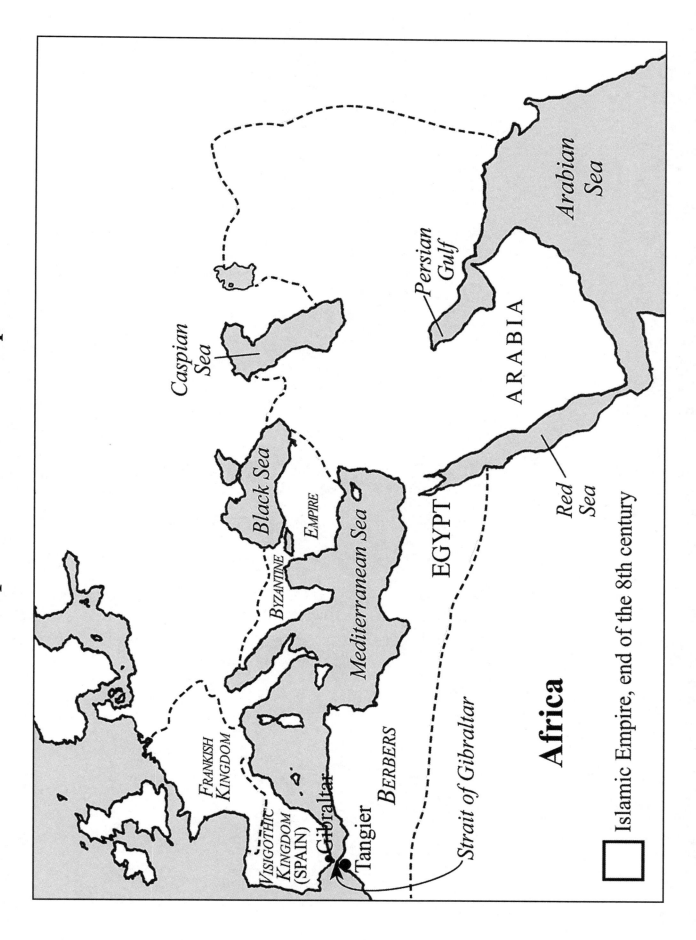

Persian
Gulf

Arabian
Sea

ARABIA

Caspian
Sea

Red
Sea

Black Sea

BYZANTINE

EMPIRE

Mediterranean Sea

EGYPT

Africa

Islamic Empire, end of the 8th century

FRANKISH
KINGDOM

BERBERS

Gibraltar

Tangier

Strait of Gibraltar

VISIGOTHIC
KINGDOM
(SPAIN)

Chapter Twelve Advanced Map Work

During this time, architectural wonders were built all over Spain, but especially in the Islamic part. Here are three examples. Color each and cut them out. Find the city each belongs in and glue it onto your map.

a. La Mezquita in Cordova. This building took two hundred years to build. Its large columns were borrowed from ruins, lifting high double arched supports with the traditional red stripe. The ceiling reaches 39 feet high.

b. La Giralda in Sevilla. This grandest of minarets was begun by the master mason Ahmad ibn Basi in the 11th century and finished by Abu Ya' qub, his apprentice.

c. The Alhambra in Granada. This collection of palaces took refuge behind formidable walls surrounding the mountaintop that overlooked the city. It has been the source of wonderful stories in both the eastern and western cultures.

Moorish Mosque and Fountain

Moorish Stamps

Juice Can Wind-chime Lid Decorations

Chapter 13: The Empire of Charlemagne

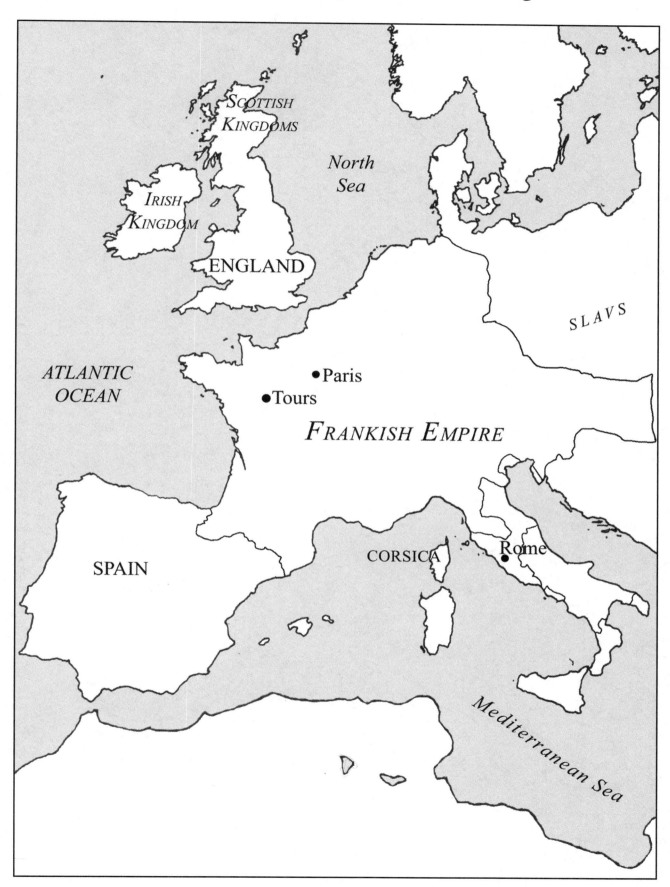

Chapter Thirteen Advanced Map Work

A-Witikind **B-Charlemagne** **C-Louis** **D-Einhard** **E-Hildegard**

F-Alcuin **G-Carloman/Pepin** **H-Charles** **I-Roland** **J-Ganalon**

Color these symbols. Then, follow the directions. First enlarge the copy of the map on Student Page 47. Then cut out the pictures and paste them on your map where they belong. (Glue sticks work best.)

Tours was a very important place even before Charlemagne's reign. Charles the Hammer, or Charles Martel, began his defense against the invading Muslim armies in a field between Tours and Poitiers. Tours became an important place of learning and Charlemagne's greatest advisor, Alcuin of York, became the Abbot of Tours. Place the picture of Alcuin at Tours.

The hold the Frankish kings had over the wild Saxons was not always a strong one. Though Charlemagne was able to restore some sort of order in the area, he had one enemy he could not subdue for twelve long years. Witikind led the Saxon rebels, sneaking in to the French strongholds and killing the monks in small, unguarded places. This made Charlemagne so angry that he finally dealt with the rebels with uncharacteristic brutality. Finally, Witikind surrendered, accepting Charlemagne's generous terms. Place the pictures of Charlemagne and Witikind in France.

Charlemagne had three sons with his second wife, Hildegard. Ages four and three, Carloman and Louis were crowned kings by Pope Hadrian in Rome. His oldest son, Charles, would take over his empire. To Carloman, whose name was changed to Pepin, he gave the kingdom of Italy. To Louis, he gave the kingdom of Aquitaine. Place Louis's picture just below Tours. Place Pepin's picture in northern Italy, above Rome. Place Charles' picture in the center of the empire. For most of their lives, these young sons lived Charlemagne's plans. But when Charles and Pepin died in their thirties, Louis became Charlemagne's heir. He was known as Louis the Pious.

Charlemagne

Family, Friends, and Foes of Charlemagne

Family, Friends, and Foes of Charlemagne

Family, Friends, and Foes of Charlemagne

Charlemagne Crown Template

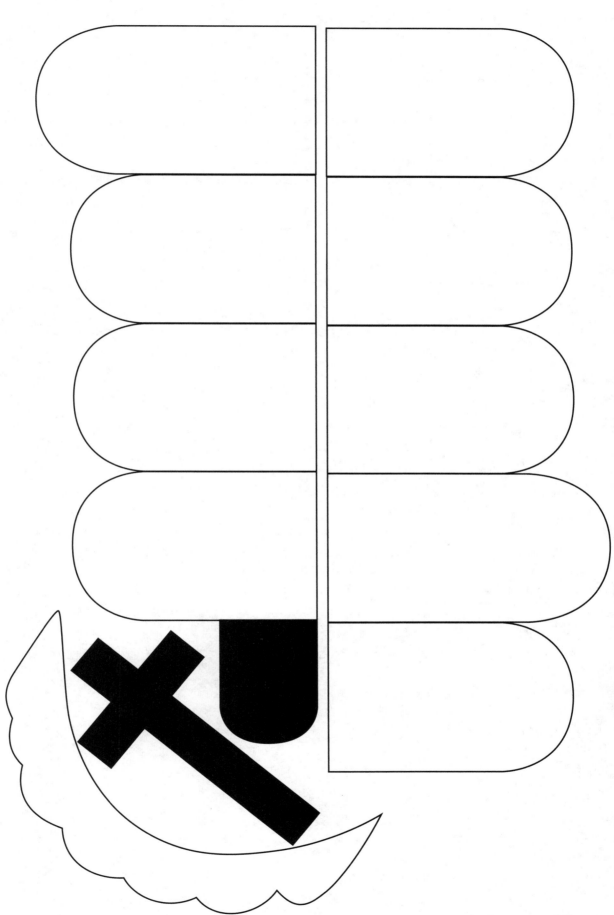

Chapter 14: Viking Lands

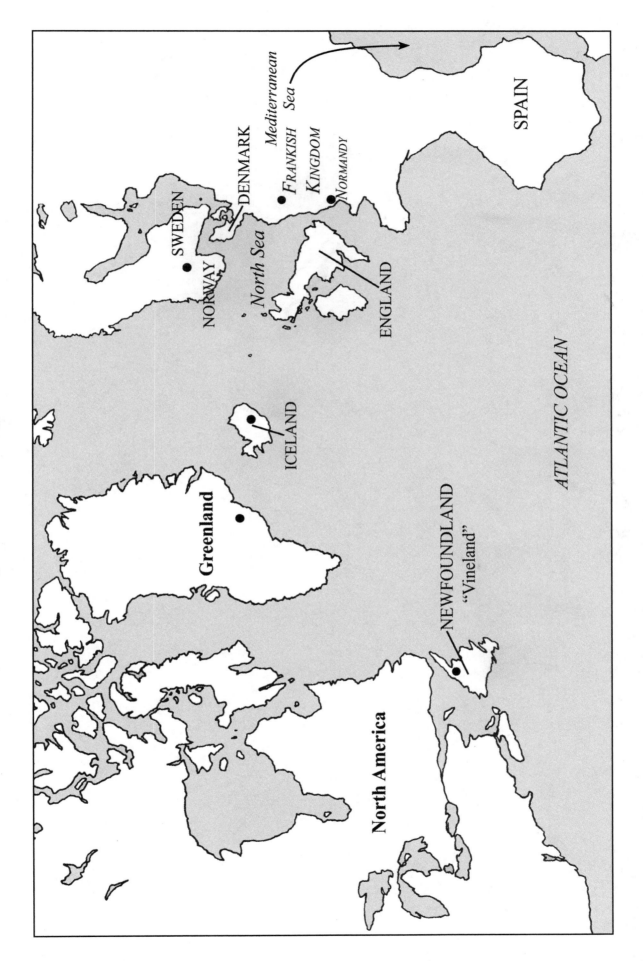

A Viking Longship

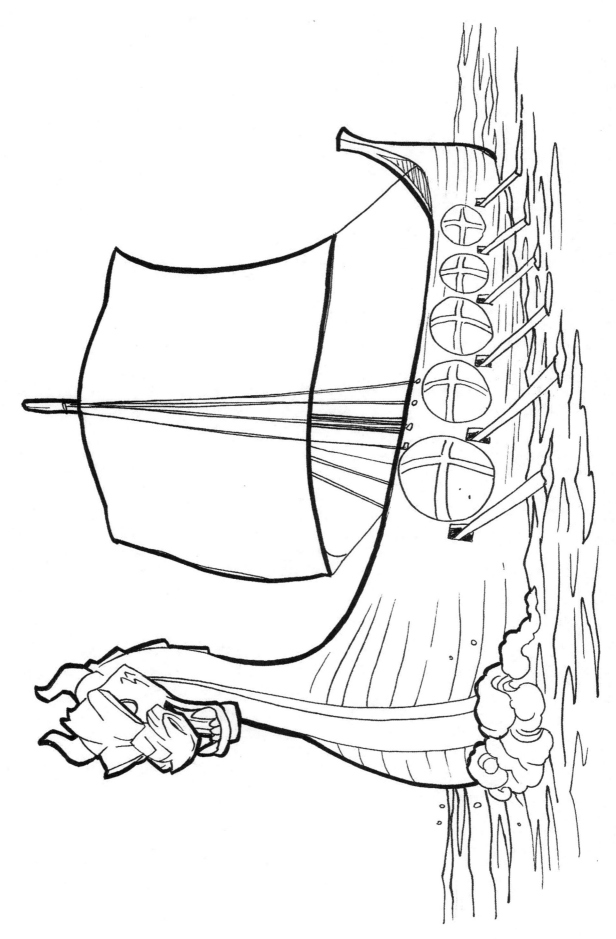

Viking Boat Template

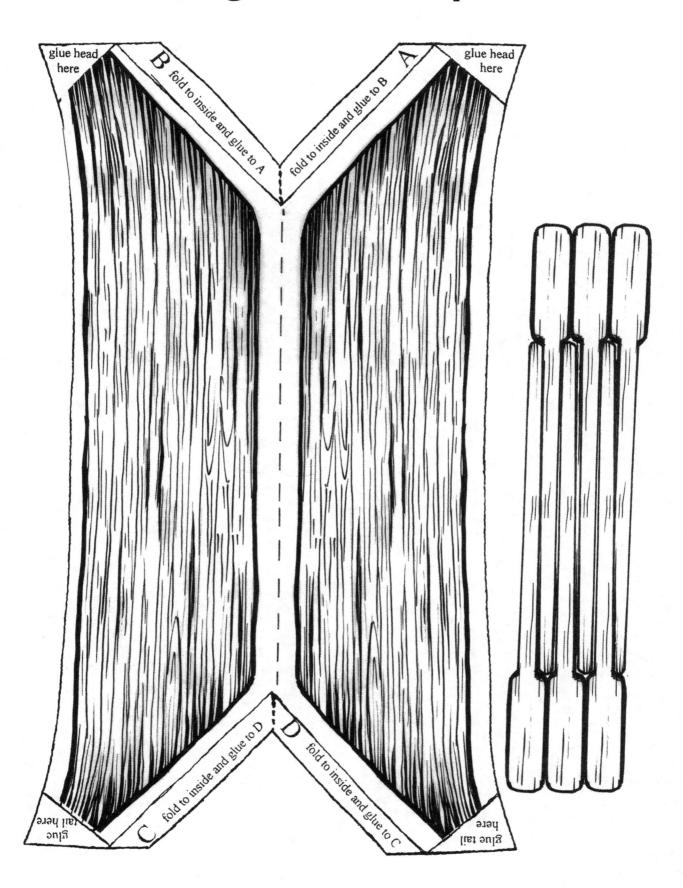

glue head here

B

fold to inside and glue to A

A

fold to inside and glue to B

glue head here

C

fold to inside and glue to D

D

fold to inside and glue to C

glue tail here

glue tail here

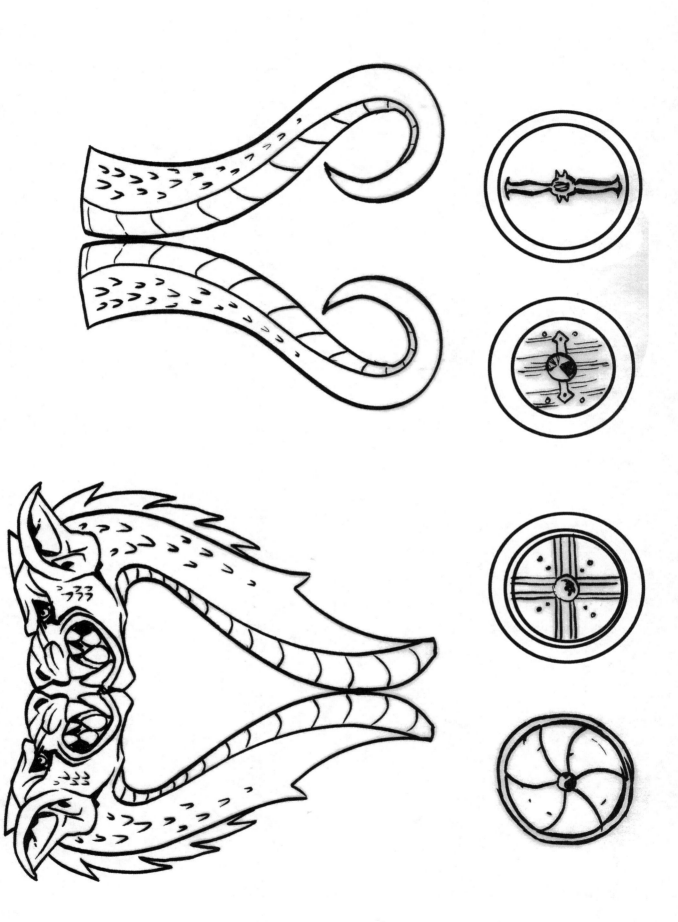

Viking Brooch and Thor's Hammer Template

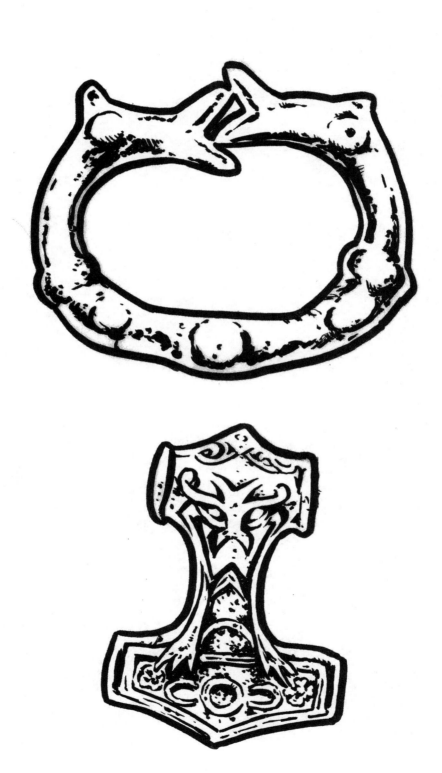

Chapter 15: England and Normandy

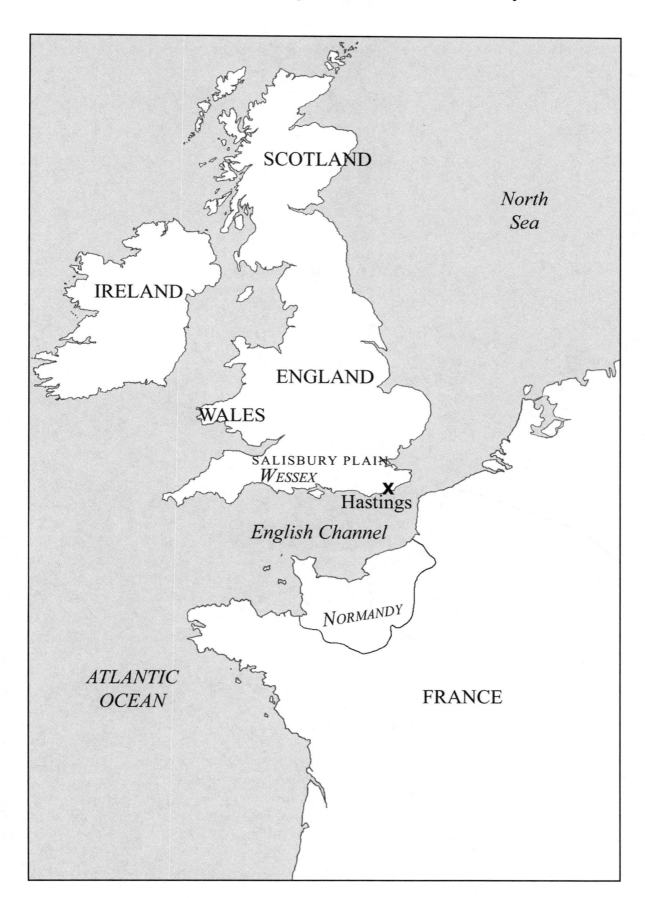

Statue of Alfred the Great

The Bayeux Tapestry

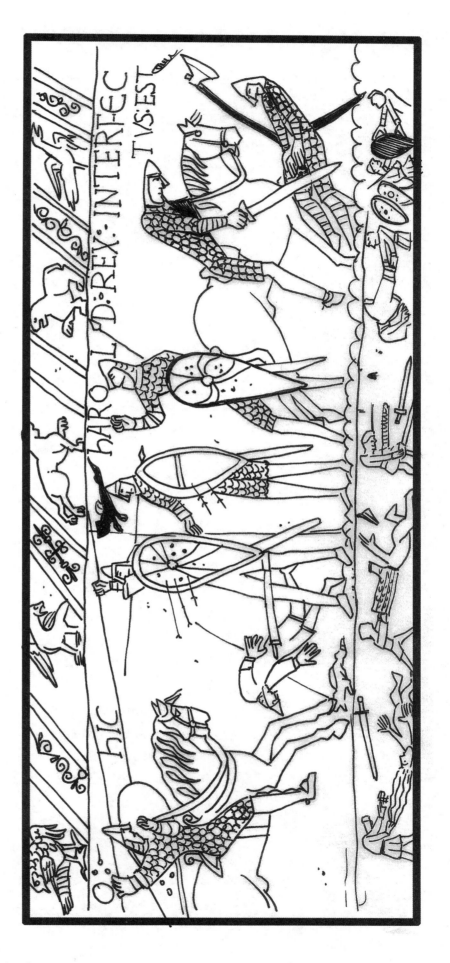

WILLIAM AND HAROLD GAME BOARD

Harold
Godwinson

William the
Conqueror

PECTORE PURO

William and Harold Game Cards

Where did the Vikings come from?	What was the name of the Viking warrior who wanted more gold from the people of Wessex?
What did the Vikings do to the monasteries and churches and to all of the things belonging to them?	When the Vikings came to their borders, what did the noblemen of Wessex do?
What did the Vikings do to the people they captured from Britain?	Guthorm's army made a surprise attack. What were the people in Wessex celebrating?
Why did the Vikings find it so easy to attack Britain?	What did Alfred do to buy time for his plans?
The Great Army landed in England. They were the Viking raiders led by two brothers. What were their names?	Guthorm invaded! Where did some of the English people run to?
After the Vikings fought in Britain for 10 years, what did they do?	What did Alfred do when Guthorm made his surprise attack?
The Vikings wanted all of England but they didn't count on meeting a strong king! What was his name?	Tell a story about Alfred when he was in hiding.
Alfred managed to think of a plan while he was in hiding. What was it?	Alfred gathered his troops in the spring. Why?

William and Harold Game Cards

What happened to Guthorm's army while Alfred hid?	By the time the two armies met, which one was stronger?
The battle between the Vikings and the people from Wessex took place on Salisbury Plain. Who won?	How did Alfred finally defeat Guthorm and his troops?
Alfred became one of the greatest kings of England. Where was he buried and what happened to the site of his burial?	In 1999, archaeologists figured out where Alfred's grave was. Where was it?
After Alfred died, was the battle against the Vikings over?	200 years after Alfred the Great, his descendent Ethelred was defeated by a Viking. What was his name?
What did King Sweyn look like and what was the name he got because of it?	The Vikings ruled England for many years after Sweyn took over. What happened to the mix of people on the island?
The English stopped thinking of themselves as "Viking" or "Anglo-Saxon." How did they now think of themselves?	Edward the Confessor ruled England for over 20 years, but he had no sons. What did the noblemen do?
The noblemen of England appointed an heir for Edward the Confessor. What was his name?	What was Edward's appointed heir, Harold, like?
Did everyone like Edward the Confessor's chosen heir?	Why did William think *he* should be Edward's heir?

William and Harold Game Cards

Why didn't the English noblemen want William to be their king?	What happened to Harold that put him under the control of William in France?
William played a trick on Harold. What was it?	Why was Harold nervous when he was in William's castle?
What is a relic and why was it bad for Harold that his hand was on it during his pledge?	Did William let Harold go back to England?
When Edward the Confessor died what message did William send to Harold?	What happened during Harold's king-making ceremony that was a bad sign?
As Harold was crowned, bad news came. What was it?	What careful planning did William do for his invasion?
By the time Harold's troops got to the battle line, what were they like?	What were William's troops like by the time Harold's troops got to them?
What was the name of the battle between Harold and William?	When William was knocked off his horse his soldiers began to shout, "The king is dead." What happened?
Harold's troops were tired so he camped on the hill. What did William do?	Who won the Battle of Hastings?
Who won the Battle of Hastings?	William was given a new name. What was it?

Chapter 16: England After the Conquest

A Stone Castle

Fox and Geese Game Board

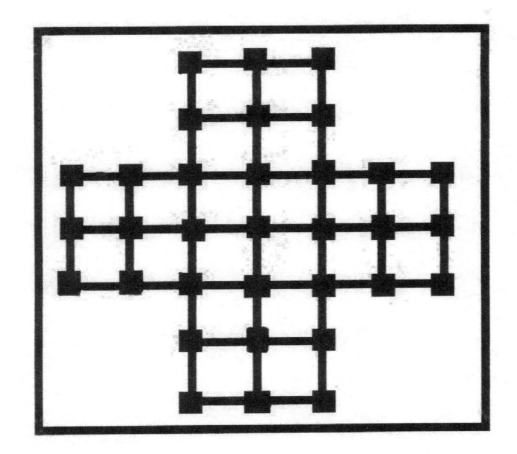

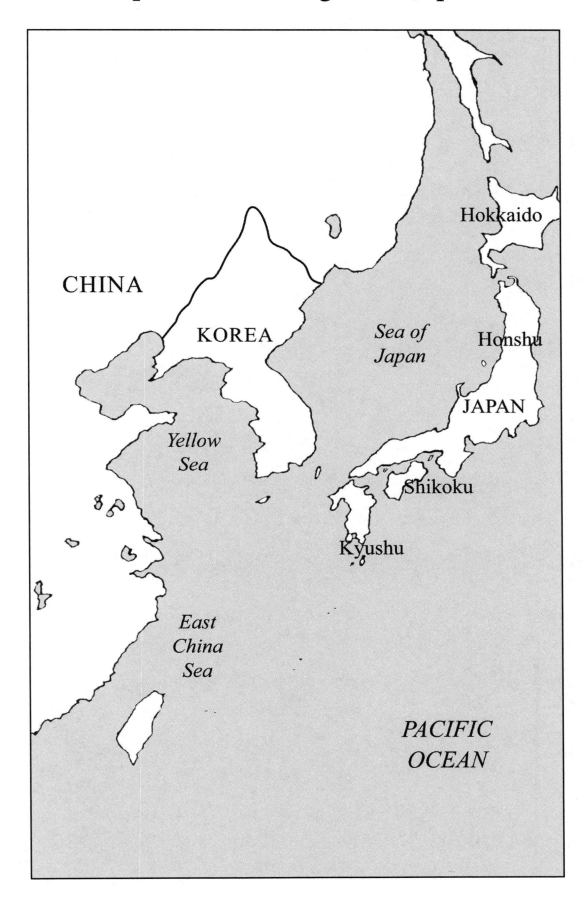

Knight

Samurai Warrior

Shield Template

Find the Knights Word Search

Find the knights' names. They may be forward, backward, vertical, horizontal, or diagonal.

ARTHUR   BEDIVERE   BORS   GAHERIS
GALAHAD   GARTH   GAWAIN   GERAINT
KAY   LAMORAK   LANCELOT   PERCIVAL
TRISTAN

```
L L K B F L K K A Y L P G C B
Y M K B X A A K M R E J O U E
L G J S R O B N B R T D H N D
C A A O V L R H C D N H W Q I
R W M K V G J I V E G A U G V
Z A V P U Q V D B L L Z T R E
L I Q B L A L Y P G U O X U R
D N F Q L N W K A X S K T H E
E A T R I S T A N K I X U D R
I Q H N G U G B P F R S O S C
V G S A G B T C N A E V G F G
U B Z C L G V Q L K H R F A P
O T W K C A N O G Z A Z R C C
T N I A R E G G S G G T A A N
E Q F C G E F D Z P H J P C Y
```

Spur Template and Rowel Pattern

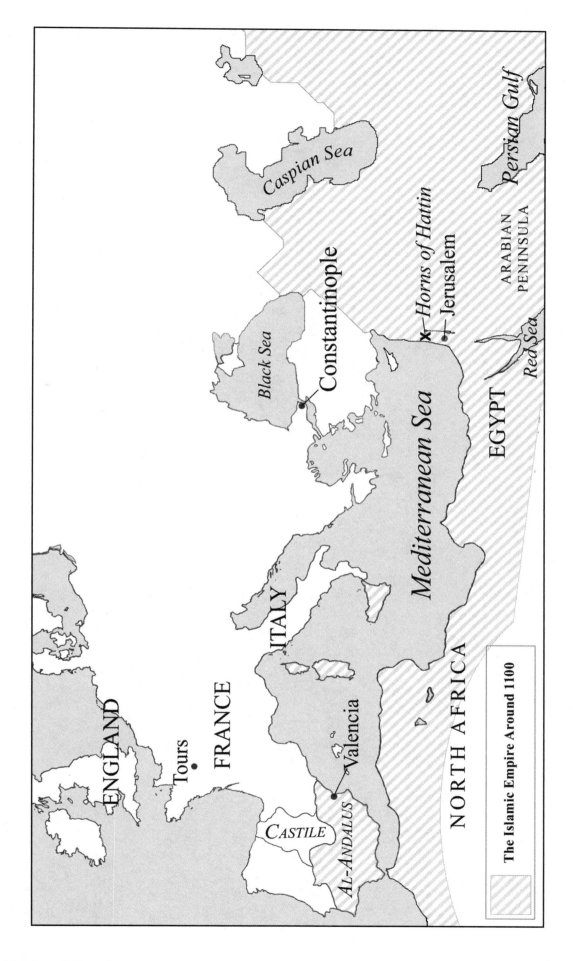

The Crusades

Pilgrim's Badges

This pilgrim badge depicts Saint Thomas Becket, whose shrine is located at Canterbury Cathedral in Canterbury, England.

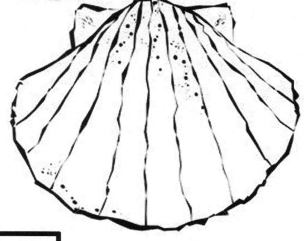

The scallop shell was the badge received for a pilgrimage to Santiago de Compostela in Spain. This was where the shrine to Saint James is located.

The cross was the pilgrim badge for visiting Saint Peter's shrine in Rome, Italy.

Spanish Conquest and Reconquest Flip Book

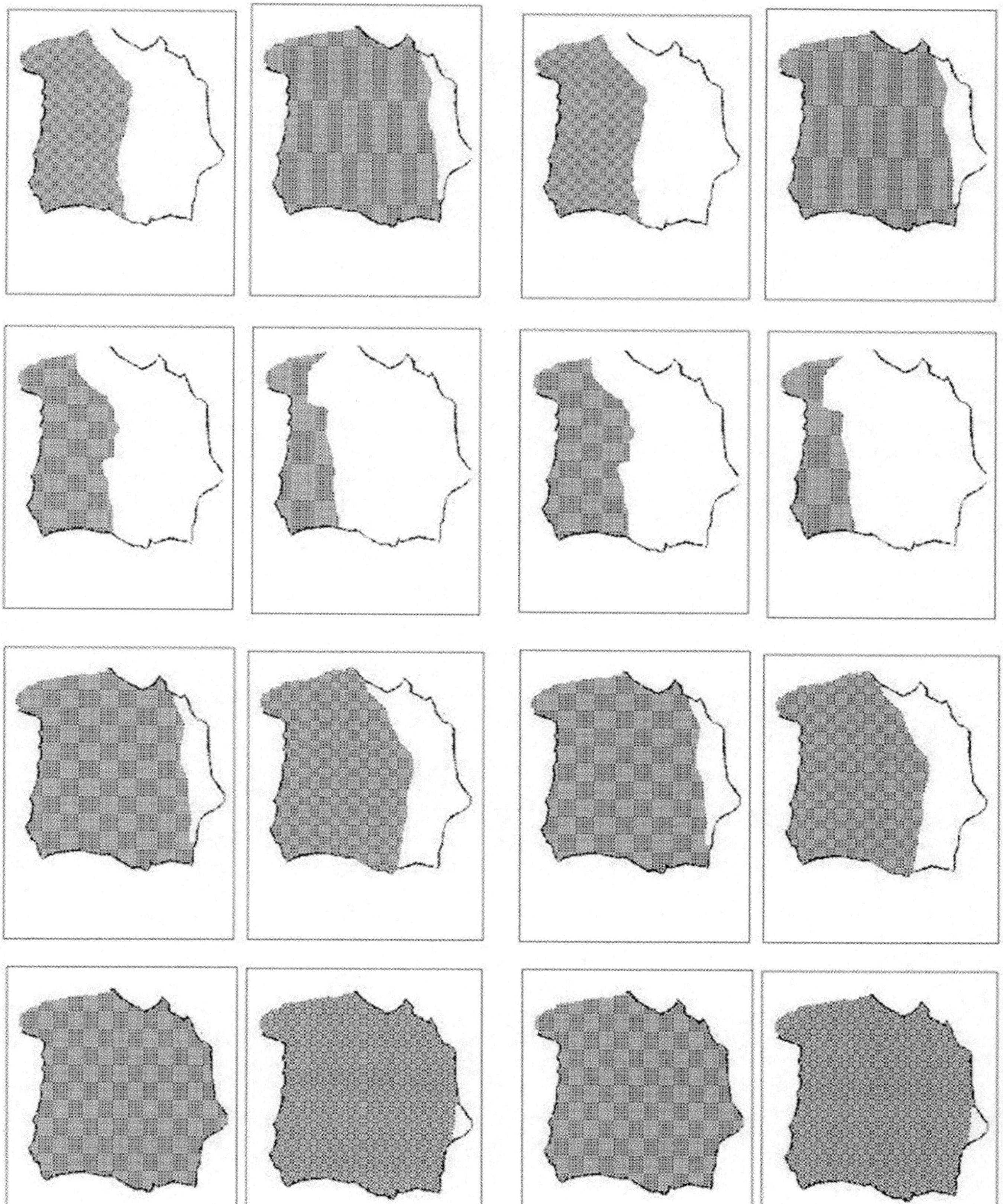

Chapter 19: Richard and the Crusades

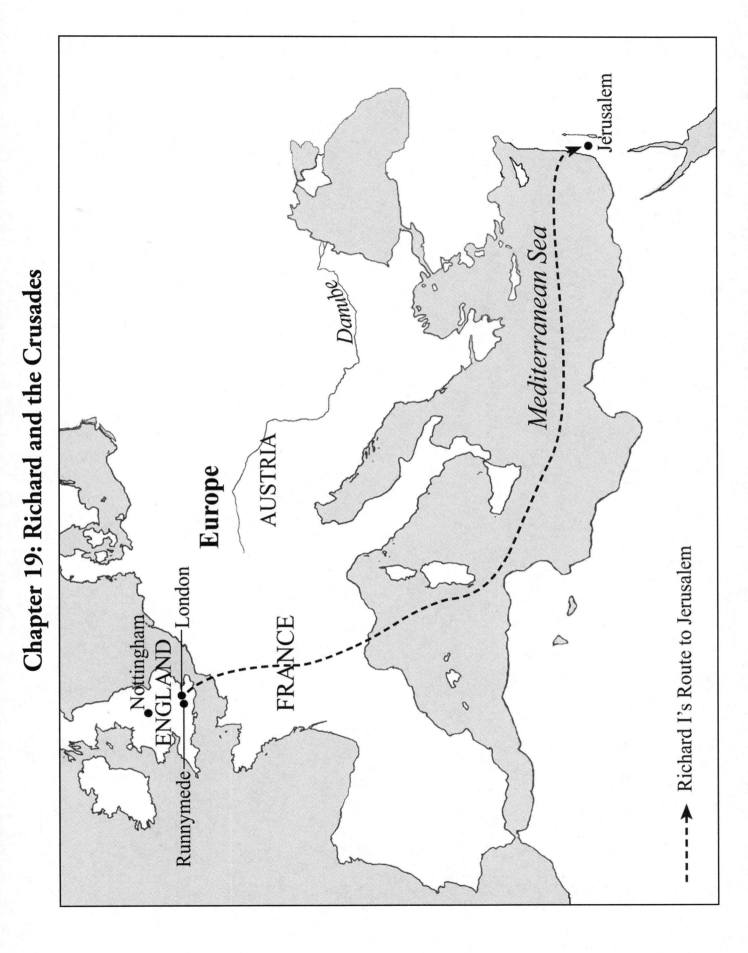

Labels on map:
Danube
AUSTRIA
Europe
FRANCE
ENGLAND
Nottingham
London
Runnymede
Mediterranean Sea
Jerusalem

Richard I's Route to Jerusalem

Robin Hood

Lion Shield Design

Chapter 20: The Scattering of the Jews

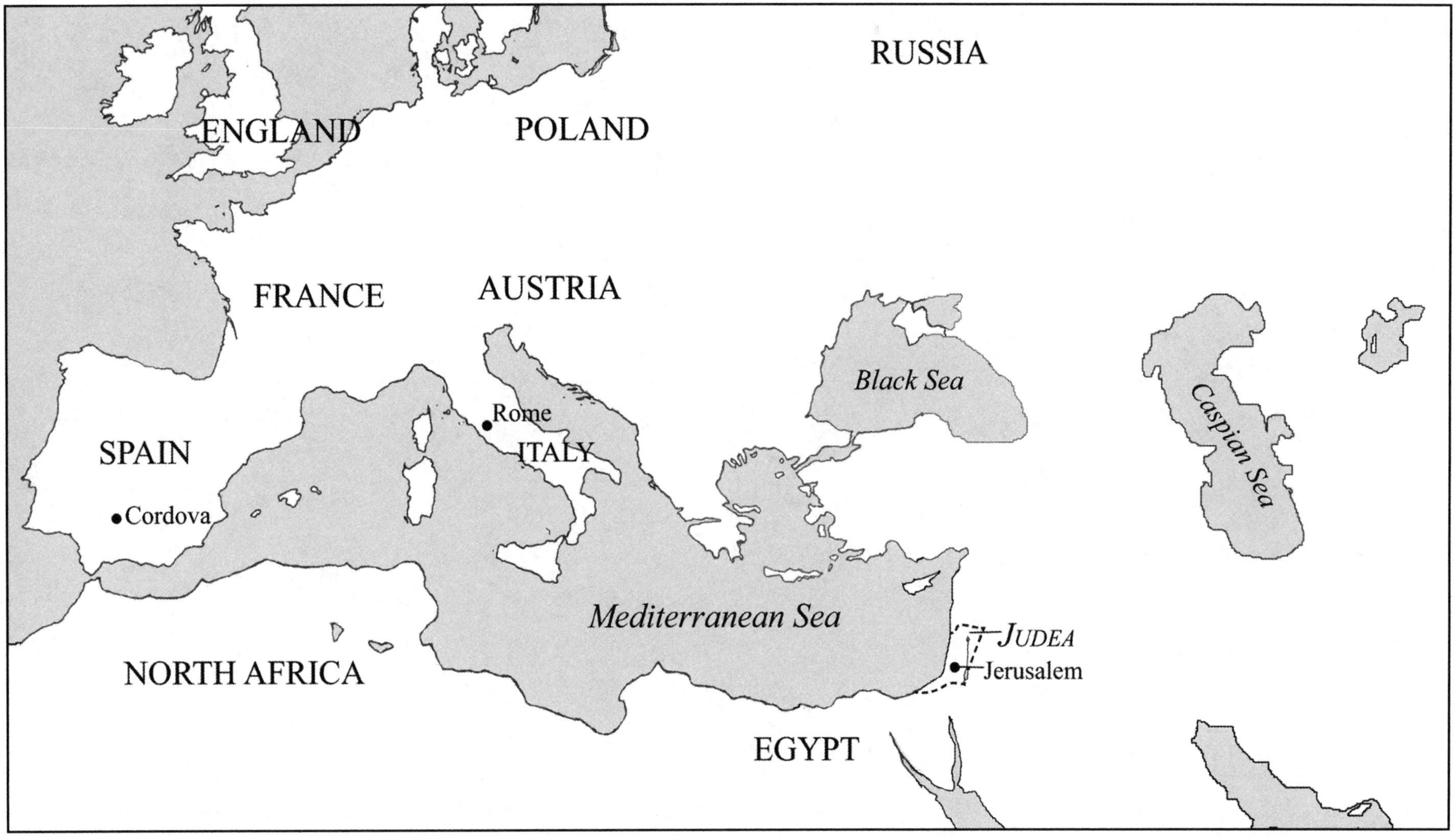

RUSSIA

POLAND

ENGLAND

FRANCE

AUSTRIA

SPAIN

●Cordova

NORTH AFRICA

Caspian Sea

Black Sea

Mediterranean Sea

ITALY

●Rome

EGYPT

JUDEA

Jerusalem
●

Herod's Temple

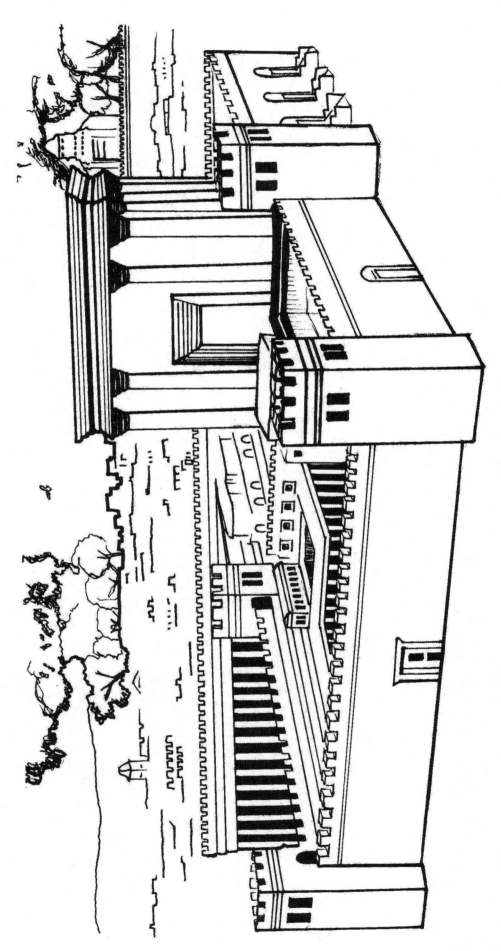

Jewish Symbols

The **Menorah** is the lamp used in the Temple for worship. It is a symbol of the Nation of Israel, acting as a light to the nations.

The **Wailing Wall** survived both the Babylonian and Roman destruction of Jerusalem. It is seen as a symbol of hope.

Though **Lions** are smaller in Judea than in Africa, their curly heads and strong figures are found in medieval architecture, symbolizing royalty, courage, and power.

Placed on a house's doorposts, the **Mezuzah** symbolizes God's presence in the home.

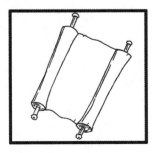

These **Scrolls** symbolize the sacred scriptures of the Jewish people, the Torah.

The Shema

"Sh" — the symbol for *Shema*

Hear O Israel!
The Lord our God,
the Lord is one!

Deuteronomy 6:4

Clever Rabbi Finger-Puppets

The Clever Rabbi   The Emir   The Emir's Servant   The Evil Advisors

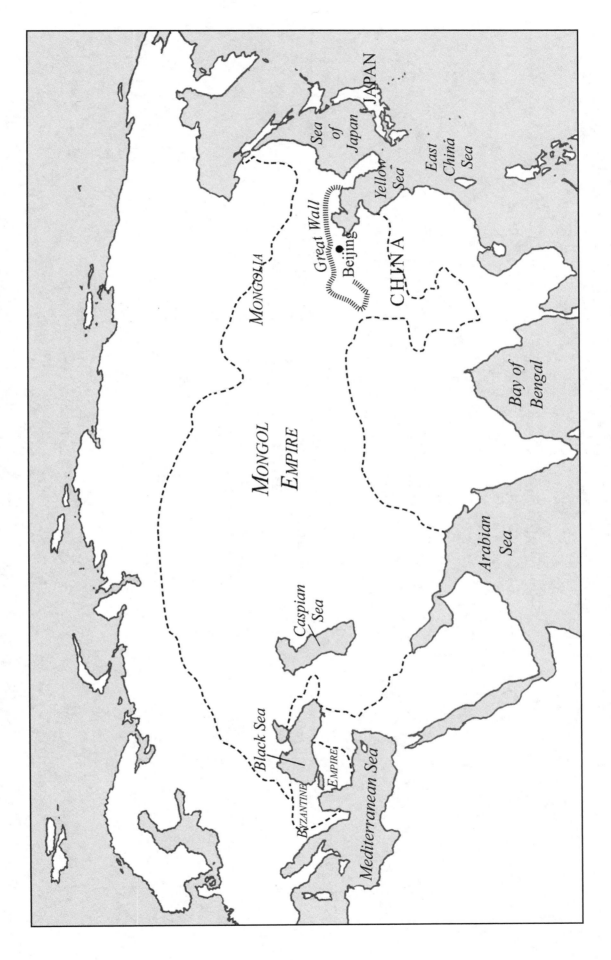

Genghis Khan

Put History Back in Order!

Genghis Khan led the unified Mongols
into China to take over villages.

Kublai Khan became the leader of the Mongol territory
and made people bow down to worship him.

Genghis Khan became the leader of the Yakka.

Genghis Khan led the Mongols
as far south as the city of Peking and conquered it.

Genghis Khan sought to unite all of
the Mongol clans—through force if necessary.

Chapter 22: The Ming Dynasty and the Silk Road

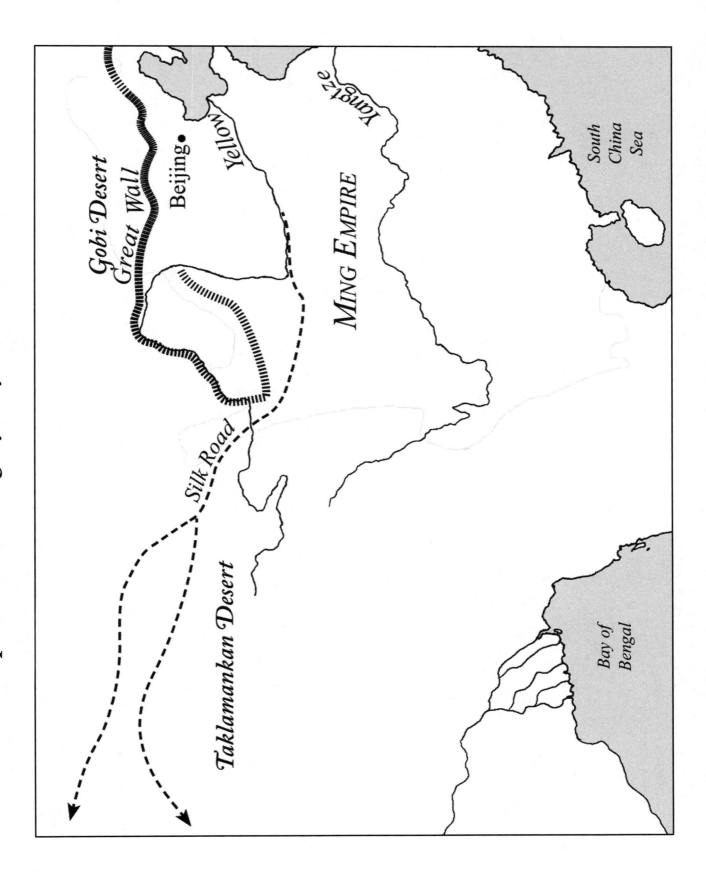

Marco Polo

Chapter 23: The Territory of the Rus

SCANDINAVIA

ENGLAND

THE LAND OF THE RUS

CENTRAL EUROPE

•Moscow

•Kiev

SLAVS

FRANCE

Constantinople

Black Sea

Rome
ITALY

Mediterranean Sea

The Kremlin

Kokoshnic Pattern

Architectural Eggs

Chapter 24: The Ottoman Empire

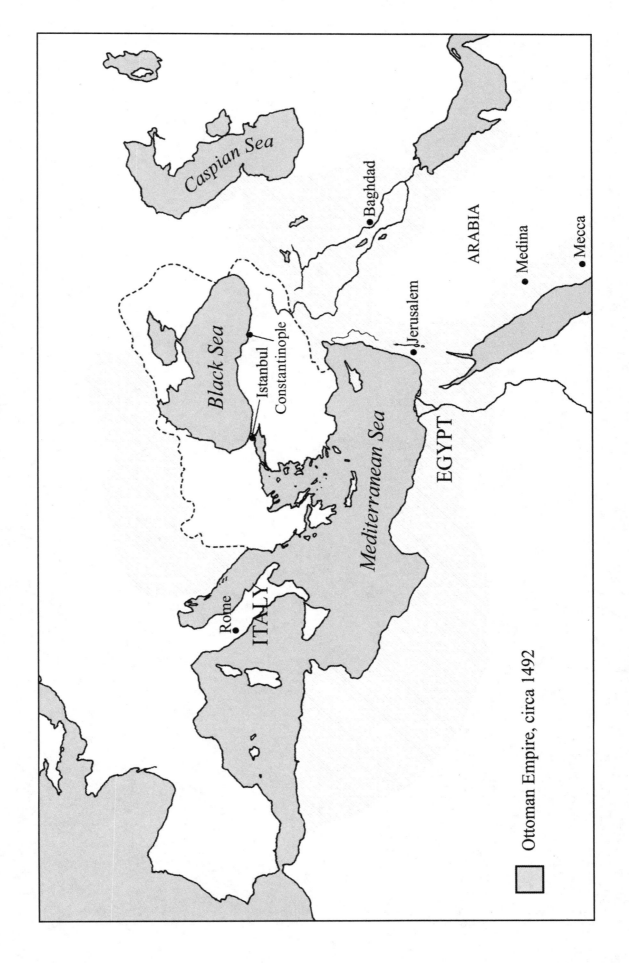

Caspian Sea

Baghdad

ARABIA

Medina

Mecca

Black Sea

Istanbul
Constantinople

Jerusalem

Mediterranean Sea

EGYPT

Rome

ITALY

Ottoman Empire, circa 1492

The Turks Overtaking Constantinople

Suleiman

Byzantine Icon

Cross Pattern

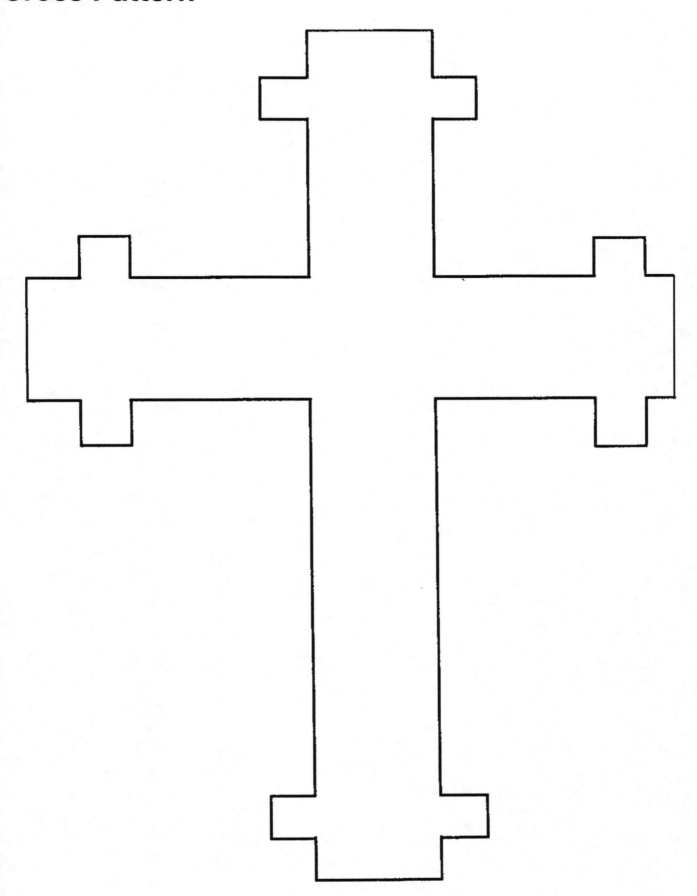

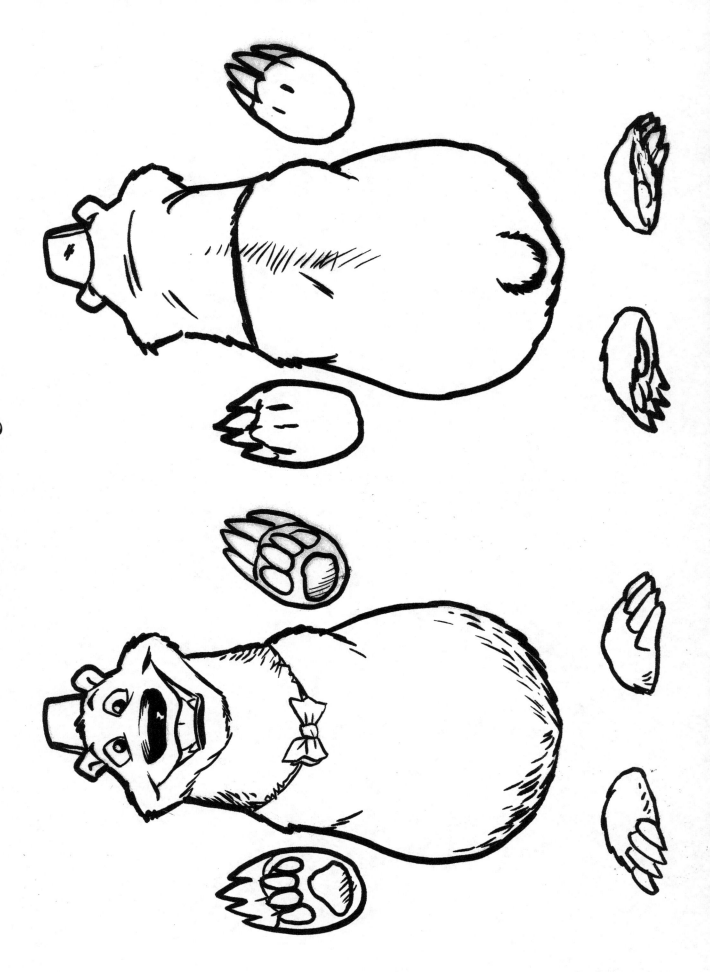

Chapter 25: Europe at the Time of the Black Death

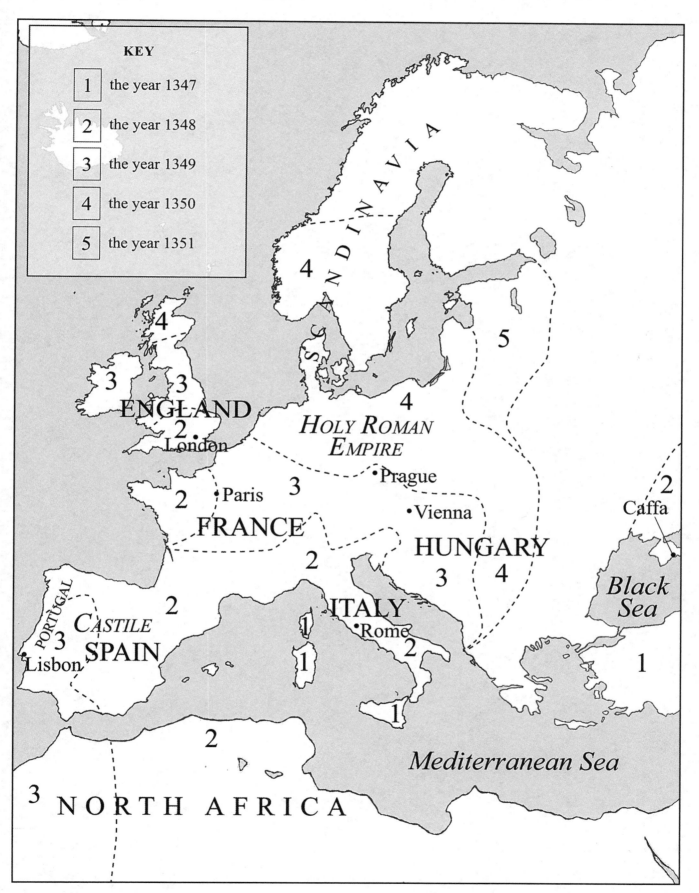

KEY

1	the year 1347
2	the year 1348
3	the year 1349
4	the year 1350
5	the year 1351

SCANDINAVIA

4

4

3

3

ENGLAND

2

London

4

HOLY ROMAN EMPIRE

Prague

3

Vienna

5

2

Paris

FRANCE

2

HUNGARY

3

4

2

Caffa

Black Sea

2

PORTUGAL

CASTILE

SPAIN

3

Lisbon

2

1

1

ITALY

Rome

1

2

1

Mediterranean Sea

2

3   NORTH AFRICA

Plague Doctor

The Cycle of the Plague

1. Rat infested with bacteria.

2. Flea bites rat and gets bacteria.

3. Flea's digestive system fills with bacteria.

4. Flea bites humans.

5. Humans become sick and die.

Beak Template

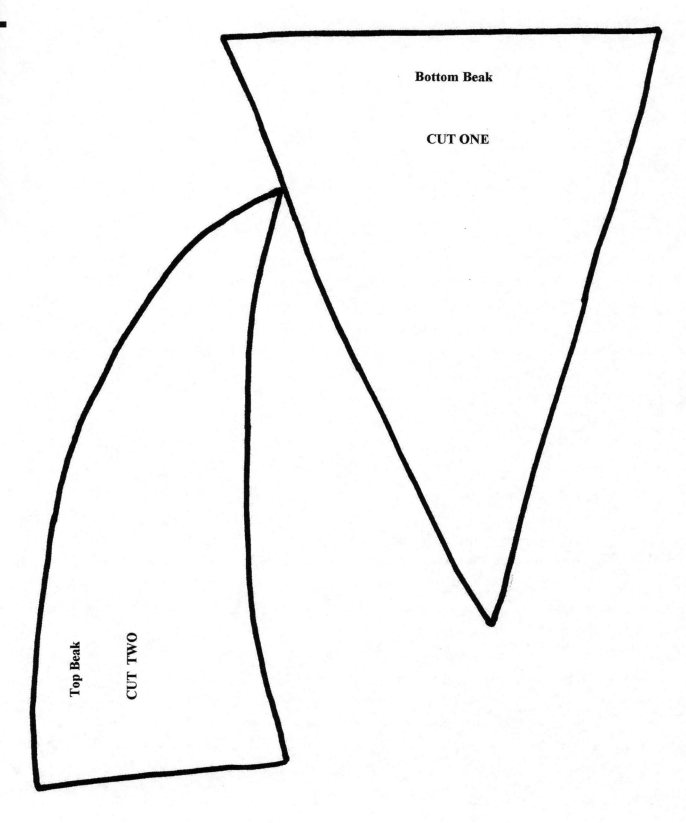

Bottom Beak

CUT ONE

Top Beak

CUT TWO

Plague Mask Template

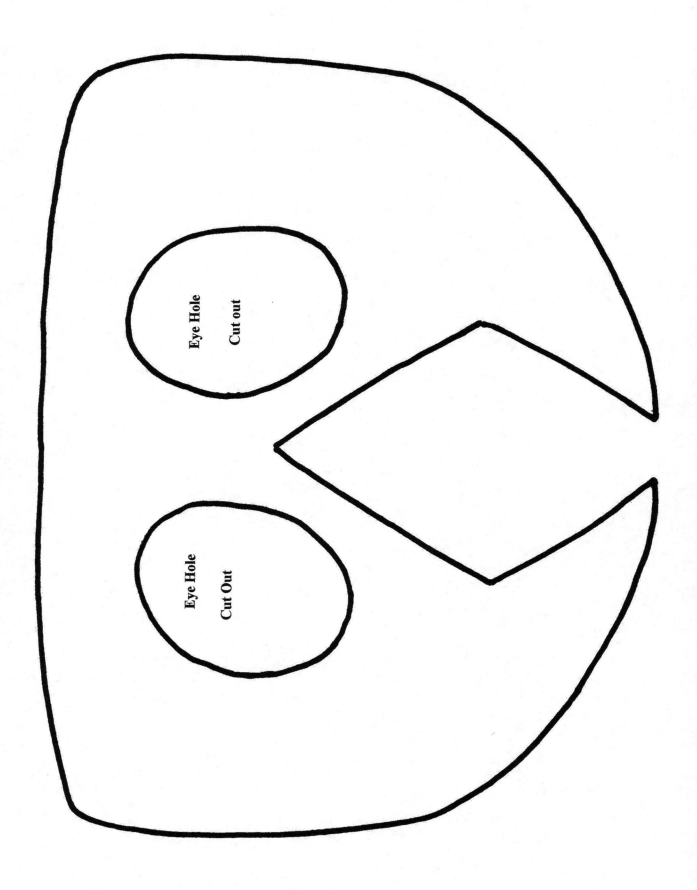

Eye Hole
Cut out

Eye Hole
Cut Out

Chapter 26: England and France

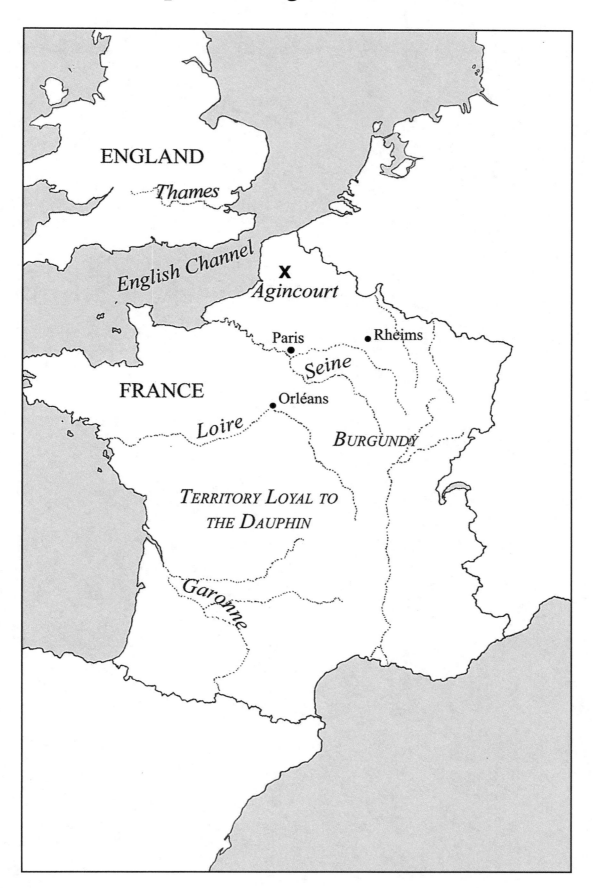

Joan of Arc

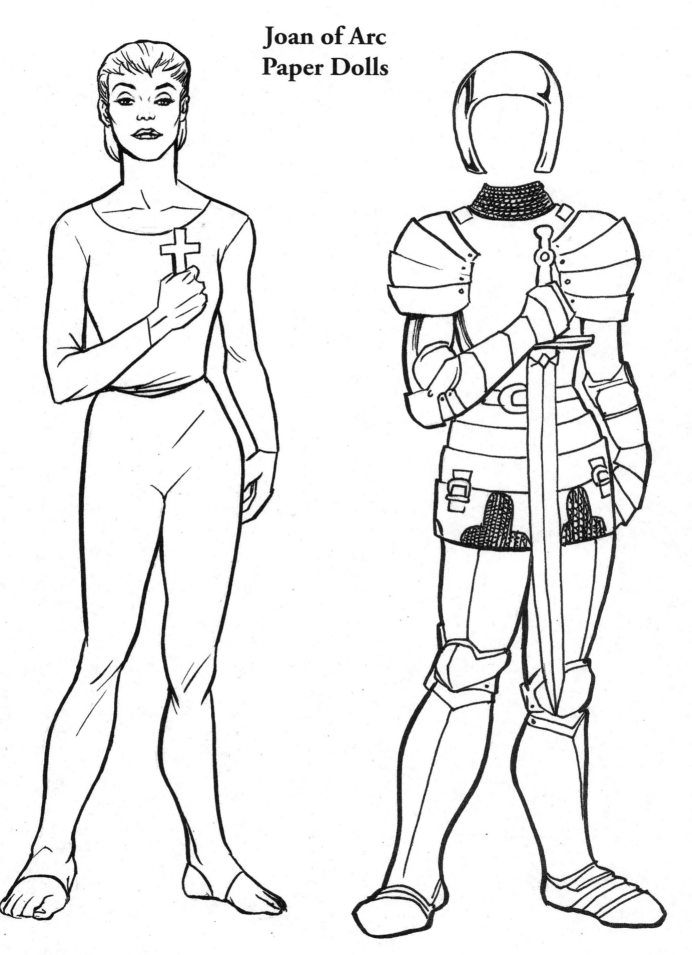

Joan of Arc
Paper Dolls

Joan of Arc
Paper Dolls

Chapter 27: England During the Time of the Wars of the Roses

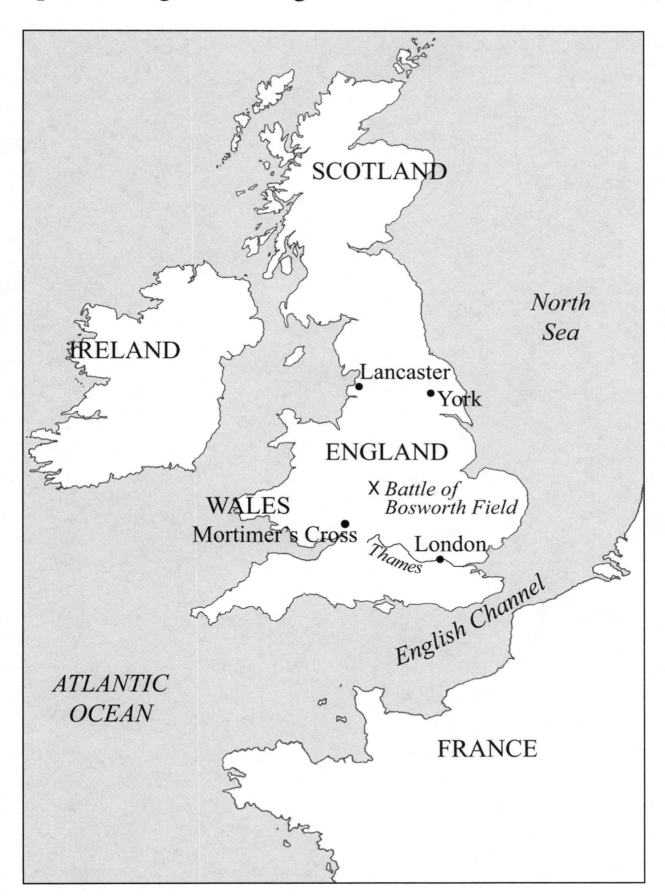

SCOTLAND

North Sea

IRELAND

Lancaster

York

ENGLAND

X *Battle of Bosworth Field*

WALES

Mortimer's Cross

Thames

London

English Channel

ATLANTIC OCEAN

FRANCE

Edward V

Richard III

York and Lancaster Roses

Rose Checker Tops

Tower of London Template

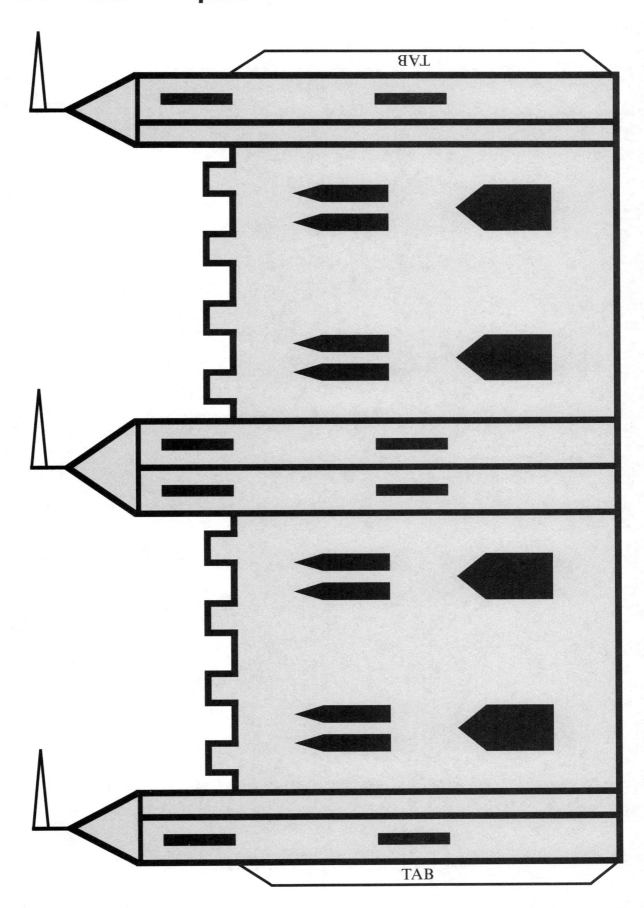

Princes in the Tower Game Board

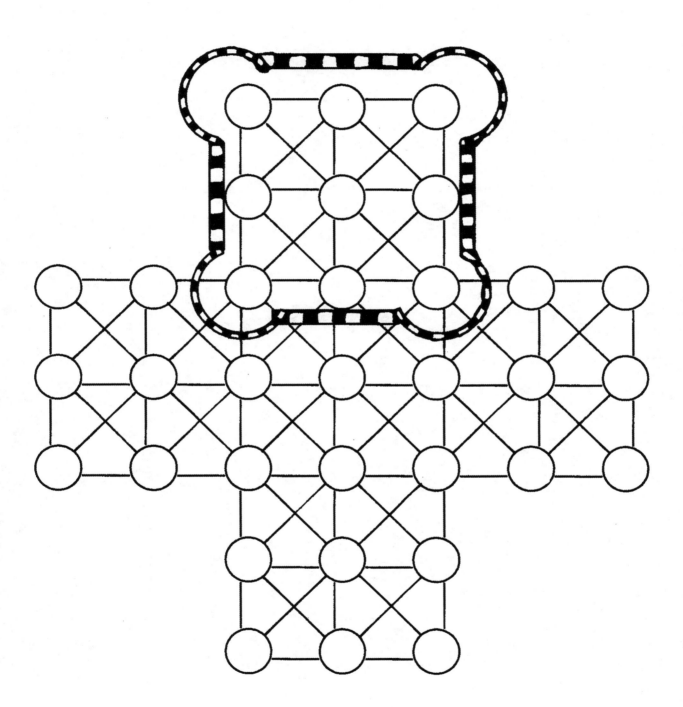

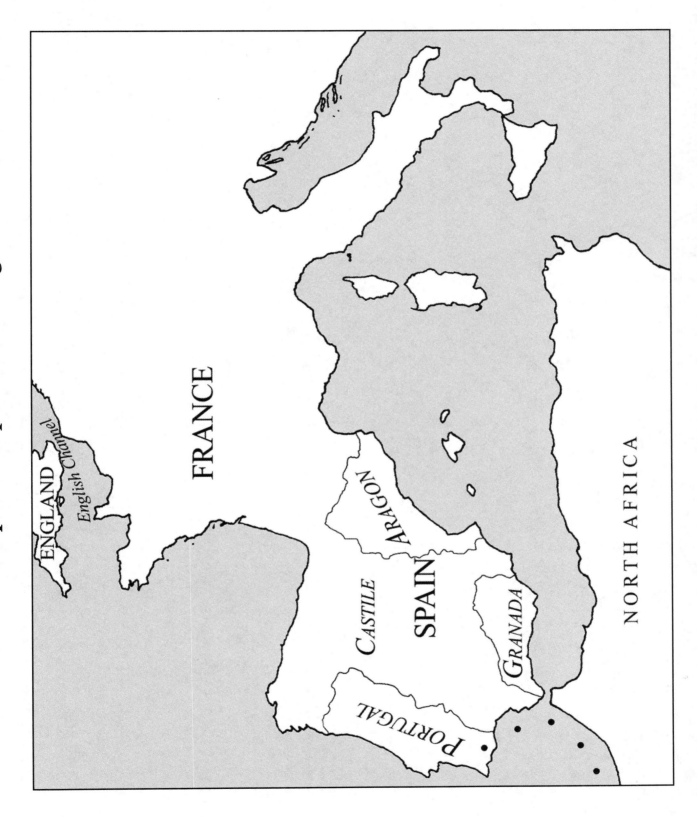

Explorer Using an Astrolabe

Chapter 29: West African Kingdoms

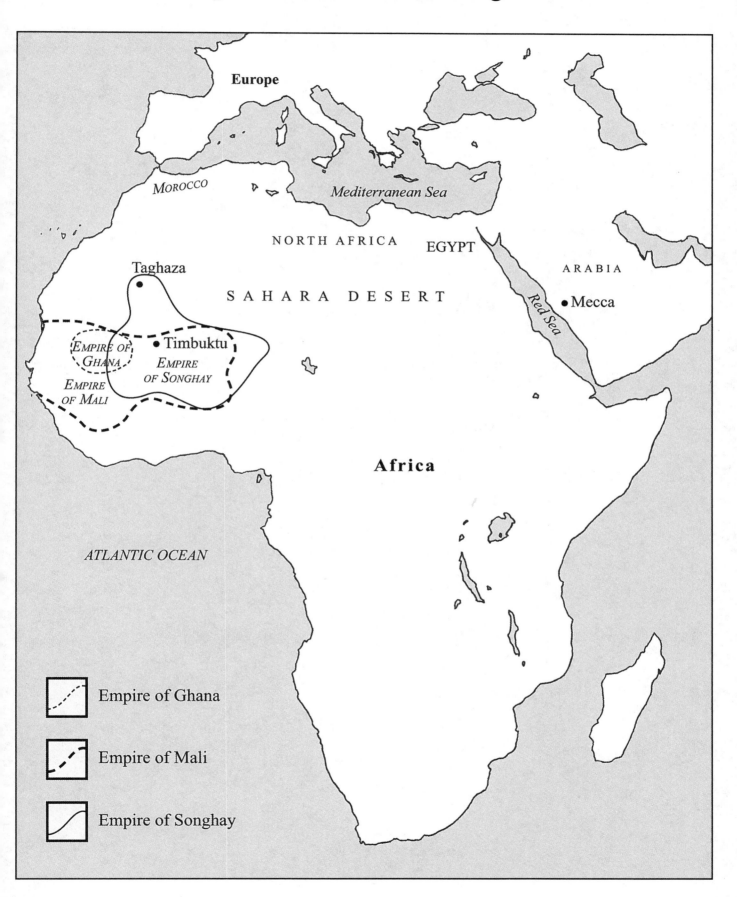

Europe

MOROCCO

Mediterranean Sea

NORTH AFRICA

EGYPT

SAHARA DESERT

ARABIA

Red Sea

●Mecca

Taghaza
●

●Timbuktu

EMPIRE OF
GHANA

EMPIRE
OF SONGHAY

EMPIRE
OF MALI

ATLANTIC OCEAN

Africa

Empire of Ghana

Empire of Mali

Empire of Songhay

Mansa Musa of Mali

Chapter 30: The Moghul Dynasty in India

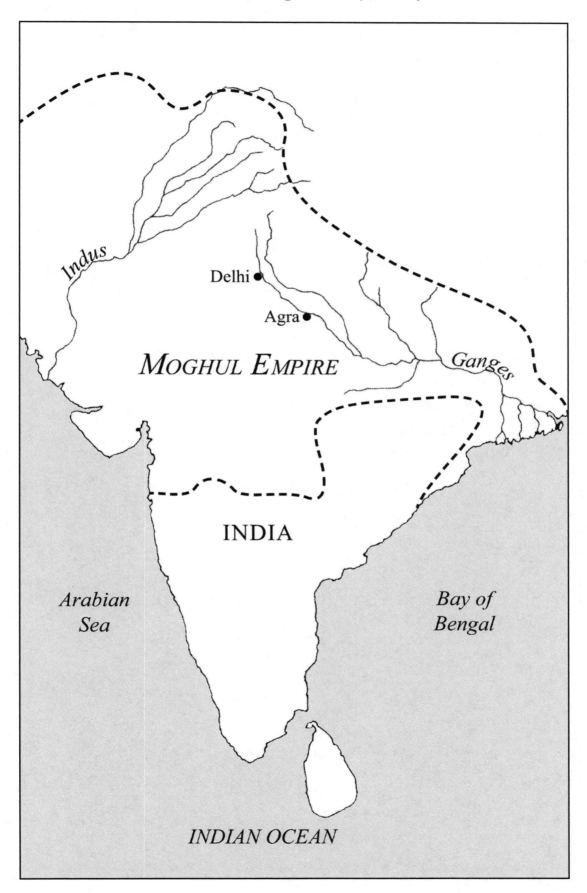

Moghul King

Babur's Garden

Chapter 31: Routes of the Great Explorers

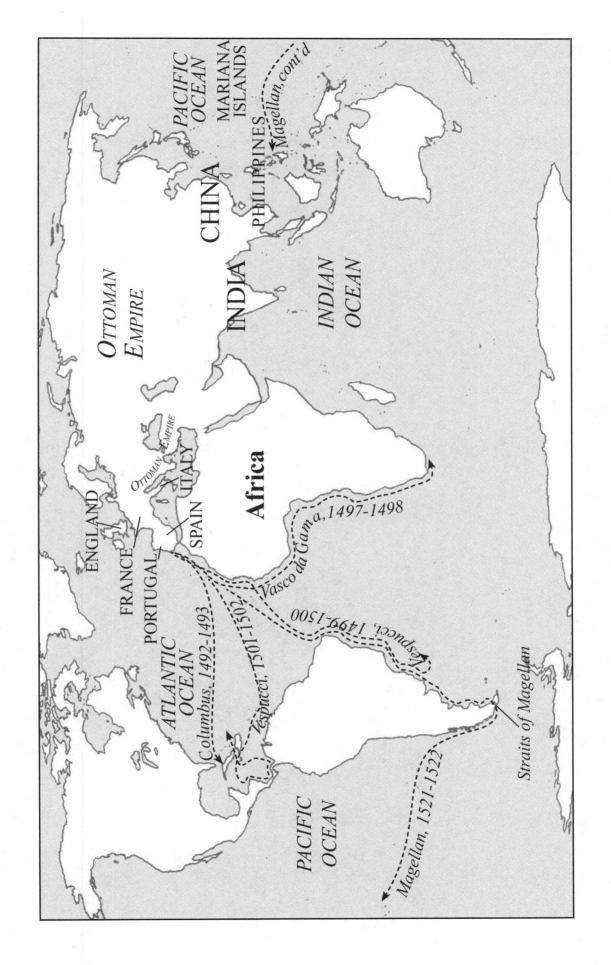

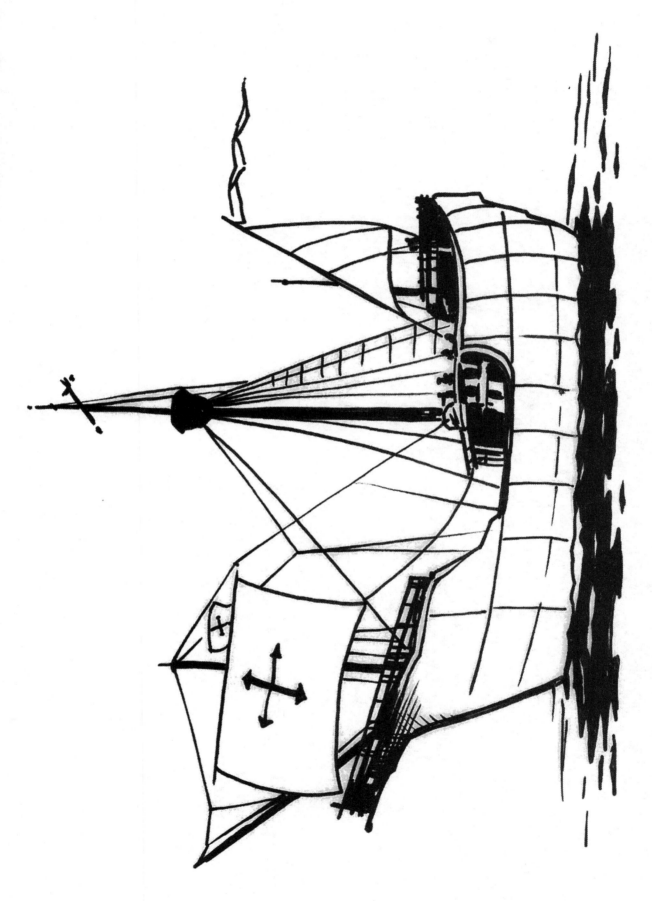

Unscramble the Explorers

1. __ __ __ __ __ __ __ __ __ __ __ __ __ __ __ __
   was an Italian explorer funded by Spain to find a western route
   to India.

   (erriophhstc bloucsum)

2. The ships that Coumbus first traveled on were the __ __ __ __,
   the __ __ __ __ __, and the __ __ __ __ __ __ __ __ __ __.

   (ainn, iatnp, aanst aaimr)

3. Columbus' men got __ __ __ __ __ __ because they went so
   long without fresh fruit or vegetables.

   (ryvusc)

4. The continents of North and South America were named after

   __ __ __ __ __ __ __ __ __ __ __ __ __ __.

   (mogriea cceipsuv)

5. __ __ __ __ __ __ __ __ __ __ __ __ __ __ __ __ was an
   explorer whose ship was the first ship to make it all around the
   world though he didn't make it alive.

   (dnnfeirda glnealam)

6. Magellan's men ate __ __ __ __ __ __ __ because they were so
   hungry.

   (dstuswa)

Chapter 32: The Mayan, Aztec, and Incan Empires

North America

MODERN
MEXICO

*Gulf of
Mexico*

*AZTEC
EMPIRE*

Tenochtitlan

Lake Texococo

*MAYAN
EMPIRE*

*ATLANTIC
OCEAN*

YUCATAN
PENINSULA

Caribbean Sea

**Central
America**

South America

*INCAN
EMPIRE*

Cuzco•

*Lake
Titicaca*

*PACIFIC
OCEAN*

Mayan Carvings

Mayan Numbers

Our number system is based on 10 perhaps because we have ten fingers. The Mayan number system is based on 20 (maybe because 10 fingers + 10 toes = 20). The Mayan symbol for zero is 👁. The Mayan number system is considered one of their greatest achievements because any whole number could be expressed using place rotation. Mayan numbers are written from top to bottom.

Fill in the missing numbers.

0	5	10	15	20
1	6	11	16	21
2	7	12	17	22
3	8	13	18	23
4	9	14	19	24

Mayan Numbers

25	30	35	40	45
26	31	36	41	46
27	32	37	42	47
28	33	38	43	48
29	34	39	44	49

Mayan Math Page

Math Activity: Mayan Mathematics
Study the logical sequence of the Mayan number chart (provided) and fill out the last row on the chart (SP 133).
Use the chart to do the Mayan mathematics.

1. Jade made ●● / ▬ / ▬ tortillas. The dog ate ● ● ● ● when she wasn't looking. How many tortillas were left for Jade's meal?
Jade had _____ tortillas left.

2. ▬ ▬ ▬ **+** ● ● ● ● **=** _____

3. Write your age using Mayan numbers.

I am _____ years and _____ months old.

BONUS QUESTIONS :   ●

4. To make a warrior's headband you need ● ● ● ● feathers. Your headband will have an equal amount of green and yellow feathers. If you have ●● / ▬ green feathers and ▬ yellow feathers, how many more of EACH color will you need?

I need _____ green feathers and _____ yellow feathers.

5. Write the number 86 using the Mayan number system.

_____

Chapter 33: The Empires of Spain and Portugal

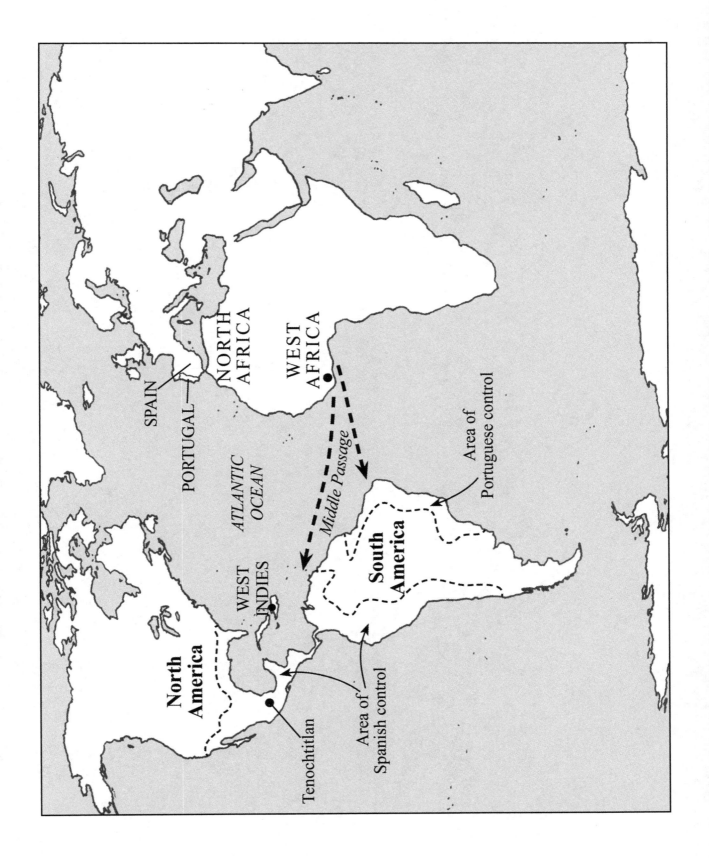

SPAIN

PORTUGAL

NORTH
AFRICA

WEST
AFRICA

ATLANTIC
OCEAN

Middle Passage

Area of
Portuguese control

**South
America**

**North
America**

WEST
INDIES

Area of
Spanish control

Tenochtitlan

A Conquistador

Conquistador
Mask Template

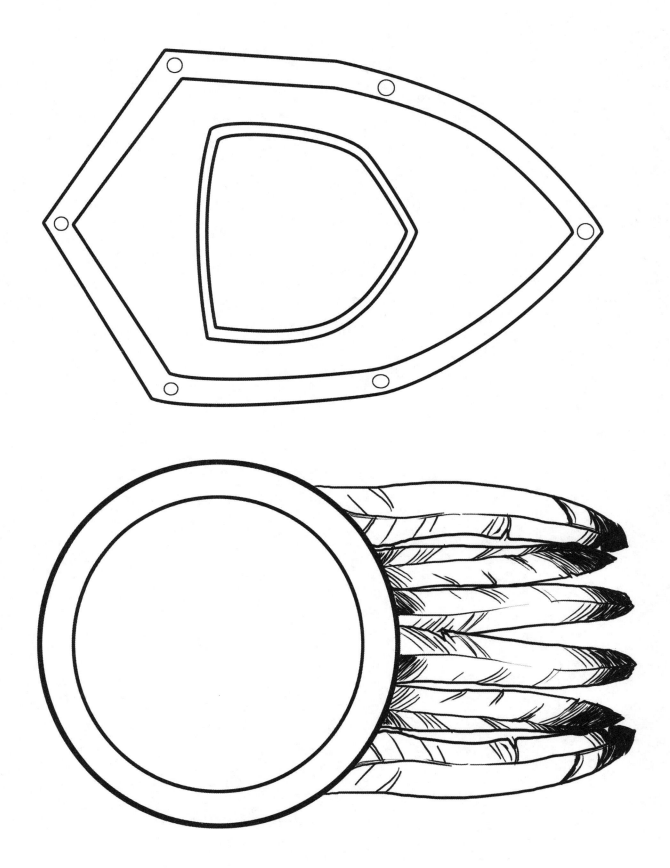

Spanish Shield Templates

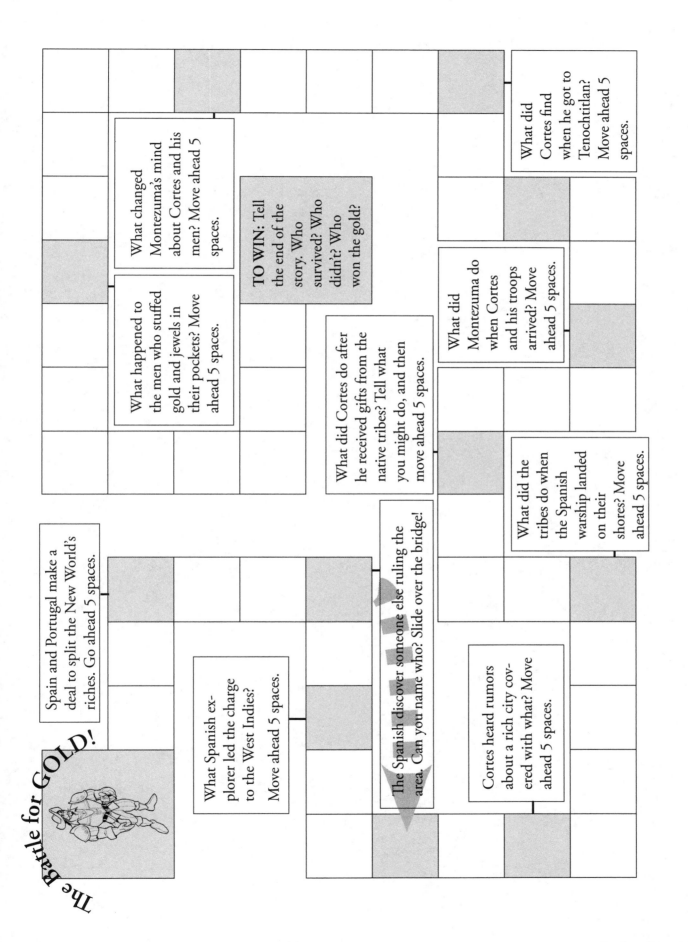

The Battle for GOLD!

Spain and Portugal make a deal to split the New World's riches. Go ahead 5 spaces.

What Spanish explorer led the charge to the West Indies? Move ahead 5 spaces.

The Spanish discover someone else ruling the area. Can you name who? Slide over the bridge!

Cortes heard rumors about a rich city covered with what? Move ahead 5 spaces.

What did the tribes do when the Spanish warship landed on their shores? Move ahead 5 spaces.

What did Cortes do after he received gifts from the native tribes? Tell what you might do, and then move ahead 5 spaces.

What did Montezuma do when Cortes and his troops arrived? Move ahead 5 spaces.

What happened to the men who stuffed gold and jewels in their pockets? Move ahead 5 spaces.

What changed Montezuma's mind about Cortes and his men? Move ahead 5 spaces.

TO WIN: Tell the end of the story. Who survived? Who didn't? Who won the gold?

What did Cortes find when he got to Tenochtitlan? Move ahead 5 spaces.

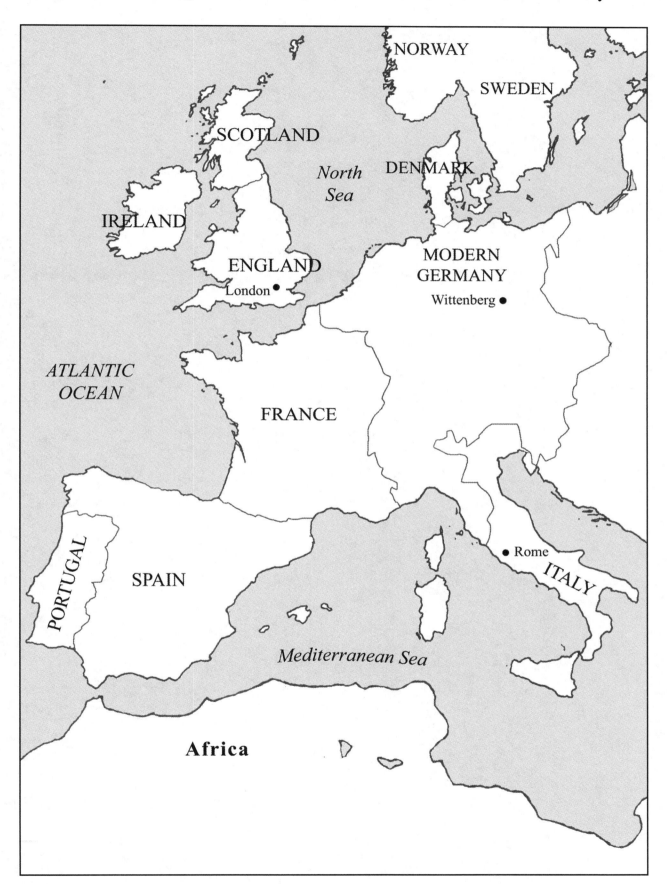

Martin Luther

Henry VIII

Illuminated "A"

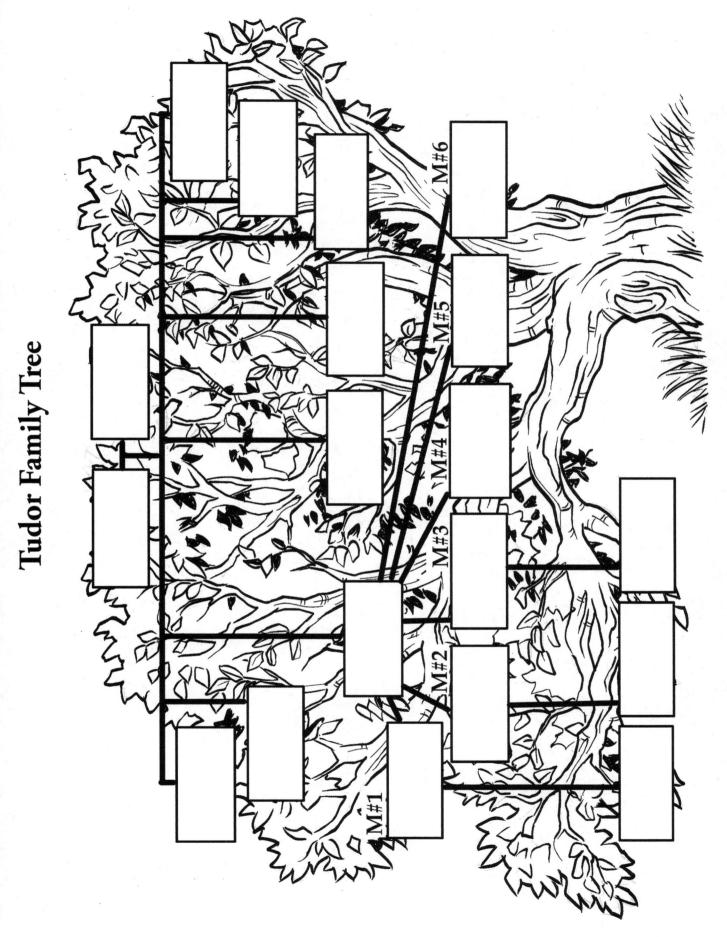

Tudor Family Tree

M#6

M#5

M#4

M#3

M#2

M#1

Chapter 35: Europe at the Time of the Renaissance

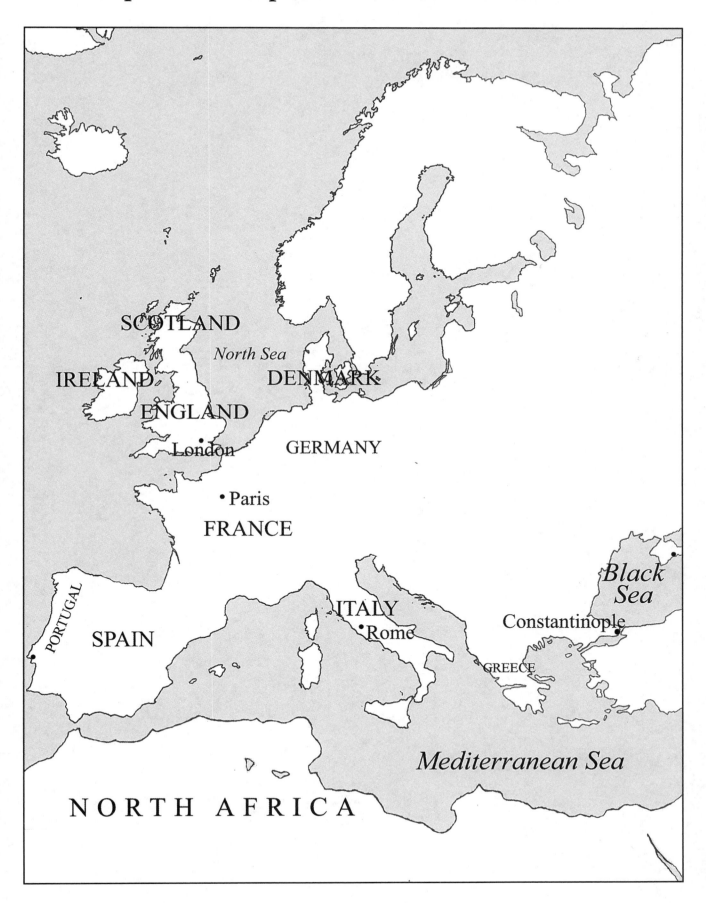

SCOTLAND

North Sea

IRELAND

DENMARK

ENGLAND

London

GERMANY

• Paris

FRANCE

PORTUGAL

SPAIN

ITALY

Rome

Black Sea

Constantinople

GREECE

Mediterranean Sea

NORTH AFRICA

A Paper Maker

Greek Columns

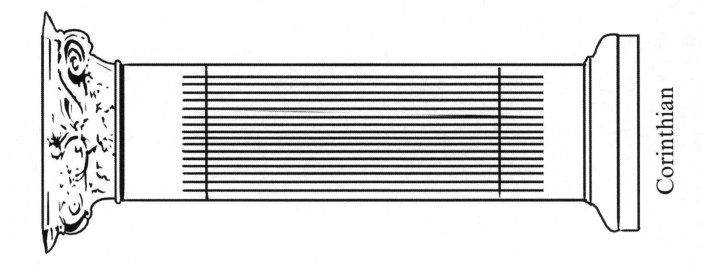

Corinthian

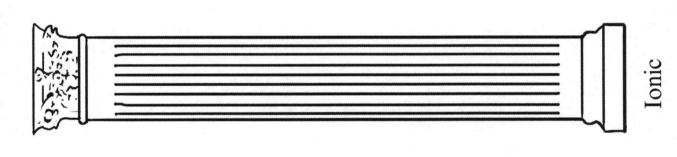

Ionic

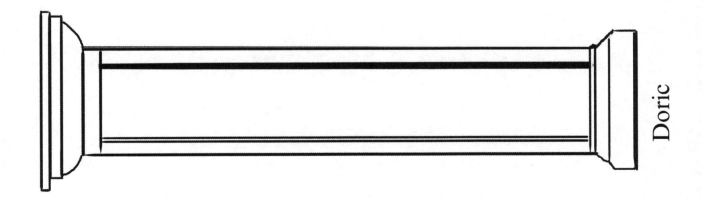

Doric

Chapter 36: The Reformation and Counter Reformation

Stained Glass

Stained Glass

Chapter 37: Poland and Italy

Nicholas Copernicus

The Solar System

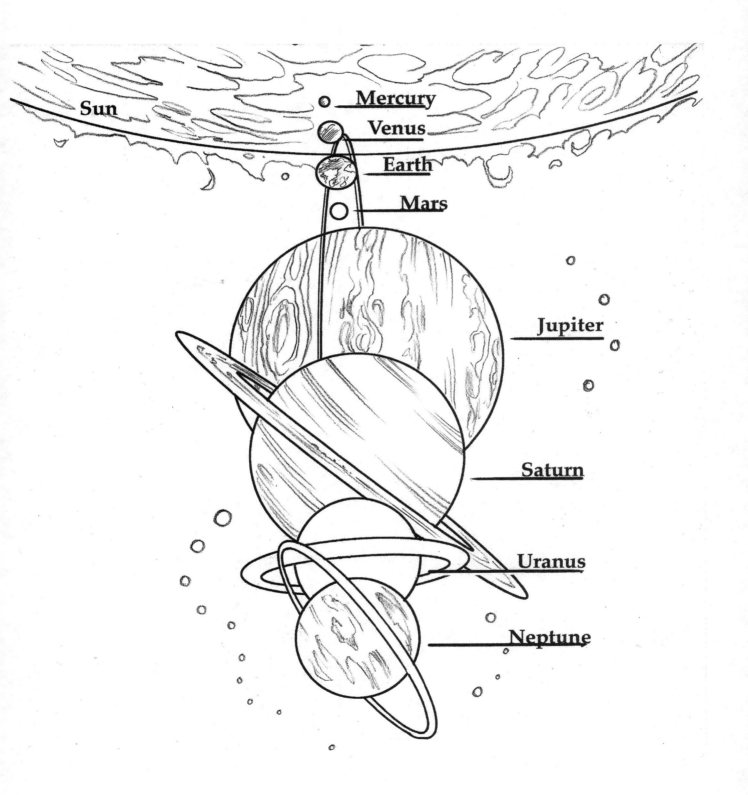

Sun

Mercury

Venus

Earth

Mars

Jupiter

Saturn

Uranus

Neptune

Chapter 38: Elizabeth's England

Queen Elizabeth

Chapter 39: England

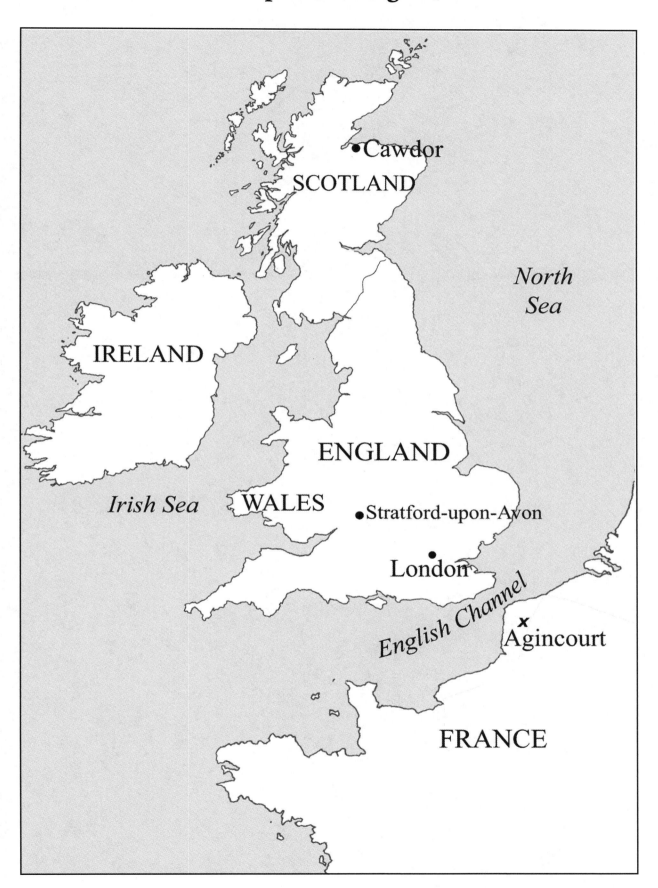

William Shakespeare

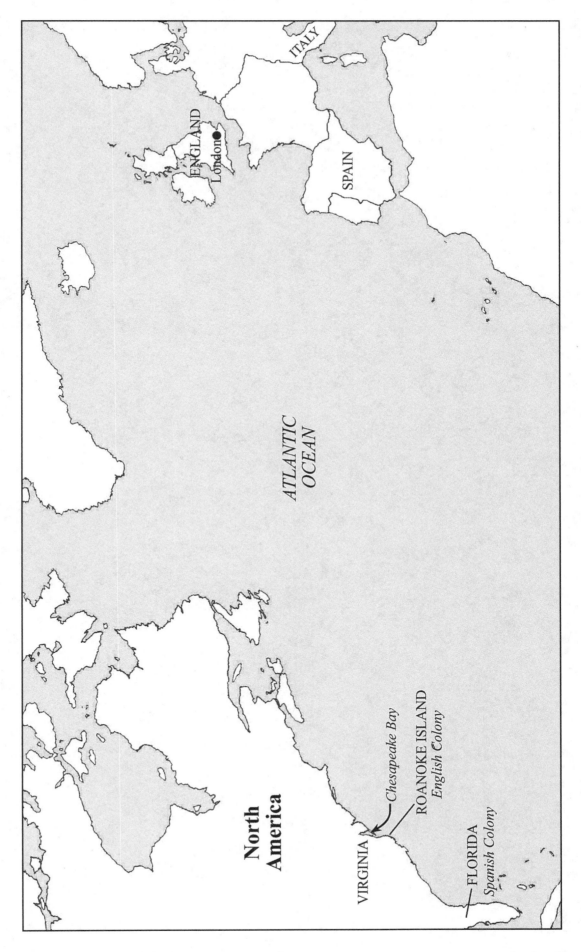

Chapter 40: English Settlements in North America

ITALY

ENGLAND

London●

SPAIN

ATLANTIC
OCEAN

North
America

Chesapeake Bay

VIRGINIA

ROANOKE ISLAND
English Colony

FLORIDA
Spanish Colony

Sir Walter Raleigh

The Lost Colony

Raleigh Quote

History hath triumphed over
time, which besides it nothing
but eternity hath triumphed
over.

~Sir Walter Raleigh
in the preface of his work, Historie of the World

Making A Map

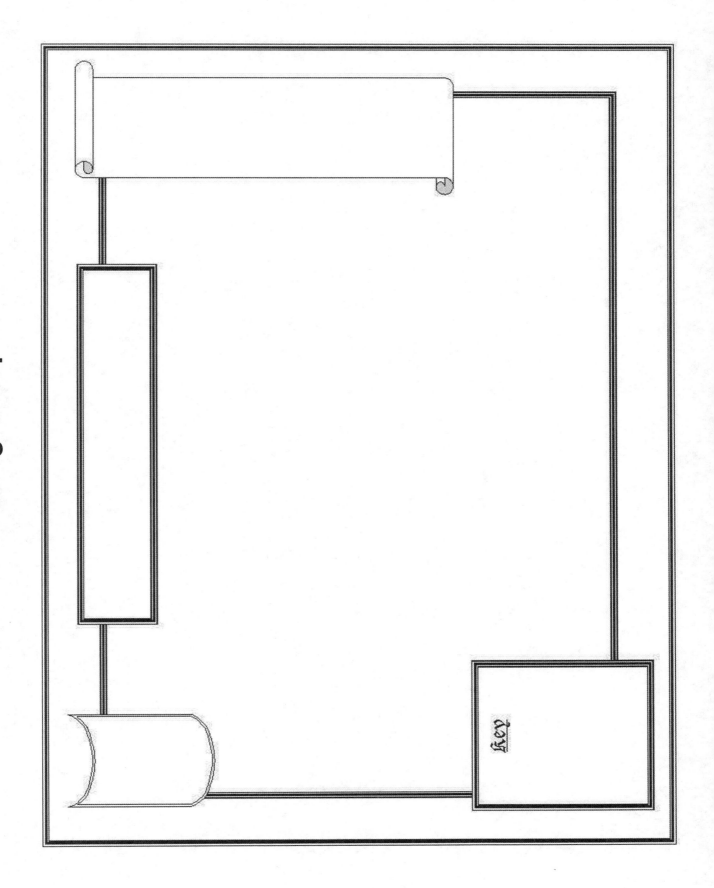

key

Chapter 41: Newfoundland

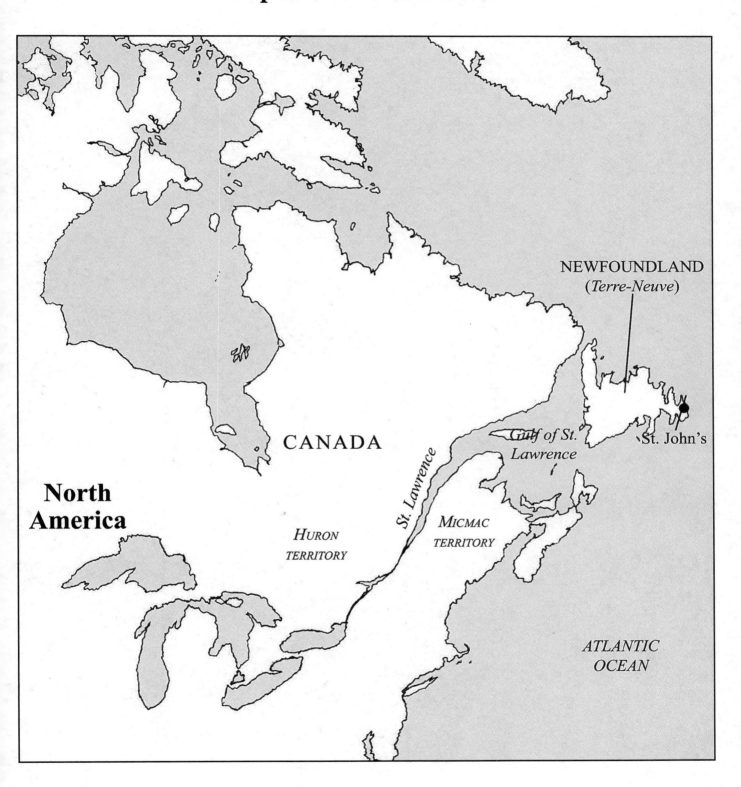

NEWFOUNDLAND
(*Terre-Neuve*)

CANADA

North America

St. Lawrence

Gulf of St. Lawrence

St. John's

HURON TERRITORY

MICMAC TERRITORY

ATLANTIC OCEAN

Statue of John Cabot

Jacques Cartier

Chapter 42: Spain and England

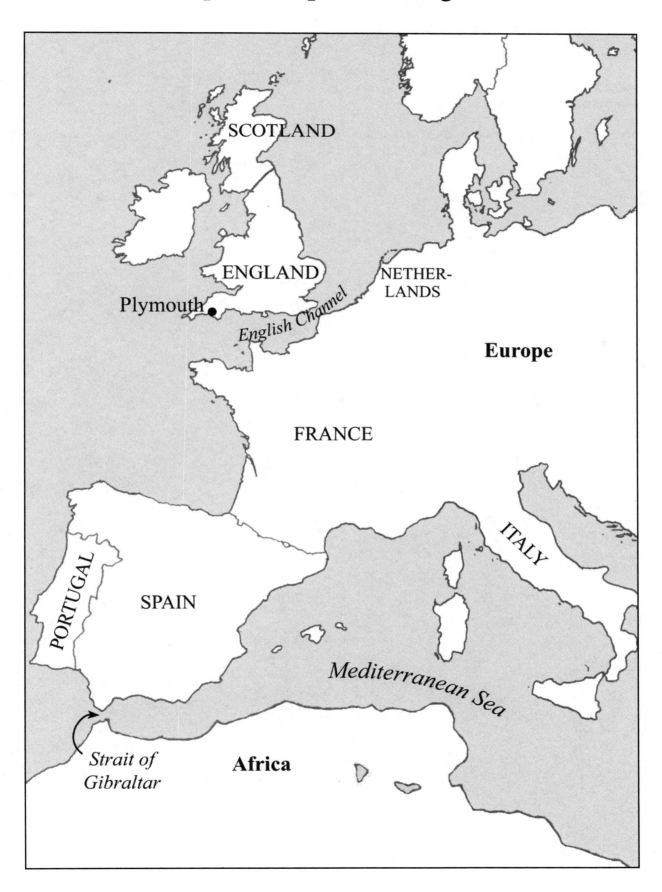

King Philip

Spanish Fighting Ships

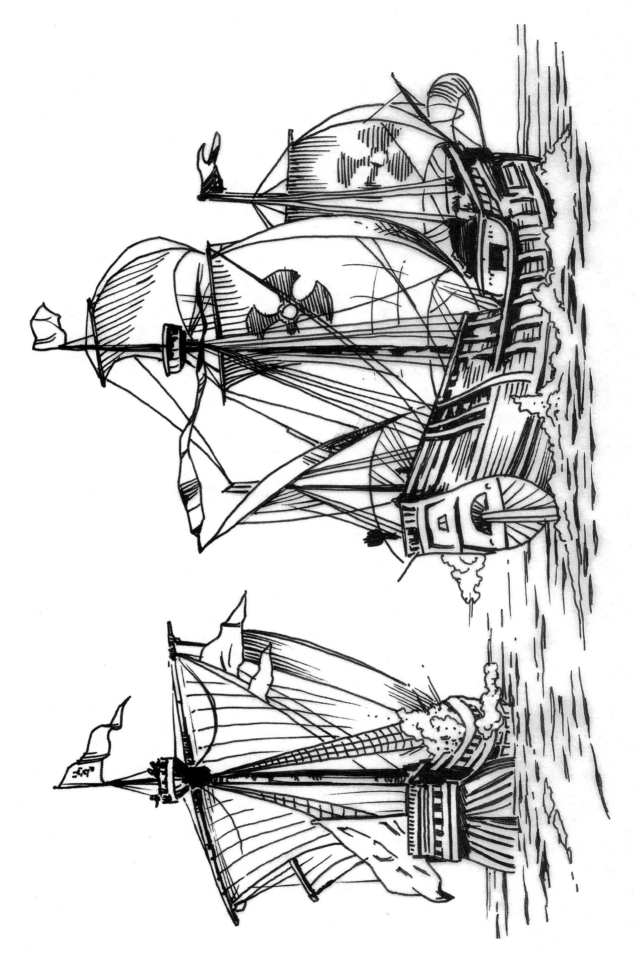

Question, Answer, Win! Cards

Four countries claim land in the Americas. Name those four countries and win 2 pieces of treasure!	This country had more settlements in the Americas than anyone else. Name the country and win 2 pieces of treasure!	What country was called "Mistress of the World and Queen of the Ocean"? Name that country and win 2 pieces of treasure!
Spain has a problem! Who keeps getting in her way? Give the answer and win 2 pieces of treasure!	How had the King of Spain become king in England? Give the answer and win 2 pieces of treasure!	When Mary died, this king lost his title of King of England. Who is it? Give the answer and win 2 pieces of treasure!
King Philip II offered to marry Elizabeth. What did she answer him? Give the answer and win 2 pieces of treasure!	How were the English traders making money? Give the answer and win 2 pieces of treasure!	What were the English explorers doing that bothered the King of Spain, Philip II? Give the answer and win 2 pieces of treasure!
Sometimes the English stopped the Spanish ships and did what with them? Give the answer and win 2 pieces of treasure!	Finally, Philip II sent a message to Queen Elizabeth because he was angry! What did the message say? Give the answer and win 2 pieces of treasure!	Queen Elizabeth didn't want to risk war with an angry Philip. What did she do? Give the answer and win 5 pieces of treasure!
Queen Elizabeth gave her English sailors a secret message. What did she say they could do? Give the answer and win 2 pieces of treasure!	English pirates knew that they could steal Spanish treasure and sink Spanish ships with no fear of punishment from whom? Give the answer and win 2 pieces of treasure!	Soon Philip decided that Elizabeth's promise had been a big lie. What did he do? Give the answer and win 2 pieces of treasure!
King Philip II believed that God had chosen him to defend Catholicism at any cost. What was one reason that he wanted to conquer England? Give the answer and win 2 pieces of treasure!	Sir Francis Drake's father had been a poor sailor turned preacher and was persecuted under the Catholic rule of Elizabeth's sister. What was her name? Give the answer and win 2 pieces of treasure!	Sir Francis Drake was known as a kind pirate, or buccaneer, because he didn't usually harm the people in the towns that he attacked. Can you name any other pirates or buccaneers? Give the answer and win 5 pieces of treasure!
King Philip assembled over 130 ships into a great floating army called the Spanish Armada. He gave strict orders to the sailors about how they should act. What did he tell them? Give the answer and win 2 pieces of treasure!	King Philip and the Spanish Armada were on their way! What did Queen Elizabeth do? Give the answer and win 2 pieces of treasure!	What did Howard and Drake first decide to do to help England against the Spanish fleet? Give the answer and win 2 pieces of treasure!
Where did the English ships wait for the Spanish Fleet? Bonus: Can you tell why that town is important to Americans? Give both answers and win 10 pieces of treasure!	What were Sir Howard and Sir Drake supposedly doing when the Spanish Fleet was first spotted? Give the answer and win 2 pieces of treasure!	How did the English ships win against the Spanish in the great battle in the English Channel? Give the answer and win 2 pieces of treasure!
How did the Spanish commanders of the Armada plan on winning against the English? Give the answer and win 2 pieces of treasure!	The defeat of the Spanish Armada changed Spain and England forever. How? Give the answer for both countries and win 5 pieces of treasure!	The merchant ships heading for North America hope to get rich. How? Give the answer and win 2 pieces of treasure!
Give the name of the famous explorer who traveled around the southern tip of Africa and back up towards India. Answer and win 2 pieces of treasure!	Along the coast of Africa you see Portuguese, Spanish, and English ships anchored at their ports. What three purchases are being made to sell elsewhere? Give the answer and win 2 pieces of treasure!	The Ottoman Empire changed the name of Constantinople to what? Give the answer and win 2 pieces of treasure!
When Suleiman the Magnificent died, what group of people began to think about taking over the Turk's empire? Give the answer and win 2 pieces of treasure!	Once China had its own ships and traded with the outside world, why did it stop? Give the answer and win 2 pieces of treasure!	Name the North American colony where you may see French, English, Portuguese, Italian, Spanish, and Dutch fishing ships. Give the answer and win 2 pieces of treasure!

Treasure! Cards

Pope Sixtus V once said, "Just look at how well she governs! She is only a woman … and yet she makes herself feared by Spain, by France, by the German Empire, by all." A good name is a treasure— collect 4 pieces.

By the end of the battle against the English, two out of three Spanish died and of the 130 Spanish ships, half returned, some severely damaged. England's navy turned the tide! Collect 4 treasure pieces.

During a lull in the war against the Spanish Armada, Hawkins is knighted for his bravery and leadership at the Isle of Wight.
Collect 4 treasure pieces.

The Queen appointed Hawkins to rebuild the navy ships. He built them lower, longer, and narrower, making them easy to handle. This helped to win against the Spanish! Collect 4 treasure pieces.

Drake led the capture of Santo Domingo, the Spanish capital of the West Indies. He gained wealth or England, but Philip never forgave him.
Collect 4 treasure pieces from each of the other players.

Drake's adventures were aided by a group of runaway slaves: the Cimaroon. Word traveled fast in the West Indies and Drake's reputation grew in the eyes of both foe and friend! Collect 4 treasure pieces.

Spies told of the Spanish build up! The Queen asked Drake to be Her Majesty's Admiral-at-the-Seas. She was telling the world that Sir Francis Drake was acting on her orders! Collect 4 treasure pieces.

Drake's coat of arms had a ship balanced on top of a globe with his Latin motto written below: Sic Parvis Magna, or "Greatness from small beginnings!" which sums him up! Collect 4 treasure pieces.

Drake marries Elizabeth Sydenham, who is younger and from a very wealthy family. He did not have children from either marriage which was a great loss to him.
Collect 4 treasure pieces.

King Philip II believed that God had chosen him to support and defend the Catholic church, especially against the growing Protestants. He used his vast wealth and power to accomplish his goal. Collect 4 treasure pieces.

Golden Hind Card!
The Queen has appointed Francis Drake to lead an expedition around the world. Drake is the first Englishman around the world, the second man ever! Collect 10 treasure pieces.

Golden Hind Card!
After 2 years, Drake came back with such wealth for England that it allowed the Queen to pay all of her debts! Drake was knighted on his ship! Collect 10 treasure pieces!

Rough Waters! Cards

 Elizabeth secretly gave her sailors permission to attack Spanish ships.

Philip realized that Elizabeth's promise to him was a big lie!

It was time to prove Spain was the most powerful!

Lose 4 treasure pieces.

 Drake and Hawkins make one more attempt to stop the Spanish for good. Both are old and set in their ways. The Queen makes the bad decision of putting them both in charge. It fails.

Lose 4 treasure pieces.

 Hawkins is betrayed by the Spanish while in San Juan De Ulua getting his ship repaired. He loses his treasure and all but two of his ships! He gives up New Spain until he is old.

Lose 4 treasure pieces.

 A man in the landing party at an early battle is captured. The Spanish torture him and discover all of the buccaneer's plans. Hawkins dies of dysentery before the Spanish attack.

Lose 4 treasure pieces.

 At 23 years old, Drake begins his career sailing with his cousin, John Hawkins. When he witnesses the betrayal of the Spanish at San Juan De Ulua, he vows a personal war with Spain.

Lose 4 treasure pieces.

 The year Drake becomes a member of Parliament, his first wife, Mary Newman, dies.

Lose 4 treasure pieces.

 Somehow, Drake discovers the secret trail of the Panama mule train, loaded with gold and jewels.

His raid is foiled by a drunken sailor who stands up too early.

Lose 4 treasure pieces.

 The Queen makes peace with Spain. Drake and crew go into hiding in Ireland.

Lose 4 treasure pieces.

 Elizabeth Sydenham, Drake's second wife, receives word that her beloved husband has died outside of Portobello of dysentery.

His last request was for his armor to be put on.

Lose 4 treasure pieces.

 Drake attacks and destroys many of Philip's ships. Then at Cape St. Vincent, Drake burns barrel staves needed to hold food and water for troops. Philip must delay war with England.

Lose 4 treasure pieces.

English Fleet Flags

Spanish Fleet Flags

World/House Map

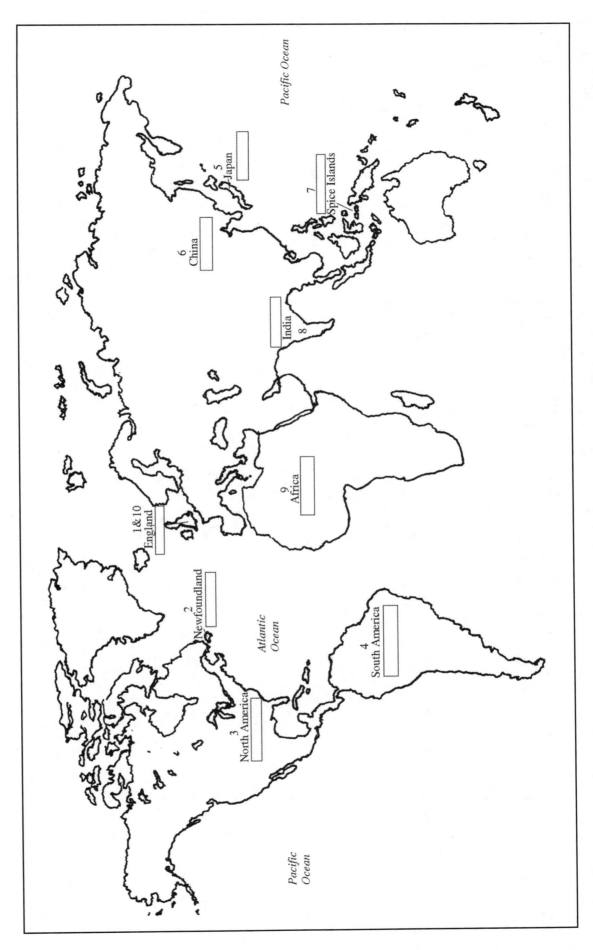

Pacific Ocean

5
Japan

7
Spice Islands

6
China

India
8

9
Africa

1&10
England

2
Newfoundland

Atlantic
Ocean

North America
3

South America
4

Pacific
Ocean

Review Cards

The Glory That Was Rome   1   SOTW2

Rome struggled against the barbarians who were trying to take over Roman territory. The Roman army had become so weak that the emperor hired barbarians to fight other barbarians. As the empire fell in the west to the barbarians, little was recorded. This was known as the dark ages, because we don't have many records of what happened in western Europe.

The Early Days of Britain   2   SOTW2

When the Romans weakened, the Celts drove them away. They had their island back! But the Celts didn't all belong to the same kingdom or obey the same king. One king asked other tribes – Angles and Saxons, from across the water – to come help him fight. They liked the green island so much, more of them came. Soon they began driving the Celts off their land.

Christianity Comes to Britain   3   SOTW2

Many people from different lands followed Christianity and most followed one leader – the Pope. After rescuing some boys from a slavery market, they told him of their home, Britain. He sent the boys with Augustine and 40 men to establish Christianity in Britain. Augustine built monasteries and churches. He became Archbishop of Canterbury, leader of the British church.

The Byzantine Empire   4   SOTW2

The Roman Empire got so big it was split in two. The Eastern part was known as the Byzantine Empire. It was small at first, but then strong emperors started to conquer the countries around them. The strongest and most famous of these emperors was named Justinian. He ruled with his wife Theodora who was smart and energetic and helped with the decisions.

The Medieval Indian Empire   5   SOTW2

A man named Chandragupta wanted to make all the little kingdoms into one large Indian empire. He founded a dynasty, and under the Guptas, India became peaceful and rich. The monks there followed Buddha and carved their monastery right out of the sides of cliffs! They decorated the cells by carving and painting frescoes on the ceiling and walls.

The Rise of Islam   6   SOTW2

Muhammad went to pray in a cave and had a vision. He saw a silk scroll floating in the air. Words were written on it in letters of fire! He told his wife and family. At first, he only had six followers, but after several years of preaching he was chased out of Mecca. Many in Medina embraced his teaching. We call the collection of his teaching the Koran.

Review Cards

Islam Becomes an Empire   7   SOTW2

Soon, Muhammad became the judge and king as well as a prophet! When Muhammad died, Abu Bakr, the first Islamic caliph, kept the Islamic rule strong. Those who came after him attacked the neighboring land and spread Islam all the way up to the Caspian Sea and to the east. They took over North Africa. Islam started with one man and became a mighty empire.

The Great Dynasties of China   8   SOTW2

Yangdi, the last Sui emperor, treated the Chinese people like his slaves. He had the Great Canal built, but the people were angry. Li Yuan founded a new dynasty – the Tang dynasty. The 300 years of Tang rule was the Golden Age of China. The people became wealthy, printing books and eating fancy food (like ice cream and dumplings) out of lacquer bowls.

East of China   9   SOTW2

In Japan, the Yamato leaders conquered and became the emperors. They knew they had to be good rulers so they borrowed ideas on how to run their country from China and Korea. Soon all the important people in Japan spoke and wrote Chinese. But when China marched into Korea, Japan cut off contact and began to write, paint, dress, and think in its own way.

The Bottom of the World   10   SOTW2

The people of Australia were nomads. They lived in small groups that moved from place to place, hunting food and gathering plants. No one knows where these nomads came from. But their own legends said that they had been in Australia from the beginning of the world. We call these nomads aborigines, from the Latin words meaning "from the beginning."

The Kingdom of the Franks   11   SOTW2

When Clovis was 20, he set out to make Gaul into one empire. He married Princess Clotilda from one tribe, fought other tribes, and became ruler over all of Gaul. While conquering his empire, Clovis became a Christian. His empire was known as the Frankish Empire. Today we call this part of the world France after the Franks.

The Islamic Invasion   12   SOTW2

The sons of the dead king in Spain were furious. So they invited the great fighter, Tariq Bin Ziyad, to bring his armies in from North Africa and help them drive Rodrigo out of power. That was a big mistake! Tariq organized men into ships that sailed to the tip of Spain. From a rock Tariq ordered the ships to be burned, saying: "We either conquer Spain or perish!"

Review Cards

The Great Kings of France 13 SOTW2

Charles Martel worked hard to win the throne of the Franks. When he heard that the Islamic armies had blown through Spain and were coming his way, he gathered his army and went to meet them. Charles hammered them at Tours. The greatest king of the Franks was Martel's grandson, Charlemagne. He made the kingdom prosperous and Christian.

The Arrival of the Norsemen 14 SOTW2

Eric the Red settled in barren Greenland. But Leif, his son, wanted to find a better place to live. Leif had heard tales of lands in the North Atlantic. He bought a boat and set off with a crew. After many, many days they found rich land, trees, and grapes. Other Green-landers followed Leif's path to his Vineland, "Land of the Grapes," or North America.

The First Kings of England 15 SOTW2

Wessex watched the Viking inva-sion with fear. They appointed Alfred to be their leader. He had to hide until he could gather a strong army. They surrounded Guthorm the Viking until he agreed to go away. Alfred truly became a king. But the kings who followed Alfred lost their land when the Normans took over at the Battle of Hastings. In came William.

England After the Conquest 16 SOTW2

After William the Conqueror be-came King, the Normans came in and changed England forever. They changed their way of living to a feu-dal system. Their language changed as French words became popular. Now it was the Norman knights who owned the land, building their castles out of stone, and allowing the peasants to farm the land for a price.

Knights and Samurai 17 SOTW2

England wasn't the only country that had a feudal system. Far to the east, Japan also had knights and lords. They were called samu-rai. They wore armor made out of iron plates with helmets that were shaped into faces, often with elabo-rate iron mustaches. They fought with curved swords, called katanas, decorated with gold and jewels.

The Age of Crusades 18 SOTW2

When the Muslim warriors fought to spread Islam across the world, other countries were frightened! Eventually the Muslims didn't let the Jews and Christians visit the holy city, Jerusalem. The Byzantine emperor asked for help. The Pope answered by calling the knights in Christian kingdoms, promising them forgiveness if they recaptured Jerusalem.

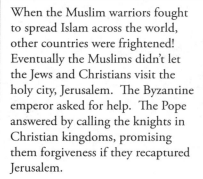

Review Cards

A New Kind of King   19   SOTW2

When Richard the Lionhearted died, John, his brother, claimed the throne. But the noblemen didn't respect him. He taxed the people so hard that the noblemen revolted. They made John sign a paper that described new laws that the king himself had to follow! He couldn't take money unless he was given permission! He couldn't throw a nobleman in jail without cause.

The Diaspora   20   SOTW2

After the Jews revolted, the Romans destroyed Jerusalem and the Jews were dispersed through many lands. The Jews were often viewed with suspicion because they believed in their God above all other authority. So the Jews were often mistreated. In Spain, they found some freedom because the Muslin rulers were friendlier towards Judaism.

The Mongols Devastate the East   21   SOTW2

The Mongol tribes never tried to invade China itself – until Genghis Khan became their leader. He unified the Mongols and led them against China, conquering Peking. He turned west and scourged the Islamic empire. No one could stop him. After he died, the Mongols ruled an enormous empire, which continued to grow.

Exploring the Mysterious East   22   SOTW2

Marco Polo traveled to China with his father. They met the emperor, Kublai Khan. He wanted foreigners to come and teach him. But after Kublai Khan, the new rulers of China, the Ming, didn't want Europeans to come. They thought China was already the best country in the world. They built the Forbidden City, where no foreigner was ever allowed to enter.

The First Russians   23   SOTW2

A Viking warrior named Rurik, wandered into central Europe and decided to stay. His descendents were the Rus. Many Rus princes ruled different cities. The prince who finally made Russia into one country is remembered as Ivan the Great. But Ivan's grandson wasn't so great. He was such a dreadful ruler that he was called Ivan the Terrible.

The Ottoman Empire   24   SOTW2

The fall of Constantinople is sometimes called the End of the Middle Ages. Constantinople was renamed Istanbul and became the capital city of the Ottoman Turks. The greatest emperor and sultan of all was Suleiman, named after the Hebrew king Solomon. He became known all over the kingdom for his fairness. He wanted all of his people treated justly and his laws followed.

Review Cards

The End of the World   25   SOTW2

The people who lived in the Middle Ages had to face one invading army after another: Muslims, Vikings, Crusaders, Mongols, Russians, and Turks! But the most dangerous enemy of all wasn't an army. It was a sickness that spread across the world – and killed more people than all these armies put together. Today we call it the bubonic plague.

France and England at War   26   SOTW2

France and England's 100 Years' War caused a French civil was. Henry V conquered France. Some French wanted Henry's son to be king, but others wanted the French prince to rule. Joan of Arc claimed that God told her to lead the French army to victory for the Dauphin. She was victorious and saw the Dauphin crowned – but then she was burned at the stake.

War for the English Throne   27   SOTW2

When Edward IV died, his 12-year-old son became king. But he was too young to rule alone. So his uncle, Richard, offered to help. That was the end of the 12-year-old king's reign! Richard took over and announced that he was now King Richard III of England. Young Edward V and his little brother disappeared. The mystery of their death was never solved.

The Kingdoms of Spain and Portugal   28   SOTW2

Spain was divided into small kingdoms. Princess Isabella of Castile married Ferdinand, the prince of Aragon, and unified the country. Although they were good rulers, they also forced the Jews of Spain to leave their homes forever. Portugal, the kingdom on Spain's coast, kept its independence and became the home of great navigators.

African Kingdoms   29   SOTW2

When Mansa Musa came to the throne of Mali, he gathered the largest army in all of West Africa. He commanded over 100,000 archers, cavalrymen, and foot soldiers. He conquered neighboring kingdoms and expanded Mali. He attracted the world's attention when he decided to make a pilgrimage, or hajj, to Mecca, along with 60,000 people.

India Under the Moghuls   30   SOTW2

Like his grandfather Babur, who established the dynasty, Akbar was a fair and just Moghul leader over India. Although he himself was a Muslim, he believed he would need to be popular with his Hindu subjects if he wanted to stay on the throne. So he married a Hindu princess and allowed Hindu worship. He became so famous that his people told stories about him.

Review Cards

Exploring New Worlds   31   SOTW2

Columbus was the first European to land in America, and Amerigo Vespucci was the first to realize that America was a new continent. But another explorer, Ferdinand Magellan, was the first to actually carry out Columbus' original plan and get to India by sailing west – all the way around the whole world.

The American Kingdoms   32   SOTW2

As the Aztecs roamed through Central America, they came to the edge of a lake. One island had a large cactus growing on it where an eagle sat holding a snake. The priests saw the eagle and told the people it was a sign that the sun god wanted them to build their capital on the island. They built a city on the marshy land – and named it Tenochtitlan.

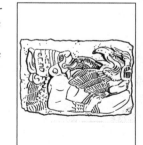

Spain, Portugal, and the New World   33   SOTW2

Before the Spanish conquistadors could settle in the New World, they had to conquer the Aztecs. And the Aztecs were skillful, fierce warriors. But when the Spanish first arrived, led by Cortes, the Aztecs didn't realize they were being invaded. They thought they were being visited by the gods.

Martin Luther's New Ideas   34   SOTW2

A monk named Martin Luther began to criticize the Catholic Church. The church taught that God would forgive sins if sinners did special deeds. Luther preached that God would forgive any sinner who believed in Jesus Christ. King Henry VIII liked Martin Luther's new ideas! He used his freedom from the Catholic Church to make his own rules.

The Renaissance   35   SOTW2

During the Renaissance, men and women began to make new theories about the world. They compared new theories with old Greek and Roman ideas. They started to ask, "Which ideas about the world are right? Let's try to find out for ourselves." When Gutenberg made a printing press, they could print these new ideas and share them with others.

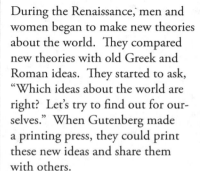

Reformation and Counter Reformation   36   SOTW2

Catholics and Protestants argued about how to understand and obey God. Protestants thought that people should be able to read the Bible and find out what God wanted. Catholics thought that the Bible could only be interpreted properly with the help of the church. Sometimes wars broke out because of the differences.

Review Cards

The New Universe   37   SOTW2

Copernicus believed that the planets went around the sun. Galileo helped to show that Copernicus as right. The ideas of Copernicus became foundational for astronomy, the study of the stars. And Galileo's discoveries are part of physics, the study of why objects behave as they do.

England's Greatest Queen   38   SOTW2

Elizabeth became queen when her older sister Mary died. She refused to marry and spent her life ruling England. She made alliances with other countries, sent out explorers, and defended the land. She also allowed her people to be either Catholics or Protestants in their private worship. She was England's greatest queen!

England's Greatest Playwright   39   SOTW2

William Shakespeare was England's most famous playwright. When he was young, he acted in a traveling company that went from town to town performing. When he grew a little older, he formed a band of actors with several friends. He acted parts, chose costumes, ran rehearsals, found props, and wrote plays – like *Hamlet* and *Macbeth*.

New Ventures to the Americas   40   SOTW2

Elizabeth didn't want Spain to become more important than England so she began to plan expeditions to North America. England needed to build its own colonies in North America! Elizabeth gave the job to one of her favorite knights, Sir Walter Raleigh. But the first colony, on Roanoke Island, disappeared without a trace!

Explorations in the North   41   SOTW2

After Columbus and Vespucci sailed across the Atlantic, other Europeans followed. The Spanish and Portuguese planted their colonies in Central and South America. The English did their best to settle in Virginia. And further north, a colony was settled by many people who loved the "New found land" for one big reason: the easiest fishing they had ever seen.

Empires Collide   42   SOTW2

Spain had a problem: the English were in the way! Philip, king of Spain, once had influence in England. But when Elizabeth allowed her sailors to attack Spanish ships, Philip built warships and sailed them towards England. Under Drake and Howard, however, the British fleet of small, quick ships defeated the Spanish Armada!